Negotiator

James B. Donovan
Photo by Bachrach. Reproduced by permission.

Negotiator

The Life and Career of James B. Donovan

Philip J. Bigger

Lehigh
University
Press

Bethlehem: Lehigh University Press

© 2006 by Philip J. Bigger

Associated University Presses
2010 Eastpark Boulevard
Cranbury, NJ 08512

The paper used in this publication meets the requirements of the American National Standard for Permanence of Paper for Printed Library Materials Z39.48-1984.

Library of Congress Cataloging-in-Publication Data

Bigger, Philip J., 1943–
  Negotiator : the life and career of James B. Donovan / Philip J. Bigger.
    p. cm.
  Includes bibliographical references and index.
  ISBN 0-934223-85-8 (alk. paper)
  1. Donovan, James B. (James Britt), 1916– 2. Lawyers—United States—
Biography. I. Title.
KF373.D589.B54   2006
340'.092—dc22

                                                              2005022901

PRINTED IN THE UNITED STATES OF AMERICA

For Mary Donovan Busch

My candle burns at both ends,
It will not last the night;
But ah, my foes, and oh, my friends—
It gives a lovely light!

—Edna St. Vincent Millay, "First Fig"

Contents

9

Preface

IT WAS CLEAR AND EIGHTY-ONE DEGREES IN CUBA ON DECEMBER 23, 1962. At San Antonio de los Banos Airport, outside of Havana, two men stood side by side on a platform near the tarmac watching a Pan Am flight board. One was the young Fidel Castro, thirty-five years old and now the premier of Cuba, a tall, patrician man dressed in crisp military fatigues. His now famous beard, a feature that he had adopted during his stay in the Sierra Madre Mountains at the start of his revolution, was full but neatly trimmed. Next to him was a New York lawyer, James B. Donovan, eleven years Castro's senior. He was shorter and stockier, with thinning gray hair, but his steel-blue eyes were piercing and alive. Both men had been negotiating for months to secure the release of the soldiers captured by Castro's forces following the ill-fated Bay of Pigs invasion in April 1961. The talks were nearly completed and now some of the prisoners were boarding planes bound for Florida and freedom.

Sharing the platform with Donovan and Castro were several aides and assistants of each, on hand to witness this momentous occasion. There were also numerous Cuban soldiers. Despite the success of the talks, there remained a deep feeling among Castro's military advisers that the United States might still try to launch an attack on Cuba, and Donovan was, at times, likened to the Japanese peace envoys in Washington at the time of the strike on Pearl Harbor. As the group watched the prisoner-laden planes take off, several Cuban pilots who were circling the airport in Russian-built MIGs sought to salute their commander. One flew in over the platform at an exceptionally low altitude causing both the Americans and Cubans, including Castro and Donovan, to fall to their knees in panic. When someone near Castro asked, "What was that?" Donovan quickly yelled to Castro, "It's the invasion!" Castro roared loudly with delight. His soldiers, though offended with the remark, joined with their leader in laughter. It was Donovan's characteristic quick wit, and it helped to break the tension of the moment, as he had done so often during his negotiations with

11

the Cuban leader. Castro had been completely taken in by Donovan's boldness, charm, humor, and integrity. The successful culmination of negotiations with Fidel Castro was a high water mark in Cuban-American relations, one that has not been replicated since. For Donovan himself, it was only one episode in a career of service that had begun in earnest in the early 1940s.

James Donovan was reared in a conservative, Irish Catholic home where concepts of family, religion, educational attainment, and patriotism were key essentials—and he lived up to all of them. The United States had entered World War II little more than a year after Donovan completed his legal education at Harvard University. By this time, a significant government agency had been created, the Office of Scientific Research and Development (OSRD). Under the leadership of Vannevar Bush, its goal was to foster development of new weapons, not the least of which was the atomic bomb, as well as new medicines for the military. Donovan was hired as a civilian attorney for the organization and quickly rose to the position of general counsel. In that capacity he was not only called upon to review military contracts with universities and write opinions on such topics as the legality of using civilian prisoners in potentially fatal military experiments, but also to participate in arranging public lands for atomic experiments.

Shortly after the creation of the OSRD in 1942, a new intelligence agency was established, the Office of Strategic Services (OSS), forerunner of the Central Intelligence Agency. Having by then received a commission in the navy, Donovan left the Office of Scientific Research and Development and was detailed to the OSS. Toward the conclusion of the war, he was designated chief of the war crimes unit within the OSS and given the responsibility for overseeing the collection and organization of data concerning Nazi atrocities. It was a smooth transition for him then, after Germany surrendered, to fill the role of one of the prosecutors at the first war crimes trial in Nuremberg. Still a member of the OSS, Donovan was given the task of organizing and presenting the shocking and effective photographic evidence against the major Nazi leaders and their organizations that contributed to their eventual criminal convictions.

Donovan returned home after completing his prosecutorial task in Nuremberg and commenced the private practice of law, specializing in insurance. It was during this time, when the Cold War and espionage were ever-present realities, that a high-ranking Soviet spy, Rudolph Abel, entered the United States for the purpose of obtaining military and atomic secrets. After Abel was captured in 1957, Donovan's legal reputation was such that he was asked to defend the

Soviet spy in criminal proceedings in the United States District Court in Brooklyn, New York. He took on this unpopular cause out of principle and provided such a meritorious defense that the outcome was only decided by the Supreme Court of the United States. Donovan's legal ability finally did not forestall a conviction for his client, but it spared Abel from the death penalty. Donovan's prophetic argument to the sentencing judge—that the court should spare Abel's life against the possibility that an American might be similarly situated in the future in the Soviet Union—an American for whom Abel could be traded—was soon realized in the capture of U-2 pilot, Francis Gary Powers.

Working with the knowledge of the Central Intelligence Agency, but as a private citizen, Donovan made several trips inside East Berlin in order to negotiate the trade of Rudolph Abel, not only for Francis Gary Powers, but also for two other Americans who Donovan had learned were in Soviet jails. He negotiated alone, usually under dangerous circumstances, and was successful.

Although the U-2 affair was an occasion for some embarrassment to the United States—and resulted in the cancelation of an international summit—it paled in comparison to the humiliation of the United States in the aftermath of the failed Bay of Pigs invasion in 1961. The United States had trained Cuban refugees in a Latin American camp, encouraged the invasion of Cuba by these forces, and once this invasion began, failed to provide adequate support for the troops. One hundred fourteen Cubans were killed and more than one thousand were captured by Fidel Castro's forces. The survivors were tried, fined, and imprisoned.

An initial attempt to negotiate for the prisoners by a civilian "Tractors for Freedom" committee failed despite the participation of such notable figures as David Eisenhower and Eleanor Roosevelt. As time passed, fears grew on the part of families of the invaders for the health and survival of their loved ones. Moreover, the responsibility for the failed invasion gnawed at President Kennedy, who had authorized it. As a result, when the new Cuban Families Committee for the Liberation of Prisoners of War approached the president's brother, Attorney General Robert F. Kennedy, he suggested that they ask James Donovan to intercede with Castro for the prisoners' release since he had been so successful in the recent Soviet negotiations for the return of Powers. And, over the course of several months, Donovan did just that. He did so in the face of a quarantine of Cuba after the discovery of Soviet missiles on the island. And he did so at great personal peril, not only because of hostile Cuban military leaders, but also because of a secret CIA plot to kill Castro using Donovan as an unwitting intermediary. The presentation of the negotiations following the quarantine is based on original records maintained by Donovan, and the fresh, new details of the CIA plot are based on interviews with one who was present with Donovan at the time. It was, in large part, Donovan's sincerity, charm, and wit that engrossed Castro and enabled the discussions to continue to a successful conclusion. The result of Donovan's work was the release of the convicted invaders, 1,113 in all. In addition, more than eight thousand relatives, political prisoners and other Cubans seeking refuge, together with a number of Americans, were also allowed to emigrate.

During Donovan's negotiations with Fidel Castro, the Cuban leader often alluded to the topic of a renewed relationship between Cuba and the United States. Donovan relayed these hopeful signs to an interested government in Washington, DC. However, with the assassination of John F. Kennedy in 1963 and the assumption of the office of president by Lyndon Johnson, that possibility abruptly ended.

*

Spurred on by the Supreme Court's decision in *Brown v. Board of Education* in 1954, which clearly prohibited segregation, many black activist groups around the country began to demand an end to the practice in public schools. The New York City public school system in the 1960s was a microcosm of the struggle toward full integration of minority and white students. The use of busing was one of the main goals to achieve that end. While black families saw this as a means for their children to have a better education, white families believed that their own children should attend local, community schools. There were school boycotts and demonstrations by each side. Standing between them was James Donovan, who had been appointed vice president of the New York City Board of Education in 1962. Even in the face of personal threats, group demonstrations, and vacillating support from the state government in Albany, Donovan was able to begin the process of change. He wasn't perfect, and sometimes his quick wit was ill advised. He supported busing for older children, but when he was challenged to provide busing for all, he once blurted out, "I am the president of a board of education, not a board of transportation." But he was also quick to apologize for his outspoken comments because at heart he was always sincere in his support for children.

Institutions of higher learning were also involved in the civil rights process, being asked, for example, to provide more courses with relevance to minorities. They were also the sites of student protests against the war in Viet Nam. And while the public school system for the lower grades faced organized demonstrations and boycotts, they were, for the most part, peaceful. Students in postsecondary institutions, however, were prone to more violent activities, such as the occupation of buildings and the destruction of property. Against this backdrop, Pratt Institute in Brooklyn, New York, asked James Donovan to assume the presidency of the school. During his brief tenure, he maintained order, met frequently with students, and ultimately developed a constructive outlet for the presentation and resolution of their legitimate demands.

James Donovan died suddenly in 1970 at the age of fifty-three following a severe heart attack. Although his life was brief, it was filled with numerous accomplishments and contributions to international relations, the law, and education. Sharing his extraordinary life and valuable contributions with others is the purpose of this work.

Acknowledgments

JOSEPH P. FRIED OF THE *New York Times* was the catalyst who first brought James Donovan's wife, Mary, and me together. He had written a very kind article about my historical exhibit on espionage, which appeared in the lobby of the United States Courthouse in Brooklyn in late 1999. After reading the article, Mary saw the exhibit. In a subsequent meeting she asked that her late husband's life be recorded so that he and his work would not be forgotten. For this I owe a special debt of gratitude to Mr. Fried.

Mary Donovan Busch's assistance was both essential and invaluable. She not only provided personal papers and photographs but most especially she offered insights into her husband that only a spouse could provide. In that same spirit, James Donovan's children, John Donovan, Jane Ann Amorosi, and Mary Ellen Fuller, were also most helpful in providing personal observations as well as in reviewing the manuscript.

James Donovan's colleagues, associates, and friends freely gave of their time and knowledge. I am particularly grateful to Daniel McNamara, Milan Miskovsky, John Nolan, Thomas Parry, and Aston George Taylor.

Librarians and research specialists provided much needed assistance in a most genial fashion and without hesitation. They include Norman Brouwer, Marine Historian, South Street Seaport Melville Library; John Celardo, Archivist, National Archives and Records Administration, Northeast Region; Elena Danielson, Archivist, and Carol Leadenham, Assistant Archivist, Hoover Institution, Stanford University; Professor Robert Fabro and Josie Caporuscio, Assistant to the President, Pratt Institute; Professor Michael Hannon, Duke University Law Library; Patrice M. Kane, Head of Archives and Special Collections, Fordham University Library; Vivian Shen, Book Preservation Librarian, Fordham University; Stephen Plotkin, Reference Archivist, John Fitzgerald Kennedy Library; Brian Quail, Election Law Counsel to the New York State Assembly Election Committee; Margaret "Peggy" Perrin, Catalogue Librarian, New York Law School; Ismael Rivera-Sierra, Librarian, St. John's University Library, Manhat-

17

tan (formerly the College of Insurance); and Scott Smothers of the Westgroup.

While I was researching the papers of James Donovan at the Hoover Institution in Palo Alto over a number of weeks, I was accorded the wonderful hospitality of Wallace and Ruth Erichsen, who opened their home to me for the duration of my work there. Their interest, warmth, and great discussions made the research trip an enjoyable and productive one.

Five people whom I am proud to call friends and colleagues—but whose retirement I wantonly intruded upon—performed the imposing task of reading the entire manuscript and offering their much appreciated comments, suggestions, and corrections. A special thank you, therefore, is tendered to Carol Erichsen, Deputy Chief U.S. Probation Officer for the Western District of Michigan (Ret.); her husband, Wally Erichsen, Special Agent of the Federal Bureau of Investigation (Ret.); John Moccia, Chief U.S. Pretrial Services Officer for the District of Hawaii (Ret.); and Fred Howes and Richard P. Maxey of Raleigh, North Carolina.

One other individual also read the entire manuscript and somehow managed to maintain professionalism and patience in editing the work, enhancing both its literary quality and technical compliance. Not only is Judi Mayer of Lehigh University Press an editor, but a valued mentor as well.

Finally, were it not for the tolerance of my wife, Lois, in accepting my many hours, days, and weeks away from home that the research required, in reading the drafts of the biography chapter by chapter, and in general offering all the support that she could possibly give, this work may not have been accomplished in the time that it was—if at all. I am deeply grateful to her.

"First Fig" by Edna St. Vincent Millay. From *Collected Poems*. Harper Collins. Copyright 1922, 1950 by Edna St. Vincent Millay. All rights reserved. Used by permission. "Horror His Job, Readying Nazi Films for War Crimes Trials," *New York Daily News*, L.P., reprinted with permission; *Lake Placid News* article, December 24, 1981, reprinted courtesy of the *Lake Placid News;* Memorandum of Gordon Chase, March 4, 1963 and Note from Fidel Castro, February 12, 1964, are materials reproduced from www.nsarchive.org with the permission of the National Security Archive; "Adventure in Education" reprinted courtesy of Pratt Institute; multiple quotations from the *New York Times* are copyrighted and reprinted with permission from the New York Times Co.; quotations from sources in the personal papers of James B. Donovan in the Hoover Institution are reprinted courtesy of Mary Donovan Busch.

Negotiator

1

The Early Years

In 1963, Robert F. Wagner, the mayor of the City of New York, presented James Donovan with a bronze medallion in recognition of his role in the release of the Bay of Pigs prisoners. As the mayor was draping the ribboned medal on Donovan, the successful negotiator was particularly moved, not only for the award itself, but also because, many years earlier, his father, John Donovan, MD, had received a similar medallion from another mayor for his heroic efforts to assist the victims of the worst maritime disaster to occur in the history of New York City.

June 15, 1904, the East River: The sun was bright this summer Wednesday morning. Picnickers from St. Mark's Evangelical Lutheran Church in lower Manhattan were in a festive mood as their steamboat headed up the river on their way to Locust Grove Picnic Grounds on Long Island. Suddenly, smoke began seeping from a forward storage area. A cabin boy's first warnings of danger went unheeded until a fire had engulfed the area. An alarm was sounded, but the forward motion of the boat created a strong breeze that quickly spread the fire throughout the ship. Claudia Glen Dowling, writing much later in *Life* magazine, described the survival of one child: "Catherine and her family were on the top deck. People were rushing to the stern, away from the fire, screaming, jumping into the water in their heavy petticoats, with life preservers too rotted to be of any use. Catherine's mother clutched at her, but the girl broke away and was swept to the rail. There a man picked her up and dumped her over the side, onto the deck of a tugboat."[1]

Catherine Gallagher, eleven years old, was one of 310 people who survived when the excursion boat *General Slocum* caught fire and burned in New York's East River near North Brother Island. Her mother, younger brother, and her baby-sitter were among the 1,021 others, mainly women and children, who died from drowning or

21

from being burned to death. New York had not witnessed such a maritime disaster either before or since.

Rescuers were almost immediately on the scene since the smoke and then the fire could be seen from the shorelines of Manhattan and Queens, and word spread rapidly. They came in tugboats, fire and police boats, ferries, and private vessels. Doctors, nurses, and even patients at the sanatorium on North Brother Island raced to the water's edge. Among those individuals who sought to assist was a young doctor, John Joseph Donovan, then an intern at Harlem Hospital. Hearing of the fire, he took a ferry to the disaster and worked for fifty hours, many of them in the water, treating the injured and the dying at the shoreline to which they had been pulled by rescuers or carried by the current.[2]

The disaster virtually wiped out the small German community known as *Kleindeutschland*.[3] A monument was erected in 1906 in Tompkins Square, in lower Manhattan, as a memorial to the dead. However, even before the completion of the monument, New York City mayor George B. McClellan presented Medals of Honor to a number of the rescuers. Among the recipients was Dr. Donovan.[4]

John Joseph Donovan had been born in the Bronx on May 21, 1879.[5] At the time of John's birth, his parents, both Irish immigrants, were living in a four-family apartment house, in the Mott Haven section of what is now the Bronx.[6]

Mott Haven in 1879 was still a part of New York County, having been annexed by New York City four years earlier. In fact, it was termed "the Annexed District" and contained the Twenty-third Ward, in which the family was living.[7] The Harlem River formed the western and southern boundaries, and the Bronx River, the eastern. To the immediate north were tracts of farms and estates, accentuated by villages such as Melrose and Morrisania. East 146th Street, where the family home was located, was a suburban area, just a few blocks south of a developing section known as "The Hub." At 149th Street and Third Avenue, the Hub was a location for movie palaces and vaudeville performances, as well as department stores such as Alexander's. Travel in 1880 was by horse cars and private horse-drawn vehicles. In order to reach the island of Manhattan from the mainland of Mott Haven, the Donovan family would have found it necessary to take a horse car south across the Third Avenue Bridge to 129th Street, where they and other travelers could get on New York City's elevated subway line. The more pastoral atmosphere of Mott Haven changed dramatically after 1886, however, when the city's transit system extended into the Annexed District and brought many Manhattan tenement dwellers north to settle in less crowded housing. Residences seemed to follow the train line along Third Avenue, and trolleys began to run east and west, connecting with the trains. The fare for each form of transportation was five cents.

After graduating high school, John Donovan entered the College of the City of New York. Thereafter, he went on to New York University and Bellevue Hospital Medical College, supporting his medical studies by tutoring students at City College in Latin and Greek. He graduated in 1902. Following receipt of his degree, he interned at Harlem Hospital and eventually went into private practice. A religious man, he was a member of the Xavier High School Alumni Sodality, a significant Catholic layman's association in the city in the early part of the twentieth century.[8]

On September 28, 1910, John married the former Harriet F. O'Connor at St. Jerome's Church, the same church in which his parents were wed. Harriet had been orphaned at an early age and was raised in Manhattan by an uncle, Maurice Power, a sculptor and foundry owner. She later graduated from Hunter College, and worked as a recital pianist and teacher. The couple made their home in a brownstone at 413 East 139th Street.[9] A grand piano occupied a prominent place on the first floor where Harriet continued to give lessons for many years. The couple's two sons were born here, John Joseph Jr. on February 14, 1913, and James Joseph on February 29, 1916.[10] Dr. Donovan, a surgeon by the time of James's birth, had been an assistant professor of Operative Surgery at Fordham University Medical School and was soon to join the staffs of Misericordia Hospital and the House of Calvary in the Bronx.[11] John and James were baptized in the church of their parents.[12] John attended St. Jerome's Elementary School while James went to All Hallows Elementary School, a Manhattan day school run by the Christian Brothers of Ireland. While still in All Hallows, James was already interested in reading and in books, particularly rare ones. In later years, he recalled discovering a Manhattan bookstore in 1929 where he made his first purchase:

When I was about thirteen and on a normal Saturday exploration of Manhattan, I chanced upon the Oxford Book Shop ("Sign of the Sparrow") located at 24th Street and Lexington Avenue. Many of you will remember its disarmingly modest appearance and how one would be greeted downstairs by Alfred Goldsmith and his charming wife. Mr. Goldsmith enjoyed telling in later years how I appeared that winter's day in tweed knickerbockers and inquired whether he had an issue of "The Yellow Book."[13] When Mr. Goldsmith peered down at me and asked the reason for my rather esoteric search, I confessed interest in the drawings of Aubrey Beardsley. He became sufficiently intrigued to invite me for a cup of tea with Mrs. Goldsmith and himself.[14]

Donovan explained that his interest grew to include illuminated manuscripts, incunabula, fine press books, and fine bindings. The teenager became an habitué of the Oxford Book Shop over the years, and he recalled meeting other literary regulars such as Alexander Woollcott and Carolyn Wells.[15]

Donovan entered All Hallows High School in 1929. He edited the school newspaper, played varsity basketball, and captained the tennis team.[16] He was active in dramatics and debating, as well, all the while maintaining high grades. One of his teachers, Brother Patrick A. Gleeson, recalled him as "a scrappy little chap, a real live wire."[17] Perhaps "scrappy" was an understatement. According to family history, one day at All Hallows an inkwell was tossed at a teacher. Several days later, the Donovan family donated a statue to the school.[18] The gesture of atonement was apparently accepted, and their younger son graduated in 1933.

The Donovan family was fortunate in these years, and they appear not to have been affected by the economic depression that began in the same year that James entered All Hallows. During his summers, James vacationed in Lake Placid and worked on a newspaper there and on another at Camp Ticonderoga near Lake George. A friend, Edward J. Calhoun, recalled some of their camp days in a later letter, describing how a certain Mr. French would pay the boys with checks that bounced. Calhoun, a junior in medical school at the time, also remembered how James's father helped him treat the fractured arm of another boy when Calhoun himself was unsure of what to do.[19]

James's brother, John, entered Fordham University in 1931. With an interest in politics, John was already president of the Young Men's Democratic Club in the Bronx. James followed his brother to Fordham two years later, one of an entry class of five hundred students. His love of journalism prompted him to try out immediately for a position on the school newspaper, the *Ram*, which held a competition for freshman staff each October. James was one of eight selected for a probationary period. John, then a junior at the university, already had his own byline on the *Ram* with his column, "Ramblings." Within four months, James completed his trial period and was made a permanent member of the newspaper staff.

In his freshman year, James ran unsuccessfully for class president, but was elected treasurer the next year. He also submitted his first literary effort in the Freshman One-Act Play Contest. Entitled *Deadline*, it survived a first round of eliminations before losing after a stage performance in April 1934.[20] James finished his first year with a satisfactory academic average and was accorded an honorable mention by the university for his scholastic attainment. Cited with him were classmates Vince Lombardi and Wellington Mara.[21] While at Fordham, James became a lifetime friend of another student, David N. Edelstein, later a federal judge in Manhattan. After James graduated, Edelstein remained at Fordham to pursue a master's degree and, immediately after, a degree in law. Meanwhile, brother John graduated in 1935. He had served on the *Ram* staff for four years, was an editor of the yearbook, and a college debater.

Shortly after John graduated, his parents celebrated their twenty-fifth wedding anniversary on September 28, 1935, in a gala event at the Starlight Roof Garden of the Waldorf Astoria Hotel.[22] James and John were among those in attendance. In this same month, James began his junior year at Fordham.

James was named editor-in-chief of the *Ram* in 1935 and was the first student to hold this position for two years. During his tenure he wrote all of the paper's editorials. Some of them were quite passionate attacks on the ogres of the time; most revealed a deep conservatism, both political and religious. He encouraged freshman to wear the maroon tie as a sign of loyalty to Fordham; he criticized students for tearing down the goal posts at the Polo Grounds when their football team won; he forcefully opposed euthanasia, nonreligious Christmas cards, interfaith marriage, jokes about the Irish, and everything about *Esquire*, a magazine that he called "a mass of stupid smut." [23] He believed that students had very limited rights.[24] And while he encouraged praying for peace, he opposed pacifism and spoke out against the antiwar strike of April 22, 1937, in which one million students around the country refused to attend class.[25] He was convinced that the Communists were behind the strike and even wrote an article in *America* magazine to prove his case.[26] In the latter essay, he traced the development of Communist youth organizations and their leaders and concluded with:

> The heads of our largest universities have permitted a radical minority such as the A.S.U. [American Student Union] to dictate the day, and exact hour of that day, on which they are to conduct demonstrations for peace. Kow-towing before such groups has only served to exaggerate their already bloated importance. And meanwhile, unwittingly or not, they are playing into the hands of those who wish a united front for their own insidious purposes.
>
> A careful consideration of the new tactics adopted by Communism leads one to conclude that the greatest danger in the United States does

not lie with the violent radicals but rather with those who are neither fish nor flesh but poor red herring.[27]

Earlier, he had attacked communism in an editorial entitled "Anti-Christ has Risen":

The Communist Party in the United States, illegitimate child of the Bill of Rights, is making far more headway than Hearst-haters would have us believe. There is an amazingly communistic trend in the average American University, riding free under the guise of "Anti-Fascism." We maintain that six of seven "Leagues Against Fascism" are as pro-Communist as anti-Fascist. The rising generation is at a cross-road and many a Marxist is more than anxious to direct it down the path to Moscow.[28]

In another fiery editorial, Donovan objected vigorously to President Roosevelt's "packing" of the Supreme Court. In doing so, he critiqued the Court as well, with an outspokenness and brashness that he demonstrated throughout his life:

He [President Roosevelt] evidently believes that some five of the present Supreme Court are economic ante-diluvians who steadfastly refuse to take cognizance of the people's needs. More than a modicum of truth underlies this contention, despite the wailings of those who bemoan desecration of hallowed ground. . . . If ever a scheme were conducive to Fascism, it is this. A distraught nation, a powerful executive, a rubber-stamped legislature and now an impotent judiciary! Such a combination paves the road to dictatorship.[29]

In a Thanksgiving editorial in 1935, Donovan expressed his gratitude for being insulated in a Catholic university. It drew praise from the Jesuit magazine, *America*,[30] but it was severely criticized as illiberal by other student papers, such as *Campus* of the College of the City of New York, soon after it was published. When another Catholic newspaper, *The Quadrangle*, of Manhattan College, published an article attacking the Catholic Alfred E. Smith, former governor of New York, because Smith, now a private citizen, was attacking President Roosevelt, Manhattan's administration moved to halt the paper. James supported the administration.[31] Far from being the inkwell-tossing prankster of several years before, James now believed that "Sensible if not prim decorum is truly a requisite of a gentleman."[32] He was also quite pragmatic in his views on the purposes of a college education:

We hate to be crass. But despite our appreciation of factual knowledge and love of romanticism, in which the four years of college should abound, we feel it our duty to remind that neither winding elms nor sheer study will ever fill the family larder. There is a great deal more to be considered. . . . First, there are the contacts which you make during these years. They are friendships which, to be frank, in the future may be reckoned in dollars and cents. . . . And remember that when you are an alumnus, you will attend your dinners and renew friendships not only for the spiritual beauty of the thing but also because you sell radiators.[33]

When *Vogue* magazine asked a number of male college editors for their viewpoint on feminine fashions through a questionnaire, Donovan was one of those solicited. The article appeared in the 1935 Christmas issue of *Vogue*. While most of the responses were presented in tallied form, Donovan's response was quoted in detail and presented as the ending for the magazine article:

> To me, the most important rôle [*sic*] which dress can play in a woman's life is to accentuate her natural beauty and if possible withdraw a man's attention from what she physically lacks. . . . It would seem more important that a man does not notice individual points of attire. It is the beautiful entity which appeals to a man . . .
>
> It is thus that such an expression as a "vision in white" has become popular. . . . In a vision we would hardly notice individual points, but rather the beauty of the complete image. And so it is with a girl. We would prefer to think of her as something remotely lovely and intriguing—not as a rational animal.[34]

Fordham's newspaper joked that *Vogue*'s cancellation rate rose markedly after Donovan's contribution.[35]

In his senior year, Donovan completed his second one-act play, *Alcazar,* and entered it in competition. It was not successful. The play centered on a foreign correspondent covering the civil war in Spain and that reporter's personal struggle in choosing between the rebels and loyalists. Ultimately, amid the bombed ruins of the fortress of Alcazar, the reporter finds justice in the rebel cause.[36]

Donovan did have a lighter side. According to a story in the Fordham *Ram* just before his graduation in 1937, he could "be seen most Friday or Saturday nights at the Stork Club or the Sapphire Room. Drives about in a Ford Phaeton, which still can't tell the difference between gasoline, rye or kerosene. Visited Europe last summer and took in the Olympics."[37]

Patrick Cardinal Hayes presided over Fordham's commencement exercises on June 16, 1937, when James received his bachelor of arts degree. The yearbook, *Maroon,* noted that Donovan had the twofold honor of being voted by his classmates as both *Best All-Around Man* and the member of his class who *Did Most For Fordham.* Donovan had majored in English, wrote the draft of the Student Council's constitution, and was a debater, varsity tennis player, and assistant band manager. He also contributed to the university's literary magazine, *The Fordham Monthly*.[38]

Donovan went on to attend Harvard Law School in September 1937, living in Walter Hastings Hall. According to family legend, at about this time, he asked his father to buy him a small-town newspaper because of his love for journalism. The elder Donovan, according to the story, agreed, but only if his son completed law school first and if he was still interested in a newspaper career at the later time.

In 1939, as chair of the law school yearbook, Donovan decided to honor one of his former law professors at Harvard, Felix Frankfurter, who had recently been elevated to the United States Supreme Court, by dedicating the yearbook to him. The Supreme Court Justice acknowledged: "I bow with humility and pride that you wish to dedicate next year's Law School Yearbook to me. For me the ultimate tribunal of approval will always be the students of law, and, more particularly, the students of Harvard Law School. Your kindness in this offering is one more powerful spur for me to merit the good opinion of fellow students at the Harvard Law School."[39]

In addition to Frankfurter, the faculty of the law school at the time Donovan attended included Roscoe Pound, who later became its dean, and James McCauley Landis, a future chairman of the Securities and Exchange Commission. After completing a thesis on the law of libel in New York State,[40] Donovan received his LLB degree in 1940.

Edelstein and Donovan had always remained friends. In 1941, when each was preparing for the New York State Bar examination, they traveled together to study at the Lake Placid Club where the Donovan family maintained a cottage. In his later years, Edelstein, who had since been appointed as a United States District Judge for the Southern District of New York, recalled his time at the Lake Placid Club in a talk at a holiday gathering of Donovan's law firm at Windows on the World Restaurant atop the World Trade Center in about 1977. What made a lasting impression on him, Judge Edelstein said, was an action of his friend's father in his behalf. In the early 1900s the Lake Placid Club did not admit Jews, Edelstein related. Even as a visitor, Edelstein, as a Jew, was made to feel uncomfortable, especially in the dining hall. When Dr. Donovan heard of the difficulties of his son's friend, he went directly to the club's manager. As Edelstein recalled, Dr. Donovan asked for a piece of paper and a pencil—to tender his resignation from membership over the poor behavior directed toward David. His treatment, said Judge Edelstein, improved appreciably during the remainder of his stay.[41]

It was at Lake Placid, too, that James Donovan met his own "vision in white," the lovely Mary E. McKenna, in about 1939. Mary, then twenty-one, had vacationed with her family at Lake Placid yearly, as did the Donovans. Mary was the daughter of John F. McKenna and the former Elizabeth L. Farrell. She attended Marymount Academy, a boarding school in Tarrytown, New York, and later completed an associate's program at Marymount Junior College on the academy's grounds.

Soon after Mary met Donovan their courtship began. They were engaged in the spring of 1941, and as an engagement gift, Mary gave him a collector's copy of Housman's *A Shropshire Lad*. Although the United States was not yet a participant in the war that was engulfing Europe, Donovan was somewhat reluctant to plan a wedding in the near future. Mary saw no advantage in waiting, however, and as a result, on June 30, 1941, they were married. The service took place in Mary's home parish of St. Anselm's in Brooklyn. As a wedding present, Dr. Donovan provided the couple with their first home in one of his brownstone townhouses in Manhattan at 432 East Fifty-eighth Street.

In 1940, having graduated from law school, Donovan secured a position with Townley, Updike, and Carter, a general practice law firm located in the *Daily News* building at 220 East Forty-second Street in New York City. He had learned of this firm while he was a senior at Harvard. At that time, he was introduced to a patient of his father who was an officer of the Metropolitan Life Insurance Company. The patient referred the younger Donovan to Churchill Rodgers, later the general counsel for Metropolitan Life who, in turn, sent Donovan with a note of referral to Townley, Updike and Carter. Following an interview, Donovan was hired at an annual salary of $1,800, to begin upon graduation.

At the time Donovan joined the firm, it was defending insurance companies as well as newspapers. In one particular case, a sensational radio commentator and insurance agent named Morris H. Siegel had been telling his listeners on the radio to drop the ordinary life insurance policies of Metropolitan Life Insurance Company and buy term insurance through him and his associates instead. Metropolitan Life informed its field staff about Siegel in a memorandum and also engaged in rebuttal radio programming. As a result, some of Metropolitan Life's own policy holders sued the insurance company because they believed that its actions were too aggressive and were hurting the company's reputation and hence their profits. A second group of policyholders sued the insurance company for not being aggressive enough by failing to take civil action to restrain Siegel. Donovan worked briefly on the suits against the company until the court finally dismissed them based essentially on the fact that Metropolitan Life's directors made their decisions in good faith.[42]

Donovan took the New York State Bar examination in October 1940. Of 979 who sat for the examination, Donovan was one of 447 who passed.[43] He was admitted to the New York Bar in 1941. According to Donovan himself, he had by this time become irretrievably "hooked" on the practice of law.[44] While at Townley, he dealt with publication law as well as insurance law and represented the *Daily News* in several actions. After the Siegel suit, one of the earliest cases to which he was assigned was that of *Henry Louis Gehrig, also known as Lou Gehrig v. News Syndicate Co., Inc. and James Powers, also known as Jimmy Powers.*[45] In this instance, Powers, the sports editor for the *Daily News*, had written an article suggesting that the Yankees had been hit by a polio epidemic. He wrote that Lou Gehrig's infantile paralysis had infected other Yankees, thus causing their losing streak. Gehrig, actually suffering from amyotrophic lateral schlerosis (ALS), not poliomyelitis, felt offended by the article and sued the paper in the Supreme Court of Bronx County, charging that his reputation and credit were hurt. Townley, Updike and Carter provided the defense for the *News*. Powers subsequently wrote a public apology on September 6, 1940,[46] and the case was resolved out of court.

In another interesting libel case on which Donovan worked, the *Daily News* had published an article about a raid by federal agents on a location that was said to be quartering Nazis. A photograph of a house appeared with the story. The homeowners sued because the photographer had taken a picture of the wrong dwelling, and the court ruled in favor of the owners.[47]

Donovan was an associate of Townley, Updike and Carter for two years.[48] After the United States's entry into World War II, he took a leave of absence from the firm and joined the United States Office of Scientific Research and Development in Washington, DC, as associate general counsel in 1942. Mary returned to her parents' home, thankful to be back in more suburban Brooklyn, but unhappy at the prospect of a lengthy separation. It would not be the first and, as she later quipped of their time together, "I could just as well have been married to a traveling salesman."[49]

2

The Lawyer in World War II

THE UNITED STATES MAY NOT HAVE BEEN PREPARED MILITARILY BE-
fore its entry into World War II in 1941, but a number of scientists
had begun to take some initiatives following Germany's invasion of
Poland two years earlier. In 1939, Vannevar Bush, president of the
Carnegie Institution in Washington, DC, recommended to President
Roosevelt that an organization be established that would conduct
research in behalf of the military. Thereafter, on June 27, 1940, the
Council of National Defense ordered the creation of a National
Defense Research Committee (NDRC). A year later, the NDRC was
reorganized by Executive Order 8807, and the United States Office
of Scientific Research and Development (OSRD) was formed. The
OSRD became the primary organization while the National Defense
Research Committee and a Committee on Medical Research served
as its two components. The goal of the agency was the coordination
of research efforts by scientists and technicians involving weaponry,
military hardware, and medicine. The research was to be carried out
through contracts with existing academic institutions, industrial organizations, and governmental groups. At the peak of OSRD's activity during the war, it had fourteen hundred contracts with two
hundred laboratories and one hundred colleges and universities and
a multimillion-dollar annual budget.

The OSRD's governing committees included Vannevar Bush as
chair, together with Robert A. Millikin and Ernest O. Lawrence of the
University of California; James B. Conant, president of Harvard University; Karl T. Compton, president of Massachusetts Institute of Technology; and Harold C. Urey, a professor at Columbia University.[1] In
the years that followed, the atomic bomb was developed, as were radar
and sonar, rockets, the bazooka, and synthetic antimalaria drugs. A
new invention, the proximity fuse, was also created at the time. It had
the advanced electronics to allow an artillery shell to explode near its
target without having to hit it directly. In addition, the OSRD oversaw
the perfecting of penicillin and sulfa drugs for use in wartime.

31

Administering such a large and expensive program necessitated the advice of counsel on many occasions. When an opening in the OSRD occurred, James Donovan sought it. In 1942 he left private practice and obtained an appointment as an associate general counsel at the agency's headquarters at 1530 P Street, NW in Washington, DC Soon after, he and Mary found an apartment at 4801 Connecticut Avenue, NW in the District.

While working for the OSRD, Donovan had to address numerous war-related legal concerns such as the legitimacy of using human test subjects in life-threatening medical experiments and the possible right by individual scientists to patent certain mechanisms that they had invented while constructing the atomic bomb.[2] Later, as general counsel, Donovan was responsible for the highly secret contracts that were developed between OSRD and universities and research laboratories for the development of the latter weapon. In this effort, he worked with his former Harvard classmate, John T. Connor, later president of the pharmaceutical firm, Merck. In cooperation with Secretary of the Interior Harold Ickes, "they secretly withdrew from the United States Public Reserve in New Mexico all of the land required to be used for atomic bomb experiments."[3]

In addition to the above, accident insurance for the workers on these potentially deadly projects had to be secured. As it was briefly written in a later senatorial campaign bulletin: "All Donovan had to do was to find U.S. insurers willing to underwrite a hazard they could know nothing about, on insureds whose names and precise jobs they could not be told, at rates which could not be based on experience. On top of this, the companies had to agree to pay claims they could not even investigate!"[4]

Donovan negotiated this insurance contract in behalf of the government with Hale Anderson Sr., vice-president of the Fidelity and Casualty Co. of New York, who represented a syndicate of insurance companies for this purpose.[5] The plan called for $10,000 accidental death, dismemberment, and disability coverage, a $50 weekly indemnity and full hospitalization, all at a cost of $150 yearly. Thus, scientists just off campuses in the United States were protected in the event of exposure to radiation or harmful diseases, as well as while they watched bazooka tests in deserts, or while traveling high over the Atlantic Ocean in experimental balloons.

In addition to evaluating contracts and developing insurance plans, Donovan sought to fulfill the many requests from personnel for wills and waivers of various kinds, and to provide numerous legal opinions ranging from questions of delegation of authority and exemptions from federal excise taxes for contractors to the use of conscientious objectors in defense work. He also wrote an opinion sanctioning the use of a Russian transmitter located in the United States. He noted that it was not illegal although it could be prevented by policy statement.[6]

Donovan applied for an officer's commission in the navy while he was still with the OSRD. On August 2, 1942, he was admitted into the naval reserves. It was also during his time in the OSRD that he and Mary had their first child, Jane Ann or "Jan."

Donovan received his commission as an ensign in the United States Navy on August 2, 1943, and was assigned to the Naval Command of a newly created agency, the Office of Strategic Services (OSS). He immediately took leave from his civilian post at the OSRD and was designated as assistant general counsel to the OSS.

The Office of Strategic Services was the outgrowth of an earlier agency known as the Coordinator of Information. Prior to 1941, several organizations were responsible for collecting intelligence information, such as the Office of Naval Intelligence, the Department of State, and the War Department's Military Intelligence Division (G2). However, there was no central core of individuals who would sift through and collate the disparate information that was developed. President Roosevelt desired a coordinated, strategic approach to intelligence. Thus, on July 11, 1941, he appointed William J. Donovan as the Coordinator of Information (COI).[7] According to Michael Warner of the Central Intelligence Agency history staff, the office of the COI was the first intelligence agency created to operate in a time of peace. Its purpose was to gather and evaluate information affecting the national defense.[8]

In September 1941, William Donovan's COI was given the additional task of espionage using little-audited presidential funds to conduct activities. Director Donovan, himself, developed a Research and Analysis Branch for the purpose of presenting reports on German and Italian strengths and weaknesses. On June 13, 1942, six months after America's entry into World War II, President Roosevelt split the Coordinator of Information's organization into two separate units, one public, the Office of War Information, and the other clandestine, the new Office of Strategic Services (OSS). William Donovan was given command of the latter, and within a very short time, he was sending operatives to all parts of the world to gather information, conduct subversive activities, and guide invading allied troops. In 1943, William Donovan was recommissioned as an army officer and appointed a brigadier general since he represented the

Joint Chiefs of Staff as head of the OSS. By 1944 the office had a staff of thirteen thousand men and women of whom 25 percent were nonmilitary. More than half of the employees served overseas.[9]

James Donovan was not at the OSS two months before he was directed to report to the Naval Training School, located on the grounds of Princeton University in New Jersey, in October 1943 in order to fulfill officer-training requirements.

During the time that James was stationed in Princeton, Mary and Jan moved back to the home of her parents in Brooklyn. Then, when his training was completed, James returned to the Office of Strategic Services under General Donovan, of the same name, but unrelated to him. Among other notable figures that General Donovan hired at about this same time were Arthur M. Schlesinger Jr., Richard M. Helms, Arthur J. Goldberg, and Allen W. Dulles.[10] In fact, based upon the appointment of so many such socially prominent figures the OSS gained the nickname, "Oh So Social."

James Donovan was appointed chief of the Legal Division in December 1943 and, on April 1, 1944, he was named general counsel of the agency. In February of the following year, he was promoted to lieutenant. As in his position with the OSRD, many legal problems were brought to him, ranging from the more usual, such as how to establish fictitious businesses as fronts for spying, to the more fantastic, as in the legality of inserting an acrid but nonlethal chemical in the enemy's water supply in order to make drinking more difficult.[11]

The Office of Strategic Services was composed primarily of military personnel, and from time to time, charges were brought against servicemen that resulted in a court-martial. After one of these trials, an officer who had represented a defendant approached Donovan to request his aid in seeking a new trial for his client. The officer explained that his client, an army sergeant, had been found guilty of attempted assault upon a commissioned officer and was sentenced to twenty years' hard labor and a dishonorable discharge. As Donovan read the trial transcript he learned that an army unit, scheduled to go overseas, was given liberty one evening. Several soldiers went to a local bar and, after some drinking, found themselves in a brawl with a cadre of military police. As the melee spilled outside, a police captain took his pistol and beat one of the enlisted personnel, a Sergeant Musica. The sergeant was taken to a hospital and treated for his injuries. When the captain later visited Musica and saw the damage that he had done, he chose a course to cover his brutality by charging the sergeant with a crime, falsely claiming that the sergeant moved as if to hit him, thus prompting his use of force.[12]

At the first trial, the captain presented himself as a professional policeman who would never use excessive force based upon his training and experience as the chief of police in the northern New York State town of Whiteface Manor before the war. Having vacationed on numerous occasions in the Adirondack Mountains, Donovan immediately knew that no such town existed. Whiteface Manor was actually a resort.[13]

Donovan later spoke with the manager of the Whiteface Manor resort, one Mr. Simpson, who explained that the M.P. captain was known there as "Blackie," and worked as a night watchmen before the war, but with no police under his control. The manager agreed to attend a rehearing on the original court-martial and traveled at his own expense. At that rehearing, the captain reiterated his earlier, sworn testimony about his police background in the nonexistent town of Whiteface Manor. At the conclusion of his testimony, Musica's defense attorney, whom Donovan was assisting, brought the hotel manager into the hearing room. The startling impact that Simpson's presence had upon the captain was obvious.[14] Following Simpson's testimony, the defense rested, and within minutes, the court found the defendant, Musica, not guilty. Two days later, the captain committed suicide.

While Donovan was working with the OSS in Washington, Mary, Jan, and the Donovan's newlyborn son, John, joined him. They lived in a wing of a stately home at 2301 North Uhle Street in Arlington, Virginia. John English, an OSS officer, and his wife, Ottilie, had quarters in the opposite wing. While the friendship between these couples grew, there was apparently some discord from time to time. A biographer of General Donovan, Richard Dunlop, recorded John English as having gone to the general at one time because of friction between the wives. The general, trying to give sage advice, reportedly told him, "You can't put a German girl [Ottilie] and an English girl [Mary] in one house and expect them to get along."[15] "Irish," Mary hastily corrected in a recent conversation with the author, adding "and we always got along."[16] At some point during their time together, the couples even coined a name for their home, "Engdon," from a consolidation of their last names.

On March 15, 1945, General Donovan designated James Donovan, now a lieutenant (jg), as chief of a new unit within the OSS, the War Crimes Division. Earlier, in a separate action, the United Nations Commission for the Investigation of War Crimes, with seventeen participating nations, had been established in London in 1943.[17] Each body had as its goal the amassing of sufficient evidence to warrant prosecution for the atrocities committed by the Nazis during the war.

At the request of China, a subcommission was also established for the Far East with respect to the actions of Japan. In 1944, President Roosevelt gave the Department of War the responsibility for deciding how best to try war criminals. U.S. Army Colonel Murray Bernays, as Head of the Special Projects Branch of the War Department, worked for nine months on these procedures, and by September 15, 1944, he had drafted a document entitled "Trial of European War Criminals."[18]Before his military service, Bernays had been an attorney in New York with a special concern for American prisoners of war as well as German atrocities.

With the War Crimes Division in place, James Donovan's staff was enhanced by two men from Hollywood who were now in service, E. Ray Kellogg and George C. Stevens. Kellogg had been a director of photographic effects for 20th-Century Fox Studios between 1929 and 1941. He now had the responsibility of locating and compiling photographic evidence against the Nazi regime. Stevens, a producer and director, was given the duty of photographing the concentration camps as they were liberated.[19]

Many of the photography experts were actually assembled long beforehand by Hollywood director John Ford. Ford, a navy commander, was ordered for duty in Washington, DC, in September 1941. He developed a Field Photographic Branch that included Kellogg, Budd and Stewart Schulberg, Robert Parish, Joseph Ziegler, and Robert Webb. Ford had, in fact, fifteen complete film crews in Washington. His first assignment in the war was to prepare a film report on the condition of the Atlantic fleet. He later prepared a top-secret report on the Pearl Harbor attack. When the OSS was given the mission of gathering evidence against the Nazis, some of Ford's units were assigned to Europe.[20]

Assembling and organizing evidence, however, was only one of James's responsibilities. He had also been directed early in April 1945 by General Donovan to "get us a top-flight staff on war crimes."[21] One such member was not recruited, but actually showed up on his own initiative. Drexel A. Sprecher, an attorney, was a first lieutenant in the army, serving in the Midwest. When Sprecher learned of the formation of a prosecution team, he took a leave and flew to Washington, DC. Through a previous friendship with an individual on the National Labor Relations Board, Sprecher was brought to James Donovan for an interview. After a half hour of discussion, James said he would make the necessary arrangements to take Sprecher into the OSS.[22]

Meanwhile, Harry Truman, who had ascended to the presidency on Roosevelt's death on April 12, named Associate Supreme Court

Justice Robert H. Jackson as Chief of Counsel for the Prosecution of Nazi War Criminals on May 2, 1945.[23] Jackson, in turn, asked William Donovan to be his lead counsel at the suggestion of Sen. Alben Barkley.[24] On May 16, Jackson issued a press release naming the first of his prosecution team, including William Donovan, Sidney S. Alderman (a lawyer for the Southern Pacific Railway who had impressed Jackson in the past with his arguments before the Supreme Court), Francis M. Shea (former assistant attorney general), Lt. James Donovan and Lt. Gordon Dean (a special assistant to Jackson when the latter was attorney general and a former press officer at the Department of Justice).[25] The main office of the prosecutors was in the Pentagon. Colonel Bernays was the executive officer of the unit. Among James Donovan's responsibilities was the preparation of visual evidence against the Nazis in anticipation of a trial. According to Telford Taylor, an Army Intelligence officer who would later join the team, "James Donovan made an excellent impression on Jackson and joined the inner circle of his advisors."[26]

When news of his latest assignment reached Donovan's parents, they immediately sent him a telegram that reflected their love and religious devotion:

> Congratulations and best wishes on your new assignment May God bless you and direct you always in the way of holiness and truth and spare you to Mary and children and the folks back home for many years to come Love= Mother and Father[27]

The new team worked quite rapidly and on May 30, 1945, James Donovan sent a program report on the preparation of the prosecution to Alderman. He noted that the basic task of organizing the prosecution was complete and included twenty-five trial briefs and a list of the top fifty major German war criminals. James added, "The basic Field Photography program is designed to prove all five charges in the indictment by photographic means."[28] Telford Taylor was not so convinced. He wrote afterward:

> As for the OSS, James Donovan had previously assured Bernays that his agency had "done a great deal of work" and "assembled much material" on its assigned subjects. But his progress report of May 30 did not encourage me to believe that the OSS would be much more productive of real evidence than the JAG. In fact, the OSS staff included a number of able and learned experts on the Third Reich [these included Franz Neuman, author of *Behemoth—The Structure and Practice of National Socialism* (1944); Raphael Lemkin, coiner of the word "genocide" and author of *Axis Rule in Occupied Europe* (1944); Carl Schorske; and William L. Langer], but

most of what they had to offer, however valuable as background information, was neither documentary nor testimonial evidence suitable for court use.[29]

Taylor, however, was always somewhat cool in his references to James Donovan, perhaps resentful of a thirty-year-old already having strong ties to both General Donovan and Justice Jackson.[30] It should be noted, too, that the visual material provided by the OSS was only a part of their work. As will be seen, they also collected valuable Nazi documents for the prosecution.

World War II ended in Europe on May 7, 1945. At this same time, Donovan received orders to travel to England. In addition to his regular wages, he was to receive a per diem pay of seven dollars for overseas work. By mid-June, it was time to leave for Europe. On Sunday, June 17, Justice Jackson invited James Donovan and other staff who had been recruited into the prosecution group, to his home in McLean, Virginia for a get-acquainted party.[31] They had to get acquainted quickly. The next day most left for London.

Separated again, this time with her husband overseas, Mary, the children, and their housekeeper, Rose, remained in Virginia for several more months before deciding to return to New York.

3

The Aftermath of War: Trying Its Criminals

BY THE TIME THAT GERMANY SURRENDERED IN APRIL 1945, EUROPE was virtually prostrate. Whole cities had been demolished, particularly in Germany; western Russia was in ruins; and England was reeling from the nefarious V-1 and V-2 rocket attacks on its cities and towns. The historians R. R. Palmer and Joel Colton have already provided a picture of the war's broad devastation:

> The war damage, chiefly bomb damage, destroyed the capital accumulation of generations—housing, paved streets, utilities plants, foundries, factories. And the ruin of freight yards, rolling stock, and bridges brought the interchange of commodities to a standstill. Town was cutoff from country. City people dispersed to live with their country cousins, or reverted to primitive methods of hunting for food and fuel.[1]

Harbors were also severely damaged as were the merchant fleets. In addition to homes, farms and farm animals were destroyed, as were schools, government complexes, and administrative centers. Shortages abounded in food, fertilizers, raw materials, and equipment. Essential services, such as fire fighting and health care, were severely impaired. Unable to export goods, Europe became primarily an importer, which obviously had a substantially negative impact on its trade balances. While the United States began massive aid shipments immediately after the war ended in Europe, it would be two more years before the successful Marshall Plan was instituted.

If the material losses were staggering, the human toll was beyond the grasp of human feeling. Nearly 13 million individuals were displaced and homeless. Estimates of deaths from the war in Europe have reached upwards of 40 million, more than half of these civilian. "No one could begin to estimate the complete toll of human lives lost in the war, directly or indirectly, from the bombings, the mass extermination and deportation policies of the Germans, the post-war famines and epidemics," wrote Palmer and Colton. "Perhaps the losses came to thirty-five or forty million, but at such figures the human mind retreats and human sensibilities are dulled."[2]

39

Against this backdrop of the horrors caused by the war, the Allied governments were determined to exact justice from its perpetrators. The process began in London and ended in Nuremberg.

On June 18, 1945, Justice Jackson and a number of his personal staff flew to London. They included his son, U.S. Navy Ens. William E. Jackson, Maj. Lawrence Coleman, and Jackson's secretary, Elsie Douglas. In addition, there were several trial counsels and support staff, Sidney B. Alderman; Francis M. Shea; Shea's secretary, Elizabeth Leonard; Col. Murray C. Bernays, Capt. Ralph L. Morgan; Navy lieutenants Gordon Dean and James Donovan; and five other secretarial assistants. The group took up residence in the fashionable Claridge Hotel and constituted the advance unit who would begin the process of setting up a military tribunal. On June 23 Robert Storey, a Texas lawyer and Air Corps colonel who had just come back from a war crime trial in Bulgaria, and Gen. William Donovan, joined them. This relatively small American staff would quickly grow to approximately seven hundred, including 150 attorneys, before the start of the trial. The British, by comparison, had a total staff of 168.

As soon as he arrived in Europe, Donovan began to write Mary regularly. He was homesick and missed Mary from the outset, never hesitating to tell her, but his letters were also informative. Some of the information in the material that follows was gleaned from the letters that Donovan wrote to his wife during the period.[3] He described the people with whom he worked, the places he visited, and his role in the progress leading up to and including the first Nuremberg trial. In fact, they provide a brief, personal summary of the postwar justice exercised by the Allied powers in Europe. After the first trial of the major war criminals and organizations others would follow, although Donovan had returned to the United States before those later trials commenced. Tribunals were also held in Japan for the same purpose.

Upon his arrival in London, Donovan immediately began working with British representatives for the purpose of developing an international agreement that would create a tribunal to hear charges against the Nazi leaders. The French quickly joined the conference, as did, somewhat belatedly, the Soviets. The intended agreement was essential for an international prosecution. It was also important both to formulate a military tribunal to conduct the trial as well as to establish an underlying philosophy, building on the earlier work of Bernays. All of this had to be done simultaneously with gathering, analyzing, and sorting evidence and preparing trial briefs and memoranda. A place for the trial had to be found, and the prisoners, who were still being captured, eventually had to be transferred to the trial site. To accomplish much of this, Jackson made use of both civilian and military lawyers, together with the vast resources of the Office of Strategic Services. While there were difficulties in this process, the trial preparations did move forward.

On June 22, Alderman, Bernays, and James Donovan conferred to review and extend the list of war criminals beyond the ten proposed by the British. They also sought to include several organizations in the indictment, such as the Nazi Party leadership and the SS. The group brought the list up to sixteen at that time, and the British found it generally acceptable.[4]

Writing home to Mary, Donovan described his initial activities:

On Monday we begin our conferences with the Russians and the French. My role thus far has been one to my liking. We have a group of six dealing on behalf of the United States; Justice Jackson, Alderman, Shea, Col. Bernays, Bill Whitney and I.[5] Opposite us is a rather imposing array; Sir David Fyfe (Attorney General), Sir Thomas Barnes (Solicitor to the Treasury), Sir Basil Newton of the Foreign Office, General Lord Bridgeman (British Judge Advocate General) and some others, including one Hon. Roberts, K.C., the foremost British criminal lawyer. Despite all the titles, they have no more to offer than our side and we have seen eye to eye on almost all things. Mr. Alderman and I represent the U.S. on the subcommittee charged with preparing an indictment, selecting the defendants and preparing the case itself. As soon as the other nations arrive on Monday, that subcommittee will then proceed to join similar subcommittees from the other countries.[6]

At about the same time that Donovan was writing to Mary, Justice Jackson was writing to Secretary of the Navy James Forrestal, on Donovan's behalf:

We have commenced negotiations with British. Next Monday we will begin them with French and Russians. A most important role in this international program is being carried out for me by Lieutenant James Britt Donovan, USNR, 297681, to whom a spot promotion to commander should be given as soon as possible. Due to the requirement of his work he must remain in uniform. It will be appreciated if you view this matter as urgent and give it your personal attention.
R.H. Jackson[7]

Meanwhile, John English, Donovan's friend and associate from Engdon days, left London for Paris on June 28. The work of OSS agent English was directed toward finding enemy documents, an effort that resulted in a mass of evidence, collected not only by the

OSS but by Allied forces as well. The problem for the prosecution quickly became not one of the scantiness of evidence, but rather its sheer volume. When English arrived in Paris, for example, he met Col. Robert G. Storey, named by Jackson as the chief of the Documentation Division who was just setting up an office at No. 7 Rue de Presbourg, near the Arc de Triomphe.[8] Storey, whose responsibilities included assembling, analyzing, and selecting documents for trial, informed English that he needed high-level documents if the prosecution against the Nazis was going to be successful. English replied that he was going into Germany and would attempt to assist him.

Within days, English telephoned Storey and told him that he had just found forty-seven crates of documents hidden behind the brick wall of a German barn. On examination it was discovered that the papers, original correspondence among the Nazis who were about to be tried, were hidden by Alfred Rosenberg, former Nazi minister of the occupied eastern territory. Soon after English's discovery, Allied troops found 485 tons of German Foreign Office documents in an abandoned castle near Kassel and numerous top-secret Luftwaffe documents hidden earlier by Herman Goering in a salt mine near Berchtesgaden.[9] The finds were becoming typical of other discoveries all around Europe.

While part of Jackson's prosecution team were poring through seized enemy documents, another group, which included James Donovan, were continuing to develop a judicial process with the French, English, and Soviets. It could be a laborious task: "The negotiations are still going on [Donovan wrote]. We hope to reach an agreement but thus far have not done so. Trying to unite four legal systems into one proceeding is a difficult job. But there are common objectives, so I hope that it will work out. Meantime, however, it is a slow and difficult process."[10]

After ten days' discussion among the Allied powers, the group agreed on naming the trial court as the International Military Tribunal, and in early July they began to search for a site. Jackson insisted upon the trial being held on German soil, and the Russians pushed strongly for Berlin. Gen. Lucius Clay, in seeking a location for the court, found the Palace of Justice in Nuremberg,[11] and he decided that it contained adequate jail space with ready access to the courthouse. Also the buildings had suffered little damage from bombings. Upon Jackson's arrival in Nuremberg he immediately resolved to use that city, especially because he saw it as the philosophical center of National Socialism and the ideal location to try the criminal proponents of that creed. Later in July, Jackson accompanied the English and French to Nuremberg, and they, too, agreed on the location. The Soviets ultimately concurred as well. At about this same time, the secretary of the navy acted on Justice Jackson's request and Donovan was promoted on July 10, 1945, to full commander.

It was not lost on Telford Taylor that Jackson had actually secured a double promotion for James Donovan.[12] Prior to the promotion, Donovan was a lieutenant. The next step in the navy was normally lieutenant commander before becoming eligible for the superior position of commander. Donovan, himself, was elated.

Wasn't that wonderful news about my being made a full Commander? Three broad stripes & a new cap with "scrambled eggs" on the visor. Veddy handsome, indeed. I know you will be proud when you see me. It was done by Presidential order on request from the Secretary of the Navy, in turn based on a request of a Supreme Court Justice. To think that in December I was an Ensign. Everyone here (from Admiral Stark down) thinks it is unprecedented in Navy history. I am now a "Senior Naval Officer." In all OSS we have only a couple . . .

By the way, you may see me in the newsreels—at the International Conference, with the Russians, French, etc. Watch for it. I'll have a print made for us anyway. Ask Ray Kellogg to let you know as soon as the films get back to the U.S.[13]

According to Telford Taylor, dissatisfaction among the American participants over the slow process of multinational planning started to become manifest in June. In the first week, Taylor admitted he was not an administrator; General Donovan warned that anyone who was dissatisfied with the progress of the work could take the next flight home; and two weeks later, Bernays wrote a personal letter blaming Jackson and Shea for the staff disorganization. On July 13, "bad luck Friday," Jackson antagonized the British. And then, in the dead of a hot night on July 19, when all the windows overlooking the courtyard of Claridge's Hotel were open, Jackson and Shea were awakened by James Donovan's shouting into the telephone on a long distance call to General Donovan. Taylor, in his recounting of the incident, said James Donovan was overheard telling the general that "Jackson was too much under the influence of his son, Bill, that the Justice had turned over to Shea 'the economic side of the case' and so there was no use in trying to push one Dickenson for that job and that Jackson had promised that 'he would not embarrass [General] Donovan and he hoped [General] Donovan would not embarrass him.' Jackson and Shea were much disturbed by this gross indiscretion."[14]

In a footnote, Taylor added "Whether or not as a result of this episode, after my arrival in London, I only rarely encountered James

Donovan at staff conferences, and his responsibility at the trial was limited, as far as I could determine, to the presentation of visual evidence, such as charts and films."[15]

It is not certain if a leave Donovan had sought for a long time was finally granted as a result of this "incident," but he did fly home from England on August 8. He was not "limited" to the responsibility for presenting visual evidence as Taylor mentions, however, for that assignment was always his. If Jackson was upset at Donovan's remarks, it did not reveal itself in his assignments or in Jackson's behavior toward him, as later events would show.

The agreement that established the International Military Tribunal on which Donovan had been working with the English, the French and the Russians was signed just prior to his departure for home on leave.[16] It included a constitution and governing principles together with a charter.[17] The concept of a charter was used rather than an international law or statute in order to avoid later accusations of ex post facto justice. Under the illicit ex post facto concept, an act is defined as a crime after the act is committed. The essence of the Allies' problem was finding documentation that existed prior to the war that made the Nazi crimes illegal before they were committed. Under the agreement's principles, defendants were entitled to have a copy of the indictment, to offer a defense against the charges, to have an attorney, and to have the opportunity to cross-examine witnesses.

According to the agreement, the tribunal was to consist of four members, one each from the United States, Britain, France, and the Soviet Union. There was also one alternate member from each of these countries. A president was to be chosen from the four members for each trial. Decisions were to be made by majority vote. The tribunal was characterized as "military," but it was composed almost entirely of civilians.

The document also defined a war criminal. Briefly, a war criminal was an individual who committed any one of three acts:

1. *Crimes against peace* such as the "planning, preparation, initiation or waging of a war of aggression, or a war in violation of international treaties . . . or conspiracy for the accomplishment of any of the foregoing."
2. *Violations of the laws of war or customs of war* including murder, ill-treatment, or deportation to slave labor of civilians; ill-treatment or murder of civilians; ill-treatment or murder of war prisoners or hostages; and other offenses.
3. *Crimes against humanity* such as "inhumane acts committed against any civilian population, before or during the war, or persecutions on political, racial or religious grounds."[18]

On August 12, 1945, a U.S. C-47 aircraft carried the alleged war criminals from the Bad Mondorf prison in Luxembourg, where they were held following capture, to the city of Nuremberg. Work had also begun at this time on refurbishing the Palace of Justice to accommodate the many prisoners, defense and prosecution staffs, trial needs, and the expected visitors. On August 15, Colonel Bernays resigned from Jackson's staff, presumably because of poor health, but in fact because of continuing disagreements with the justice.[19] Coincidentally, on this same day in the Far East, Japan accepted the terms of unconditional surrender following the two atomic bomb attacks on Hiroshima and Nagasaki.

On August 27, 1945, twenty-four Nazis were named in an indictment with four counts: Count 1 charged the defendants with conspiracy to commit counts 2–4. Count 2 charged that under the defendants' leadership, Germany began aggressive war contrary to treaties; Count 3 charged that Germany resorted to murder, pillage, and destruction in violation of the laws of all civilized nations and the country where the crimes were committed; and Count 4 charged crimes against humanity including extermination, enslavement, and deportation of civilian populations and persecutions on political, racial, and religious grounds.[20]

The chief prosecutors who would be presenting the case shortly were Robert H. Jackson for the United States; Roman A. Rudenko for the Soviet Union; Sir Hartley W. Shawcross for Britain;[21] and François de Menthon for France. Although Justice Jackson had originally predicted that the first trial would begin on September 1, 1945, the start was actually delayed until well into November.

Donovan returned to Europe on September 9. While he had been home on a thirty-day leave, he and Mary spent some time in Virginia with the children and some time traveling to Brooklyn in search of a new home. The couple ultimately found a house at 102 Eighty-second Street into which Mary would move after her husband returned to Europe. The family remained in this home for the next ten years.

On his return to Europe, Donovan flew directly to Paris and remained there for three days in order to begin evaluating the photographic evidence for the forthcoming trial. On September 12, he went back to London and to Claridge's, where he wrote to Mary on his arrival. Some of his observations concerned the military point system that governed when service personnel could return home:

Arrived after an uneventful trip via Paris. Am remaining here until Tuesday or Wednesday, then leaving for Nuremberg. Thereafter I expect to shuttle between Nuremberg & Berlin, with an occasional side-trip to Paris or London.

Everything is going well. I have complete charge of the photographic evidence for the trial. I'm more interested in that than anything else. It includes old newsreels, captured enemy film, etc. Jackson, by the way, is ultra friendly . . .

Delighted to see that Congress is looking into the Navy demobilization program. It's an outrage. For an officer to get out you must be over forty almost, have dependents and have been in around three years. You then about add up to the 49 points . . . The Navy can get along on the officers & men it's taken in within the past two years—plus the regular Navy and those Reservists who would like to stay in. If they passed a law that any officer or enlisted man who has honorably served for over two years is entitled to a discharge the Army & Navy would still have all they need.

From now on, please send all letters to me at . . . Nuremberg.[22]

Jackson and some of his staff arrived in Nuremberg on September 14. James Donovan arrived six days later, simultaneously with the British and the French. Prior to this time, and after, he was flying among London, Paris, and Berlin overseeing the preparation of the photographic evidence for the trial.[23] He was, in fact, responsible for all visual evidence against those charged, including captured motion pictures and photographs.[24]

After his arrival in Nuremberg, Donovan began to provide Mary with his impressions of the city and the people:

To begin, Nurnberg used to be one of the most beautiful cities in Germany. I have some moving pictures of it before the war. It survived from medieval times and within the modern city was an ancient walled city, fully preserved. Beautiful spires, old trees, quaint shops, etc. Because it was such an ancient German city, it was sort of a national shrine and it was here that the Nazi Party each year held its Party Congress. And again because it meant so much to all Germans, the RAF deliberately pounded it. After the air raids, in the last days of the war, the SS made a last desperate stand within the walled city and the American 7th Army had to use artillery on it for five days. You simply cannot imagine the result. It is the most complete picture of devastation that could be conceived. You stand in the "Grand Hotel" (about 50 percent of which is intact but frightfully damaged) and so far as you can see it looks like the ruins of Carthage. You can drive for ten minutes in any direction and cannot see a building standing. The damage to London is negligible compared with this. The walled city is simply a huge mass (for several miles in every direction) of rubble, twisted steel and great concrete slabs. Parts of the wall can still be seen in places, but very little of it.

I cannot believe that this city could be re-built in anything less than a century. I think they would be better off to allow it just to stand—and begin to build on another site.

Where the people who survived now live, is beyond me. They are fed on bread lines and you see some walking along the streets in the day, looking dazed and haggard. If we are going to establish in our trial—the main point—that to plan and launch a war of aggression is a crime, punishable under international law, we certainly came to the right place in which to hold the trial. Anyone who looks at this and doesn't believe that it is a crime—punishable in the most severe way and yet necessarily an insufficient way—to begin a war, must be insane. The destruction, waste, misery, suffering—all that goes with war—is here on permanent exhibit.

The trial will be held in the Criminal Courthouse, a good portion of which survived by some miracle. It is out from the center of the city and gradually, with hundreds of SS prisoners working on it, is beginning to resemble a building. I have a very lovely office in it, just down from Justice Jackson's and directly adjoining the General's. It used to be the chambers of some Court of Appeal judge.

George Demas, Dr. Pathy and I live together in a beautiful house outside the city, up on a hill. It was formerly occupied by some Nazi bigwig and his family. I have the master bed-room, with a breakfast balcony outside it. We have four servants (all of this is provided by the Military Government and charged to German reparations). I have a staff car and driver, etc. As probably the only full Commander in all Bavaria, they give me the best of everything, right after Jackson and the General.

Despite all of the above, I'd give anything to be home. All that I do is try to find ways of cutting the trial short. But the problems are enormous. Everything has to be translated into four languages, etc. The prisoners, Goering, Ribbentrop et al., are housed in a big jail just behind the courthouse. From a window across from my office you can look down into the exercise-yard and see them walking around. They are not allowed to speak to each other and are under heavy guard. We are awaiting the General, who no doubt is busy winding up OSS. You probably know that it goes out of business on Oct. 1. So far as I know, however, it's almost a paper change for administrative purposes and I'll go right on liquidating its affairs for the War Department. I certainly hope that the Navy point system goes down by December. I'll have $40\frac{1}{2}$ points (you still need 49 at present).[25]

Although Donovan does not mention them, evening seminars were given daily for a time by Rafael Lemkin and Robert W. Klempner on the "principles, background and documentary proofs of the organization of the Nazi Party and the administration of the German government under the Nazis."[26] According to Robert Storey, these seminars were useful and informative because most of the staff was unfamiliar with the technical aspects of the Nazi government.[27]

At the beginning of October, Donovan was back in Paris guiding his film work and anticipating the formal filing of the indictment of the Nazi leaders:

I came to Paris on a short trip to consult with the Signal Corps about making a film for me. Am returning first thing tomorrow morning.

On Thursday I am going to Berlin with Justice Jackson, for the filing of the indictment. That pleases me a lot, because you can figure that the trial will begin one month from the day of the filing of the indictment. Also that the trial will last about three or four weeks. If we can keep to that schedule it will mean that I'll be home before Christmas. Believe me, I better be.

France is very poor—little in the shops, what there is is very expensive. There is no night life, etc. other than some clip joints in which the GI's get into battles every night. The Navy has wonderful quarters in the Royal Monceau Hotel, where they gave me a fine single room with bath. But it's a hurried trip and aside from being able to stroll along the Seine looking in the bookstalls I've been busy every minute of the two days.[28]

In preparation for the forthcoming tribunal, the eight judges finally met in Nuremberg on October 9 for the first time to plan the trial. They included, for the United States: Attorney General Francis J. Biddle and Judge John Parker, U.S. Court of Appeals, Fourth Circuit (alternate); for the Soviet Union: Maj. Gen. I.T. Nikitchenko and A. F. Volkhov (alternate); for Britain: Sir Geoffrey Lawrence, Lord Justice of the Court of Appeals and Sir William Norman Birkett (alternate); and for France: Henri Donnedieu de Vabre and Robert Falco (alternate). That same night, General Donovan, together with Ambassador Robert Murphy and John English, went over to James Donovan's residence in Berlin to watch the commander's film on the Nazi concentration camps.[29]

On Sunday, October 14 the tribunal in Berlin postponed meeting again for three days at the request of the Soviet Union, as they required more time to translate the documents related to the indictment. On this same day British troops in Berlin cracked down on a very public black market in the Tiergarten, arresting two thousand individuals. Donovan, curious about the black market, apparently just missed being caught up in the British sweep. He wrote to Mary on the day following the arrests, unaware that the arrests were conducted.

I am still here, working away on my film. I think it will be really sensational. What we have done is to take all the old German newsreels from 1922 on and we put them together so as to show how the Nazi's seized power in Germany and then prepared for & launched aggressive war. It's fascinating to review the history of the past fifteen years—tho it makes you wonder whether the whole world went mad.

Life is very comfortable here. We live in a beautiful home run by a very interesting woman who speaks excellent English. She is middle-aged, a good housekeeper, and still has her own servants, for whom the Allied

Government now pays while we are here. I have just been talking with her—what experiences she has had during the past few years, with the war, then the Russian occupation, etc. She has a little girl about ten, who is very cute.

I looked in yesterday on the famous Alexanderstrasse black market in the Russian zone. People are milling all around, trading everything you can imagine—gold, watches, rings, books, suits, furs, etc. Money's not so much the medium of exchange—cigarettes are the main item. A carton of cigarettes here sells for $100.00 on the black market. Can you imagine. As for girls—it's really pathetic. All over Berlin there are hundreds and hundreds, who'll sleep with you for a chocolate bar. Some beautiful. But practically all are diseased. Tho our troops are warned of it every day, the Army venereal disease rate is simply enormous. I suppose that the boys—most of whom are battle veterans overseas a couple of years—get a few drinks and run wild. They must be crazy when by now it's almost a certainty that even to be around one of those girls means at least that you get some sort of lice.[30]

On the following day, Donovan described the Russian occupiers:

This is a miserable day—pouring rain, cold, etc. and no electricity in the house. The power plant for Wansee is in the Russian zone and every once in awhile they just shut it off. After enough protests have been made, they turn it on again.

The Russians are real characters—every one of them. Our house is just inside the Russian zone, so we have them go by all the time. They are uniformly big, simple and direct. While I haven't been approached by any, Budd Schulberg, Commander Monroe, etc. have all had Russians come up, finger their uniforms & say "How much?" They will spend any amount of money for anything—clothes, watches, etc. The reasons, I think, are two-fold; first, they haven't much in Russia of anything and second, by what I think is a real fraud on the part of the Russian government, all soldiers coming to Berlin are paid all arrears in occupation marks. Since most of them haven't been paid for three years, the amount is quite large. But the catch is that the Russian marks are not good back in Russia, so that they must be spent here. That's why the Russians offer such fantastic prices for American cigarettes.

You hear fabulous stories about them all over. They love women and make approaches to them all day long. The regular troops are not above rape, of course, but the officers are a trifle more polished and offer such items as a half-pound of sugar. Mrs. Sprecher, our housekeeper, told me that last week a Russian officer about twenty two came to the door, looked at her and said in German, "How old are you?" "Forty three," said Mrs. S. "That will do," said the Russian, "Where is your bedroom?" Mrs. S. said she was not interested, whereupon he produced a quarter-pound of butter. It took ten minutes to convince him that the butter wasn't wanted. After he left, Mrs. S. said, she turned and found the maid looking longingly after the Russian and the maid said, "And we could have made such nice cakes out of it, Mrs. Sprecher!"[31]

Three days later, on October 19, the indictment of twenty-four Nazis was presented to the military tribunal.

On October 22 Jackson issued General Memorandum No. 5 on "Trial Organization." It created a Board of Review with Storey as chair. The other members included General Donovan, Thomas Dodd, and several others. The board's tasks were to oversee and guide in the preparation of the trial briefs and evidence. The memo also named as consultants to the Board of Review Sidney Alderman, Shea, James Donovan, and Telford Taylor.[32]

Before the trial, Donovan was also involved in an exercise that sought to determine whether or not Rudolf Hess had amnesia. Previously, Associate Trial Counsel John Harlan Amen,[33] in October, had placed Hess in a cell with Goering and Hess's mentor, Dr. Karl Haushofer, in order to determine if Hess would acknowledge either person. He didn't. Donovan, in a letter home described the subsequent plan:

> Tomorrow we are going to make a very interesting experiment and I will write you all about it. Hess has been claiming that his memory is bad and that he suffers from total amnesia. He met Goering in one of the rooms and simply passed him by. Well, we are going to take him in tomorrow and run for him some sound movies of himself when he was at the height of his power, next to Hitler in all Germany. I wonder what will go through his mind when he sees them. We are quite sure—by medical testimony, Etc.—that he is a fakir. But I'm going to sit there and just watch his reactions.[34]

On November 5 Justice Jackson selected the initial trial counsel. They included Executive Trial Counsel Robert G. Storey, and Gen. William Donovan, Sidney S. Alderman, Gen. Telford Taylor, Col. John Harlan Amen, Ralph G. Albrecht, Thomas J. Dodd, Lt. Col. Benjamin Kaplan, Lt. Col. Murray Gurfein, and Maj. Frank B. Wallis.[35] James Donovan, meanwhile, was back in Paris in search of more film material.

> Back in Paris for two days. We ran across a wonderful piece of evidence a couple of weeks ago & I'm up here to track it down. A Colonel sent home to his wife, as a war souvenir, a film (movie) of SS guards in a concentration camp beating up their prisoners. Nice souvenir! Anyway, we had the FBI locate the film in the U.S. and had it shipped here to Paris. Now I'm trying to get it made up into regular movie size, etc.
> Paris is very depressing (by now, as you realize, all Europe is) but our

billet at the Royal Monceau is very lovely. One of the finest hotels in Paris. Because of my rank (ahem!) they assign me as quarters a three-room suite. What I'm supposed to do in the other two rooms is beyond me.[36]

The "experiment" with Hess that Donovan had written about to Mary on the first of the month, took place several days later. The results, however, were not conclusive, but ultimately, Hess admitted his sham behavior.

We had our showing of the old newsreels to Hess yesterday. It was the most fascinating thing I have ever attended. He sat handcuffed to guards and we [William Donovan, Justice Jackson, James Donovan, Colonel Amen, and several Russian and American psychiatrists[37]] placed some dim lights in such a way that we could study his face. Then we saw these newsreels of Hess, Hitler, Goering, etc. at the height of their power, being worshipped by tens of thousands of people. There were close-ups of Hess speaking. It was terrific, looking at the screen and then back at the man in the chair—about thirty pounds lighter, haggard, etc. He has been claiming complete amnesia and it is terribly difficult to figure out whether he is faking.[38]

In early November, Donovan wrote home, still homesick, but nevertheless full of news. He told Mary that General Donovan, whom he idolized, was leaving Nuremberg before the trial even started. He and Justice Jackson had had serious disagreements from the beginning, first as to who would be charged in the tribunal and later about how the trial evidence ought to be presented. It finally came to a head and, in the end, the general withdrew from the prosecution. Essentially, General Donovan wanted to have the defendants testify against each other since he believed that live testimony would lend credibility to the evidence. In addition, he didn't want to prosecute organizations, such as the German High Command. On the other hand, Jackson wanted the trial to be based on documentary evidence that, he believed, could not be assailed as easily as a live witness could. He also wanted to prosecute those military groups.[39] In a letter home in early November, Donovan touched on his feelings about the rift between his friend and mentor and that of the chief prosecutor:

The General is leaving within a couple of weeks. He is too big a man for Jackson to have around him and the General is dissatisfied with the way Jackson runs his show. I am too and the inside story on this whole case is that Jackson is being held up by a group of men who dislike him personally but are trying to support a national position. I haven't changed my opinion one bit since I was in Washington. But he is sweet as honey to me—because I control the most important evidence in the case.[40]

The photographic evidence that had been compiled for the trial had the attention of the media since it created a powerful, visual impact that the documentary evidence simply could not do. On November 16, 1945, Tenold Sunde of the *New York Daily News* interviewed Donovan about this work:

> The man in charge of the biggest motion picture job in the world is Comdr. James B. Donovan of the U.S. Naval Reserve, whose home is 102 82d St., Brooklyn.
>
> Directing the Special-Projects Division of Justice, Jackson's war criminals prosecution staff, it's his task to gather, process, classify and catalogue millions upon millions of feet of movie film for possible use in trials of war criminals before international tribunals.
>
> Donovan is a young man with tired eyes who would soon like to get back to his law practice . . . and to his wife (and children) . . .
>
> But right now he's racing against time in laboratories and projected [*sic*] rooms to be ready for the trials scheduled to open Tuesday. Donovan doesn't know how much film he's got.
>
> "There were 10,000,000 feet in the first batch we processed last summer," he recalled, "and it keeps pouring in."
>
> And it's a wonderful film—official German records of the war and the preparations for it, Nazi Party films, official recordings of speeches by Hitler and other German bigwigs, Luftwaffe and Wehrmacht pictures, strictly personal stuff found in the homes of Nazi leaders, pictures of horror camps and other atrocities and films of pre-war rioting against the Jews.
>
> "The complete recording of the 1938 trial of the assassin of von Rath (Ernst von Rath, member of the Germany Embassy staff in Paris, who was slain by Herschel Grynzpan, Polish Jew), which was made the excuse for an anti-Semitic campaign, takes 10 hours to screen and it's absolutely fascinating," Donovan said.
>
> "We have pictures of top Nazi secrets, also, and scientific experiments. Priceless stuff!"[41]

On Tuesday, November 20, the trial began. Of the twenty-four Nazis indicted, twenty-one were being tried initially.[42] These included Reich Marshal Hermann Wilhelm Goering, 42, Luftwaffe commander and the designated successor to Adolf Hitler; Rudolf Hess, 47, deputy Nazi party leader up to 1941 when he fled to England; Joachim von Ribbentrop, 53, foreign minister dubbed "Hitler's errand boy"; Field Marshal Wilhelm Keitel, 64, chief of the German High Command who signed the German surrender in Berlin; Col. Gen. Alfred Jodl, 54, chief of the general staff; Grand Adm. Karl Doenitz, 55, navy commander and Hitler's choice as president of the Third Reich; Grand Adm. Erich Raeder, 70, navy commander up to 1943 and the designer of the "pocket battleship"; Hjalmar Schacht,

67, former Reichsbank president, who had been in a concentration camp since 1944 for his role in the plot to kill Hitler; Walther Funk, 56, economics minister and a director of the Reichsbank; Wilhelm Frick, 60, interior minister in Hitler's first cabinet and Reich protector in Bohemia-Moravia; Franz von Papen, 67, ambassador to Turkey; Alfred Rosenberg, 53, minister for the occupied eastern territory and official Nazi philosopher; Hans Frank, 46, governor of occupied Poland, who admitted his guilt; Fritz Sauckel, 52, Reich defense commissioner and director of forced labor; Albert Speer, 41, minister of armaments and chief of Todt construction organization; Arthur Seyss-Inquart, 54, Nazi chancellor of Austria; Julius Streicher, 61, editor of *Der Stuermer* and a leading anti-Semite; Hans Fritzsche, 46, head of the propaganda ministry's broadcasting division; Konstantin von Neurath, 73, foreign minister to 1939 and protector for Czechoslovakia; Baldur von Schirach, 39, Hitler Youth leader; Martin Bormann, Hitler's assistant, who was believed to be dead, but was, nevertheless, to be tried in absentia; and Ernest Kaltenbrunner, 43, chief of the Reich security (secret) police. Kaltenbrunner was not present at the beginning of the trial. He had suffered a cranial hemorrhage two days before the start of the trial. Ultimately, he recovered and first appeared in court on December 10.

On the same day of the opening, Donovan wrote home to describe it:

20 Nov.

The trial opened . . . by having the eight judges—two from each country—walk in. The courtroom was very crowded. All my old friends from London, such as Lord Wright & Lord Bridgman, were there, in the gallery for distinguished visitors. Directly opposite my seat at the table is the entire panel of defendants. They look like this:

Doenitz	Raeder	v. Schirach	Sauckel	Jodl	Seyss-Inquart	v. Papen	Speer	Fritzsche	v. Neurath
Goering	Hess	Rosenberg	v. Ribbentrop	Keitel	Frick	Frank	Streicher	Funk	Schacht

The first day was taken up with reading the indictment. The most interesting part of that came when they read the individual charges against the defendants. As each man's name was mentioned his face would change and he would lean forward. Then the particular prosecutor would begin with a recital of the positions he had held and the crimes charged against him. Goering was wonderful. He would nod along on some things and then shake his head on others. Ribbentrop couldn't stand it. He kept blinking to hold back the tears, as all his past honors were read to him, and then he just gave way. He asked for permission to leave the court and did so.

When you look at them as individuals, you keep thinking of their wives & their families, and you feel rather sorry for them. But when you think of each and the lives he has cost, you lose all that. I went thru every shade of emotion but wound up believing that when the trials are over, if all goes right, the people of the world would be certain that these were men who fell under the spell of an evil genius and now must pay the penalty. So far as I know every one of them will wind up by having the pseudo-statesman laurels taken from him and emerging as a man who, for all his high station in society by reason of its being a criminal regime, is an enemy of humanity who should be done away with for the good of all.

On Wednesday, November 21, the twenty defendants present pleaded not guilty before the tribunal, whereupon Justice Robert H. Jackson opened the American case. He said, in part:

In justice to the nations and the men associated in this prosecution, I must remind you of certain difficulties that may leave their mark on this case. Never before in legal history has an effort been made to bring within the scope of a single litigation the developments of a decade, covering a whole continent, and involving a score of nations, countless individuals, and innumerable events. Despite the magnitude of the task, the world has demanded immediate action. This demand has had to be met, though perhaps at the cost of finished craftsmanship. In my country, established courts, following familiar procedures, applying well-thumbed precedents, and dealing with the legal consequences of local and limited events, seldom commence a trial within a year of the event in litigation. Yet less than eight months ago today the courtroom in which you sit was an enemy fortress in the hands of the German SS troops. Less than eight months ago nearly all our witnesses and documents were in enemy hands. The law had not been codified, no procedures had been established, no Tribunal was in existence, no usable courthouse stood here, none of the hundreds of tons of official German documents had been examined, no prosecuting staff had been assembled, nearly all of the present defendants were at large, and the four prosecuting powers had not yet joined in common cause to try them. I should be the last to deny that the case may suffer from incomplete researches and quite likely will not be the example of professional work that any of the prosecuting nations would normally wish to sponsor. It is, however, a completely adequate case to the judgment we shall ask you to render, and its full development we shall be obliged to leave to historians.[43]

The full statement lasted for four hours, at the conclusion of which the defense moved to have the court declared incompetent and the trial dismissed on the ground that there was no basis in international law for it. The motion was denied.

Each allied prosecution team was responsible for a part of the charges against the Nazis. The American case was the first to be presented. Several days into the trial, Donovan wrote:

> This is the greatest experience of my life—probably the greatest I shall ever have. I sit at the counsel table and within a few feet are sitting all the defendants, Goering being closest. I could just sit there all day, studying their reactions to the evidence going in against them. They suddenly have become human beings fighting for their lives instead of names known in the abstract all over the world.
>
> Everyone imaginable is here. Hundreds of newspapers, all over the world, have correspondents. The courtroom is very ingeniously designed—we did it (Presentation Branch) you know. It looks like an ordinary courtroom but in every wall are hidden broadcasting booths, photographers, etc. Talk about your historic occasions.
>
> I haven't put in any films yet but expect to next week. When I do I feel sure that you will hear about it because my evidence is really the most significant in the case.[44]

On Thursday, November 29, 1945, the result of Donovan's many months of work was going to be presented. As Joseph E. Persico related, "Navy Commander James Donovan was about to provide Jackson's answer to the complaint that his paperwork prosecution was too dry." Persico continued:

> A projector began whirring and cut a cone of light through the room, delivering images to a screen on the back wall behind the witness stand. Later generations might become hardened by repeated exposure to these sights, but scenes of bulldozers shoving moon-white corpses into mass graves were being seen for the first time by this audience . . .
>
> The films went on for over two hours, a phantasmagoria of broken, charred, gray bodies, ribs protruding, legs like sticks, hollow eyes gaping. When it was over, the lights went on. Silence hung like a pall over the room.[45]

Even the prisoners were moved by the film as the *New York Times* later reported. All, that is, except for Schacht, who kept his back to the screen for the entire showing.[46]

As the trial moved on, Donovan wrote of some of the tedium:

> We still are wading through the case on "aggressive war" by Germany. The court recently ruled that any document we offer in evidence must be read into the record—so that it goes over the IBM system and is translated.[47] So the trial has really become quite dull, with a lot of reading all day long.

I expect to make my next appearance early next week when I present the major photographic evidence—a film called "The Nazi Plan." It's composed of captured German film and chronicles the history of the Nazi Party from 1921 to 1945. Really fascinating.[48]

On December 11, 1945, the other film Donovan had written Mary about, one that he had convinced Jackson would strengthen their case, was presented. Called *The Nazi Plan,* it was compiled from captured footage by George Stevens. Budd Schulberg managed the continuity, and Ray Kellogg, the cutting, all under the direction of Capt. John Ford.[49] Joel Sayre of the *New Yorker* described a preview as powerful.[50] Stoddard White of *Stars and Stripes* wrote, "To the lay observer, all the thousands of documents in evidence before the International Military Tribunal could not accomplish a fraction of the task done by this film in four hours to clarify the prosecution's case against major war criminals."[51] One of the prosecutors, Drexel Sprecher, related that many on the staff praised the films. He noted, "All of us, I believe, felt that Donovan's initiatives in producing the concentration camp film and 'The Nazi Plan' had added a significant dimension to the great trial."[52]

Powerful though this film was, it had a very different effect on the defendants. Tania Long reported in the *New York Times* that they "acted like excited school children." Schacht, who had his back to the earlier film, watched this one with interest. They looked with pride on themselves and especially on Hitler as they viewed his filmed speeches.[53] Two days later, however, a third film considerably offset the defendants' elation. It had been made by a German soldier on a personal movie camera. Donovan presented it to the Tribunal on December 13:

> COMMANDER DONOVAN: May it please the Tribunal, the United States now offers in evidence Document Number 3052-PS, Exhibit Number USA-280, entitled "Original German 8-millimeter Film of Atrocities against Jews."
> This is a strip of motion pictures taken, we believe, by a member of the SS and captured by the United States military forces in an SS barracks near Augsburg, Germany, as described in the affidavits now before the Tribunal.
> We have not been able to establish beyond doubt in which area these films were made, but we believe that to be immaterial.
> The film offers undeniable evidence, made by the Germans themselves, of almost incredible brutality to Jewish people in the custody of the Nazis, including German military units.
> It is believed by the Prosecution that the scene is the extermination of a ghetto by Gestapo agents, assisted by military units. And, as the other

evidence to be presented by the Prosecution will indicate, the scene presented to the Tribunal is probably one which occurred a thousand times all over Europe under the Nazi rule of terror.

This film was made on an 8-millimeter home camera. We have not wished even to reprint it, and so shall present the original, untouched film captured by our troops. The pictures obviously were taken by an amateur photographer. Because of this, because of the fact that part of it is burned, because of the fact that it runs for only 1½ minutes, and because of the confusion on every hand shown on this film, we do not believe that the Tribunal can properly view the evidence if it is shown only once. We therefore ask the Tribunal's permission to project the film twice as we did before Defense Counsel.

This is a silent film. The film has been made available to all Defense Counsel, and they have a copy of the supporting affidavits, duly translated. [*The film was shown.*]

COMMANDER DONOVAN: [*Continuing*] May it please the Tribunal, while the film is being rewound I wish to say that attached to the affidavits ordered in evidence is a description of every picture shown in this film. And, with the Tribunal's permission, I wish to read a few selections from that at this time, before again projecting the film, in order to direct the Tribunal's attention to certain of the scenes:

Scene 2—A naked girl running across the courtyard.
Scene 3—An older woman being pushed past the camera, and a man in SS uniform standing at the right of the scene.
Scene 5—A man with a skullcap and a woman are manhandled.
Number 14—A half-naked woman runs through the crowd.
Number 15—Another half-naked woman runs out of the house.
Number 16—Two men drag an old man out.
Number 18—A man in German military uniform, with his back to the camera, watches.
Number 24—A general shot of the street, showing fallen bodies and naked women running.
Number 32—A shot of the street, showing five fallen bodies.
Number 37—A man with a bleeding head is hit again.
Number 39—A soldier in German military uniform, with a rifle, stands by as a crowd centers on a man coming out of the house.
Number 44 —A soldier with a rifle, in German military uniform, walks past a woman clinging to a torn blouse.
Number 45—A woman is dragged by her hair across the street.

[*The film was shown again.*]

COMMANDER DONOVAN: [*Continuing*] We submit to the Tribunal for its permanent records this strip of 8-millimeter film.[54]

It was to be Donovan's last act as a prosecutor in Nuremberg. As of December 13, he had acquired the necessary points to earn a discharge from active duty. [55] Two days later Donovan was at Le Havre.

He surrendered his .38 cal. pistol, a shoulder holster, one clip and one hundred rounds of ammunition and then boarded the USS *Philadelphia*. The ship arrived in Brooklyn on Christmas Day.

Gen. William "Wild Bill" Donovan had departed before the first trial began. However, before he left he provided his protégé with a letter of commendation that remained on the latter's library wall at home until he died. The general summed up his young commander's work in preparation for the Nuremberg trial as well as his accomplishments within the OSS earlier. He said, in part:

> As General Counsel you established a reputation for careful analysis, constructive imagination and speedy decision in all matters submitted to you. In fact, no major question of organization policy was determined without obtaining your opinion. The arrangement made by you with various departments of the Government, particularly the Treasury and the Comptroller General, in the control and distribution of funds, and your advice to the Board of Review in the allocation of such funds, was of the greatest value in the establishment of confidence on the part of governmental departments in our handling of our appropriation . . .
>
> It may be that you will not receive due credit for the materials gathered and studies made in preparation for the war trials. You were the first to evolve a comprehensive plan, not only for translating operational intelligence into evidence for trial but also for the mobilization of experts; the constitution of the court; the coordination of the efforts of other agencies with those of OSS; the comprehensive photographic study and film evidence of the activities of the Nazi Party through our Field Photographic Branch, but more than anything else the stimulation to a commonsense activity of the various groups concerned. It was because of this that you were designated in OSS to head the Branch dealing with all phases of the study and the presentation and the actual trial.[56]

The first trial recessed from December 20, 1945, until January 2, 1946. When it resumed, only thirteen of the original 150 American lawyers remained.[57] The prosecution ended its case on February 27, 1946. After the defense provided its case and summation from March 8 to July 25, 1946 (with a brief gap in between when Martin Bormann was tried in absentia), Jackson delivered his summation on July 26, 1946. Four days later, he left Nuremberg but returned in the fall for the verdict. In the meantime, his deputy, Thomas Dodd, took his place. The defense of seven Nazi organizations was presented throughout the month of August, and on September 2, the judges began their deliberations. On the last day of the month, they announced their verdicts as to the organizations. Found guilty were the Leadership Corps of the Nazi Party, the Gestapo (*Geheime Staatspolizei*) and the SD (*Sicherheitsdienst*). Acquitted were the SA (*Sturmab-*

teilung), the Reich Cabinet, and the German General Staff and High Command of the Armed Forces.

On October 1, 1946, after 218 court sessions, the tribunal issued the verdicts as to the individual defendants. Nineteen of the twenty-two defendants were found guilty. Acquitted were Schacht, von Papen, and Fritzsche. In the process, the court rejected the two major defenses offered: that only a state could be found guilty of war crimes, not individuals; and that the trial represented ex post facto justice.

The sentences were imposed immediately. Twelve defendants were sentenced to death by hanging: Goerring, von Ribbentrop, Kaltenbrunner, Keitel, Rosenberg, Frank, Frick, Streicher, Sauckel, Jodl, Seyss-Inquart, and Bormann (in absentia). Three defendants were sentenced to life imprisonment: Hess, Funk, and Raeder. Von Schirach and Speer received twenty years; von Neurath, fifteen years; and Doenitz, ten years. After 315 days, the tribunal had completed its work. The death sentences were carried out on October 16. Goering committed suicide just before his execution; the others were hung.[58]

By the time that the verdicts were issued, Donovan had been home for nearly ten months. Fully involved in the private practice of law, he did not see a need to return to Nuremberg for the verdicts or sentences. He was satisfied that justice had been done, and he was happy to resume his civilian life.

4

Private Practice, 1946–1957

DONOVAN'S CHRISTMAS HOLIDAY WITH HIS FAMILY WAS BRIEF. After arriving in Brooklyn on the USS *Philadelphia* on December 25, 1945, he was required to report for duty in Washington, DC, on the twenty-sixth, and he remained on active duty in the District until February. During the course of Donovan's stay in the capital, the Joint Chiefs of Staff, in a special ceremony, honored him on January 8. At that time he was awarded the Legion of Merit by Brig. Gen. John Magruder on behalf of the Joint Chiefs for his past service with the OSS.[1]

While in Washington, Donovan used some of his spare moments pursing an idea that he and Justice Jackson had about the subsequent use of his film, "The Nazi Plan." On January 10 he met with a White House aide, David K. Niles, to discuss the film. Donovan related that it was Jackson's and his intention to try to distribute that work for educational purposes. He wrote a letter to Niles that same day confirming their earlier discussion:

> As I explained to you, the film was presented in Nuremberg as a photographic summation of the American prosecution, with respect to the nature of the Nazi conspiracy and its wars of aggression. It is the hope of Mr. Justice Jackson and the undersigned that ultimately the film will serve a permanent educational purpose through schools and other media in the United States. The British Government has already requested prints of it and it is being shown to King George VI at his request.[2]

In the end, however, despite additional work on the idea, the film did not receive the widespread distribution that Donovan sought. After several more weeks, on February 12, 1946, he was detached from active duty with a letter of thanks sent soon after from the Secretary of the Navy James Forrestal. In March, Donovan and Mary took a long-anticipated three-week vacation in Florida.

That vacation was apparently long overdue because in February, Donovan suffered what appears to have been an episode of severe chest pains and possible angina pectoris. Others had apparently seen it coming, as Ray Kellogg was quick to point out in a letter after Donovan told him about it. "If you rem'ber old boy, I warned you of such a thing a long time ago. I don't want to say 'I told you so,' but Jim, I saw it coming then, and I felt at the time that you'd crack up if you didn't back off. I still believe the only reason you didn't was because of your willpower alone."[3]

Before Donovan and Mary went on vacation, he had secured the position of general counsel for the National Bureau of Casualty Underwriters at 60 John Street in downtown Manhattan. He would begin on March 20, 1946, after his return from Florida. Donovan found this position largely through Hale Anderson, Sr. It was Anderson to whom Donovan had turned in order to obtain insurance for the OSRD staff and contractors. At that time, Anderson was unaware of OSRD's work in the development of the atomic bomb but he learned of it later. He wrote to Donovan while he was in Nuremberg and proposed that when he returned to the United States, they meet to discuss the bomb and the related insurance issues attached to nuclear weaponry. In January, while still in uniform, Donovan met with Anderson and his son, Hale who was at that time, associate general counsel for the Hartford Fire, Accident and Indemnity Group, and the three had a productive discussion, especially for Donovan.

When Hale, senior, learned during the meeting that Donovan was planning to enter private practice, he called William Leslie, general manager of the National Bureau of Casualty Underwriters (NBCU).[4] Anderson suggested that Donovan was the right person to replace Judge E.W. Sawyer, their former general counsel who had just retired. Leslie, who had three sons and a daughter in the Armed Forces during the war, asked Donovan during a subsequent interview if he was interested in the position. Donovan informed him that he was.[5]

Since Donovan was still formally on military leave from the OSRD at this time, he notified his former agency on March 4 of his intent not to return to his position as senior attorney since he was taking a private position in New York. The OSRD, a temporary wartime agency, was dissolved later in the year.

During the first months after the Nuremberg trial, Donovan kept in contact with Justice Jackson about the educational distribution of the Nuremberg films. In the spring of 1946, he was still trying to have an English sound track added to the main film. Participants of the trials were also frequently called upon to talk about its various aspects, particularly the ex post facto issue. Robert Storey, for example, discussed the "Legal Aspects of the Nuremberg Trial" before the Annual Meeting of the State Bar of Texas in July 1946.[6] Later, in

October, Donovan, himself, addressed the Federal Bar Association on "The Nuernberg (*sic*) Trials" describing the search for evidence, the types of offenses and the tactics of the prosecution.[7] And there were reunions of the Nuremberg trial staff. Donovan attended one such event at the Faculty Club of New York University on November 20, 1948.[8]

By the time of his discharge from active duty, Donovan was a member of the bar of the United States Supreme Court, the United States Court of Claims and local New York State and federal district courts. He was also a member of the American Bar Association, the American Society of International Law, the Federal Bar Association, the Association of the Bar of the City of New York, the Harvard Club of New York, and the Lake Placid Club.

In the late 1940s the legal aspects of the insurance business kept Donovan extremely busy. Prompting much of his activity was a decision of the United States Supreme Court in 1944 in which it broke from its historical position that the regulation of insurance was a function of the individual states. Until this time, the Court viewed the insurance industry as unique and not subject to federal control. With their revised opinion in *United States v. South-Eastern Underwriters Association,* a majority of the justices found that insurance was a commercial activity and, like all other industries engaged in interstate commerce, was subject to the regulatory powers of Congress under the Commerce Clause of the Constitution. In addition, they found that the fixing of noncompetitive rates by insurance companies was a violation of the federal antitrust acts.[9] Donovan later wrote that because of this decision "many officials, insurance executives and counsel feared that the foundations of State regulation and taxation had been shaken."[10]

Faced with what they perceived as a Hobson's choice between federal or state control, the insurance industry elected the latter as the lesser of two evils[11] and began to pressure Congress to act in their behalf. In response, Congress quickly began to consider a number of bills that would exempt the insurance industry from federal antitrust legislation, such as the Sherman Act and the Clayton Act. Their work resulted in the passage of the McCarran-Ferguson Act commonly referred to as simply the McCarran Act that became law on March 9, 1945.[12] The act provided that the states could continue to regulate and tax insurance, and that for a period of approximately three years from the time of passage of the bill, the federal antitrust statutes would not apply to the insurance business. After the three-year period, the antitrust acts would apply to the industry *to the extent the industry was not regulated by the states.* Thus, the states, with the willing assistance of the insurance industry, had a mandate to bring their insurance laws into conformity with the decision of the Supreme Court in the South-Eastern Underwriters case during this three-year moratorium.

Donovan had joined the NBCU a year into the three-year waiting period set by the McCarran Act. As general counsel representing numerous insurance companies, he immediately began to participate in the All-Industry [Insurance] Conferences for the purpose of drafting legislation and preparing model rating laws for the various states so that they would be in a position to regulate the industry by 1948, the deadline established by the McCarran Act.

Under the model rating laws, the rates had to meet certain standards, that is, they could not be excessive or discriminatory and they had to be filed with the appropriate state commissioner of insurance. Further, the model laws provided that companies could combine in fixing rates if they were licensed and supervised by the states.[13]

In support of these model laws, Donovan began to travel extensively around the country, representing the NBCU at numerous public hearings. His goals were twofold: first, to foster legislation that adopted these model statutes, and second, to standardize the variety of practices, procedures, forms, and exclusions followed in the business. At a lunch meeting of the Automobile Casualty Underwriters Association in Manhattan on November 13, 1946, for example, Donovan told the attendees of the diverse interests that had to be reconciled in drafting such rate regulatory legislation. "The proposed rating laws, he said, 'provide for the legislative delegation of regulatory powers to administrative agencies, granting to those agencies norms of conduct which are concrete but permit a certain flexibility in administration.'"[14] Similarly, in a talk in Cleveland, Ohio, before the American Bar Association's Law Section in 1947, Donovan discussed the wording of duplicate coverage in insurance policies and urged greater uniformity so that insured individuals would not suffer and much litigation could be avoided.[15]

In addition to legislative action to bring administrative uniformity to a highly diverse industry through state control, there was also a need to reconcile conflicts within the industry itself, such as between members of the NBCU and nonmembers, between mutual companies and stock companies, between agents and insurers and the like.[16]

Toward his goal of bringing uniformity to the insurance industry, Donovan chaired the Joint Forms Committee on behalf of the stock companies and directed the national standard policy program for liability insurance. He also helped to develop the standard atomic warfare policy exclusions.

A word should be said about uniformity in the insurance industry. Uniformity as it applies to forms, additions, and exclusions in policies is one thing. But the term "uniformity," when applied to insurance rates, is quite another matter and could be viewed as a euphemism for price-fixing. Why is it considered legitimate in this field? Addressing this issue in 1950, Donovan wrote, "Cooperative action in rating matters has long been considered to be essential in the business; it is by the pooling of experience that rates normally are made, and it is by a stabilized rate structure that rate wars, disastrous to industry and policyholders alike, are avoided."[17] On this same topic, in a talk at the University of Wisconsin ten years later, Donovan quoted from a subcommittee report of the National Association of Insurance Commissioners:

> Experience has demonstrated that unrestricted competition in the insurance business is not in the public interest. Practically every state in the Union has upon its statute books provisions prohibiting unfair discrimination in rates. If unfair discrimination is to be avoided, there must be reasonable uniformity in the rates. Such uniformity can be obtained only by cooperation in obtaining statistical data and in the promulgation of rates based thereon. This result can be obtained only through concert of action.[18]

By 1950 nearly all states had adopted the model statutes that were proposed by the NBCU, the All-Industry Conference and the National Association of Insurance Commissioners. During this legislative process, there were bound to be those who took issue with the idea of legalized price-fixing,[19] and it fell to Donovan, himself, to defend the NBCU as chief counsel in one of the most important cases which threatened the state regulation of insurance, that of *North Little Rock Transportation Co. v. Casualty Reciprocal Exchange et al.*[20] In this instance, an Arkansas taxicab company that was unable to obtain liability insurance because of its bad record of accidents applied to the Arkansas Automobile Assigned Risk Plan for coverage. The plan assigned the company to the Aetna Casualty and Surety Company who then charged a premium determined by the NBCU of which it was a member. Unhappy with the premium, the taxi company sued the NBCU and all the insurance companies involved, charging price-fixing and conspiracy in restraint of trade, in addition to alleging that parts of the McCarran Act were unconstitutional and that the defendants proceeded by intimidation and coercion.

After presenting his arguments, Donovan and the attorneys for the defendants denied the charges and motioned that the court dismiss the case by summary judgment without trial. The court agreed, finding that intimidation and coercion did not exist in the case. Further, it found that the McCarran-Ferguson Act was constitutional and that the Sherman Act was not violated since the insurance companies were regulated by state statute. Although the cab company subsequently appealed, the United States Court of Appeals for the Eighth Circuit affirmed the lower court ruling on April 5, 1950. An appeal by the cab company to the United States Supreme Court similarly failed. There was thus established, through the efforts headed by Donovan, the legal principles of state regulation of insurance.

While Donovan's primary legal work was in the field of insurance, there were times when he became involved in other issues, often as amicus curiae, or "friend of the court." One of the more interesting cases he handled in the early years involved the New York City Board of Education and the *Nation* magazine. Briefly, the New York City Board of Superintendents and the board of education, because of the *Nation*'s anti-Catholic articles from November 1947 to June 1948, excluded that publication from the list of approved reading material. The board, in particular, felt that the material was not suitable for high school libraries. Attorneys for the *Nation* argued that the board had "no right to promulgate an exclusive list of periodicals approved for high school libraries, that its action in not including the *Nation* in its approved list abridged the constitutional guaranties of freedom of the press, due process and equal protection of the laws."[21] Counsel for the board of education argued for the need to control the reading matter of its children. On appeal, supporters on both sides submitted amicus curiae briefs arguing their own positions. Donovan filed one such brief with Herbert F. Dimond and Godfrey P. Schmidt in behalf of the Catholic Lawyers Guild of the Diocese of Brooklyn. Other submitters, both for and against, included Archibald MacLeish, the Guild of Catholic Lawyers of the City of New York, the Authors League of America, the *Ad Hoc* Committee to Lift the Ban on the *Nation,* the New York State Council of the Knights of Columbus, and the American Labor Party. On May 25, 1949, ruling in favor of the board of education, the New York State Commissioner of Education stated (in part):

It is my opinion that under the Education Law a board of education has not merely the right to determine the periodicals to which it wishes to subscribe or which it will accept for deposit in its school libraries, but a fundamental responsibility so to determine, in accordance with its best judgement of the educational welfare of its pupils. . . . The principle of freedom of the press applies to the right of publication; it does not impose on boards of education, which stand *in loco parentis,* any more than it imposes on parents, an obligation to purchase or accept any particular publication for the children in their charge.[22]

The Donovan household, at the time of the decision in the *Nation* case, was continuing to grow. Mary and Donovan had a second daughter, Mary Ellen. Their first child,, Jan, was six and John was four. The family was still living in the Bay Ridge section of Brooklyn in the home they had purchased in 1946. Meanwhile, Donovan's brother, John, a successful prosecutor, was about to enter politics. John had been engaged as an assistant U.S. attorney in the Southern District of New York since 1944 (as was David Edelstein at this time, before his appointment to the federal bench). He first served in the Criminal Division, and while in that position, received some notoriety when he was able to solve a mistaken identity case for which the wrong man was serving a lengthy prison sentence.[23] In that case, a Wall Street broker, Bertram M. Campbell, was convicted of forgery in 1938. The crime, John Donovan discovered, was actually committed by one Alexander "Whitey" Thiel, a Campbell look-alike and a master forger. Thiel was ultimately convicted and Campbell, then on parole after serving three years of a five- to ten-year sentence, was pardoned. John Donovan later went on to the Appeals and Civil Divisions of the U.S. Attorney's Office. However, on September 11, 1950, he was designated by the Democratic Party to replace New York State Senator Sidney A. Fine of the Bronx in the Twenty-fourth Senate District.[24] John was elected in his own right on November 7, 1950.[25] He lived on the Grand Concourse in the Bronx and had been active in the borough's Democratic politics since 1933. He was also a partner in the Manhattan law firm of Manes, Sturim, Donovan and Laufer at 70 Pine Street.

In addition to his public speaking engagements and his law practice, James Donovan, by 1951, was involved with a number of associations. He was chairman of the Insurance Section of the New York State Bar Association, and chairman, as well, of the Automobile Insurance Law Committee of the American Bar Association. He was active, too, with the Association of the Bar of the City of New York, the International Association of Insurance Counsel, and the Federal Bar Association of Government Counsel. Then, in May of that year, he became a partner in the firm of Watters, Cowan and Baldridge, a firm that for many years had represented clients in the fire insurance industry.

Donovan's firm, which changed its name on his entry to Watters, Cowen and Donovan, had offices in the Shoreham Building in Washington, DC, and at 116 John Street in Manhattan, but by December 1951 the New York office moved to more spacious quarters in a then newly constructed building at 161 William Street in lower Manhattan. It readily accommodated the seven attorneys and support staff on the nineteenth floor and part of the eighteenth, joined by an internal, spiral staircase. The principal lawyers included Thomas Watters Jr., who, before private practice, had been the deputy insurance commissioner in Iowa from 1919 to 1921; Myron T. Cowen, assigned to the Washington office, but on leave at this time as the American ambassador to the Republic of the Philippines; and John P. Walsh, soon to be a partner in the firm and a close friend of Donovan, who had been an assistant district attorney in Manhattan.

A reporter for the *Eastern Underwriter,* after a visit to the firm in 1951, remarked that "the rooms are light and airy with soft-toned decorations. They look more like individual libraries than mine-run offices and there is ample room for the staff. The biggest room houses a magnificent law library."[26] The view from Donovan's window looked east toward the Brooklyn and Manhattan Bridges and most of Brooklyn's western shoreline. In his own office, with its burlap-covered walls, marine clock and seascapes, Donovan brought from home many of his prized sixteenth- and seventeenth-century law books, together with some of his illuminated manuscripts. By this time, his collection of rare books numbered in the thousands. After Donovan's arrival, the firm's practice was expanded to include corporate, insurance and tax law, as well as general practice cases. Donovan also continued in his position as general counsel to the National Bureau of Casualty Underwriters.

The Federation of Insurance Counsel, based upon Donovan's work in insurance law, presented him in 1953 with the George Henry Tyne Award for outstanding achievement.[27] However, in the two years following Donovan's receipt of the award, two major tragedies struck his family. He and Mary had a daughter, Clare, who was born in 1954. Soon after birth, Clare was diagnosed as being profoundly retarded and has required hospitalization all her life. Six months after Clare's birth, Donovan's brother, John, suffered a fatal heart attack and passed away at St. Elizabeth's Hospital on March 12, 1955.[28]

After working for the Department of Justice as an Assistant U.S. Attorney in the Southern District of New York, John had served New York as a State Senator from 1950, winning reelection in 1952 and 1954. In the latter year, he was one of a four-member ethics committee of the Senate. During his terms in office, John introduced legislation authorizing lotteries, strengthening police in dealing with after-hours bottle clubs, requiring periodic eye examinations and fingerprinting for drivers, barring sales of leased, rented, or demonstration cars without a sign stating their prior use and sponsoring bills to grant New York City $2.2 million to operate day care centers for children of working mothers.[29] He had never married. John Donovan was a highly regarded state senator, as evidenced, in part, by those who attended his funeral. As the *New York Times* reported:

> Funeral services for John Donovan were conducted on March 15 at St. Jerome's Church. Mayor of the City of New York, Robert Wagner, headed the honorary pall bearers who included Peter Campbell Brown, a classmate of John and currently Corporation Counsel, Senate Minority Leader Francis J. Mahoney of Manhattan, Senator John H. Hughes of Syracuse, United States District Judges Thomas F. Murphy and John F.X. McGohey, and Victor J. Emmanuel and Mathew Manes. Senator Walter J. Mahoney, Republican leader and temporary President of the State Senate had designated the entire Senate two days earlier as a committee to attend John Donovan's funeral. In all, five hundred individuals attended the funeral including Lieutenant Governor George B. DeLuca and seventy-five members of the state legislature. Interment was at Gate of Heaven Cemetery in Hawthorne, New York.[30]

During the 1950s, Donovan and his firm prospered and came to represent a number of large organizations including the American Insurance Association, the Western Actuarial Bureau, Underwriters Salvage Company, the National Board of Fire Underwriters, the National Automobile Underwriters' Association (which would merge with the National Bureau of Casualty Underwriters in 1968), the Surety Association of America, the New York Board of Title Underwriters, the Nuclear Energy Liability Insurance Association, and the Nuclear Energy Property Insurance Association. Donovan also continued to write for legal periodicals[31] and was even asked occasionally to review a book.[32]

In defending his clients' interests, he was not always the primary counsel or attorney-of-record. However, by following cases that involved members of the insurance industry, he could, when he thought necessary, submit an amicus curiae brief to the court in support of an insurance company's position. It allowed Donovan to defend the interests of insurance companies, even though he was not the legal representative for a particular defendant or plaintiff. One such case, whose outcome was important to the industry, arose in the State of Washington after an insured driver ran into five individuals on motorcycles. The important question to be answered in the case was whether the incident was viewed as one accident or a series of accidents.[33] Donovan, representing the Association of Casualty and Surety Companies, flew out to Olympia in order to submit his amicus brief. When he traveled on this occasion, he took his now ten-year-old son, John, with him. (At times, when he saw that their school schedule permitted, Donovan tried to bring one of his children with him on his trips.) After submitting his brief, Donovan presented his oral argument in behalf of the insurance company on December 5, 1955. The Supreme Court, in an unusual step, ordered the attorneys to reargue the case later. After the second round of presentations, Donovan and the industry prevailed when the court ruled on November 8, 1956, that while each of the cyclists might have separate claims, the "character of the event" was that of a single accident.[34]

During court appearances at home and around the country, various associates usually accompanied Donovan. One such person was Daniel McNamara, an actuary as well as an attorney, who joined him when cases were related to insurance pricing or the interpretation of state regulatory laws. McNamara had graduated from Fordham Law School in 1955 and was employed by W. R. Grace and Company before joining the NBCU in 1953 where he first met Donovan. McNamara was impressed with Donovan, he said, because of his integrity and keen intelligence, coupled with warmth and a sophisticated Irish charm. He thought, too, that when Donovan focused on a legal issue he was brilliant, but he also believed that Donovan was restless and had a need to pursue a variety of goals in order to satisfy his wide-ranging interests. To say that he burned the candle at both ends, according to McNamara, was understating Donovan's relentless drive.[35]

One of these pursuits was Donovan's participation in a public policy group in early 1957. It began when he was named as one of thirty-four individuals forming an advisory committee to the Project for Effective Justice. Maurice Rosenberg, associate professor of law at Columbia University, chaired the group. Also on the committee were, among others, William A. Brennan, associate justice of the Supreme Court; Edward S. Greenbaum, U.S. delegate to the United Nations General Assembly; A. Leo Levin, a professor at the University of Pennsylvania; Louis M. Loeb, president of the Association of the Bar of the City of New York; and Harold R. Medina, judge of the Court of Appeals for the Second Circuit Court of Appeals.[36] The first effort of the group was a survey of automobile accident claims and the delays they were believed to cause in the civil courts.

By the year 1957, Donovan and his family had moved from their Bay Ridge home to a fifteen-room, bi-level apartment at 35 Prospect Park West in Brooklyn, overlooking Prospect Park. His library there contained several thousand rare books and illuminated manuscripts. The Donovan children were also growing: Jan, fourteen, was in Marymount High School; John was thirteen, Mary Ellen, eight, and Clare, three. In what spare time he availed himself, he could be found at his favorite Brooklyn club, the Rembrandt, or golfing occasionally on Staten Island.

Not long after a business trip to England in May 1957, Donovan was presented with an unanticipated opportunity to exercise all of his legal talents in the field of criminal law, a field that he had not practiced since Nuremberg. But even his Nuremberg experience, which was in international criminal law, was as a prosecutor, not as a defense attorney. And it was a defense attorney who was needed soon after the Federal Bureau of Investigation arrested a master spy of the Soviet Union, Col. Rudolf Abel, in a Manhattan hotel room on June 21, 1957.

5

The Arrest and Trial of Col. Rudolf Abel

SINCE MID-MAY 1957, THE FEDERAL BUREAU OF INVESTIGATION HAD the Soviet master spy, Rudolf Ivanovich Abel, under surveillance following information received from a defector, Reino Hayhanen. Then, during the early morning hours of June 21,1957 at the Latham Hotel, 4 East Twenty-eighth Street in New York City, three agents, led by Special Agent Edward F. Gamber, approached Room 839, Abel's $25-per-week, single-room apartment where he had lived under the name of Martin Collins. Abel, lying nude on top of his sheets, and just awakened by the knock at his door, groggily arose and opened the door slightly. Agents quickly pushed their way in, addressing Abel by his Soviet title of "Colonel." For his part, Abel refused to speak. When he continued in his refusal to talk, the FBI asked several officers of the U.S. Immigration and Naturalization Service (INS), who were waiting just outside, to come into the room. Still maintaining silence, Abel was arrested by the immigration officers and charged with illegal entry into the United States. He was then brought to the INS office at 70 Columbus Avenue, Manhattan, at which time he was photographed and fingerprinted.[1]

After the arrest and while Abel was being processed, agents searched his hotel room. They found $6,000 in cash, warehouse storage receipts for property at the Lincoln Warehouse in Brooklyn, a European passport for Andrew Kayotis (by means of which Abel had entered the United States illegally in 1948). They also found a safe deposit box receipt at a branch of the Manufacturers Trust Company in Manhattan and coded documents that described espionage meetings in New York City; Quincy, Massachusetts; and Salida, Colorado; as well as in Mexico and England. The deposit box belonged to one of Abel's few friends, Alan Winston, a box, it would be later learned, that Abel had borrowed in order to secrete $15,000 in cash. Agents also found a birth certificate in the name of Emil R. Goldfus with a birth date of 1902, the approximate year of Abel's own birth.[2]

FBI agents were aware that Abel also maintained a $35-per-month

71

studio apartment on the top floor of 252 Fulton Street, Brooklyn, which he had established in December 1953, ostensibly as a photography studio. He had rented it under the name of Emil Goldfus, and, ironically, it was located less than a block from the federal courthouse where he would later be prosecuted. (In the only egregious error of his espionage career, he had once brought his underling, Reino Hayhanen, to this photo studio and thus revealed its location.)

A search of the Fulton Street studio resulted in the discovery of a shortwave radio receiver, warehouse storage receipts for some of Abel's property at the Lincoln Warehouse and about fifty paintings done by Abel. The paintings, primarily oils on canvas, were characterized by a later critic as depicting "Socialist realism."[3] Among the works were a self-portrait, three nudes, several watercolors, and an abstract.

Thirty agents worked on the evidence seized in the multiple searches following Abel's arrest. In addition to that already mentioned, some of the more exotic evidence included hollowed-out pencils, coins, batteries, bolts, nails, cufflinks and earrings, together with code books, coded messages, and maps of the United States highlighting areas involved in the national defense. References were found to secret drops in the Newark, New Jersey, station of the Pennsylvania Railroad; another in the vicinity of a naval air station in Quincy, Massachusetts; and a third near a center for missile electronics research in New Hyde Park, New York. Agents also discovered an abandoned 250-foot telephone wire across Clinton and Clark Streets that appeared to have been spliced for use as an antenna.

Meanwhile, Abel was transferred from the Immigration Office in Manhattan to the Federal Alien Detention Camp in McAllen, Texas. He was held here incommunicado for five days and was subjected to constant questioning. Finally, at an immigration hearing in McAllen on June 27, Abel admitted his identity[4] and his Soviet citizenship. He also admitted that he had failed to notify the attorney general of his address changes in 1956 and 1957 in violation of the Immigration and Nationality Act. He added that he had entered the United States through Canada on November 5, 1948. At this time, Abel was represented by Morris Atlas of the McAllen firm of Stafford, Atlas, and Stillman. Following the hearing, deportation was postponed pending a federal indictment for espionage. In keeping with the Consular Agreement of November 16, 1933, Atlas wrote to the Soviet embassy asking what the Soviets would like the firm to do in behalf of Abel. There was no response.

During the time that Abel spent in the Immigration Detention facility in Texas, agents of the FBI interviewed him daily. However, he never offered to cooperate and never provided information about his activities in the United States. In Brooklyn at this time, William F. Tompkins, assistant attorney general in charge of the Internal Security Division of the Department of Justice, was convening a grand jury. On August 7, after the testimony of Colonel Abel's assistant, Lt. Col. Reino Hayhanen, an indictment was obtained. Abel was charged in three counts and nineteen overt acts with conspiracy to transmit United States defense and atomic secrets to the Soviet Union; conspiracy to gather secrets; and failure to register as a foreign agent. Named as unindicted coconspirators were Reino Hayhanen; Alekssandr Mikhailovich Korotkov, assistant director of the PGU (Ministry of State Security, First Division, Espionage) and a coconspirator in another case, that of Morton Sobell; Mikhail Sverin, first secretary of the Soviet delegation to the United Nations; and Vitali G. Pavlov, a former second secretary at the Soviet mission in Ottawa who was indicted with a Canadian spy ring in 1946. On the same day as the indictment, Abel was transferred to a jail in Edinburg, Texas, to await return to Brooklyn.

On August 8, 1957, Deputy U.S. Marshal Neil Matthews of Houston escorted Rudolf Abel on the plane to Newark, New Jersey. The Justice Department had booked eight seats on the regularly scheduled flight in order to maintain a distance between the other passengers and Abel. During the flight Abel spoke with Matthews about conditions in the Soviet Union as compared with the United States. He also expressed the opinion that better relations between the United States and Russia could develop if citizens of each country knew the other's language.[5] On leaving the plane at Newark, Abel spoke briefly with reporters saying, "I'm feeling fine"; "I'm getting a lot of publicity" but adding, in response to a question, that he did not seek a lawyer through his embassy.[6] He was then brought to the Federal Detention Headquarters on West Street in Manhattan, to await his initial appearance on the following day.

Abel appeared before Judge Matthew T. Abruzzo of the U.S. District Court for the Eastern District of New York in Brooklyn on August 9. There were neither counsel nor friends with him. He asked for time to obtain a lawyer, and when the court asked how long it would take, Abel replied, "I really couldn't say. I don't know. I have no experience in these matters."[7] Judge Abruzzo entered a plea of not guilty for Abel, ordered him held without bail, and adjourned the case until August 13. After the hearing, Abel asked the marshals if they could locate an attorney for him with the last name of Abt, and they found a John J. Abt of 320 Broadway, Manhattan. A correspondent of the *New York Times* located Abt on vacation in Maine. Abt was counsel for the Communist Party and had represented many party leaders who had been charged with belonging to a group that advocated the violent overthrow of the government in violation of the Smith Act of 1940.[8] On this occasion, however, Abt stated that he thought he would be too busy to take on Abel's case, and even said that he had never heard of him. In fact, Abel was viewed as a very unpopular defendant whom many defense counsels were reluctant to represent.

The *New York Times*, however, was quick to make a distinction between a spy, who might be unpopular because he was an enemy, and a traitor, who was far more nefarious because he turned on his own country. It was a distinction James Donovan also made immediately after his appointment as defense counsel: "Colonel Abel is a spy. Americans who helped him are traitors. There is a difference and it should be borne in mind."[9] Abt eventually did visit with Abel, spending fifteen minutes with him on the day before his next appearance. After the interview, according to a press statement, he told Abel that he had too many other commitments. Abel, however, later told Donovan that Abt wanted too much money for a defense and thus Abel declined his services.[10] Finding an attorney for the spy was not going to be easy. As the *New York Times* reported on August 13, "A New York lawyer who has been active in civil rights cases said that, in view of the nature of this case, he doubted there would be any volunteer counsel."[11]

The adjourned hearing took place as scheduled on the thirteenth. If Abel could not obtain counsel, the judge declared, one would be appointed for him. A special prosecutor, James J. Featherstone, told the court that Abel could use the funds found in his room at arrest, together with any other funds he might have, to obtain counsel. Abel then stated, "I understand that a request can be made to the Bar Association" for a recommendation as to a defense attorney.[12] Judge Abruzzo assured the defendant that a request would be made and then adjourned the case for three days. Despite Abel's understanding of the role of the Bar Association, Louis M. Loeb, then president of the Association of the Bar of the City of New York, said the bar had never been approached with such a request in the past, and that there was no set procedure. He would, however, canvas the larger New York law firms if such a request was made.[13]

By Friday, August 16, Abel still had no attorney and Judge Abruzzo informed him that he would appoint one through the Brooklyn Bar Association. At this time Abel also asked for the release of some money to be able to make purchases at the prison commissary. Judge Abruzzo released $250 with the comment, "You see, you're in a democracy here, sir. This is the way we do things here. I hope you appreciate that. You will before you're through."[14] The hearing concluded with the setting of a trial date on September 16 before Judge Mortimer W. Byers.

Within a few days, the Selection Committee of the Brooklyn Bar Association, headed by Lynn Goodnough, decided that James B. Donovan would be the best choice to represent Rudolf Abel. Goodnough was a neighbor of Donovan, as well as a professional colleague, and had heard him speak previously on the Nuremberg trial. On August 19, Ed Gross of Donovan's law firm, telephoned his boss at the family's Lake Placid retreat where he and Mary had just arrived to begin a vacation. Gross relayed Goodnough's proposal to nominate Donovan and asked if he would accept. Fearing that her husband would again be deprived of a much needed rest, Mary was none too pleased with Gross's communication.[15]

Donovan used the library of a friend and attorney, Judge Harold R. Soden, in Lake Placid to review a number of legal issues as he considered accepting the defense.[16] After much thought that day and the following night, Donovan decided to take the case. On August 20 he met with Judge Byers. Prior to accepting the appointment, Donovan had expressed some concern to Judge Byers about whether or not it would be a conflict for him to take the case since he was then involved in an insurance case with a Soviet state.[17] Byers dismissed the concern. Later that day, Donovan held a press conference in his law office. He said that he decided to assist the alleged spy "as a public duty" to ensure that Abel received the fairest possible hearing.[18] He then described a significant difference between his client and some other spies:

> A careful distinction should be drawn between the position of the defendant and people such as Alger Hiss and the Rosenbergs . . . If the allegations are true, it means that instead of dealing with Americans who have betrayed their country, we are dealing with a Russian citizen, in a quasimilitary capacity, who has served his country on an extraordinarily dangerous mission.
>
> I would hope, as an American, that the United States Government has similar men on similar missions in many countries of the world.
>
> The nature of a secret agent's work is always dangerous and unrewarding, since he is called on to accept the knowledge that if discovered he is automatically disavowed by his Government. Nevertheless, there are many statues of Nathan Hale in the United States.[19]

Immediately upon receipt of his appointment, Donovan began to study the case in detail. He realized at once, however, that he would need at least one associate who was knowledgeable about federal criminal procedures. He thought his best chance of finding someone would be through a large law firm. Thus, Donovan obtained a list of former assistant United States attorneys, and on August 28, he visited the offices of Dewey, Ballantine, Bushby, Palmer and Wood where he met Arnold Fraiman. Impressed with Fraiman, Donovan brought him that same day to the Selection Committee of the Brooklyn Bar Association.[20] Fraiman had been an assistant U.S. attorney in the Southern District of New York for three years prior to the end of his term in May 1957. A graduate of Princeton University (1947) and Columbia Law School (1954), he was appointed to the Abel defense team by Judge Abruzzo on August 29. Former governor Thomas E. Dewey, of Fraiman's firm, had approved the selection and agreed to continue his salary during the pendancy of Abel's case.[21]

Donovan met with another potential member of the team, Thomas M. Debevoise, on September 6. He found the graduate of Columbia Law School and former assistant U.S. attorney equally qualified to help with the defense, and so the team was complete.[22] For the next two months the three worked tirelessly each day and on many nights.

On August 21, 1957, Donovan met Rudolf Abel for the first time. He informed his client that he would do his utmost in presenting a defense, but it would be done with respectability. Abel responded that he did not want Donovan to do anything that would impugn the character of a soldier in the service of his country.[23]

While a dignified defense might be important to Abel, Donovan was always aware that this was a capital offense case because the first count of the indictment charged conspiracy to transmit atomic and military information to the Soviet Union. On the one hand, he knew that no modern, foreign spy had been executed in the United States or Europe for peacetime espionage. On the other hand, he was also aware that all of these cases preceded the so-called "Rosenberg Law,"[24] which made such an execution quite possible. His defense, therefore, had to be aggressive toward the prosecution's witnesses, especially Abel's associate, who had betrayed him. In addition, Donovan had to try to separate, in the jurors' minds, the trial of Rudolf Abel from a trial of communism.[25]

Donovan also discussed a fee with Abel at this first meeting. Judge Byers had earlier suggested that $10,000 plus expenses would be appropriate. Donovan mentioned this to Abel since it would be deducted from Abel's own confiscated funds. When he said he thought the amount was fair, Donovan informed him that whatever fee the court approved would be donated to charity.[26] Once he announced this intention publicly, Donovan was deluged with requests for money from numerous charities.

As the trial date neared, Donovan and his assistants worked intensely on a motion to suppress the evidence obtained from Abel's quarters based upon a purported illegal search. In a memorandum to the court, he summarized the affidavit in support of the motion:

> Sometime prior to June 21, 1957, the Department of Justice, believing Abel to be a spy, had to make a decision with respect to him. The FBI possesses the dual functions of a law enforcement agency and of a counter-espionage arm of our national intelligence forces. The decision had to be as to whether:
>
> (a) As law enforcement officers, they should arrest Abel on charges of espionage, conduct any lawful search and seizure, and follow all other procedures established under the Constitution and other laws of the United Stated; or
>
> (b) As counter-espionage agents, fulfilling a national intelligence function, they should seize Abel, conceal his detention from his co-conspirators for the longest possible time, and meanwhile seek to induce him to come over to our side.
>
> The election between the two alternate courses of action was made. While that election may have been prospectively in the best interest of the United States, it did not succeed. The government thereafter cannot pretend that such an election was not made, or attempt to pay lipservice to due process of law.[27]

On Saturday, September 14, Thomas Debevoise filed the motion in the U.S. District Court for the Southern District of New York since the first search took place in Manhattan, a borough within the jurisdiction of the Southern District. Judge Sylvester J. Ryan ultimately declined jurisdiction and referred the matter back to the trial judge, Mortimer Byers in the Eastern District of New York (Brooklyn).

The defense was also unsuccessful in postponing the trial until the beginning of November in order to have adequate time to prepare. Judge Byers ordered a trial date of October 2, although he added that, once a jury was selected, the defense could ask for an adjournment to gain more preparation time. The government provided Donovan with a list of 69 potential prosecution witnesses including 32 FBI agents, 13 INS agents, and 24 others. On October 3, 125 potential jurors reported for duty. By the following day, a jury of nine men and three women was selected, together with four alternate jurors. Judge Byers then adjourned the case, at the request of the defense, until October 14. During this hiatus in the trial, Judge Byers ruled on Donovan's motion, originally submitted to the federal judge sitting in Manhattan, to suppress evidence seized in the alleged illegal search. In denying Donovan's motion, Judge Byers said: "The Department of Justice owes its first allegiance to the United States and it is not perceived that an alien unlawfully in this country has suffered any deprivation of his constitutional rights in respect to the matters brought to light at this hearing."[28]

While Donovan had to address numerous legal issues in court throughout his defense of Abel, he also had to contend with a serious matter closer to home that grew out of this trial. That concern was the extremely negative reaction of many individuals, including members of the judiciary and the bar, to the fact that he would defend a person who represented a country hostile to the United States.[29] Even Donovan's wife, Mary, and their children were not shielded from the barbs of others, in their neighborhood and in school.[30]

On October 14, the trial began. The prosecutor, William F. Tompkins, an assistant attorney general from Washington, DC, made his opening statement to the jury. In it, he described the contents of the indictment against Abel and discussed his witnesses, trying to preempt what he anticipated to be Donovan's planned attack against them. He also provided the activities of Abel since his arrival in the United States. It lasted forty minutes.

When Tompkins finished, Donovan rose to address the jury. Ten hours of preparation went into his twenty-minute opening. He sought to drive home two points: that this was not a trial against the Soviet Union and that the main government witness, Reino Hayhanen, was, as a spy, necessarily untruthful. He said, in part:

> The defendant is a man named Abel. Now, it is most important that you keep that fact uppermost in your mind throughout the days ahead. This is not a case against Communism. It is not a case against Soviet Russia. Our grievances against Russia have been voiced and are being voiced every day in the United Nations and in various other forums; but the sole issues in the case on which you are going to render the verdict deal with whether or not this man Abel, has been proven guilty beyond a reasonable doubt of the specific crimes with which he is now charged.
>
> Now, the prosecution has just told you that among the principal witnesses against the defendant will be a man, whose name is Hayhanen, who claims that he helped the defendant to spy against the United States.
>
> This means that within a very short while this man will take the stand and testify before you. Observe his demeanor very carefully. Bear in mind that if what the Government says is true, it means that this man who will take the stand has been here for some years living amongst us, spying on behalf of Soviet Russia. Now, in order to do this it means, and it is so charged in the indictment, that he entered the United States on false papers, that he swore falsely in order to obtain these papers, that he has lived here every day only by lying about his true identity, about his back-

ground, about every fact of his everyday life. Furthermore, if what the Government says is true, he was being paid to do this by Soviet Russia and we can assume if Russia properly trains her spies, that he was trained abroad in what his cover should be here, meaning that he was trained in the art of deception. He was trained to lie. In short, assuming that what the Government says is true, this man is literally a professional liar.[31]

Despite sound opening remarks, Donovan was well aware, as he took his seat, of the lingering fear and shock experienced by the public in general, let alone the jury before him, upon hearing of the launching by the Soviet Union ten days earlier of the world's first satellite, Sputnik I. He was also sensitive to the strong, lingering anti-Communist feelings of the McCarthy era.

At the conclusion of the opening statements, Tompkins called his first witness, Lt. Col. Reino Hayhanen. Hayhanen, a stocky man with dark hair and mustache,[32] testified in limited English that Abel was the Soviet Union's resident officer in the United States for espionage. Hayhanen, himself, was sent to the United States in 1952 under the assumed name of Eugene Nikolai Maki, ostensibly born in Idaho in 1927 of Russian-born parents who eventually returned to the Soviet Union. Hayhanen said he was sent to work with Colonel Abel, a KGB[33] officer, whom he only knew as "Mark." His own cover name, he said, was "Vik." He related that he would be paid $400 per month in addition to $100 for expenses. If he successfully passed an important piece of information, he said, he would receive a bonus of $5,000. During his testimony that first day, Hayhanen added that one of his other contacts in the United States was Mikhail Sverin, former member of the USSR delegation to the United Nations, who passed coded messages to him in a theater.

Hayhanen told the court that he was informed in Moscow where his secret "drops" would be, such as Prospect Park in Brooklyn and Fort Tryon Park in Manhattan. Containers used to hide messages included hollow bolts, coins, flashlight batteries and pencils. Some were magnetic so as to be able to adhere to metal objects such as gates and lampposts. The coded information that was to be transmitted was recorded on "soft film" which could be rolled into a tiny ball. Later, the photographic film could be chemically treated to become hard for developing.

On the following day, Hayhanen, again on the witness stand, described how he and Abel were ordered to give $10,000 in two payments to Helen Sobell, wife of Morton Sobell, who was serving a thirty-year sentence for his part in the Julius and Ethel Rosenberg spy case, which was heard in the Southern District of New York. Hayhanen said that $5,000 was buried in Bear Mountain State Park, and another $5,000 had been deposited in a bank. He added that Mrs. Sobell received none of the money. Hayhanen related that he was also told to find out if Helen Sobell would serve as an agent, but he said that he never asked. In addition, Hayhanen testified that Abel had instructed him to find several individuals, ostensibly potential agents, including one Roy Rhodes.

After nearly two days of testimony for the government by Hayhanen, it was the defense's opportunity for cross-examination. The United States Supreme Court had recently ruled in *U.S. v. Jencks* that the defense could view statements made by government witnesses to the FBI relevant to the matter at hand since these statements might be helpful during cross-examination.[34] Donovan, therefore, at the conclusion of Hayhanen's direct testimony, moved to see such notes, but Judge Byers ultimately ruled against the motion. Nevertheless, Donovan did have reports from a private detective agency, the Hooper-Holmes Bureau, whom he had hired to look into Hayhanen and so was able to launch into an aggressive cross-examination. He was able to elicit the fact that Hayhanen was a bigamist, with a wife in Russia and a second "wife" in the United States, and that he mistreated and humiliated the latter woman. He also elicited the fact that Hayhanen was an alcoholic; that he stole money that was provided by the Soviet Union and intended for a potential agent; that he was unsuccessful in establishing a Newark, New Jersey, photo studio as he was directed; and finally, that he could not locate certain people that his superiors asked him to. Donovan asked, then, given the foregoing, if it was possible that this witness could ever have been a lieutenant colonel in the Russian Secret Service.[35]

After Donovan completed his cross-examination of Hayhanen, Tompkins called several FBI agents to the stand, together with a sister of Roy Rhodes, the soldier who was due to testify the following week.

On Monday, October 21, the prosecution called several witnesses including an artist whom Abel befriended in his Brooklyn studio building. He was a critical witness in that a typewriter that he borrowed from Abel was introduced into evidence through him. Later in the day, a secret message that was found in a hollow bolt was introduced, and an FBI agent testified that the message was typed on that typewriter.

On this same day, the now-famous hollow nickel story was presented in evidence. The *New York Times* had carried the story of the coin in the month before the trial began. Briefly, James Bozart, a fourteen-year-old newsboy for the *Brooklyn Daily Eagle*, had received five nickels on his delivery collection route in 1953 from two women. On the stairs leading from the ladies' apartment he accidentally dropped the coins, and one of them split open. Inside one of the halves was a piece of microfilm. Young Bozart told his father, Fulton, a mail handler for the New York Central Railroad, about the coin and was instructed by him to turn it over to the police. Bozart brought it to Patrolman Frank R. Miley, the father of one of his schoolmates who, in turn, gave it to the FBI. Several days after the incident, the FBI visited the boy at home, but he had not heard from the FBI again until September 1957 when he was informed that he might be a witness in the Abel case.[36] The microfilm in the coin contained a message, the first of many, to Hayhanen upon his arrival in New York to work as Abel's assistant.

The last witness that the prosecution called on October 21 was U.S. Army M. Sgt. Roy A. Rhodes of Ft. Meyers, Virginia. The witness was originally identified through a microfilm found in Hayhanen's Peekskill home. Rhodes testified that in December 1951, after a drinking bout in Moscow, he woke up with a Russian woman in his bed. Thereafter, he had sold military and other information to the Russians while he was stationed at the U.S. Embassy garage in Moscow between 1952 and 1953. His code name, he said, was "Quebec." There was no indication from his testimony, however, that he ever heard of Rudolf Abel, and Donovan motioned to have his testimony stricken. The motion, upon which decision was initially reserved, was denied later in the day. On cross-examination Donovan brought out that Rhodes was a heavy drinker, as was Hayhanen, that he provided inconsistent information and that he had never known Abel. In his concluding questions to Rhodes, Donovan asked if Rhodes had ever heard of Benedict Arnold. Rhodes said that he had. Donovan continued:

Q. How does he stay in your mind as a figure in American history?
A. Not so good.
Q. I didn't ask you that.
A. Yes, you did.
Q. I didn't hear your answer.
A. I said, not so good.
Q. I asked you, how would you think of him?
A. I answered that. I said not so good.
Q. Why?
A. I—
Q. Isn't it because he betrayed his country?
A. I think so.
Q. Do you know enough history to know that even Benedict Arnold didn't do it for money?
A. I know it.

Q. Sergeant, Benedict Arnold may have been the greatest traitor in American military history, but it was only until today.[37]

After some additional testimony from agents on the following day, October 23, the government introduced a letter from Abel's wife. With that opening, Donovan introduced all of the letters that Abel's wife had sent since Abel was arrested, all of which tended to portray a warm and loving relationship and Abel as a devoted husband and father. They were the next best things to a character witness. Thereafter, because Abel had elected not to take the stand, and because there were no defense witnesses, both sides rested. The next day, October 24, would be the day for summations.

According to procedure, the defense would be first to make a closing argument, to be followed by the government. As Donovan spoke to the jury, his main thrust was the continued attack on the credibility of the two main government witnesses. He said, in part:

So, on the one hand, assuming that all this is true, you have a very brave patriotic man serving his country on an extremely hazardous military mission and who lived among us in peace during these years. And, on the other hand, you have the two people that you heard testify as his principal accusers.

Hayhanen, a renegade by any measure. Originally, there had been talk about Hayhanen being a man who, and I quote, "defected to the West" and you might have the picture of some high-minded individual who finally "chose freedom" and so on. You saw what he was. A bum. A renegade. A liar. A thief. You could just run down the adjectives to describe such a man.

He was succeeded by, so far as my knowledge would go, the only soldier in American history who has ever confessed to selling out his country for money.

These are the two principal witnesses against this man.[38]

Donovan went on to summarize the testimony of Hayhanen and Rhodes:

Now let's review a few of the things of what this man Hayhanen says that he did in the furtherance of this conspiracy.

He went out to Colorado to find a man, whom he never met to this day. He went down to Atlantic City to find another man; but he never met up with him. He went up to Quincy, Massachusetts to locate another man and to date, to this day, he is not sure that he found the right man. He was told, he says, that he should open a photographic shop as a cover. He never opened the shop. He was told to learn the Morse Code; he never learned the Morse Code.

By the time that man got through, including the fact that he was given money to give to a woman, Mrs. Sobell, but he never met up with her and he pocketed the money, five thousand dollars, for himself. Now, by the time that man got through telling his story, all that I could think of was that new best-selling book about children Where Did You Go? Out. What Did You Do? Nothing.

If that man was a spy, history will certainly record he is the most fumbling, self-defeating, inefficient spy that any country ever sent on any conceivable mission. It is virtually an incredible story and we are to believe that this is a lieutenant colonel in Russian military intelligence, sent here to obtain our highest defense secrets. That bum wouldn't have private first class stripes in the American Army.[39]

Donovan then proceeded to go after Rhodes:

Sergeant Rhodes appeared. You all had an opportunity to see the type he was: dissolute, a drunkard, betraying his own country. Words can hardly describe the depths to which that man has fallen.

Now, remember that Rhodes testified he never met Hayhanen, he never heard of him, he never met this man the defendant, he never heard of him, he never heard of any of the conspirators named in the indictment. Meanwhile, he told in detail here of his own life in Moscow, selling us out for money, and how is this related to this defendant? Those events in Moscow occurred two years before Hayhanen says Abel sent him to locate a man named Rhodes, two years. How did these relate to this man? The answer is, they don't relate in any way.

Now, it is on evidence of that kind that you are being asked to convict this man . . . this is the kind of evidence that is before you to send this man possibly to his death.[40]

The prosecutor, Tompkins, gave his summation next. It lasted for nearly an hour, and even Donovan agreed that it was thorough and powerfully given. Tompkins stressed that on re-cross-examination, Hayhanen had admitted he was a spy. He didn't apologize for Rhodes, but tried to reduce the impact of Donovan's argument saying, "Now, in other words, I think the defense discredited an already discredited witness."[41] He discussed the typewriter that Abel used in preparing codes and pointed to the great amount of evidence collected from the searches of Abel's rooms. When Tompkins was finished Judge Byers adjourned the case until the next day.

On Friday morning, October 25, Judge Byers charged the jury, a process through which the court explains the law to the jurors, advises them on what to consider and what should not become involved in the process, such as their emotions. When he had finished, the jury left the room to deliberate.

While the jury was out, reporters asked Donovan if he thought that Abel had received a fair trial. Donovan was aware that by commenting upon fairness, he could prejudice any future appeal. In his memoir of the trial, he mentioned that the defense in the Rosenberg espionage trial had thanked the Court for its fair manner. It plagued that attorney throughout the later appeals process.[42] Instead, Donovan presented to the press a statement that his client had written at the conclusion of the trial. It was a brief note, written in long hand, in which Abel thanked his attorneys for their work and demonstrated talents in his defense.[43]

After deliberating for three and a half hours the jury returned with a verdict of guilty on each of the three counts. Judge Byers set sentencing for November 15, 1957. It was only at this time, it should be noted, that Moscow finally spoke out about the Abel case through a periodical, *Literaturnaya Gazeta.* As could be expected, it denounced the trial as "low-brow science fiction" without having the merits of the evidence argued.[44]

It now befell Donovan to try to avert the imposition of the death penalty on his client. He submitted his argument to Judge Byers in a letter before sentence and outlined what would later be described as the "social utility" theory of justice, that is, that the defendant might be more useful to society alive.[45] Based upon the assumption that the jury verdict was correct, Donovan addressed the court (in part, emphasis added):

First, it will be my contention that the interest's of justice and the national interests of the United States dictate that the death penalty should not be considered. This is because:

  (a) No evidence was introduced by the Government to show that the defendant actually gathered or transmitted any information pertaining to the national defense;

  (b) Normal justification of the death penalty is its possible effect as a deterrent; it is absurd to believe that the execution of this man would deter the Russian military;

  (c) The effect of imposing the death penalty upon a foreign national, for peacetime conspiracy to commit espionage, should be weighed by the government with respect to the activities of our own citizens abroad;

  (d) To date the government has not received from the defendant what it would regard as "cooperation"; however, it of course remains possible that in the event of various contingencies this situation would be altered in the future, and accordingly it would appear to be in the national interest to keep the man available for a reasonable period of time;

(e) *It is possible that in the foreseeable future an American of equivalent rank will be captured by Soviet Russia or an ally; at such time an exchange of prisoners through diplomatic channels could be considered to be in the best interest of the United States.*[46]

Prior to the imposition of sentence on Friday, November 15, Donovan read the letter in court in its entirety. He also provided some additional remarks. Thereafter, William Tompkins addressed the court, and although he asked for a substantial sentence, he did not specifically ask that the death penalty be imposed. Judge Byers then spoke briefly and imposed a total sentence of thirty years and fines amounting to $3,000.

After the sentencing, Abel was taken to the detention pen of the courthouse to await transfer to the Bureau of Prisons facility in Manhattan. There, Donovan caught up with him. Abel again complimented his attorney and then inquired about subsequent court actions. Donovan explained that they had ten days in which to begin the appeal process, and a decision was made to do so.[47]

On November 25, 1957, Donovan filed a notice of appeal with the Second Circuit Court of Appeals. Later in the year, on December 23, the New York City Police Department awarded a civilian commendation to James Bozart, the newsboy who had found the hollow nickel in 1953. On that same day, Frank Miley of the Snyder Avenue Police Station was promoted to detective second grade.[48]

During the early months of 1958 Donovan met with Abel at the West Street Detention facility. Occasionally, his son, John, then thirteen years old, would accompany him. Some of the discussions centered on art and covert intelligence, others on the forthcoming appeal. That appeal was prepared by Tom Debevoise and Donovan (Fraiman was relieved at the conclusion of the trial) and filed with the Second Circuit Court of Appeals on February 15, 1958.

The substance of the appeal focused on the proposition that the search and seizure were illegal, thus violating the Fourth and Fifth Amendments to the Constitution. The defense added that no proof was offered that connected Abel to a conspiracy and that Rhodes's testimony should not have been admitted. The third contention presented the opinion that there were minor errors by the trial court that had the cumulative effect of depriving Abel of a fair trial. On April 16, in an oral presentation before the court, Donovan argued belatedly that the government prosecuted Abel with unconstitutional evidence after failing to persuade him to defect. Three months later, on July 11, the Court of Appeals affirmed the conviction and sentence.[49] The three-judge panel rejected the defense notion that

Abel was not shown to be part of the conspiracy. They also ruled that the search and seizure by agents was legal and that the minor errors the trial court may have made did not have a cumulative effect since the evidence clearly revealed the defendant's guilt.

Following the Appeals Court decision, the next step was an application to the Supreme Court for certiorari, that is, the granting of permission by that court for an attorney to present a case. During August 1958, Donovan and Debevoise, who had traveled from Vermont, worked on the application at the Lake Placid retreat. Two months later the court agreed to hear the case but restricted arguments to two questions regarding search and seizure, namely the legality of a search without a warrant in an immigration matter and the admissibility of evidence seized that was unrelated to the immigration arrest.[50] Donovan, ill for ten days with a virus, worked on the brief at his Brooklyn home. Debevoise joined him for several days. Donovan's daughter, Jan, was a senior at Marymount High School at this time and had expected, just at this time, that her father would take her to the school's square dance, but his illness prevented it. In fact, Donovan had been leaving his office early to take surreptitious dance lessons in anticipation of Jan's event.

On February 24, 1959, Donovan presented his oral argument before the Supreme Court.[51] He described the experience at the time as thrilling and the atmosphere of the court as one of great dignity and decorum.[52] Speaking to the justices, he quickly reached the core of his argument. According to FBI procedures, he summarized, agents had the option of treating Abel as a possible spy, detain him, search his premises and then attempt to persuade him to cooperate against his own government. In the alternative, they could charge him with a crime involving espionage, and then proceed according to established rules of criminal procedure and obtain a search warrant for his premises. However, Donovan pointed out to the justices,

> Having gone down that road, employed such a process, having (Abel) drop out of sight for three days, then for six weeks hold him down in Texas, offering him a job, offering every other inducement to come over to our side . . . I say, that having taken that gamble and having lost, that then you cannot come back up the other road and seek to get an indictment and pretend that due process of law has been followed.[53]

In short, the government used a civil detention writ of the Immigration and Naturalization Service to seize evidence against Abel when it should have used a criminal search warrant.

At the conclusion of the arguments, Chief Justice Warren extended an unusually high compliment to Donovan: "I think I can say that in my time on this Court no man has undertaken a more arduous, more self-sacrificing task. We feel indebted to you and your associate counsel. It gives us great comfort to know that members of our bar associations are willing to undertake this sort of public service in this type of case, which normally would be offensive to them."[54]

Several weeks after the hearing, Donovan was informed the justices wanted to hear additional arguments in the matter, a request quite out of the ordinary. That hearing ultimately took place during the following November.

Prior to the next Supreme Court hearing, a shocking development in Abel's case occurred. Donovan had reluctantly accepted responsibility to pack and ship his client's belongings back to his home in the Soviet Union. However, he was very insistent that those belongings be inspected first in order to avoid inadvertently sending espionage material with them. Thus, on May 15, 1959, when a crate of Abel's property was delivered to Donovan's office on William Street, two FBI agents arrived as well. They immediately began a detailed search of the crate's contents. As one of the agents examined Abel's wallet, he noticed a small pocket in it. A closer look revealed a thin piece of film secreted in it. Using a magnifying glass, the film was found to contain a numeric code, similar to that found in the hollow nickel. Discovered earlier, it would have solidly linked Abel to Hayhanen, and if the Supreme Court ordered a new trial it would severely damage the defense's case. In the end, the matter did not have a bearing on the conclusion of the case other than to provide an astounding aside.

In the following months, Donovan's fee for the defense of Abel was paid in two installments through an East German attorney, Wolfgang Vogel, ostensibly from family funds, but actually from the foreign currency accounts of the East German Secret Police.[55] Vogel had written to Donovan in July 1959 that he was engaged by Abel's wife to represent her interests, the first concern being the payment of Donovan's fee. The second concern was for a possible commutation of Abel's sentence or other form of relief that would return the convicted spy to his homeland. Of the total amount Donovan received, $10,000, he donated $5,000 to his alma mater, Fordham University; $2,500 to his law school, Harvard University; and $2,500 to Columbia University in behalf of Fraiman and Debevoise, graduates of that school.[56]

The hearing before the Supreme Court for reargument was originally scheduled for October 12, 1959, but rescheduled to November

9 because of the press of an earlier government case. During this time, as Donovan was trying to set another date, he wrote to a friend, "I am afraid that by now the whole Federal Government has concluded that they have a very intransigent Irishman on their hands."[57]

On Monday, November 9, 1959, Donovan made his final argument in Abel's behalf to the Supreme Court. He had 2,500 copies of his brief printed and sent to associates. His son, John, even wrote his own "brief" on the case that he "submitted" to his father. In a press statement in the following year, before the Supreme Court reached its decision, Donovan tried to put the Abel case in perspective: "The very fact that Abel has been receiving due process of law in the United States is far more significant, both here and behind the Iron Curtain, than the particular outcome of the case."[58]

Five months later, the court affirmed the conviction in a five-to-four decision.[59] Donovan requested another rehearing, based upon his concern that the justices' majority opinion permitted too much latitude to law enforcement officers and would adversely impact upon aliens residing in the United States.[60] His request was denied, and on May 16, 1960, the court ruled that Abel's conviction would stand.[61] The judicial process was over. The ultimate resolution of the Abel case, however, was yet to come through the far more secretive processes of international politics in which Donovan would play a central role. Meanwhile, however, Donovan resumed his civil practice. For example, two major cases involving the integrity of the insurance ratemaking process by rating bureaus saw Donovan before the Supreme Courts of New York and Wisconsin in 1958.[62] Based upon Donovan's work in these cases, as well as others, the General Insurance Brokers Association of New York presented him with a gold medal at the thirty-third annual meeting of the association at the Waldorf Astoria Hotel on October 29, 1958.[63]

6

The Abel-Powers Exchange

AT THE END OF THE APPEALS PROCESS, RUDOLF ABEL WAS TRANS-ferred from the Bureau of Prison's Detention Center in Manhattan to the United States Penitentiary in Atlanta, Georgia, to begin the service of his sentence. He was peacefully integrated into the general population of the prison and began to pursue his artistic interests. He designed and printed Christmas cards for the other inmates, painted a seascape for James and Mary, and even painted a portrait of President Kennedy. Some of his works were eventually given to Larry Houston, general counsel of the CIA. Others were given to Judge Joseph C. Zavatt of the U.S. District Court in Brooklyn. One of Abel's main concerns at this time, however, was in securing writing privileges so that he could reestablish communication with his family. His other, of course, was in being released.

In fact, it was Abel, himself, who first broached the idea of an exchange on February 12, 1958, suggesting that a neutral country such as India might broker a swap that would include Americans imprisoned in China for himself. In the following month, in connection with trying to secure the opportunity for Abel to write to his family, Donovan traveled to Washington where he met with CIA director Allen Dulles and the agency's general counsel, Larry Houston. Donovan had known both men from their days in the OSS. When Donovan mentioned the idea of a swap, Dulles replied that he didn't believe that the Soviet Union was then holding any prominent Americans as spies. However, he became interested when Donovan told him of Abel's idea, and he indicated that he would discuss the suggestion with his brother, John Foster Dulles, then secretary of state.

While the two CIA officials said that they had no problem with Abel corresponding with his family, they did caution Donovan about dealing directly with individual representatives of the Soviet Union with respect to a possible exchange of prisoners. They suggested that he send copies of all correspondence both to Houston and the Justice

89

Department before they were sent out, and Donovan agreed. Later, the State Department informed him that any trade for Abel would be opposed unless it included recognition of Abel by the Soviet Union. It would be some time, however, before there were any significant developments.

The Soviet Union, for all of its public silence about Rudolf Abel, definitely wanted him back and was preparing to negotiate for his release, albeit indirectly, well before Francis Gary Powers was shot down in his U-2 over Russia. Toward this end, the Soviets had begun to look for a negotiator and asked Heinz Volpert of the East German Secret Police, or Stasi,[1] to find someone suitable. Volpert, in turn, selected a lawyer, Wolfgang Vogel, for the task. Vogel was thirty-two years old when Abel was convicted. He had been born in Lower Silesia, then part of Poland, and during World War II served in the German infantry. After the war he studied law and subsequently joined the German civil service as an attorney in the Ministry of Justice. While at the ministry, he met Joseph Streit, later the chief prosecutor of East Germany, and became his close associate. By 1959, Vogel left his civil service position and went into private practice. Although he was a Catholic and denied ever being a member of the Communist Party,[2] he had received and continued to maintain the trust of the East German government.

When Vogel accepted Volpert's assignment, he was informed that he would receive his instructions from his friend, Josef Streit. In order to ensure that Vogel would not appear to be acting for Moscow, the Soviets created "relatives" of Rudolf Abel whom Vogel, as an attorney, would represent.[3] Thus, when Vogel first wrote to Donovan in behalf of Abel's "wife," concerning the matter of Donovan's fee, she was actually a character created by Moscow.

Francis Gary Powers was shot down near Sverdlovsk, Russia on May 1, 1960. He had been flying an aerial espionage mission, primarily to photograph Soviet missile sites. The journey began in Pakistan and was to have concluded in Norway. Powers survived as did the airplane, the latter much to the dismay of many Americans who believed that the pilot should have destroyed it, even if he didn't do the same to himself. Eleven days later, the *New York Times* suggested an exchange.[4] Powers's father, Oliver, too, immediately wrote to Abel in the federal penitentiary in Atlanta, Georgia proposing that his son be exchanged for the Russian spy. Abel then sent a copy of the letter to Donovan, suggesting that Donovan meet with Wolfgang Vogel when he was next in Europe.[5] Donovan and his son, John, did sail to

Europe in connection with business on June 13, and while he visited the American embassies in London and Paris, he only off-handedly discussed the case. Donovan did not meet with Vogel at this time.

The U-2 incident had created an international incident that Soviet premier Nikita Khrushchev used to his advantage for propaganda purposes. The four-power summit meeting that had just opened in Paris was canceled. When the Soviet leader demanded an apology from President Eisenhower, the American president quickly pointed out the espionage activity of the Soviets, themselves, citing the case of Rudolf Abel in particular. Khrushchev, of course, was well aware of Abel's activities, although he never admitted or conceded that Abel was a spy. If there was going to be an exchange for Abel, however, it would have to come after a conviction of Powers for espionage. Khrushchev would even wait until the election of John F. Kennedy to consider an exchange because he disliked Eisenhower and, even more so, Nixon.[6]

While Francis Gary Powers was not of the stature to the Central Intelligence Agency that Rudolf Abel was to the Russian Committee for State Security (KGB), the Americans did not want to abandon him in a foreign prison. Their first plan focused on the trial. It was hoped some international legal principle could be crafted that would bring about Powers's release. Toward this end, the CIA's assistant general counsel, Milan C. Miskovsky, was given the task of preparing such an argument. Miskovsky, in turn, recruited two respected Virginia attorneys, Alexander W. Parker and Frank Rogers, to assist him on a pro bono basis.[7] Essentially, the legal brief was based on the concept that Powers's overflight did not violate Russian airspace anymore than the Soviet satellite, Sputnik, violated American airspace in its passes over the United States.[8] As the three men were working on the brief, it was learned that the Soviet court was not going to permit Powers to have foreign defense counsel. As a result, Mikhail K. Grinyov, selected by the Moscow bar, was assigned to represent Powers, and the legal brief of Miskovsky, Parker and Rogers would have to be submitted through him. With the brief completed, Parker and Rogers flew to Moscow under the guise of being the attorneys for Gary Powers's wife, Barbara. While they were able to speak with Grinyov, he did not use their argument. Grinyov, in contrast to Donovan, was more a spokesperson for the Russian government than he was of his own client.

The Powers trial opened on August 17, 1960, in the Hall of Trade Unions in Moscow, a facility large enough to hold two thousand spectators. Present for the thirty-one-year-old defendant were his father and mother, Oliver and Ida Ford Powers, his wife, Barbara, and some friends.[9] Opposing Grinyov, the Soviet prosecutor was Roman A. Rudenko, the same individual who had participated at Nuremberg with Donovan. The trial before a three-judge court, presided over by Viktor V. Borisoglebsky, lasted three days and culminated in an apology from Powers. At its conclusion, Powers was adjudged guilty and sentenced to three years imprisonment and seven years in a labor camp.[10] Donovan discussed the trial briefly in an interview for *America* magazine in 1960 and repeated Abel's idea to employ a neutral country to act as a go-between for a possible exchange.[11]

With Powers now serving his sentence in a Soviet prison, officials of the Central Intelligence Agency began to discuss the possibility of an exchange. In fact, there were two schools of thought on the subject. One group believed that, given more time before a trade, Abel might be persuaded to give up important information. The other group was of the opinion that since Abel hadn't broken down since his capture in 1957, little could be gained by waiting longer. In addition, their over-riding concern was the imprisonment of one of their own in a Russian jail.[12] Miskovsky continued to have the responsibility for the return of Powers to the United States.

As the exchange of Abel for Powers was being discussed in the United States, the first foreign hint of an exchange came through Abel's "wife." She, as "Frau Abel," had started writing to Donovan in February 1959, inquiring about the health of her "husband," Rudolf. The style of her first and future letters was so substantially different from those Abel received from his true wife while he was in custody before trial, that Donovan correctly surmised that she must be an intermediary for the Soviet Union.[13] Frau Abel had written several letters, including one to President Kennedy, between 1959 and 1961. On May 8, 1961, however, Donovan received a letter that seemed to suggest the possibility of exchange of prisoners. He shared the letter with Miskovsky of the CIA and the latter prepared an innocuous response. Three additional letters from Frau Abel, written from Vienna, gradually moved toward a firmer offer of a trade. In each case, Donovan would sign the return letter that had been prepared by Miskovsky. After four months, Frau Abel finally proposed the simultaneous release of Powers and Abel. After receiving this news, Donovan traveled to Washington, DC, in January 1962.

Meeting with Milan Miskovsky on the eleventh of January, Donovan received authority to negotiate a trade. However, Donovan was informed that he would be traveling as a civilian and not as a representative of the government. In addition, he was sworn to secrecy so that the future negotiations would not be compromised in any way. At the conclusion of this meeting Donovan proposed that he use his usual business trip to London as a cover for his presence in Europe and suggested sending a letter to Frau Abel with an offer to meet her at the Soviet Embassy in East Berlin at noon on February 3. When the plan was agreed, Donovan wrote the note while still in Washington. If the date and time were acceptable, Frau Abel was to cable him at his office with the simple statement, "Happy New Year." He also received a letter from the United States pardon attorney that he would take with him to show the good faith of his country in pursuing the exchange.[14] Two weeks later, Frau Abel's cable arrived.

On January 27, Donovan met with Miskovsky at the Harvard Club in New York City for a final briefing before his trip. At this time he first learned of the existence of two other Americans who were imprisoned behind the Iron Curtain, Frederic L. Pryor and Marvin W. Makinen. Pryor was a Yale University student who had been working on a thesis concerning the economy of the German Democratic Republic. When he brought copies of the thesis to several professors in East Germany who had helped him in its development, he was arrested. Makinen was also a student, from the University of Pennsylvania, who was arrested in Kiev in July 1961 for taking photographs of a military reservation. He was tried and sentenced to eight years in prison. Miskovsky also informed Donovan that Wolfgang Vogel had gone to the United States Mission in West Berlin to advise that he was now representing both the Abel and Pryor families. Donovan was instructed that he should travel alone to meet Vogel and, in response to a question, was cautioned against bringing either a recording device or a weapon, despite the fact that his mission was fraught with danger.[15] He was also told that it would be preferable to secure the release of Powers, Pryor, and Makinen, but his concentration should be on Powers. Donovan, true to his character, decided to negotiate for all three American prisoners.[16] Three days later, Donovan arrived in London and checked in at the Claridge Hotel where he had stayed in the days before going to Nuremberg. Upon his arrival, he was met by another contact, a "Mr. White," who said that for the rest of the mission Donovan would use the code name of "Mr. Dennis."

On February 2, Donovan proceeded to an airbase about two hours from London. Upon arrival, he entered a C-45 aircraft and was flown to Templehof Airdrome in Berlin where "Bob," later identified as CIA base chief, William Graver, met him and took him to some modest accommodations in the city where he would remain for the duration of the negotiations.[17] On the following day, Donovan had a brief meeting with Graver. A security specialist was also on hand, and he checked the contents of Donovan's wallet and items on his person in order to avoid the possibility that Donovan, himself, be held hostage since he did not have any official status.[18] The meeting over, Donovan took the S-Bahn in West Berlin and traveled to Friedrichstrasse in the eastern sector where he walked from the train station to the Soviet embassy on Unter den Linden.

At the embassy, Donovan first met Frau Abel. Accompanying the lady was her "daughter," Lydia, and a "cousin," Herr Drews, a man who would act as interpreter when needed. The four spoke for about an hour before Ivan Alexandrovich Schischkin, the reported second secretary of the Soviet Embassy, entered. Donovan again correctly concluded that he was associated with the KGB in Western Europe. In this first session, Donovan sought to have Pryor and Makinen added to the anticipated swap. Schischkin, however, put off further discussion until February 5, and Donovan returned to West Berlin. This evening, and after each visit to East Berlin, Donovan prepared a report of his activities and the progress of the discussions and submitted them to Graver.

As arranged, Donovan made his second trip to East Berlin on the fifth. In an attempt to cover his stay in Germany, Donovan telegrammed his office:

2/5/62: To: Watters and Donovan in Scotland on brief business trip Returning to New York Saturday inform family —Donovan[19]

At the time of this second visit, Schischkin reported that the Soviet government would trade Powers or Makinen for Abel, but would not include both. He added that Pryor's release would have to be handled by Wolfgang Vogel as the representative of the East German government. Lydia and Drews sat quietly through the meeting, but later that day accompanied Donovan to Vogel's office at 113 Alt-Friedrichsfelde in East Berlin.

Vogel informed Donovan that he received a letter from the chief prosecutor of East Berlin (Josef Streit, who had just been promoted to the position and from whom Vogel took his instructions). Streit agreed that Vogel's client, Pryor, could be released if the Americans met certain conditions that were known to Vogel. Donovan asked if the East Germans were ready to release both Pryor and Makinen simultaneously with Powers. Although Vogel answered in the affirmative, Donovan received a message from him when he returned to West Berlin later in the evening. Vogel asked Donovan to come to his office on the following day because some difficulties had developed. In fact, Streit had told Vogel that the Soviets now wanted to see if they could swap Pryor for Abel, leaving Powers in prison.[20] This was just a bargaining ploy, however, because the Soviets were well aware that Powers was key to the trade. At this point Vogel was furious at having been caught between the competing interests of the Soviet Union and East Germany. Although the German Democratic Republic (East Germany) was a puppet government of the Soviet Union, Vogel was equally aware as the Russians that for the exchange to proceed, Powers had to be included. In response, Donovan and Graver decided that Donovan should go back to Schischkin rather than Vogel.

When Donovan visited Schischkin the next day he said that the United States would take Powers and Pryor for Abel and that Makinen could follow later. Schischkin suggested that he speak with Vogel before proceeding. Accepting that, Donovan, accompanied by Drews who was at the embassy, taxied to Vogel's office. While at Vogel's, the latter received a telephone call from Streit, which he took alone. Vogel then drove Donovan and Drews to a restaurant for lunch. On the way, four East German police officers who were following pulled them over and ostensibly gave Vogel a ticket for speeding. Donovan felt certain, however, that the purpose of the stop was meant in some way to intimidate him. Vogel continued on to the restaurant where he dropped off Donovan and Drews. He, himself, continued on to see Streit. Vogel informed Streit that unless the swap included Powers, there would be no deal. Streit agreed with Vogel's assessment and instructed him to accompany Donovan back to Schischkin's office in order to make certain that Schischkin understood this as well.[21] Vogel returned to the restaurant and picked up Donovan and Drews. As they got underway again, Vogel related that Streit had approved the Abel-Powers exchange.

Once the three had arrived back at Schischkin's office, only Donovan was permitted in, and Schischkin informed him while they were alone that, contrary to Streit's decision, the Soviet government would only trade Makinen for Abel. At that point, Donovan, as angry as Vogel was, declared that it would have to be Powers for Abel or there would be no swap. He told Schischkin that he had until the next day to call him or he would be going home. It was high-risk negotiating, but Donovan was sufficiently confident in his abilities to employ the tactic, knowing full well that the Soviets wanted Abel back.

On the seventh of February, Schischkin telephoned Donovan to say that he did not have an answer yet from Moscow. Later that day, Donovan went to a small reception at Graver's residence where Gen. Lucius Clay, a personal envoy of President Kennedy, happened to be as well. Donovan had known the general since his days at Nuremberg, but he made the mistake of sharing his mission with him, contrary to his earlier instructions. Clay did not further breach this secrecy although he complained to the State Department about his lack of prior knowledge of Donovan's mission.[22]

The day after the reception, Schischkin telegrammed Donovan informing him that he received an affirmative answer on the exchange and asked Donovan to meet him at his office as soon as possible. Donovan wired his agreement. Later that same day, Donovan traveled to Schischkin's office. Pryor, Schischkin told him, would be released at Checkpoint Charlie.[23] Abel would be released at another site, yet to be determined. Schischkin also added a request that the United States not try to create propaganda on the exchange. Anticipating his success, Donovan cabled his office:

2/8/62: To: Watters and Donovan Returning Monday Advise family — Donovan[24]

On his fifth and last negotiating trip to East Germany on February 9, Donovan met with Schischkin at the Soviet Embassy and the final details of the exchange were worked out. The Soviets requested, Schischkin repeated, that any official United States press release not refer to an "exchange" and to say nothing that would connect Abel to the Soviet Union. Donovan agreed. It was also decided that the Abel-Powers transfer would occur on the Glienicker Bridge, which connects East Berlin with Potsdam, on February 10.

On the morning of the exchange, Donovan met with Abel for the last time in a cell in West Berlin. After the brief meeting, Abel was transported under guard to the western side of the Glienicker Bridge. Donovan went separately with the CIA officer, Graver. At about this same time, Pryor was picked up at his prison by Vogel and a guard. Pryor had never been made aware of the impending exchange in the Soviet hope that he still might confess to spying. The three drove to Checkpoint Charlie and awaited the arrival of Frank Meehan of the U.S. Department of State. Meehan crossed the checkpoint to the eastern side and waited with Vogel and Pryor until the accompanying guard was notified by his superiors that Meehan, Pryor, and Vogel could cross into West Berlin.[25] That signal came at 8:35 a.m.

Meanwhile, at the Glienicker Bridge, at 8:20 a.m., Donovan, Abel, a prison guard and others, including Joseph Murphy, walked to the center of the bridge. Murphy, who was familiar with Powers, from the U-2 program, was on hand to verify Powers's identity.

Simultaneously, Schischkin, Powers, and Nikolai A. Korznikov walked from the opposite end. Korznikov had been Abel's superior in the KGB and would perform the same function as Murphy. Fifteen minutes later they received word that Pryor had been released. At that moment, Abel shook hands with Donovan, expressed his thanks again and walked to the Soviet side, just as Powers walked to the American side. Immediately following the exchange, a call was made from a telephone near the bridge, a telephone that had been previously set up by the CIA with a direct line to Washington.[26] Shortly thereafter, Pierre Salinger, President Kennedy's press secretary, announced the release of Powers and Pryor under the terms that Donovan had agreed to with Schischkin, adding that in the process the United States had the cooperation and assistance of Donovan.[27]

After the exchange, Donovan and Pryor were immediately taken to the airport. On the flight back to the United States, Powers, who still faced an American inquiry into the crash of his plane, his confession and his trial, asked Donovan about representing him. Donovan responded that his retainer would be one smoked Virginia ham, delivered at Christmas.[28] As the plane neared Washington, DC, CIA general counsel, Larry Houston, called Donovan's daughter, Jan, at her school, Marymount, in Virginia. She was picked up and brought to the airport where she met her father on his arrival. Regrettably, she recalls, school officials prohibited her from traveling on to New York with him.[29]

On February 11, Donovan and Miskovsky met Supreme Court Justice William J. Brennan in Georgetown where they had all attended Sunday mass. Full of good humor, Donovan asked the justice if he would convey to Justice Frankfurter that he had, at last, found a procedure to reverse a decision of the Supreme Court.[30] That same day Donovan said in a press conference that he hoped that better relations between the United States and the Soviet Union would speed the release of Marvin Makinen. In a statement on the twelfth, he added that he was not taking an active role in that release.[31]

After the spy exchange, Donovan never saw Rudolf Abel again, but he did receive a gift from his former client. In August 1962 Abel sent him two sixteenth-century, vellum-bound editions of the *Commentaries on the Justinian Code* in Latin. Donovan later said that he didn't know where Abel had found the books, but that, on inspecting them, found that a piece of paper covered an inscription that indicated that they were originally in the possession of the Duke of

Saxony. Donovan surmised that they were among the items that the Russians had seized when they entered Germany at the end of World War II.[32]

Even before he received Abel's gift, Donovan had written to his former client asking for his intercession in the release of the third American, Marvin Makinen. Although Donovan had told the press that he would not actively seek Makinen's release, he was urged to help by the Makinen family attorney, Oliver S. Allen of Boston. On March 2, 1962, Allen had sent a petition for clemency for Makinen to Leonid I. Brezhnev as president of the presidium of the Supreme Soviet of the USSR. A copy went to Donovan. As a result, on March 19, Donovan wrote a letter to Vogel asking him to speak with Schischkin to see if the time was not now right for Makinen's release. In order to permit the quiet work of diplomacy, the press was not notified. Vogel replied through the U.S. Mission to the United Nations in Berlin suggesting that Donovan write to Abel to ask his intercession. Thus, on April 2, 1962, Donovan wrote to Abel in Leipzig. Two months later, on June 1, Donovan wrote again to Vogel informing him that the United States had lived up to its commitment.[33]

The last contact that Donovan had with Abel came in 1964 after he had sent his former client a copy of his book, *Strangers on a Bridge*. In a letter dated June 11, Abel wrote:

> Dear Jim,
> Many thanks for your book, which finally reached me after a long delay. I am well and everything is fine. I hope this letter finds you in good health.
> Please give my best regards to your family, Tom Debevoise and Mrs. McInturff.
> Very sincerely yours,
> Rudolf[34]

A little over a year later, with Abel still on his mind, Donovan, accompanied by his daughter Mary Ellen, traveled to Moscow during a tour of Europe.[35] Following their arrival in the capital, Donovan asked Soviet authorities for permission to see his former client. By this time, August 1965, the Soviet Union had already conceded that Abel was a spy. That admission came in a Moscow television program in the previous March. The broadcast noted that Abel had served with the security forces since 1927 and that after his return from the United States, he had been teaching at the KGB's Higher School.[36]

He was said to be living in Moscow.[37] While he soon received permission, Donovan was also informed that Abel was in southern Russia on vacation and was not available. It was the last attempt Donovan made to see his client.

There were other ramifications of the Abel case for Donovan. He certainly received a number of accolades for his work. As early as December 4, 1958, during the Brooklyn Bar Association's Seventieth Annual Dinner at the St. George Hotel, Donovan was singled out for his defense of Abel as representing the highest traditions of the legal profession. In March 1962, Fred Pryor, together with his mother, father, and brother visited Donovan at his office. They presented him with a crystal paperweight that contained a piece of the Berlin Wall, and on the twelfth, President Kennedy sent Donovan a letter of thanks. It read, in part: "So far as I am aware, the type of negotiation you undertook, where diplomatic channels had been unavailing, is unique, and you conducted it with the greatest skill and courage. The additional release of Frederic L. Pryor and the openings left for negotiations concerning Marvin W. Makinen could only have been accomplished by negotiation of the highest order."[38]

On the following day, in a private ceremony, CIA director John A. McCone presented Donovan with the Distinguished Intelligence Medal for his work. In an accompanying citation, the director noted that Donovan, "employing tact, firmness and the highest order of diplomatic skill, succeeded in bringing his mission to a conclusion more satisfactory than initially envisaged."[39]

On June 13, 1962, Donovan was the recipient of an honorary degree of Doctor of Laws by Fordham University at a ceremony over which Francis Cardinal Spellman presided. In awarding the degree, Fordham cited not only Donovan's contributions to education, but also his "metadiplomacy"[40] in securing the release of Francis Gary Powers.[41]

Following the exchange there was much publicity including magazine articles and books. One article, however, particularly piqued the CIA's interest. David Snell, writing for *Life* magazine in February 1962, presented details of Donovan's trips to East Berlin that could only have been provided by Donovan or from leaks of his notes by the CIA.[42] And Vogel, who had been interviewed in June of the same year, apparently made a number of remarks that incensed Donovan. The CIA conveyed these developments to Donovan, who answered by letter:[43]

June 29, 1962
PERSONAL AND CONFIDENTIAL
Lawrence R. Houston, Esquire
General Counsel
Central Intelligence Agency
Washington, D.C.
Dear Larry:
I have read with care the message concerning the meeting with lawyer Vogel on June 12th. It is perfectly clear that Vogel was acting under instructions and that the world press reaction to the exchange, which the Russians should have anticipated, has infuriated them. I fear that this does not present a good picture for the release of Makinen in the near future.

With respect to Vogel's statements, they of course are mostly nonsense, plus some half-truths. However, I think that I should deal specifically with his statements and would appreciate your communicating my comments to your correspondents:

1. I had no part in composing the Snell article and did not see it before it was printed; Snell spoke with me once for a brief period at home and subsequently once by telephone. As I have told you, most of the article came from other sources. If Vogel really believes that I cooperated in the writing of the *Life* article, he should be told that I rejected an offer of $10,000.00 from the *Saturday Evening Post* to collaborate on such a series dealing solely with the Berlin mission and furthermore, when the *New York Times* inaccurately reported that I had accepted such an offer,[44] I compelled them to print a retraction.[45]

2. What Vogel really is, is a mystery to me. Any thought that he has not collaborated with East German and Russian authorities is absurd on its face. It will interest you to know that the Pryor family expressly commented to me upon the strange office of Herr Vogel and voiced suspicions similar to those voiced by Snell. If Vogel would like to know what I personally think about him, and it is considered diplomatic to tell him, you might state that I regard him as an unprincipled whore trying to play both ends against the middle and more to be pitied than condemned. However, you might further state that he was the only East German I met who wore hand-tailored clothes, a white-on-white silk shirt and expensive matching silk ties and kerchiefs. He could hardly be regarded as one making patriotic sacrifices for either side, especially in his new sports car.

3. His statement that I asked him to give a pledge of silence on the Powers-Abel deal is an outright lie. This matter was discussed solely by Schishkin and me, as my reports set forth. I would never consider discussing so important a matter with a person who I regarded as a minor and most unreliable tool.

4. Vogel's statement of his relationship to the case is a complete fabrication. I believe that my reports show this and it is absurd to think that he would forward me my $10,000.00 fee and undertake other actions on behalf of a man convicted here of being a top Soviet espionage agent without realizing whose interests he was serving.

5. The accusation that I weakened on the Makinen deal is preposterous. As those concerned will attest, and the records bear out, I played a bid of three-for-one so strongly that official concern was raised for my personal safety and that I might lose my basic Powers mission. Furthermore, ask Vogel how he knows about my negotiations with Schishkin concerning Makinen, since my reports will show that he was not present at my crucial discussions with Schishkin.

Your official correspondent's statement with respect to my agreement on publicity is precisely accurate and was observed by our Government in every official manner. While there may have been a variety of "leaks" from governmental sources, as evidenced by the Snell article, *The U-2 Incident* and *The Secret War*,[46] these certainly did not emanate from me. Furthermore, Schishkin expressly stated that he would not hold against us what the newspapers or magazines might print, since he understood our tradition of freedom of the press. Accordingly, he agreed with me that I could be expected to give no commitment beyond the official statements of the Government.

I see no point in my writing to Vogel on these matters, since he might use it, or be instructed to use it, as the occasion for a public tirade. [Illegible], I am strongly of the opinion that they unfo[illegible] simply further prostituting his profession and [that he is] being used by the Russians as a pawn for the obvious reason that they wish a plausible excuse not to fulfill their pledge on Makinen.

I would appreciate an early call on the letter from Mr. Allen dated June 25, 1962, since I should communicate with him.

Sincerely,

JBD/mm

There is no indication that Donovan had anything further to do with Vogel. In later years, Vogel became a trusted individual in East-West prisoner exchanges and is said to have brokered the freedom of more than 33,000 East Germans over the course of his career.[47]

The publicity generated for Donovan after both the trial and exchange led to many requests for lectures on the subjects, but especially on the trial itself from educational institutions. To the extent that his schedule allowed, Donovan acquiesced. During these presentations he focused on the concept of defending unpopular causes. One of his earliest talks on the subject constituted the Stevens Lecture on April 14, 1962, at Cornell University Law School in Ithaca, New York. It was also printed in a number of journals and newsletters.[48]

Well after the Abel trial, Thomas Debevoise found a copy of the Carpentier Lectures at Columbia University given in 1963. He sent Donovan a copy that included a lecturer's remarks. In one of those talks, the speaker had said:

> No matter what the judge or the organized bar may do, in the end the reliance is on the individual lawyer. The rest of us may urge and applaud. It is he who bears the heat and burden of the case. It is so when a nation is stirred by great conflicts and emotions, as, to name a few, when Erskine defended Tom Paine during the French Revolution, when Medina defended an accused accomplice of Nazi saboteurs during World War II, and when Donovan and Debevoise defended a Russian spy during the Cold War. It is no less so when an obscure lawyer in a county town defends a member of a minority group accused of a grave crime.[49]

Donovan replied the next day, "Arnold (Fraiman, not mentioned by the lecturer) must be fit to be tied."

The last major development of the Rudolf Abel affair was Donovan's recounting of it in his book, *Strangers on a Bridge.* Chronologically prepared from thorough notes taken over several years, it is a comprehensive history of the trial and exchange. Donovan started to write it in August 1960, but when the press of other business grew to be too much, he sought the assistance of Bard Lindeman, a staff writer for the *New York World Telegram and Sun,* to complete it. Lindeman worked on *Strangers* from April to August 1962,[50] and Donovan's secretary, Minnie E. McInturff, typed each of the drafts as they were completed. When it was finished, Donovan submitted it for review to his friend from his Nuremberg days, Budd Schulberg, and to Simon Michael Bessie of Atheneum Publishing Company.

Originally, Donovan anticipated asking David Maxwell Fyfe, the lord chancellor of England and former British prosecutor at Nuremberg to write the preface to *Strangers,* and he asked Charles E. Desmond, chief judge of the New York State Court of Appeals to write the foreword. As it ultimately happened, Judge Desmond did write the foreword and Donovan, himself, the introduction. Prior to publication, he cleared the work with Allen Dulles of the CIA.[51] The title of his book was actually conceived by his daughter Mary Ellen.[52]

On May 23, 1964 *Strangers on a Bridge* was released, and it was ultimately translated into nine languages including Braille. It was a Literary Guild selection, as well as the first nonfiction recommendation of the Book of the Month Club. Later in the year, *Reader's Digest* published a condensed version. Book reviews from around the country were generally very favorable.[53] Following publication, Donovan was also called upon for a number of radio and television appearances[54] and was asked, as well, to review several manuscripts in order to provide later dust-jacket comments. Bud Kay of Four Star Television asked Donovan, on April 6, 1964, to authorize a motion picture based on his life, but he declined. Before the year ended, the Scribes, an organization of writers on legal subjects, presented Donovan with their award for his writing of *Strangers.*

As with many popular books, consideration was given to turning *Strangers* into a movie. Through the William Morris Agency, Donovan contracted with Peter Ustinov, whose father was a spy for the Tsar, to produce the film. When the film rights were sold to MGM, Donovan placed the matter in a trust. Thereafter, Gregory Peck was offered the role of Donovan and Alec Guinness, that of Rudolf Abel. The movie, however, was never made.[55]

In 1965 when the John LaFarge Institute, an organization whose purpose is the betterment of interracial relations, planned to open a new headquarters for the Catholic magazine, *America,* at 106 West Fifty-sixth Street, Donovan donated $25,000 in royalties from *Strangers* to endow the managing editor's office at the new America House.[56]

Donovan last saw Ivan Schischkin in person in 1962. Five years later, however, he received a photograph from London that revealed two Russians carrying a man, identified as Vladimir Tkachenko, into the Russian Embassy. One of the Russians could not be identified by the news media, and they forwarded it to Donovan. As soon as he saw the picture, Donovan easily identified the unknown individual as Schischkin. The KGB had apparently abducted Tkachenko in London on September 16, 1967, because they believed that he was going to defect to the West. They brought him to the Russian Embassy and later, drove to the airport. Scotland Yard, however, prevented them, at least temporarily, from taking him aboard a plane to Moscow.[57]

Rudolf Abel died a hero in Moscow on November 16, 1971, at the age sixty-eight. He had suffered with lung cancer for some time. In 1990, the Russian government honored him with his likeness on a postage stamp.

Francis Gary Powers died in a helicopter crash on August 1, 1977, in Van Nuys, California, shortly before his forty-eighth birthday. His craft had run out of fuel on his return from taking aerial photographs of a fire in Santa Barbara.

7

Cuban Negotiations: Part I

ON JANUARY 1, 1959, JAMES DONOVAN WAS PREPARING HIS ORAL arguments before the Supreme Court in behalf of Rudolf Abel. At the same time the dictator, Fulgencio Batista, was fleeing Cuba in the face of the advance of Fidel Castro Ruz and his revolutionaries. Once established in power, Castro took on the role of premier, and in the months that followed, nearly three-quarters of a million Cubans fled their homeland, many in the hope of returning again after Castro had been ousted.

Castro, born in Cuba in 1927, received a Catholic education at a local Jesuit school before attending the University of Havana, from which he graduated with a law degree in 1950. Two years later he ran for Congress, representing the Orthodox Party. However, General Batista was running for president at this time as well. When he saw that he couldn't win, Batista staged a coup, suspended the Constitution, and canceled the election. Later, in an attempt to end the dictatorship of the general, Castro unsuccessfully attacked the Moncada army barracks on July 26, 1953. Most of his compatriots were either killed or captured. Castro himself was captured, tried and sentenced to fifteen years imprisonment. Pardoned in 1955, he traveled to Mexico and soon founded the Twenty-sixth of July Movement. Within a year he returned to Cuba, hiding with his revolutionaries in the Sierra Madre Mountains, where he continued to gather support.[1] After Castro's assumption of power, the United States viewed his revolutionary Marxist government with concern and supported plans for his overthrow.

During Castro's first year in government, the Central Intelligence Agency started to make plans for an invasion of Cuba, by Cubans, from a Latin American base. Toward this end, they assisted in helping certain Cubans leaders escape from the island and began to recruit others who had already arrived in the United States. Gradually, the invasion force began to take shape. They called themselves Brigade 2506, deriving the number from the serial number of Carlos Rafael Santana, the first brigade member to die.[2]

An agreement between the United States and Guatemalan governments permitted training in the latter country. President Dwight D. Eisenhower had, on March 17, 1960, authorized the CIA to train the Cubans in guerrilla warfare. By the end of the year, that training had changed to conventional warfare tactics, a fact that some have said helped to preclude the ultimate victory of the invasion force. The Brigade, however, had many more difficult things with which to contend once the attacks were launched, including a lack of air support, insufficient ammunition and an overwhelming number of opposing forces.

The invasion commenced on Sunday, April 16, 1961. The Brigade had selected three landing sites in the area of the Bahia de Cochinos, or Bay of Pigs. Of the 1,444 men in the force only 10 percent had been professional soldiers; 20 percent were students and the remaining numbers were a complete cross-section of the Cuban population and included lawyers, teachers, mechanics, newsmen, clerks, priests, and a minister. Three days after the landings, the invasion was over: 1,180 Brigade members were captured, 114 were killed, and 150 escaped and were rescued.[3]

In the failure of the invasion, the United States had suffered a singular defeat, since it was so obvious that the American government orchestrated the ill-fated action. John F. Kennedy, who had just assumed the office of president three months before the invasion and who had given the final authorization for the Brigade to proceed, took personal responsibility for the failure and was anxious to find a means to obtain the release of the prisoners. The first opening came from Castro, when he announced on May 17, 1961, that he would be willing to exchange the prisoners for five hundred heavy-duty tractors. He then formed a "commission" consisting of ten prisoners and sent them to the United States for the purpose of negotiating for the tractors. President Kennedy, upon learning of the commission, urged the formation of the Tractors for Freedom Committee as a private agency to work with the Cuban prisoners. Among the Americans who lent their name to the Committee were Eleanor Roosevelt, former First Lady, Milton Eisenhower, president of Johns Hopkins University and Walter Reuther president of the United Auto Workers Union. Despite the prestige of these individuals, however, the Committee was short-lived. Political and public opinion viewed as blackmail any form of trade, whether it was called indemnification or exchange, and the Tractors for Freedom Committee was dissolved within two months.[4]

The prisoners' commission, however, remained in the United States for a time, and on July 5, 1961, they met in Key West, Florida, with the parents of some of the other prisoners. As a result of that meeting, a new organization was formed, the Cuban Families Committee for the Liberation of the Prisoners of War (CFC).[5]

CFC representatives obtained power of attorney from the members of the prisoners' commission and tried, unsuccessfully, to secure previous donations to the Tractors for Freedom Committee. Thereafter, they met with Richard Goodwin, a speechwriter and assistant special counsel to President Kennedy.[6] At a meeting on July 11, 1961, Goodwin told the CFC representatives that the government could not underwrite $26 million for tractors and suggested that the CFC incorporate and obtain the services of a public relations firm with a view toward gaining national support and donations for the tractors.

While the CFC did incorporate and did obtain tax-exempt status, they were unable to obtain anything approaching a groundswell of support. And although Allis Chalmers, Caterpillar, and Fiat seriously considered supplying tractors entirely on credit, Castro ended all hope for a prisoner exchange for tractors on March 10, 1962, when he withdrew the offer and announced that the prisoners would be tried.

The trial of 1,178 soldiers began on March 29.[7] After four days all were found guilty and sentenced to thirty years imprisonment or until total fines of $62 million were paid. The fines were calculated on class. Professionals were fined $100,000; those next in status, $50,000; and those least in status, $25,000. Three commanders, Manuel Artime, José San Roman, and Erneido Oliva were each fined $500,000.

Both before and immediately after the trial CFC members were in contact with Robert A. Hurwitch, special assistant to the Secretary of State for Cuban Affairs.[8] Hurwitch had assured the CFC orally that they had $26 million in agricultural credits with which to deal with Castro. On April 10 a delegation from the CFC, including Alvaro Sanchez, Enrique Llaca, Ernesto Freyre, and Virginia Betancourt de Rodriguez flew to Havana and met with Castro. The meeting took place in the home of Berta Barreto de los Heros, the CFC's liaison in Havana, who was also the mother of one of the prisoners. Castro rejected the agricultural credits, asserting that he was bound by the court's fine. However, he offered to release fifty-four wounded prisoners if their fines would be considered as a preferred obligation, to be paid before the other fines. The CFC ultimately agreed, after consulting with many of the prisoners who were to be left behind. They also successfully increased the number of wounded prisoners released to sixty.[9]

In the CFC's discussions with Castro, Enrique Llaca suggested medicine as an alternative to cash, and the premier responded that medicine could be a substitute for a portion of the fines. Thereafter, the CFC and the prisoners returned to Miami. While the Cuban community expressed their joy at the airport, Hurwitch of the State Department felt that the CFC had gone far beyond their authority in agreeing to take back the prisoners. He also withdrew the pledge of $26 million in farm credits.

By the beginning of June 1962, the CFC was acquiring sponsors but was not any further along in securing the funds for the fine payments. The prisoners had been transferred to the garrison on the Isle of Pines and their future looked bleak. It was at this point that Enrique "Harry" Ruiz-Williams approached Robert Kennedy. Ruiz-Williams, one of the wounded prisoners released by Castro, had had several previous meetings with the attorney general since the trial of the prisoners. He was a graduate of the Colorado School of Mines, had worked in Cuba, and had the respect of the other Brigade members. In a meeting on June 19, he bemoaned the fact that the CFC could not find a national chairperson to lead the fund drive. The attorney general replied, "Enrique, you don't need a chairman. You can get a chairman under any rock in the trail. What you need is a man who knows how to deal with Castro. You need someone who can represent you. I think I know of a lawyer who might help." "Who is he?" Harry asked. "Donovan," Kennedy responded.[10]

On the following day, the CFC asked Robert W. Kean Jr. to telephone Donovan on their behalf and request that he meet with representatives of the committee. Kean was a businessman who had been assisting the CFC because he was married to the sister of one of the prisoners. Donovan agreed to meet the delegation at his office that same day.

During the meeting Donovan agreed to represent the CFC without a fee once he determined that he would not be in violation of the Logan Act[11] and that his actions would be in accord with the interests of the United States. He asked for a summary of the Cuban Families Committee's activities to date and about any information that they might have concerning the Brigade as well as Castro.

Several days after their meeting with Donovan the CFC employed the services of a public relations firm, John Price Jones of New York. On June 26 the CFC announced the names of their fifty-two initial sponsors including Richard Cardinal Cushing of Boston, Gen. Lucius D. Clay, Ed Sullivan, and Dame Margot Fonteyn.[12]

On June 27 Alvaro Sanchez brought Berta Baretto to Donovan's office at the latter's request. Baretto was not only the CFC's liaison in Havana. She was also a good friend of Celia Sanchez, Castro's chief of staff and confidante. During the meeting Donovan wrote a letter to the CFC knowing that Fidel Castro would eventually see it. He said, in part:

> Fidel is a Cuban before he is a Marxist and he must have pride that fellow Cubans—however misguided or misled he may believe them to be— would risk their lives for what they thought to be in the best interests of Cuba. If reasonable conditions can be brought about, in the interests of the Cuban people, I believe he will carry out his Pledge with respect to these fellow-Cubans and demonstrate not only to Latin America but to the world that he wishes to be regarded as the compassionate leader of all the Cuban people. It is in this belief that I have agreed to assist your cause toward a prompt accomplishment of its objectives."[13]

Donovan's next step was to consult with Attorney General Robert Kennedy. Through Ruiz-Williams he obtained an appointment on July 3. Taking the train to Union Station in Washington, DC, Donovan was met by Ruiz-Williams and brought to Kennedy's office. In a private conversation, the attorney general assured Donovan that his activity with respect to Castro would not be in violation of the Logan Act and would certainly be in the interests of the United States. After a conference later in the day with Hurwitch of the State Department, Donovan returned home.

Over the next several weeks, Donovan recruited others to assist him. He hired John Ryan for this purpose and provided him with space in his office on William Street. Donovan also asked a Brooklyn attorney, Robert A. Morse, to assume the duties of assistant general counsel to the CFC.[14] Morse's first task was to review Castro's speeches following the collapse of the tractor negotiations in order to determine if there was anything Donovan could use in negotiating with the premier. He quickly found an important remark in a speech Castro made on May 19, 1961, upon receipt of the Lenin Peace Prize: "Of course, we do not exchange them the prisoners against arms, we do not exchange them against bullets, we do not exchange them against money."[15] A good arguing point for Donovan.

Originally, Donovan thought he would be working through the Cuban Mission to the United Nations, and toward this end, he met with the Cuban Ambassador to the UN, Jorge Garcia-Inchaustequi, on August 1. Donovan asked him at this time, "Can your government consider the possibility of accepting food and medicines in lieu of cash?"[16] He received the answer several days later while attending a conference in San Francisco. At that time, he was informed in a telephone call that a message was waiting for him at the Cuban mission. Donovan directed John Ryan to pick it up and learned that Castro had an offer for him.

Donovan traveled to Washington on August 23, in part to have his passport validated for travel to Cuba. He also visited the Czechoslovakian Embassy in order to apply for a visa for his Cuban travel. Once this was done, he presented himself in the office of Robert F. Kennedy. With Kennedy at the time was Hurwitch. Kennedy informed Donovan that a full indemnity of $62 million was unrealistic and that, in addition, the Central Intelligence Agency was under a direct injunction from congressional leaders not to use its unrestricted funds to help Castro with any amount of money. On the other hand, Kennedy said, "Don't be discouraged. You will receive some help. Through the cooperation of the State Department, you can be assured that between $15 million and $30 million in food and medicine can be made available . . . The play should be for emphasis on the food, Mr. Donovan. Go quiet on the medicine." "In other words," replied Donovan, "if I can settle for $20 million in food plus some cash as can be raised, and never mention medicine, you will be pleased?" "Correct," Kennedy replied.[17] The next day, in a press conference, Donovan mentioned his forthcoming trip. "When and if I do leave," he said, "it will not be in a clandestine manner. It will be done in a simple, ordinary and public manner."[18] On August 25 Donovan received a telegram with authorization to enter Cuba.

On August 29 Donovan left for Miami on a private plane and checked into the DuPont Plaza Hotel under an assumed name. He had already worked out a secret number code to use with his Washington contacts while he was in Cuba. The code was a simple one: *1* meant that the negotiations were going normally; *2* indicated that there was difficulty, but they were progressing; *13* represented that he was meeting Castro; *19* meant that his personal status was fine; *24* indicated that there was a hostile atmosphere and he was coming out.[19] The mission even had a code name, Project Mercy. The next day Pan American Airlines donated a small plane with an American pilot to transport Donovan, Alvaro Sanchez Jr., president of the CFC, and Ernesto Freyre, the CFC's secretary, to Cuba. Before takeoff it was necessary to get clearance from Cuba so that they could pass safely through the antiaircraft batteries. The short plane trip was uneventful, and once on the ground in Havana, a convoy of guards armed with machine guns greeted the visitors. Donovan, to break the tension, signed the visitors' book at the airport, "James B. Donovan, ambassador from Brooklyn, USA."[20] They were escorted to Berta Baretto's villa in Miramar, a suburb of Havana, where their first visitor was Santiago Cubas, the attorney general. The significance of this first meeting lay in the fact that Donovan immediately conceded that whatever medium might be exchanged for the prisoners, it would be called an indemnification, a concession not made before.[21]

The meeting with Castro took place on the thirty-first. Castro spoke only in Spanish and Alvaro Sanchez translated. Donovan had told Sanchez earlier that he, Donovan, would interrupt for a translation if Castro spoke for too long. As the talks began, Donovan first related that he didn't speak for the United States government. He pointed out that he had problems with money and offered some cash in addition to foodstuffs. Donovan also discussed a deal in terms of the retail value of products instead of manufacturers' costs and wondered out loud if Castro would agree to a reduction in his demands. Castro replied that there were problems for Cuba as well. He said it was difficult to fix an indemnity because "the damage done by the American government cannot be measured."[22] Then, after some expressions of humor on both sides, Castro asked for a specific proposal.

Donovan suggested that a boat from a neutral country be utilized to receive the entire Brigade in return for $5 million in cash or $20 to $25 million in products. When Castro asked what products, Donovan replied that they could include skim milk, chickens, grains, corn, rice, wheat, and the like. Castro balked, stating that foodstuffs were not acceptable because they were humiliating. He said that he could discuss values with his government, but a reduction would be difficult. When Donovan pointed out that he couldn't obtain merchandise for the values that Castro wanted, Castro replied that the only cash he was interested in was the $2.9 million for the sixty prisoners who were released earlier. The remainder of the deal could be in foodstuffs and goods whose values were sufficient to cover the court-fixed indemnity. He promised to give Donovan a list of the products most valuable to Cuba, and Donovan agreed to get the maximum quantity. Meanwhile, Cuba would evaluate the costs of the products, insurance, packing, and freight. After four hours, the meeting finally ended.[23]

On September 1, Donovan had a second meeting with Castro lasting only half as long as the day before. The two initially discussed some unrelated topics, such as Donovan's work at the board of education, and then Castro related that his government considered it possible to reach a solution to the exchange. Some ministers present at this meeting asked if, among the products, women's tailored clothing and hides for shoes could be included. Donovan replied that he didn't think so. Soon Castro began to talk at great length, so Donovan decided to inject some humor with a little story about the value of brevity, hoping that his host would get the message. There was a court case in New York, Donovan began, that involved the collision of two ships. Each ship owner hired attorneys and went to court. One of the law firms, in defending their ship captain's actions and in explaining why he was not negligent, presented a massive brief extending to 275 pages. Two weeks later, the opposing firm representing the other ship submitted a one-page, one-line answer, "Then, why didn't he blow his whistle?" It was this type of engaging humor that Castro enjoyed and that helped to promote the good-natured relationship between the two men. Sometimes, the humor could be outrageous, as will be seen, but the Cuban leader only seemed to enjoy it that much more. Prior to Donovan's departure, he and Castro had agreed that all arrangements must have the prior approval of the American government but the exchange itself would remain one between people, not between governments.[24]

On Sunday, September 2 Donovan left for home. Four days later he received the lists of goods sought by Castro's government. He immediately realized that fulfilling the amount of food products would require numerous ships, ranging in number from thirty to sixty. Thus, on this same day, September 6, Donovan visited John E. McKeen, president of Charles Pfizer, a major pharmaceutical company, who was a neighbor in Donovan's apartment building. Contrary to Robert Kennedy's advice, he asked McKeen about sending drugs and medicines to Cuba, items that were both small and valuable. McKeen said he would be willing to donate drugs from unfilled inventories, but he couldn't do it alone. Therefore, he agreed to call John Connor, a former classmate at Harvard and president of another pharmaceutical company, Merck, Sharp and Dohme. McKeen knew that Connor was concerned about the recent antitrust investigations into the drug companies by Attorney General Robert F. Kennedy and Senator Estes Kefauver. He also knew that Connor would want tax deductions for his contributions, and he shared these concerns with Donovan. Later in the day, Donovan left for Washington.[25] He met with Robert Kennedy on September 7 to discuss his meeting with Castro and the need to add medicines in place of some of the foodstuffs. Earlier, the attorney general had held a small conference concerning Donovan's efforts in liberating the brigade. Present at this meeting were Secretary of State Dean Rusk, CIA Deputy Director Marshall Carter, the CIA's assistant general counsel Milan Miskovsky, and McGeorge Bundy, the president's special assistant for national security. Kennedy, anxious for input on the relief effort went around the room asking for comments. Receiving less-than-substantive replies from Rusk and Carter, he was becoming irate. When he asked Bundy for his thoughts, the latter simply raised a concern over the Cuban affair's impact on the upcoming election.[26] Kennedy, in a loss of temper, tossed a pencil across the table that landed in Miskovsky's lap and shouted, "As long as I'm attorney general, we have a moral obligation to those people in that jail. And I don't care if we lose every election that will ever be held. We're going to get those guys out."[27] His position was also that of his brother, the president.

Little more occurred in the month of September since the primary emphasis was on acquiring the products on the Cuban lists. Donovan had sent copies of those lists to Pfizer and Merck ending each with the note, "You have my personal assurance and that of the Committee [CFC] that the officials of the U.S. Government at the very highest levels have been kept informed of our every activity in this regard, and have endorsed our contemplated action."[28] By September 30, Donovan had developed bursitis in his right shoulder and was advised by his doctor to remain in New York. Nevertheless, he resolved to return to Cuba. His wife, Mary, asked him at this point, "How long will you be gone this time? That man talks so long. Are you going to talk too?" To which Donovan replied, "I have a few things to say." "Then," Mary answered, "it could take months."[29]

At the beginning of October, Donovan arranged for a Letter of Credit from the Royal Bank of Canada to cover the delivery of drugs and medicines from members of the pharmaceutical industry. The manufacturers would provide an inventory of older drugs at cost, rather than using their newer drugs. The retail value of the drugs would be approximately $60 million. Donovan also secured a second letter of credit guaranteeing the payment of the $2,900,000 for the sixty released prisoners. With that accomplished, he flew to Havana on October 3. The next day, still in severe pain, he saw a neurosurgeon, Clemente Inclan, and received injections for his bursitis. Later, he met Attorney General Santiago Cubas and Minister of Internal Security Capt. José Abrahantes. Donovan had brought a letter from McKeen of Pfizer pledging medicines and showed it to the Cubans. Abrahantes asked if baby food and surgical equipment could be included with the medicines, and Donovan said that he believed they could. Significantly, there were a number of Cuban officials who distrusted Donovan. Abrahantes was one. However, his suspicions were accompanied by a strong dislike of the United States, and Donovan became the lightning rod of his anti-American feelings.

After this exchange, Donovan was taken on a fast, bumpy car ride, escorted by two carloads of men and machine guns, to the former DuPont estate to meet Castro. Traveling in such a fashion greatly increased the pain of his bursitis, and it was clearly the intent of

Captain Abrahantes to cause this. Upon meeting, Castro warmly shook Donovan's left hand, and they proceeded to take a walk on the beach. The night before, Celia Sanchez had mentioned that she hoped Donovan would bring a gift for Castro related to his new interest in skin diving. As they walked, Donovan told Commander Vallejo to "tell Dr. Castro that through a cousin of mine who is very familiar with such things—my cousin Tom—I had ordered some very recent skin-diving equipment from Abercrombie & Fitch . . . I hoped he would accept such a present . . . " Donovan later wrote in his chronology of the Cuban negotiations, "Castro smiled all over and said that he was deeply appreciative of this, that he wanted me to know that he would wear it in good health! I figured with what we were playing for here, this was peanuts, but he was like a child."[30]

After a walk along the beach, Castro, Donovan, Abrahantes, and Vallejo passed through a grove and found a small cottage with a porch and chairs. As they stopped and sat for a while, Castro's concern for both arranging a deal and for saving face emerged. "They are trying to make a fool of me," Castro opined of the American government. "In the beginning I told the people I would accept only cash. Now you come and talk food and medicine. Then you return and embargoes are put down, and transportation of food becomes impossible. You come back this time, and whereas only 15 percent of my package was in drugs and medicine, you want 100 percent. Meanwhile you try to explain a basis of value which makes no sense to the Cuban people. . . . The captain was under the impression when he saw you yesterday that you were offering $60 million in wholesale value of medicines and drugs."

"No, No," Donovan replied. "That is a misunderstanding, partly due to my poor presentation of the matter . . . "

"Let's drop it," Fidel said. "Let's just say it was a misunderstanding. But the captain did make a report to some of our people last night, and it will be slightly embarrassing for him to explain the situation."

Vallejo interjected at this point, bringing up the need for medical supplies such as X-ray plates. He also mentioned that baby food would also be acceptable: "Baby food doesn't present the shipping problems that bulk food would and can be classified as medicine, drugs and medical supplies. The more of it you can get, the happier we will be, and the more you can justify your position to the American public. One of your problems is that people would say, how can you guarantee that all these supplies won't be turned over to Soviet technicians or militia. That contention would be effectively eliminated if we could get a heavy shipment of infant's food."

At Castro's suggestion, he, Vallejo, and Donovan proceeded to a boat in the nearby harbor. Once on board, the discussion continued. Castro was still holding out for an increase in the wholesale value of the goods. He also wanted to release the prisoners in groups as the goods were delivered.

On this point Donovan was adamant. "In the first place, absolutely no dice on releasing these boys in groups. They all have to come out as soon as the initial delivery is made. You'll just have to rely on the fact that among other things, the relationship created here could open a channel of communication that might be of mutual benefit to all parties concerned."

"Yes," Castro seemed to agree, "we've discussed this at some length."

Donovan then tried for a little more out of the discussions and brought up the subject of Americans who were being held prisoner entirely apart from the Bay of Pigs invaders. "It is possible," Donovan said, "by resoliciting some large American corporations that have not as yet come through with pledges that I could increase this by a few million dollars if I could bring some Americans out with me." As Donovan related, "Castro gave this quite a bit of cigar chewing, then said, 'My decision is final. The question of the Americans must be separately handled from this question of the remnant of the Brigade. However, I will say to you that as soon as this matter has been concluded I believe I would like to take up with you the question of the Americans.'"

As they returned to the monetary value of the products sought by Cuba, Vallejo calculated that if a letter of credit could be issued for between $16 and $17 million, this would be sufficient to guarantee the delivery of goods with a retail value of about $50 million. When Donovan stalled on the $16 million figure, Castro remained firm. In the end, Castro summed up their tentative agreement: "Now let me see if I understand this. Drugs, medicine, baby food and medical supplies which have a recognized wholesale list price plus an estimated transportation cost amount to 50 million dollars [retail]. And this can be purchased for 17 million dollars?" Donovan replied, "According to the calculations I've made with Pfizer and Merck, yes. But, we, the Committee, will have to shop around to see if other companies with heavy inventories would be interested in cleaning them out. I cannot—and I want this made clear that John McKeen told me this—I cannot commit these two companies alone to doing something of that magnitude."[31] Actually, McKeen had originally told Donovan that Pfizer could do it alone but his own executive board objected. It was then that he asked that Merck also take part. Donovan knew, however, that the present agreement would be far too much even for two large pharmaceutical companies.

Donovan and Castro had finally arrived at a tentative agreement. Briefly, Castro would receive $50 million in drugs, medicines, and medical supplies including $1,500,000 in baby food. He also continued to demand the $2,900,000 in cash for the sixty wounded prisoners. With an increase in the deposit with the Royal Bank of Canada, Castro would accept Pfizer and Merck's guarantee for delivery. He added that he wanted 20 percent of the drugs and medicine, in addition to the cash, on the first vessel. That vessel, then, could take all of the Brigade prisoners from Cuba. The American prisoners would be considered once these negotiations were over.

When the boat returned to the dock, Castro and Vallejo shook hands with Donovan and went off in their own car. Captain Abrahantes, according to Donovan, drove him back to Mrs. Barreto's house, in a ride just as wild, if not more so, as the trip out, and similarly designed to enhance the American's pain.

Before dinner that night Donovan, in a telephone conversation, briefed Jim McIntosh, a CIA contact, of the day's events.[32] "Then," Donovan wrote, "on doctor's orders, Jesus gave me an injection. Every four hours, I was supposed to receive an injection in the rear. Now Jesus is a lawyer, but was also formerly an owner of a race-track horse. He got hold of a needle and medication from a nearby vet and treated me. For this reason I began calling him 'my horse doctor.' The joke wore thin, however, when the area became infected and I had difficulty sitting. There was no oral medicine to be had in Cuba."[33]

On October 6 Captain Abrahantes visited Donovan and told him that Castro had met with his government on the previous night. Abrahantes related that Castro was informed by his staff that they did not think Donovan would be able to guarantee delivery beyond the first one and that, therefore, all officers of the Brigade must be held. Abrahantes also relayed an increase in the Cuban government's request, to which Donovan replied that by asking for an additional $6 million in a letter of credit and $5 million in baby food and surgical instruments, Castro was asking for a miracle. Then, in a letter written immediately and boldly to Abrahantes, Donovan stated (in part), "If the Cuban government notifies me of an irrevocable decision that even one prisoner must remain as a human guarantee, I shall consider myself obliged, much against my desires, to consider my humanitarian mission hopeless and shall return to my country."[34]

An angry discussion followed between Donovan and Abrahantes, ending only upon the departure of the Cuban captain. Thereafter,

Celia Sanchez called at 8:00 p.m. and explained that they needed the officers as a guarantee. After further discussion, Donovan asked whether or not he should take a plane out the next day. He was of the opinion that the young officials, such as Abrahantes, hated the prisoners and were trying to persuade Castro that Donovan was trying to trick him. Later in the evening Celia called again. She related that she told Castro that if he continued on his present course, Cubans would see that the Americans had done everything possible, while Castro would be seen as the one who showed bad faith. Castro, Celia said, then changed his mind and agreed that Donovan should continue his negotiations. The sole remaining question was the method to guarantee the quality and quantity of merchandise. Donovan realized that he also had to find some way for Castro to save face.

On Sunday, October 7, Donovan returned to the DuPont Plaza Hotel, still using an assumed name. He called upon a physician to examine him because of his pain. The doctor informed him that he should be hospitalized, not only for his bursitis, but also for a general infection, 102-degree fever and a baseball-sized lump in his buttocks caused by unsterile injections.

Refusing treatment, Donovan returned to Havana on the following day. On Tuesday, October 9, a representative of the Royal Bank of Canada and the Canadian ambassador called Donovan. A letter of credit had been established in Montreal, and the Ottawa government instructed its ambassador to assure Cuba of the letter's validity. At a 4:00 p.m. meeting with Castro in the Presidential Palace on the following day, Donovan presented a tentative Memorandum of Agreement that essentially stated that Cuba would receive drugs, medicine, baby food, and surgical supplies valued at approximately $53 million. In addition, the CFC would pick up all charges related to transportation. Finally, the first shipment of goods would contain 20 percent of the entire indemnity and would be delivered before any prisoners were released.

Suddenly, in a change of position, Castro said the estimated retail values of the proposed goods were too high. He also hesitated about releasing all of the prisoners with only 20 percent of the indemnity paid. Castro indicated that the first list of goods sought was incorrect and had to be revised. When Donovan threatened again to go home, Ernesto Freyre, secretary of the CFC, contrary to his instructions from Donovan, suddenly interjected himself and spoke in Spanish to Castro without pausing for interpretation. Donovan felt that he had just lost his strong position and so he ended the negotiations at that point and decided to return to the United States. Before leaving, however, he sent Castro a note informing him that he would wait for the new lists, and wait, as well, for the time when Castro was ready to resume negotiations. He returned to Miami on October 11. Two days later, Donovan flew to Idlewild Airport in New York where he was met by Mary and reporters. In a press statement, he said that he was now ready to start his senatorial campaign.

The first round of negotiations was, in fact, over. The two pharmaceutical companies who were assisting, Pfizer and Merck, had actually lost at least $1 million dollars in wages, shipping costs, and related charges incident to gathering the drugs, medicines, and surgical supplies that the Cubans now did not want. Seven planes had been sitting ready at the airport in New York where all of the pharmaceuticals were also waiting in refrigerated cars. The letters of credit that had been established were withdrawn. New negotiations could not begin until Castro provided revised lists. Neither could they resume until after the missile crisis that erupted on October 22 between the Soviet Union and the United States was resolved.

8

Senate Race

DONOVAN'S INTEREST IN POLITICS DID NOT SUDDENLY DEVELOP IN 1962. As early as 1954 he was vice chairman of the State Democratic Finance Committee, and in 1956 he coordinated the annual Democratic State Dinner at the Sheraton Astor Hotel in New York City, which took place on February 2 of that year. He enjoyed inviting many of the political figures to his suite in the hotel for cocktails before dinner. In fact, he hosted the same event a year later at the Waldorf Astoria.[1]

Soon after Donovan's return from Berlin in 1962, Edward Zeltner of the *New York Mirror* was reporting that he might be drawn into politics, possibly for a seat in Congress.[2] But it was in mid-May of that year that Donovan, himself, seems to have decided to run for office if he could muster sufficient support. Beginning about May 15, Thomas Harnett, an attorney in Donovan's office, began to send out letters to influential Democrats, enclosing a biography of his employer, in order to determine their interest in his candidacy in the forthcoming November elections. Thus, despite his subsequent public statements of hesitancy in running, Donovan was definitely interested for some time.

One of the individuals to whom Harnett wrote was William H. McKeon, chair of the New York State Democratic Committee. McKeon responded that he had recently dropped Donovan's name on the *Searchlight* radio program. Harnett was also in contact with Judge Joseph Brust, former chair of the Law Committee of the Bronx County Democratic Party, who noted that there was strong sentiment for Donovan in the Bronx. The Democrats in that borough disliked Paul Screvane, the president of the city council, and felt that the former postmaster general, James A. Farley, at seventy-four years of age, was too old.[3] The Nassau County Democratic Club also indicated that his group was considering Donovan.

On May 20, the *New York Journal American* reported that powerful Wall Street figures were supporting Donovan in a race against the

118

incumbent senator, Jacob Javits.[4] Javits, however, was a formidable opponent. Born in Manhattan on May 18, 1904, to Russian Jewish parents, Jacob Koppel Javits had served in the U.S. House of Representatives from 1947 to 1955 as a liberal Republican. Between 1955 and 1957 he was New York State's attorney general. In the latter year he ran successfully for the United States Senate, defeating Robert F. Wagner. Notably, he had never been defeated in any race for public office.[5]

Despite Javits's political and public stature, momentum for Donovan began to build. Donovan began to write to county leaders. On June 8, 1962, William S. Andrews, a member of the board of supervisors of Onondaga County, replied to Donovan and detailed the plans for the latter's attendance at a County Committee dinner later in the month. He also described the current political figures in the county for Donovan's benefit prior to his arrival.[6]

In the following month, Donovan was to address a meeting of Nassau County Democrats. Just before it began, he was informed that he and Queens County District Attorney Frank D. O'Connor could not be on the same ticket in any election because both were Irish Catholics. The ticket had to be more diversified. Donovan saw this as grossly unfair and, in his own style, right from the hip, provided the audience with his opinion. A local reporter was on hand to record it:

> Donovan, still reeling from the blow [of not being able to be on the same ticket as O'Connor], told the public assemblage that such politicking was "a lot of nonsense" and an insult to the intelligence of the electorate. Candidates, said battling Donovan, should be chosen on the basis of their capabilities, regardless of race or creed, and the Democratic Party should not "stoop" to select them any other way.[7]

"His remarks on the point," the reporter noted, "were greeted with dead silence."[8]

On August 6, Donovan's friend, William C. Mattison, wrote a letter to the 1,138 delegates to the New York State Democratic Convention. Mattison said, in part, "I am chair of an informal group of Brooklynites whose objective is to persuade Jim to seek—actively and vigorously—our party's nomination for the United States Senate."[9] Donovan, at an American Bar Association meeting in San Francisco, said in response to Mattison's letter that he was not a candidate at the time. However, Mayor Robert F. Wagner, who was aware of the drive for Donovan, supported him.[10] Within a week, Donovan changed his public position at a press conference at the Overseas Press Club in Manhattan and said he would consult state Democratic leaders to determine if his running for senator or governor would help unify his party. Donovan actually deferred to Mayor Wagner as for which position he would run. Wagner wanted Robert A. Morganthau for governor and preferred that Donovan run for the senate.[11]

In early September, Donovan formally announced his candidacy to run against Javits. He had also been elected in the New York City primary election on September 6, 1962, as a delegate to the forthcoming State Democratic Convention, representing Brooklyn's Third Assembly District.[12] On September 16, the *New York Herald Tribune* described his strong points, including his popularity with the electorate and his support from Democratic leaders, especially Wagner. His weaknesses, the paper noted, were his lack of legislative experience, the fact he had never run for public office, and the possibility that he would not have the support of the liberal and labor segments of the party.[13] Donovan, at this time, was actually one of six individuals under consideration for the Senate by the Democratic Party leadership. The others included Paul O'Dwyer, a liberal labor lawyer and the brother of former New York City Mayor William O'Dwyer; Telford Taylor, the retired brigadier general and Justice Jackson's successor as chief counsel at Nuremberg; R. Peter Strauss, a radio station owner; William L. Cary, chair of the Securities and Exchange Commission; and Rep. Samuel S. Stratton of Schenectady. Several other figures— Eleanor Roosevelt, Edward R. Murrow, and Ralph J. Bunche—let it be known they were not interested, in running. Only Donovan, O'Dwyer, and Taylor had declared themselves available. Donovan's friend District Attorney O'Connor said he was only interested in the governor's position.[14]

On September 17 the State Democratic Convention opened in the War Memorial Auditorium in Syracuse. One of the first orders of business was the passage of a party platform.[15] It was an orderly gathering up to this point, but late in the day, following Robert Morganthau's selection as the nominee for governor, his opponents, primarily supporters of O'Connor, became riotous.[16] They cursed, yelled, hissed, booed, and rushed the platform, necessitating that all of the auditorium's lights be shut off in order to restore order.[17] After the convention adjourned for the day, Donovan prepared a "prenomination campaign" of his own. He had his biography mimeographed and purchased some paper to be used for homemade campaign posters. Then he, his daughter Jan, Thomas Harnett, and Miles McDonald Jr., a law student, worked until 3:00 a.m. pasting the candidate's picture on the posters with rubber cement. They were distributed later in the day. The total cost of the "campaign" was $165.[18] With Morganthau, who was Jewish, as the Democratic candidate for governor, Straus, who was also Jewish, was ruled out as a possibility for senator. Farley declined further consideration. O'Dwyer was still a strong candidate but had already lost once to Javits. Among the remaining candidates—Taylor, Donovan, and Cary—Donovan was seen as the strongest, although there was some concern that he was too involved in negotiations with Castro.

The fourth and final session of the Convention was opened by Erastus Corning II, Mayor of Albany at 2:35 p.m. on September 18.[19] It was at this juncture that all of the remaining posts would be filled, including comptroller, an associate judgeship for the court of appeals, attorney general, lieutenant governor, and United States senator. The first three positions were decided quickly. Mayor Robert F. Wagner nominated incumbent Arthur Levitt for state comptroller. He received the nomination unanimously by voice vote. Similarly, John F. Scileppi, a state supreme court justice, won the nomination for judge of the court of appeals and Edward Richard Riley, Manhattan borough president, received the nomination for attorney general. The next nomination was for the position of lieutenant governor. John J. Burns, the mayor of Binghamton, was nominated and received two seconds. Several other individuals were also nominated but withdrew in favor of Burns.

The final position to be considered was that of United States senator. James O'Shea of the city of Rome rose and spoke of the background of James Donovan and then placed his name in nomination. Immediately, there was "applause, cheers and demonstration."[20] He was seconded for the office four times: by William B. McKeown of Westchester County, state senator from Kings County Jeremiah B. Bloom, Jerome Weinstein of Queens County, and Donald Kramer, former mayor of Binghamton. Nominated at this time, as well, was Paul O'Dwyer who also received recognition from the delegates but not to the extent that Donovan had. The voting between Donovan and O'Dwyer then began. After Donovan had received 803 delegate votes and O'Dwyer had garnered 256, Paul O'Dwyer took the floor and moved that Donovan receive a unanimous vote. All of the delegates agreed.[21] Donovan, himself, described the outcome: "In a comparatively dull final session, I won the nomination for Senator from the Reform candidate, Paul O'Dwyer. . . . The Brooklyn delegation went wild. I was the first Brooklynite to run for the U.S. Senate since the late John Cashmore was trounced by Irving Ives in 1950. The last Brooklynite to serve in the Senate was elected in World War I."[22]

Donovan was one of the last speakers at the convention. After his nomination, Mary and the children were asked to wait under the speaker's platform until Donovan's turn came to accept the nomination. When he was called by Chairman Erastus Corning, Donovan approached the platform and addressed the delegates:

Chairman Corning, Convention delegates and fellow Democrats:

I am deeply honored to accept the nomination of this convention for the United States Senate. I thank every one of you who have made this possible. It is a great privilege to be a candidate with Governor Morganthau and the other distinguished Democrats nominated by this convention.

I pledge to you, as we unite today for a Democratic victory, to bring a hard-hitting campaign into every corner of this State. Every man and woman in the Empire State of New York should understand the vital importance of having President Kennedy supported—in these critical times—by a Democratic Senator from this State.

The people of New York, whether Democrats or Republicans, are tired of being bamboozled by Republican office-holders who may best be characterized as "counterfeit Democrats"—men who cynically proclaim what they call "liberalism" when they are downstate—but who upstate are proud of the notorious Republican Manifesto. To paraphrase a declaration made famous by President Harry Truman, I am too young to talk out of both sides of my mouth.

Our party's platform is clear and should appeal to every thinking voter in this state. May I add a few specifics, in areas of my particular experience and deep concern.

1. Our foreign policy must always be a policy heading from strength and not from weakness;

2. Every resource of our nation should be devoted to assuring that all our children, without discrimination of any kind, have the equal opportunity to obtain the finest education available in a free society. In our firm determination to maintain world leadership, we can afford no less;

3. Finally, in the field of civil rights, we must strive now—and without deliberate delay—to end once and for all conditions which exist only because of the extraordinary patience of citizens still waiting for what they were guaranteed a hundred years ago. This is not only justice; it is a necessity for our survival in a world which probes our every weakness.

It is with these beliefs—and confidence in the common sense of the people of the State of New York—that I humbly accept the great honor you have conferred upon me. (Applause and cheering)[23]

It was a good speech, brief and to the point, but no one apparently remembered to bring Mary and his daughters up from under the platform.[24]

In a statement to the press after having received the nomination, Donovan said, "I thoroughly enjoy the ones that look difficult," adding that "my campaign will be a positive one to have people realize that their interests would be better served in the Senate by a Democrat working with President Kennedy."[25]

With respect to the Cuban negotiations, Donovan said soon after his nomination that he would "refrain from making political capital out of my past services to my country" unless Javits forced the issue.[26]

On September 23, 1962, Donovan formally opened his campaign at a picnic of the Ulster County Democratic Women's Club in St. Remy, New York. He and Morganthau then went on to Washington on the twenty-eighth to meet with President Kennedy. Kennedy hoped that he would be able to appear in New York to campaign for the candidates, and he agreed with Donovan's campaign strategy of attacking Javits and presenting himself as the true supporter of the president's politics.

The campaign headquarters for Donovan was Room 740 of the Hotel Commodore in Manhattan. He had a campaign staff of two, consisting of Thomas A. Harnett from his office and a press representative, Alexander Feinberg. When not speaking extemporaneously, Donovan wrote his own speeches. He estimated that his budget would approach $25,000. Javits's anticipated budget was substantially more, approximately $500,000. In a general mailing, the senator's brother, Benjamin Javits, had even sent a request for a campaign contribution to Donovan. Replying to it was an opportunity that Donovan could not resist:

> I appreciate receiving your letter dated September 24, 1962, inviting me to contribute to your brother's campaign for re-election to the United States Senate. I note with interest your budget of half a million dollars, "of which about $150,000 has been raised."
>
> I strongly believe in solvent campaigns and have already paid the $165 in expenses which I incurred in becoming the Democratic candidate for your brother's post.
>
> I know you will appreciate that a possible conflict of interest requires my declining your invitation.[27]

As Donovan was flying in from Havana on October 13, Javits was campaigning on Long Island. He accused Donovan of "waging his campaign from the shores of Cuba. . . . I believe Donovan is on a Government mission and not that he is negotiating for private parties."[28] Once Donovan landed at Idlewild Airport that evening, he immediately flew to New City, New York, to address a Rockland County Democratic meeting. Accompanying him on this trip, as well as on numerous others, was his wife, Mary.

Mary was accustomed to her husband's being away, but she wasn't happy with it. Donovan often traveled during their marriage, to

Nuremberg, Berlin, London, or Havana or throughout the United States on speaking engagements and court cases. The campaign gave her the unusual opportunity to spend time with him. Ironically, if he were successful in his pursuit of the Senate seat, he would be away still more. She had mixed feelings about this that she shared with a reporter at the time. "It is a great honor, but it means that he will be away from home more. I don't know how he felt. Men are different creatures."[29] She told the reporter that she didn't have any intention of moving to Washington, at least in the immediate future, because their daughter Mary Ellen, thirteen, was in the eighth grade at St. Savior's School in Brooklyn. Jan, now nineteen, was away at Marymount College in Arlington, Virginia, and John, seventeen, was at the Northwood School in Lake Placid. Mary told the interviewing reporter that she occupied herself by keeping a quiet "haven" for James with the help of a maid. The family had, by this time, moved to a fourteen-room duplex apartment at 35 Prospect Park West, opposite the park's war memorial. She did volunteer work for the Immaculate Conception Day Nursery, took art courses at the Brooklyn Museum, and occasionally bowled and played tennis. She noted, however, "I don't think the wife of a busy man should be overly ambitious or a club woman type. It would be unnerving to him."[30]

While at New City with Mary, Donovan took the opportunity to respond to Javits's Cuban remarks. He told the gathering that he had no intention of using the Cuban issue in the election and pointed out that his involvement there began prior to his nomination.[31] Donovan's involvement with freeing the Cuban prisoners, however, was always a negative political factor lurking in the background, and it never really helped his campaign. In a television conversation with Dallas Townsend on WCBS–TV's *Newsmakers* on October 14, Donovan even said, in response to a question, that he regarded Cuba as having the "highest priority" in comparison to his Senate race.[32] That acknowledged, Donovan still conducted a frenetic campaign in the few remaining weeks before the election. At that time Mary saw one of his pictures in the newspaper, which Donovan himself characterized as "gruesome." Mary quipped that he was beginning to look a lot like Castro and was scaring the children. He also had to contend with a lack of support from the United States attorney general, who was unhappy about his candidacy. Donovan wrote at the time "If the President or Attorney General had asked me to withdraw before September 25th I would have. I'm not obsessed with toga. But now it is illegal."[33]

Throughout the campaign, Donovan essentially followed the two-pronged strategy he had discussed with President Kennedy: attack

Javits and encourage voting for a Democratic senator who supported a Democratic president. What the plan lacked, however, was the presentation of well-thought-out alternative policies to those of his opponent after the attacks ended. Absent these, he could only persist in invective.

In his criticisms of Javits, Donovan tried to press home the idea that his opponent was a "counterfeit Republican" because he worked with Southern Democrats and conservative Republicans in Congress, but then voted as a liberal in order to get reelected in New York. He also liked to say that Senator Javits supported 74 percent of all Democratic legislation and opposed Republican matters 51 percent of the time. Donovan would add, "He's been talking out of both sides of his mouth long enough, acting like a Republican upstate and the most liberal of all liberals downstate."[34] The message was the same at each town that he stopped. Toward the end of the brief campaign, Donovan also resorted to calling Javits a "pin wheel" in a series of articles for which the *New York Post* provided space for both candidates.[35] Called "The Battle Page," it allowed Javits and Donovan to present written statements concerning their ideas, beliefs, and goals in a venue removed from the arena of oral debate and extemporaneous speech that could become heated. Javits, an experienced politician, articulate, calm, and matter-of-fact, took advantage of the newspaper's concept. Donovan used it to continue his verbal assault.

When Donovan would emphasize the second aspect of his strategy, that Javits did not support Kennedy, the senator came back quickly that he supported the president when he agreed with him and voted against him when he did not. He said on one occasion that "New Yorkers 'don't want a yes man, don't want a rubber stamp, don't want an advisor whom the President can hire any day he wants to.' "[36]

Donovan's lack of experience in campaigning and in political debate outside the collegiate arena was demonstrated in several instances. For example, one of his campaign stops was a garment factory in New York City. As soon as he arrived, a number of the women who were working there rushed to him with tears in their eyes, thanking him for his efforts to release the Cuban prisoners. While appreciative of their comments, he never wanted to capitalize on their feelings. As a result, he never used the incident, as a true politician might, toward his own ends. In another instance, when he charged Javits with being ineffective in obtaining defense contracts for New York because he was a Republican during a Democratic administration, he did so in the town of Sydney that then had a boom in defense contracts. Over five thousand workers of the Bendix Corporation were employed on round-the-clock shifts.[37] Donovan's statements in debate, too, could be glib. In his second televised debate with Javits on WCBS–TV on October 21, Donovan suggested that he could go to the Middle East alone and be able to negotiate the region's problems. He added that he thought there were "enough backslapping trips to Israel."[38] Five days later, in a multi-candidate address at the Dalton School in Manhattan, one that Senator Javits was unable to attend, a thirteen-year-old eighth grader asked Donovan what he thought the main campaign issues were. Donovan didn't hear the boy's name, but provided a fairly standard answer. When the assembly was over, he was informed that the boy was Josh Javits, the senator's son.[39]

Several days before the Dalton School talk, Donovan led a ten-car motorcade to his place of birth at 419 East 139th Street in the Mott Haven section of the Bronx on the afternoon of October 20. After posing for pictures with Mary, two aunts and an uncle on the steps of the two-story, red brick building, Donovan explained to onlookers that his grandmother and grandfather were married at St. Jerome's Church nearby. His father was baptized and married there as well. Soon after, the motorcade took off again, led by a forty-four-year-old, double-decked bus with bag pipers playing—as they toured through the predominantly Puerto Rican communities of the southeast Bronx. Stopping at shopping centers, the motorcade was greeted by cordial, but sparse, crowds.

One of Donovan's more egregious, off-the-cuff, remarks occurred in a debate with Javits on civil rights a few days before the election. Javits had spoken of the need for new laws to implement the 1954 Supreme Court decision banning "separate but equal" facilities for blacks. Donovan quickly retorted, "No great wave of new legislation is needed. Most of these [laws] are not needed. Most of them can come later, but priority must be given to the basic human rights that were guaranteed 100 years ago and what's been needed is courageous enforcement."[40] His response came too quickly. It gave the impression that he was unaware of the 160 deputy U.S. marshals who were wounded, including twenty-eight who were shot, a month before, while defending James Meredith's admission to the University of Mississippi. In this one incident alone, 375 people were hurt and two were killed.[41] And only the year before, the Congress of Racial Equality (CORE) had organized Freedom Rides to test the 1960 Supreme Court decision prohibiting segregation in bus terminals on interstate routes. In pursuing their goal, the Freedom Riders, both black and white, were threatened, beaten, arrested, and imprisoned in Mississippi. One bus had been burned, and the attackers even tried to prevent its occupants from escaping the fire.[42] Clearly, there had been no lack of courage.

Black community leaders were irate with Donovan. Basil Paterson, chair of the political action committee of the New York City branch of the National Association for the Advancement of Colored People (NAACP), sent him a telegram, urging that he correct his position immediately.[43] Eugene T. Reed, president of the New York State division of the NAACP sent telegrams to William H. McKeon, the New York State chair of the Democratic Party and to Timothy Costillo, chair of the Liberal Party urging the parties to "disavow this misrepresentation of their party platform pledges."[44] The next day Donovan did elaborate and apologized for the appearance of insensitivity. He based it, he said, on the short time he had to respond to Javits in the debate. He emphasized that he certainly supported legislation to abolish the poll tax, for example, as well as to provide for a uniform test of literacy for voters and to enable the Commission on Human Rights to initiate investigations.[45] But the damage was done in the eyes of the many of the electorate. Donovan was certainly not a bigot, but his remarks, often terse and pointed, reflected his rigid, conservative ideology on issues that required more complex thought beforehand, as well as in response afterward.

The two other significant issues in the election campaign concerned federal aid to education and medical care for the aged. As to the first, despite some bantering back and forth, both candidates agreed that the role of the federal government had to be increased and that all students in both public and private schools should receive assistance if needed as long as such aid did not violate the constitutional requirement of separation of church and state. They differed, however, in how that could be accomplished. Javits thought in terms of direct aid to schools to support nonreligious courses. Donovan suggested tax credits and low interest government loans to students and their families.

With respect to medical care for the aged, Javits had already drafted legislation with Clinton P. Anderson, the Anderson-Javits bill, which provided that hospital and medical care benefits would be financed through Social Security and constitute the foundation on which additional private insurance could rest. Donovan, on the other hand, believed that every means to pay for medical care for the elderly privately should be exhausted before the government stepped in. He did agree, that if Social Security proved to be the only way to provide medical coverage, he would support it.[46]

Donovan's campaign began on September 23 and ended on November 4. In that forty-two day period, he was in one television interview and five televised debates. He visited President Kennedy in Washington, toured and spoke in twenty-seven New York counties, attended numerous breakfasts, lunches, and dinners and held several press conferences. He also spent a week in Cuba during this same period negotiating with Castro. But as the *New York Herald Tribune* had predicted earlier, Donovan came to the eve of the elections without the support of labor, liberals, and many major newspapers.

The voting results on November 6 were definitive. Donovan received 2,211,758 votes, Javits 3,131,661. Even Democratic New York City gave the, albeit slim, majority of its votes to Javits. The Republicans also obtained the reelection of Governor Nelson Rockefeller and the attorney general, Louis J. Lefkowitz. The only Democrat to be successful was the incumbent state comptroller, Arthur Levitt.[47]

Had Donovan allowed for more preparation and greater time to wage his campaign, the results might have been different. Or, as Donovan, himself, summed it up, "When United States News asked for an under 50 word statement about the reasons for the outcome, I replied, 'Lack of time, organization, funds and votes.'"[48] As it was, he was then the vice-president of the New York City Board of Education, the negotiator for the Cuban Families Committee, and the principal officer in an active law firm, in addition to holding office in a variety of professional and private organizations. Taking on the added burden of a Senate campaign was a near impossibility, even for such an adept person. However, now with the intensity of his campaign at an end, Donovan was freer to pursue what he always characterized as his "highest priority," the release of the Cuban prisoners.

1. The Donovan Family circa 1922.
L to R James; John Donovan, MD; Harriet; John
Photograph courtesy of Mary Donovan Busch.

2. James B. Donovan at Fordham *Ram* office. Donovan, with suspenders, is seated center.
Photograph courtesy of Archives and Special Collections, Fordham University.

Nuremberg Trial

Official U.S. photograph of courtroom at Nuremberg Trials of Nazi war criminals. Democratic Senatorial candidate James B. Donovan, then a Navy Commander (uniformed figure circled), is shown facing major Nazi figures. In third row of prisoners' benches are Goering and Hess (arms folded), von Ribbentrop, Field Marshal Keitel, von Schirach. Von Papen is among prisoners in fourth row.

Jim Donovan was Associate Prosecutor under the late U.S. Supreme Court Justice Robert H. Jackson. He was in charge of the presentation of all visual evidence. In this capacity, he amassed the damning evidence obtained in concentration camp photographs, sending in Signal Corps units as soon as each camp was liberated by our forces.

this is
JIM DONOVAN
YOUR CANDIDATE FOR U. S. SENATOR

A Man Who Has Served His Country Well...
Well Qualified to Serve You in Washington!

3. Donovan at the International Military Tribunal, 1945.
Copy of a Donovan senatorial campaign poster courtesy of Mary Donovan Busch.

4. The trial judge, Mortimer Byers, presides as the witness, Reino Hayhanen, identifies Rudolf Abel as his superior. Standing next to Hayhanen is the prosecutor William Tompkins, with an assistant seated behind him. At the defense table, from left to right, are James Donovan, Arnold Fraiman, and Thomas Debevoise. Standing, facing his assistant is Rudolf Abel.

"The Abel Spy Trial," copy of a signed original lithograph by William Sharp. Courtesy of Donovan, Parry, McDermott and Radzik, New York, New York.

5. James Donovan and Fidel Castro, Cuba, 1963.
Photograph courtesy of John Donovan.

6. Robert F. Kennedy and James Donovan during Cuban negotiations, 1963.
Photograph courtesy of Tony Rollo.

7. Donovan family at Lake Placid, New York circa 1967. L. to R. Edward and Jan Amorosi; Mary Ellen, James Donovan, John, and Mary. Photograph courtesy of John Donovan.

9

Cuban Negotiations: Part II

DONOVAN NEVER ALLOWED HIS SENATE CAMPAIGN TO INTERFERE with the progress of the Cuban Families Committee's efforts. On Sunday, October 20, 1962, Harry Ruiz-Williams brought him the new lists of drugs and medicines that had been prepared by the Cubans. In reviewing the lists, Donovan noticed that Cuban officials quoted prices from Japan, Poland, and Italy that were lower than those of the United States. In doing so, the Cubans hoped to be able to obtain more pharmaceuticals than they could at American prices. However, Donovan had already anticipated this ploy. In his notes on the meeting of October 10, he wrote that Castro's assistants "talked as though they had a certain amount of cash on hand and were asking for bids from the world market (including the committee) so that they could select the cheapest . . . To put the question in [*sic*] other way, if this negotiation fails, to whom else could the Cuban Government sell the boys. There is no world market for lives."[1] Within three days, Donovan had the lists sent to Merck and Pfizer. The Cuban lists, if filled, would cost between $25 million and $40 million. Pfizer felt that they could make an acceptable counteroffer of about $17 million.[2]

On October 22, one day before the drug companies received the new lists, President Kennedy announced the quarantine of Cuba to force the removal of Soviet missiles there.[3] Donovan was in Oneonta, New York, about to give a talk to the students of the State Teachers College when the president's speech was broadcast. As he described the moment for Haynes Johnson, Donovan said:

> I sat down in the lounge crowded with students and faculty members and watched Kennedy make his famous missile speech on TV. Then and there I had to decide what to say—"no comment" or "wait and see" or what. As soon as the speech was over I made the following statement: "The President exhibited his characteristic combination of firm courage and statesmanlike restraint. In my opinion if he firmly adheres to the position set forth in his speech the missiles will be removed, the Russians will leave and not a shot will be fired." This was the most difficult decision I had to

134

make during the negotiations. I knew whatever I said would be read by Castro, and I ran the risk of irreparably destroying my mission.[4]

In fact, the mission was not ruined and the work of the CFC progressed during the crisis, although Donovan did give passing thought to working with Secretary General U Thant of the United Nations if all else failed. On November 1, Alvaro Sanchez telephoned Donovan from Cuba to say that KLM Airlines was offering free flights when needed. He added that he thought the time now seemed favorable for continuing the negotiations. That same day, Donovan met with McKeen to work on Pfizer's counteroffer. In order to ease the concerns of the pharmaceutical manufacturers, Donovan asked Robert Kennedy on the eighth for a letter confirming that the government would not prosecute the companies, or himself, for violations of the Logan Act or the antitrust acts.[5]

In early November, the Cubans followed up their submission of new lists with a request that the pharmaceuticals and foodstuffs that they sought have a minimum expiration date of at least twenty-four months. They also indicated a desire to be able to inspect the shipments prior to delivery. For his part, Donovan continued to solicit possible donors, sending cables to individuals who had pledged money earlier. He also discussed obtaining large quantities of powdered milk at reduced rates from Borden International. At midmonth, Donovan received a letter from Berta Baretto indicating that the Cuban airport was open, that the Bank of Canada guarantees were acceptable and that the Cuban government was ready to conclude negotiations.

Donovan passed on Baretto's information to Washington on November 20, adding that he felt Berta and Alvaro were bitter toward the United States. In the latter regard, he thought that they might go to the press if some action was not taken soon. Soon after receiving Donovan's message Robert Kennedy called a meeting with Louis Oberdorfer, the assistant attorney general in the Tax Division,[6] and Milan Miskovsky. At this time he asked the two officials to take responsibility for the government's role in the relief efforts. He also asked that that the prisoners be home for Christmas, barely one month off.[7] Four days later, the attorney general met with Ruiz-Williams, Alvaro Sanchez and Roberto San Roman at the Waldorf Astoria Hotel in New York City. The Cubans impressed on Robert Kennedy their fear that the prisoners could die if not rescued soon and added that they believed the time was right to proceed with Castro. San Roman asked the attorney general what he thought their chances of succeeding were. Kennedy replied, "Fifty-fifty,"[8] but he agreed that it was necessary to make a concerted effort now. He also revealed his plan to secure the release of the prisoners by Christmas.

On the morning of November 30, Deputy Attorney General Nicholas Katzenbach asked Oberdorfer about the tax consequences of giving money, goods and services to the CFC.[9] Oberdorfer recalled a case from the 1940s in which a court overturned an IRS decision and permitted the deduction of the market value of property to charity.[10]

Later that same day, Oberdorfer had lunch with the Robert Kennedy and Ramsey Clark, assistant attorney general of the Lands Division, at the attorney general's home. During their conversation Kennedy stressed the importance of the prisoner exchange and the need to assist the men.

In the afternoon following lunch, Kennedy held a meeting with representatives of the State Department, his own staff in the Justice Department, the CIA, and the Treasury Department. Among the individuals attending were Lawrence R. Houston, general counsel to the CIA;[11] Milan Miskovsky, the CIA's assistant general counsel; Nicholas Katzenbach; Louis F. Oberdorfer; Stanley S. Surrey, the assistant treasury secretary for tax policy; Mitchell Rogovin, assistant to the commissioner of the IRS; and Robert Hurwitch of the State Department. (Several days earlier, Treasury Secretary Douglas Dillon had met with IRS Commissioner Mortimer M. Caplin and Stanley S. Surrey, in order to develop possible tax advantages for pharmaceutical companies and other manufacturers who would be asked to donate supplies.[12]) The larger group now discussed the overall planning. It was believed that the goods desired by Cuba could be provided at a manufacturer's cost of about $17 million. This would roughly correspond to the $53 million at full market value that Castro sought.[13] In order to induce large donations from American manufacturers, it was going to be necessary to offer tax deductions and protection against prosecution for antitrust violations, aspects that Dillon's group were already working on. It was agreed that Oberdorfer would prepare a memorandum outlining specific procedures over the following weekend for review by the attorney general and the president.[14] Robert Kennedy, in fact, asked Oberdorfer to "Lean on it."[15]

That same evening of November 30, Oberdorfer had dinner with Lloyd Cutler, his former law partner at Wilmer, Cutler, and Pickering. Cutler was then counsel to the Pharmaceutical Manufacturers Association (PMA). The two discussed the need for a favorable tax ruling and the removal of antitrust consequences that the pharmaceutical companies would face if they assisted in the prisoner release project. Cutler also indicated that his clients would feel more assured if the president publicly made a statement to the effect that their help would be in the national interest.[16] Over the following Saturday and Sunday, Oberdorfer worked on the memorandum requested by the attorney general. Assisting him were Mitchell Rogovin; Crane Hauser, chief counsel of the IRS; Stanley Surrey; and Mortimer Caplin. The conclusion of the memorandum drafted was that contributions to the prisoner release project would be deductible at market value.[17] On December 3, Oberdorfer gave the attorney general the memo, following which the attorney general briefed the president who also approved. The process then quickened measurably.

The Cuban Families Committee did not have the capacity to carry out a large-scale project for the transfer of goods. Thus, Oberdorfer and Katzenbach met with the Red Cross on December 5. The conference took place at the American National Red Cross (ANRC) headquarters in Washington, DC, with John C. Wilson, executive vice-president of the ANRC and his chief counsel, Harold Starr. Katzenbach explained the problem of gathering and shipping supplies to Cuba and asked if the ANRC "was capable of handling a supply operation of this magnitude, and for humanitarian reasons would the Red Cross be willing to assume responsibility of delivering the supplies."[18] Katzenbach said that the matter was urgent, and Wilson responded that he would discuss it immediately with the ANRC vice-presidents. Wilson noted that he, himself, was interested in participating.[19]

Following the meeting, Wilson met with his agency's officers who unanimously favored the idea of assistance. Wilson then spoke with E. Roland Harriman, chairman of the ANRC board of governors, who approved as well. With Robert F. Shea, an ANRC vice-president designated to manage operations, Wilson confirmed the Red Cross decision with Katzenbach.[20] Oberdorfer then designated his first assistant, John B. Jones, to act as liaison with the Red Cross.

It was clear to Robert Kennedy that Donovan was going to need assistance in meeting the demands of the Castro government. In fact, it was going to take the herculean involvement of numerous individuals, government agencies, and businesses to accomplish the task.[21] On December 7, several attorneys in private practice were asked to assist Donovan in soliciting drug companies and baby food manufacturers for contributions and for arranging transportation of all goods from around the country to Miami for transshipment to Cuba. In Washington, DC, they included John E. Nolan Jr. of the firm of Steptoe and Johnson; E. Barrett Prettyman Jr. of Hogan and Hartson; John W. Douglas of Covington and Burling; and Ray Rasenburger of

Bowen and Rasenburger. In New York, Robert H. Knight, who had just resigned as general counsel to the Treasury Department two months earlier, was called upon. With Knight came Henry Harfield of the firm of Shearman, Sterling, and Wright, nationally recognized experts on letters of credit.

The recruitment of John Nolan was typical of how the attorneys were brought in. Milan Miskovsky called him and asked if he wouldn't mind doing "a little" pro bono work.[22] Nolan recalled that he had received the telephone call from Miskovsky asking if he could meet at Louis Oberdorfer's office to discuss getting the Bay of Pigs prisoners out of Cuba. Nolan went that same day. Joseph F. Dolan, assistant deputy attorney general was in Oberdorfer's office before Nolan arrived. He related later, "Everyone who came in was asked whether he knew anybody in private practice in town who could shake loose for a few days' hard work, who would be our guy, which around here means a fellow who is a utility infielder, that is, someone who will do anything he is asked to and will take care of any problem that comes up whether it is emptying the ash trays or going to see the President. A few people were suggested—John Douglas, Ray Rasenburger, and John Nolan."[23]

The group was interested in knowing about Nolan's relationship with Donovan and if he would be willing to work with him on the Cuban exchange. Nolan answered that he would.[24] Soon after the conversation, Nolan flew to New York and went to Donovan's office. He found the negotiator sitting at his desk, almost perplexed at what to do with the many documents related to securing goods for Castro. Nolan has later reflected that Donovan was much more interested in dealing with Castro than with the details of securing the required goods, and he was happy to have Nolan on the team. After reviewing what Donovan had, Nolan returned to Washington.

John Nolan recalls that the first telephone calls for donations started with the baby food manufacturers. He reached several from Donovan's office on the day of his visit. To others, he sent telegrams on the following Saturday. In addition to presenting the need for baby food, Nolan asked them to come to a meeting the next day in Washington to discuss the matter in more detail with the attorney general. That Sunday the company representatives came. Robert Kennedy "pitched it pretty hard," said Nolan. They had a lot of questions, but they agreed to help. After the meeting, individual company representatives met separately with Nolan and his associates because they were reluctant to discuss in a group their pricing and their inventory including products they had in excess and those of which they were short. At the end of each discussion, the representatives made an informal pledge of goods to be donated. Nolan remembered that the total was about \$3 million.[25]

Telephone requests for donations were made over several weeks. New telephone lines and a number of extensions had to be installed for use by the solicitors. Louis Oberdorfer's office became the command post from which everyone in Washington operated and made the necessary calls, and he used a large bulletin board to display the progress of the solicitations. Telephones were covered twenty-four hours a day.[26] Frank Michaelman, an attorney and assistant to Oberdorfer, maintained master lists and records of the values of goods promised. Those individuals who were contacting companies had their own rough areas of specialty. Prettyman, for example, handled maritime shipments; Dolan, pharmaceuticals and air transport; and Douglas, foods. The New York group of attorneys, including Harfield, Knight, William C. Carroll, and Bruce Thompson concentrated on financial problems, particularly letters of credit, but everyone called whoever was necessary.[27] Making telephone calls, Rogovin said, sometimes took a little ingenuity:

> Once while trying to reach the president of a large food company in the Midwest it turned out that the man had a private line and there was no way of finding out the number. Through ingenuity someone in the Department of Justice (the FBI) was able to get the telephone number. When the president was reached at home and the lawyer spelled out the whole story, the president said, "Fine, our corporation is signed up. Just work out the details with our lawyers." Then he said, "How did you get my phone number?" The lawyer replied, "The White House has it." I'm sure the president grew two feet at that point.[28]

Several days later, in order to present the plan to as many pharmaceutical firms as possible, as well as to address the concerns that the companies had with respect to the attitude of the government regarding their role in the process, Robert Kennedy and James Donovan held an initial meeting with several officials of the Pharmaceutical Manufacturers Association (PMA) on December 7 including, among others, Lloyd Cutler; Edward Foley, cocounsel of the PMA and a former Under Secretary of the Treasury;[29] Eugene N. Beesley, president of the PMA as well as president of the Eli Lilly pharmaceutical company; and William Graham, president of Baxter Laboratories, together with Surrey and Rogovin.

Oberdorfer had a clear recollection of the meeting. He related

> that a very strong wind was blowing. The Attorney General's office runs east to west, and therefore this wind had stood the flag behind his window

out like a picture. From where I was sitting (he was between me and the bristling flag) it was just an extremely dramatic experience to see and hear him talking about the responsibility of both the United States and the people of the United States for the rescue of these prisoners who had risked their lives in what was, of course, they thought, in their interests, but also in an effort to protect and safeguard all of us.[30]

Briefly, Kennedy explained that the government felt a moral obligation to assist in the negotiations and was asking for the help of pharmaceutical companies. He pointed out that their help was entirely voluntary and would bring no penalties to them if they participated. Neither would there be any adverse action against them if they chose not to assist. He explained Donovan's activities as well as why the United States could not directly fund the operation. Most importantly, he told the group that the Red Cross was committed to participating. "There would be some political risks," Oberdorfer remembered Kennedy saying, "but he [Kennedy] couldn't imagine that either the business risk or the political risk would survive the picture of people being brought home to their wives and children on Christmas day."[31]

The next day Katzenbach sent a letter to the chair of the PMA advising that the antitrust laws would not be enforced against intercorporate communications about price lists of goods to be sent to Cuba.[32] On December 9, Attorney General Kennedy informed the baby food manufacturers of the decision. In another action important to the manufacturers of all products to be delivered in the Cuban deal, Mortimer Caplin, commissioner of the Internal Revenue Service, issued a ruling which declared that all contributions to the Red Cross for the purpose of the prisoner exchange would be tax deductible at a value measured by the lowest wholesale catalogue prices at which manufacturers customarily sell their products.[33]

Problems and questions that arose were handled far more rapidly than normal. As Donovan described it: "In two hours the Civil Aeronautics Board handed down a ruling permitting airlines to donate their planes to haul prisoners and freight. The railroads and the truckers received a similar ruling from the Interstate Commerce Commission."[34] Similarly, Miskovsky recalled the initial reluctance of the Maritime Administration to issue permits for American ships to carry goods to Cuba. Oberdorfer, he related, called the head of the agency and rather calmly pointed out that he was sorry that the Maritime Administration couldn't find an exception in their regulations to issue the permits, and he regretted that he would have to give this bad news to the president. Oberdorfer received a call back within minutes with word that the exception had been found.[35]

Although rulings were made quickly, care was still taken that they were legally correct. Rogovin pointed out, "One thing that marked the whole project, as far as Treasury was concerned, was that we had to rule in an even-handed fashion—right in line with existing law. We couldn't waiver."[36] John B. Jones added that it was not even "possible to give the transportation companies the same favorable ruling given the drug industry. Every time it came down to the fact that we could not give a ruling which would allow transportation to deduct the value of transportation services."[37] The same held true for insurance companies. Personal services were simply not allowable as charitable contributions.[38] Thus, neither did Donovan receive tax credit for his pro bono work in behalf of the prisoners.

Other agencies set up procedures to process prisoners, have hospital beds available, if needed, and have export licenses expedited for the goods bound for Cuba. President Kennedy publicly announced his support of these efforts in a press conference on December 12.[39]

On December 11 Donovan, Katzenbach, and Oberdorfer went to the Waldorf Astoria Hotel in New York City to meet with the full board of directors of the American Pharmaceutical Association. They brought a list of drugs provided by the Cuban government that contained 10,000 items in 237 pages by brand name, manufacturer, desired quantity, and dollar value. Katzenbach was asked if the government was encouraging them to make these contributions. He replied, "The government is not asking any company to do one blessed thing. The CFC is asking you to make these donations to the American Red Cross for this specific objective . . . If you do decide to do it, there is no violation of the Sherman Act or of the Logan Act, and you will, by written ruling of the Internal Revenue Department, have the tax deductibility at the wholesale price."[40] Before the group broke up that day, Ely Lilly offered to contribute $1 million in products.[41] That same day Donovan met with the board of directors of Borden Milk and provided the same information.

The attorney general and Donovan dealt with each other in a professional manner, yet there was always strong friction between the two personally. Neither individual ever let their personal feelings interfere with the prisoner exchange, but at times frustration came close to the surface. On the evening after the Waldorf Astoria meeting, for example, Katzenbach and Oberdorfer had dinner at Donovan's home. While they were there, the telephone rang and Donovan's daughter Mary Ellen answered it. The attorney general was calling, and Mary Ellen, in awe of the caller, remained on the line as Kennedy first spoke to Katzenbach. What left the greatest impression on her that night was the attorney general's criticism of her father as he complained to Katzenbach of Donovan's slow, methodical manner in proceeding with the exchange.[42] When Donovan himself finally got on the telephone, Kennedy repeated the importance he attached to Donovan returning to Cuba as soon as possible.[43] As Oberdorfer summarized, "The Attorney General felt very strongly that it was necessary for Mr. Donovan to go to Cuba as early as possible, and at the same time Mr. Donovan was reluctant to go to Cuba until the contributions had accumulated in some considerable depth and actually, as I recall it, until he could give unequivocal assurance that the letter of credit was inextricably on track."[44] These differences, however, occurred in the respective approaches each took, not in basic philosophy or goals. Kennedy would focus very sharply on one issue, to the exclusion of all others, while Donovan would see the issue in a much broader context—and wouldn't hesitate to talk about all the ramifications of it, a fact that generally irritated the attorney general.

Meanwhile, the Red Cross set up a special operations unit within headquarters in Washington and treated the situation as they would a national disaster. They assigned their General Supply Office and Disaster Services branch the responsibility for accepting donated products and moving them to points of embarkation to Cuba.[45] In this regard, the Red Cross set up working relationships with the Maritime Administration, the Civil Aeronautics Board, the Departments of Labor, State, Commerce, and Agriculture, the Interstate Commerce Commission, and the Immigration and Naturalization Service.[46] As to the private sector, the Air Transport Association and the Association of American Railroads assigned their own staff to the Red Cross's Washington headquarters. "They had to be able to tell us at any time," Robert Shea recalled, "where railroad cars were, what supplies were being moved to what airports, when they would arrive in the greater Miami area, by rail or by air, and how the supplies would be moved from their arrival points to Port Everglades, where the ships would be loaded, and to Opa Locka airfield that would become the major airbase for the project."[47] Shea continued:

> The American Trucking Association also played a key role in enlisting truck transport, and the Committee of American Steamship Lines donated the first ships for actual transport of supplies to Cuba. Subsequently, the other maritime associations and the United and Standard Fruit Companies also contributed ships. Pan American Airways agreed to donate an airlift capability from Florida to Cuba to take supplies in and bring prisoners out.[48]

In addition to transportation, the Red Cross also solicited the Continental Can Company, of which Lucius Clay was chairman, asking that tin cans be provided to the food and drug companies for the purpose of packaging their goods. Ultimately, the Red Cross pulled 150 staff from a variety of its operations around the country. Their initial task was obtaining and shipping, in the first delivery to Cuba, 20 percent of the total amount of goods on Castro's lists. Their second task was overseeing the products as they arrived in Cuba. Toward the latter end, the Red Cross placed its staff on all planes and boats going to Cuba and established a residence in Cuba for the duration of the project. They also had the only twenty-four-hour Teletype on the island that provided an uninterrupted link between the Red Cross staffs in Havana, Miami, and Washington. The third task of the Red Cross developed after the first shipment of products. It was the care of the hundreds of refugees who were coming out of Cuba on each returning transport. John Wilson credited his staff and hundreds of volunteers with the Red Cross Chapters in Miami and Fort Lauderdale with providing the most valuable assistance to the agency's doctors, nurses and nurses' aides who were treating these refugees on arrival in the United States.[49]

By December 12, fourteen drug companies committed themselves to $14 million in drugs, Gerber and Beechnut pledged $2 million in baby foods and Atlas Chemical pledged $150,000 in vitamins. More was still to come, but Donovan was now ready and cabled Castro that the merchandise was being obtained and requested an interview.

There were three significant obstacles remaining: first, the need for the great amount of milk that appeared on the Cuban lists; second, the demand by Castro for an irrevocable letter of credit that would guarantee that, if he did not receive any part of the entire shipment, he would then receive cash; and third, Castro's longstanding demand that he receive $2.9 million in cash for the sixty previously released prisoners.

With respect to milk, the Cubans had requested approximately $10 million worth, but the milk industry could only provide a tenth of that. In order to meet the demand, John Jones said that it was necessary to use government surplus stocks of dry skim milk to make up the difference. The government had purchased this milk at 18¢ per pound. However, the world market price was only 6¢ per pound. It was necessary, therefore, to develop an agreement with the Cubans to accept the higher domestic value.[50] Jones continued that there were no government funds that could be used to purchase this milk for donation, but there was a section in the law that would allow the Agency for International Development to donate surplus commodities to "friendly peoples."[51] Since this project was considered a people-to-people exchange, the Secretary of Agriculture authorized the donation from the Commodity Credit Corporation. The government was "reimbursed" in the following manner: A company had donated $2 million worth of a particular insecticide that the Department of Commerce had ruled was unacceptable for delivery to Cuba. That insecticide was then diverted to India and Pakistan who could use it and who were willing to pay for transportation. The $2 million was then credited to the Department of Agriculture for the purchase of milk.[52]

When it was obvious that Castro was adamant about having the irrevocable letter of credit, Donovan turned to Henry Harfield, the New York attorney. On December 14, Harfield accompanied Assistant Attorney General Katzenbach and Henry Rathbun, an attorney for the PMA, on a trip to the Royal Bank of Canada in Montreal. Briefly, the bank said that it would not provide such a letter unless it was backed by American banks. Further, the bank insisted that the Red Cross agree to be bound by such a letter of credit, and, finally, that an insurance company had to underwrite the Red Cross's commitment. As Katzenbach is reported to have said about the atmosphere in Montreal, "It was zero-zero. Zero outside and even colder inside the bank."[53]

The next day, Katzenbach, Oberdorfer, and Robert Knight met in New York to work on the problems posed by the Canadian bank. Oberdorfer related that after his meeting with Knight and Katzenbach, he and Henry Harfield rode to Idlewild Airport with a vice-president of the Bank of America. It was the only opportunity that they had to meet with him. Oberdorfer and Harfield explained the problem posed by the Royal Bank of Canada and the need for backing the letters of credit by an American bank or banks. Once the official was on the plane, Oberdorfer called the attorney general from the airport and suggested that he, Kennedy, call S. Clark Beise, the president of the Bank of America, and without any kind of coercion, repeat the discussion that Oberdorfer had had with Beise's vice-president. Oberdorfer does not know whether Kennedy made the call, but the Bank of America came through with a guarantee within two days for $26 million.[54] Morgan Guaranty Trust Company made a matching guarantee in the same time period.

For its part, the Red Cross acted very quickly on guaranteeing the Letter of Credit. Katzenbach personally flew to New York to speak with Roland Harriman and John Wilson. When Harriman asked Wilson about approaching the board of governors, Wilson suggested cabling the members of the board, which they did. They received an immediate, unanimous response to back the Letter of Credit to be issued by the Royal Bank of Canada.[55] It now fell to Donovan to convince an insurance company to underwrite the Red Cross.

Donovan called on Victor Herd, board chair of the America Fore Insurance Group. Herd, in turn, brought in surety vice-president, Alan O. Robinson, an old friend of Donovan's, and Donovan explained the problem. As Donovan described the exchange later:

> The Surety Vice President . . . said, growing a little whiter all the time, "A $53 million bond? What would be the collateral?" I gave him a severe look and said, "You mean you would require the American Red Cross to post collateral?"
>
> By now he was feeling vaguely unpatriotic and subsided a bit, but then came back with another question—I would say, after all, a very reasonable question. He said, "What would be the premium for this bond?" Before I was only shocked, but now I displayed outraged feelings. I said in an incredulous voice, "You mean you would actually charge the American Red Cross?"
>
> Believe it or not, I walked out of that room that day with a hand-written binder [on a sheet of legal-size, lined paper] for $53 million, signed by the Chairman of the Board, a binder with no collateral and no premium.[56]

On December 16, Louis Oberdorfer gave the go-ahead for the first shipments to be moved to Florida. Some would be loaded on Pan American Airlines planes, still others on the S.S. *African Pilot,* the first of nine ships donated to the project.[57] On this same day, Donovan arrived in Washington at 7:30 p.m. and went directly to Oberdorfer's home. He met Katzenbach here and the three discussed various aspects of the mission. After they left, they proceeded to Oberdorfer's office at the Justice Department. A little after midnight, Jim McIntosh of the CIA and Donovan left for Miami. (McIntosh had worked out a simple code based on the *Wall Street Journal*'s year-end stock quotes under which Donovan would give buy and sell orders of certain stocks that, in turn, would actually translate into how his discussions with Castro were going.)

At about this time, Donovan, who was staying in a CIA "safe house" in Miami, learned that one of Castro's negotiators had a sick child and needed specific medicine. He called Katzenbach who, in turn, called John Nolan. He asked Nolan to pick up ten vials of a rare medicine at Bethesda Naval Hospital. It was after midnight, Nolan remembers, when he went home to get some clothes before picking up the medicine and bringing it to Florida. His wife had just given birth to their fifth child and was still in the hospital. The other four children were being cared for at home by a housekeeper, Emma. As Nolan slipped into his home, being careful not to wake up the sleeping residents, he went up to his bedroom. He soon sensed that someone was in the room with him. As he turned, he saw Emma, a large woman, standing with folded arms over him. "I was convinced," Nolan said, "that she thought I was preparing to abandon my growing family in the middle of the night." Nolan gathered his traveling clothes and proceeded to Bethesda. Standing in a trench coat at the hospital at 2:00 a.m., he felt like he was in a cloak and dagger scene as he asked for the medicine that was quickly given to him with little talk. He then flew that night with the medicine to Miami where he changed planes for Havana.[58]

On December 18, Donovan received his final briefing and went off to Havana with Alvaro Sánchez, Berta Barreto, and Virginia Betancourt. The plane had a two-man crew and was the personal aircraft of the vice-president of Pan American Airways. When they landed at Havana airport, Castro's minister of Foreign Affairs greeted Donovan and informed him that a special inlaid-wood humidor had been prepared for him at Celia's request as a special gift from Castro. Soon after, René Vallejo, Regino Boti, Castro, Berta Barreto, Virginia Betancourt, and Sanchez met. Donovan opined that he would like the negotiations to be over by Christmas and Castro agreed. Donovan then provided a new list of products together with a letter from the Red Cross. He explained the prices used by companies in making deductions and said that 20 percent was added on for shipping, handling, insurance, etc. He also explained the letter of credit, the American banks' role and the surety bond. Boti, the minister of Planning and a Harvard Business School graduate, indicated that he understood.

Donovan, always the negotiator, tried at this time to replace goods for the $2.9 million in cash that Castro wanted for the prisoners who were released earlier. Castro, however, immediately became angry, and Donovan backed off. Still trying to push, however, Donovan brought up the twenty-one Americans being held, but Castro held to his original position and said that their fate would have to be decided after that of the initial prisoners.

Early in the day of December 19, Vallejo informed Donovan that his current offer was not acceptable to his experts because there was no surgical or dental equipment, nor was there any baby food. When Vallejo returned at 4:00 p.m. he added that a pharmaceutical expert was also needed to explain the drugs on the lists. Their own people, he said, didn't have the knowledge. Donovan suggested that Sanchez call Miami to request such an individual. Later, Donovan flew to Miami and met Oberdorfer and Dr. Leonard Scheele, the senior vice-president of Warner-Lambert Pharmaceutical Company and former surgeon general of the United States, whom President Kennedy had asked to assist Donovan at this crucial moment. That night Dr. Scheele reviewed the list of drugs and then returned to Havana with Donovan the next day.

Dr. Scheele remained in Havana throughout December 20 explaining the drugs on the list to the Cuban officials. That same day, the letter of credit from the Royal Bank of Canada was received by the Banco Nacional de Cuba. At 6:00 p.m., Scheele returned to Miami. Meanwhile, Donovan, Boti, Sanchez, and Vallejo reached an agreement that Donovan immediately wrote up. It was the Memorandum of Agreement in its final form that would be signed the next day. At this point, however, Castro was still suspicious about the value and size of the first shipment. Donovan suggested that Castro send his own inspectors to look at the cargo of the first ship, the *African Pilot*. Donovan called Washington and secured authorization for three Cuban technicians to fly to Miami to inspect the goods. It was understood that this aspect of the process was not to be made public.

On December 21, Donovan called Miami for new lists and called Washington to inform them of the signed Memorandum of Agreement.[59] Given Castro's concerns, he also asked if the first shipment could contain a high proportion of products really needed. Meanwhile, Harry Williams called Robert Kennedy at home. Kennedy informed him, "You got it, Enrique, this is it. The man with the beard has accepted. Now what you've got to do is move fast."[60]

Three members of the Cuban Red Cross, including Dr. Cervantes, the president of that group, left Havana and arrived in Miami where they were met by Dr. Scheele, John Nolan, Barrett Prettyman, Ruiz-Williams, and Ben Lovejoy of the American Red Cross. They were taken to Port Everglades where they checked the shipment on the *African Pilot* until daybreak. But there was a general atmosphere of ill will, and they tried to refuse items such as aspirin, Listerine, and Alka-Seltzer.[61] Dr. Scheele and John Nolan tried to be cordial, but when the Cubans demanded that some cargo be removed, Nolan finally declared, "That's impossible. They're already aboard and we can't disrupt everything now. We're not going to unload that ship. Everything that's on there is going to Cuba."[62] During December 22, these same personnel tried to stall the shipment until Christmas Day. In the end, however, Nolan suggested that they might want to consider the attitude toward them of the many thousands in the Cuban exile community in Miami if they learned that they were there. Certainly, Nolan pointed out, every effort would be made to protect them, but it could be dangerous. Soon after, the Cubans telephoned home and were recalled.[63]

To add more complications, during the day a forty-seven-year-old navy reserve officer, Douglas Voorhees, grabbed a carton of insecticide and threatened to throw it into the water near the *African Pilot,* screaming that the United States was paying blackmail. He was arrested. On the same Saturday, Oberdorfer, who had flown to Opa Locka to oversee the final loading, could not find the inventory of the goods to be shipped. Knowing that Castro would expect such a document, he called his assistant, Frank Michaelman, who Teletyped a duplicate list by midnight.

On December 23 at 9:30 a.m., the first planeload of goods arrived at San Antonio de los Banos Airport. In a conversation at the time between Castro and Donovan, the former opined that the two could do more together. Castro said, "I would like to resume at great length the interesting discussion we had last night. As soon as you can, I wish you would come back so that we would have the opportunity for a lengthy discussion of the more important, broader aspects of the future relations between Cuba, the United States and Latin America, than while we were occupied with the specifics of this mission."[64] While Castro and Donovan were talking at the airport, the Red Cross staff was ready with their lists of prisoners. More than two hundred Brigade soldiers had already arrived.

Although the exchange was progressing well, some of Castro's advisers still believed that Donovan was acting in the same role as the Japanese peace envoys who were in Washington at the time of the attack on Pearl Harbor, a belief that Donovan was aware of and would turn into humor. As Castro, Donovan, Nolan, and several others were watching the cargo planes land, four Russian MIGs, piloted by Cubans, passed low over the field. They had learned that Castro was there and sought to salute him. John Nolan remembered their next move. One of the pilots, Nolan said, returned and swooped in low. "He couldn't have been more than 100 feet above us. We all dropped to the pavement, including Castro. When some asked, "What is it?" Donovan turned to Castro and whispered in a strong voice, "It's the invasion." Castro roared in delight.[65]

That afternoon, the *African Pilot* arrived in Cuba. Donovan thought that the mood was right to broach the subject of the relatives of the prisoners with Castro. After some discussion, the latter agreed to let one thousand board the empty *African Pilot* on its return. In fact, 923 would do so.[66] It was Castro's Christmas "bonus." Donovan signaled the ship to begin unloading and shortly thereafter, the first of four planes with prisoners took off for Florida. However, after the first four flights left, Castro demanded the $2.9 million for the original sixty prisoners who were released earlier in the year. He would let no other prisoners go until he was assured of the money.[67]

Castro's resolve would put a halt to the remainder of the exchange if something was not done quickly. At first, Donovan and Nolan left the airport and went to Berta Barreto's home. Alvaro Sanchez was also there in a very distraught state. His son was among those prisoners who were not yet released and he began to threaten to go to the press blaming the United States for his son's continued custody. Donovan called Washington from Barreto's house in order to let them know Castro's position, as well as to pass on Sanchez's feelings. During that first call, according to John Nolan, Donovan was asked, with everything else on his mind, to try to obtain the release of the Americans held by Castro. Putting his hand over the receiver, Donovan announced to the room, "Jesus Christ, I've already done the loaves and fishes. Now they want me to walk on water, too."[68]

Shortly after the telephone call, Donovan and Nolan went to Boti's home. Donovan said to Boti, without mentioning the $2.9 million, that Nolan was going to go back to Miami that night to work on some details of the exchange. Boti, however, knew exactly why Nolan was returning and said that he would do whatever was necessary to assist Nolan. He offered to call the airport to hold a plane for him. Then Donovan, ever the humorist, pulled Boti aside and said, "There is only one thing you can do when you get Nolan to the airport." Boti leaned forward, very excited to help, and asked what it was. Donovan replied, "When you get him out there—" "Yes, yes," interrupted Boti. "When you get him out there and that big plane has its engines running, waiting to take off for Miami, there's just one thing you can do." "What is it?" asked the eagerly impatient Boti. "Don't defect." Right after this exchange, Boti left the room for a few moments. Being alone with Nolan, Donovan immediately ran to Boti's desk and began to search through it. Panicked, Nolan whispered loudly, "Jeez, Jim, what the hell are you doing? Do you want to get us killed?" Donovan looked up and quite calmly said, "You know me, John, once in the clandestine service, always in the clandestine service." Donovan only found several forms of no real value, however, but he took them anyway and turned them over to the CIA.[69]

Thus, in the early hours of Monday, Christmas Eve, John Nolan and Harry Ruiz-Williams flew to Miami, where Louis Oberdorfer met them. They first called Nicholas Katzenbach, and at 4:45 a.m. Katzenbach called Ruiz-Williams at his home. Ruiz-Williams informed him that there was no way that the Cuban Families Committee could get the money. In the search for a solution, Nolan reached Robert Kennedy at his home at 5:00 a.m. In a three-way conversation among Nolan, Katzenbach, and Kennedy, Kennedy asked Nolan, "Do you think our position is stronger once we have made the payment of the 2.9 million than it is just before? Are we in a stronger position then or in a weaker position?" Nolan replied, "I don't think our position is stronger after we've made the payment. I think it's weaker. But I don't think that we can carry out the exchange without the payment having been made at some point."[70] Kennedy then asked Nolan what he was going to do, and Nolan answered that he was going to fly back to Cuba. Kennedy then asked, "Don't you think you ought to wait until you see whether we can get the money or not?" Nolan answered, "No, I think I'll just rely on you to do that because I don't . . . You know, I'll just assume that you're going to get it. And I think, really, that's the only way we can play it." Kennedy replied, "Okay," and the conversation ended.[71]

Shortly thereafter Kennedy called Richard Cardinal Cushing of Boston who pledged $1 million.[72] He then called Gen. Lucius Clay who borrowed $1.9 million on his own signature.[73] With the funds secured on Christmas Eve, the Royal Bank of Canada informed the Cuban government that $2.9 million could be released on Donovan's written authorization. Then, at 10:00 p.m., Donovan signed for the last 108 prisoners as they boarded the Pan American Airlines clipper, *Sam Houston*, for the trip to Florida.

Before Donovan himself boarded the last flight, Castro told him that he had been in more danger than he might have thought. He related that he had had explosives placed in twelve prisons in the event of an invasion by the United States. At the end of their conversation, to inject his typical levity, Donovan told Castro that he (Donovan) had done so much for the Cuban people that he might come back and beat him in the next election. After a moment Castro replied, "You know, Doctor, I think you may be right. So there will be no elections."[74]

After the last prisoners to be airlifted from Havana had boarded the aircraft, Donovan joined them. On the flight back to Miami, he was given a hand-carved rosary strung on a fish line by a prisoner. Upon his arrival at Homestead Air Force Base, south of Miami, on Christmas Eve, 1962, Donovan first called Robert Kennedy to advise him of the successful return of the prisoners. However, instead of simply conveying this information to the attorney general, Donovan felt compelled to rile him a little with, "Well, General, mission accomplished!" According to Milan Miskovsky, the title of general was appropriate for the attorney general, but it was never used. It was especially never used with Robert Kennedy who disdained the military inference—except by James Donovan.

The weary negotiator called Mary next, but he was uncertain as to when he would rejoin his family. An Air Force colonel approached him and the result was later recounted in the *Lake Placid* (NY) *News:*

"Mr. Donovan," the Colonel said. "We were told by Washington that you had a date to spend Christmas at Lake Placid with your family. We've laid out a program to do just that." And in the end, the Air Force did just that. Soon after, Donovan was put aboard one of Homestead's newest and fastest light bombers. In no time at all they were landing their distinguished guest at New York's Idlewild airport. Donovan was still wearing the clothes he'd worn all week in Cuba. While his military escort waited, Donovan taxied across town to his home near Prospect Park. When he returned he was dressed for winter in the Adirondacks. The aircraft took off again. Next stop was the Air Force base at Plattsburgh. Time out there for a quick breakfast with the officer in command. Then, for Donovan, it was into that officer's own limousine, with his uniformed chauffeur at the wheel. Fifty-odd miles, and maybe sixty-odd minutes later, James Britt Donovan was being greeted at the door of his cottage on the grounds of the Lake Placid Club.

"So what kept you, Santa Claus?" said his family in unison.[75]

The return of the 1,113 Bay of Pigs prisoners generally satisfied public attention. It was not, however, the end of Donovan's involvement. There were still a number of Americans being held in Cuban jails for whom he wanted to obtain release; there would be additional American skin divers on a fishing vessel who accidentally intruded on Cuban waters and who were apprehended; and there were recurring problems with the type of goods being shipped to Cuba.[76] In addition, Castro was allowing relatives of the former prisoners, and others, to leave the island on the otherwise empty cargo ships returning to the United States.[77] And lingering in the background, as well, was the possibility of improved American-Cuban diplomatic relations.

On January 2, 1963, Donovan sent a telegram to Castro to express his appreciation for the courtesies that had been extended to him during the negotiations. Actually, he was very concerned about how President Kennedy's remarks at the Orange Bowl four days earlier would affect his ability to secure the release of the American prisoners. The president had said on that Sunday in December, in accepting the flag of Brigade 2506 for safekeeping, "I can assure you that this flag will be returned to this Brigade in a free Havana."[78] A lofty sentiment on President Kennedy's part, it would not be helpful to a negotiator trying to persuade the current government in Havana to release Americans.

Toward the end of the month, on January 26, Donovan left Miami on the personal executive plane of Juan Trippe, president of Pan American Airlines. In a three-hour talk that day, Castro and Donovan first discussed American and Cuban prisons. Donovan then proposed amnesty for several Cubans being held in United States prisons—Francisco Molina, Roberto Santiestaban, Antonio Suercio, and Jose Garcia—in return for the Americans whom Castro held. Molina was serving a prison term for killing a young girl; Santiestaban, an attaché to the Cuban mission to the U.N., and his two associates, Suercio and Garcia, were under indictment for planning to bomb various locations in New York City. To Donovan, Castro appeared interested in such a swap, but no definitive agreement emerged at that time. On his return, Donovan told reporters that a plan to release the American prisoners was in the works.

During the following month, Castro continued to release relatives of the former prisoners and other refugees on returning American ships. Donovan and Vallejo spoke twice about the possibility of releasing imprisoned Americans but nothing further developed in the negotiations. However, at just about this time nine more Americans were captured and imprisoned in Cuba, suspected of being saboteurs, but they were actually harmless skin divers. The group was on a fishing vessel, the *Shrub*, when they lost a rudder in a storm. The ship sank, but the crew was able to save themselves in a lifeboat that eventually washed up on a Cuban beach, where they were seized. Almost jokingly, Dr. Scheele wrote to Donovan soon after, "Now if Americans will just stop getting themselves jailed in Cuba so that the numbers grow about as rapidly as you persuade Castro to release them, we'll all be in good shape."[79]

At the beginning of March, Donovan cabled Vallejo about the urgency to proceed with the negotiations. After several days he received a response and made plans to travel first to Washington and then to Cuba.

On March 11, Donovan met with Milan Miskovsky and then attended a Grid Iron Club dinner. The next day, he met with Robert Kennedy to receive his final instructions on the continuing negotiations with Castro. Donovan noted his objectives as they were discussed with the attorney general including the release of all American citizens in Cuban prisons, the receipt of assurances that bona fide immediate family members of the Brigade could leave Cuba on available transportation and a resolution of the price disagreements on the Commodities Credit Corporation's milk.[80] Donovan also noted:

The AG pointed out several advantages on my side. Castro had already promised to review the cases of U.S. citizens in jail with a view toward amnesty, provided he felt that the Brigade exchange was being consummated in good faith, and provided 3 Cubans (arrested in the UN incidents)[81] were returned to Cuba. In addition, I could point out to Castro that one half of the promised goods had already been delivered, and there is no question of the remainder of the transaction being consummated in good faith. I also have the authority to state that the American government is prepared to release the 3 Cubans in question . . . The AG then warned me of action that should not be taken.

"Do not," he said, "initiate any discussions of a political nature with Castro. Should he begin such a discussion, listen carefully, but reply with only the minimum dictated by common courtesy.

Secondly," the AG continued, "Agree neither to the reduction of the milk prices nor the elimination of further milk shipments. Do not agree to the release of any U.S. held Cuban other than the three involved in the UN incident. Lastly, you should not push the resumption of Pan Am service to Havana[82] until you've concluded to your own satisfaction and to our satisfaction, an agreement with Castro guaranteeing the release of Geddes and the American prisoners."[83]

On March 14, Donovan left again for Havana, arriving the next day. In a discussion with Castro about the skin divers, the latter said that he would allow Donovan the opportunity to prove their innocence. When the two discussed the other American prisoners, Castro indicated that he could not release seventeen Americans for the few Cubans the United States was holding. In the alternative, he suggested that he would release the Americans as a recognition of the completion of the medical deliveries. Then, according to Castro, it would not appear as an exchange, and the United States, recognizing this clemency, could follow up by releasing the Cubans.

When Donovan saw that he would be taking no one out on this trip to Cuba, he brought up his awareness that Castro was holding two American women, Martha O'Neal and Geraldine Shamma. Each had been arrested in 1960 in separate incidents, and each was serving a lengthy prison sentence. In what appeared to Castro was going to be a lengthy speech, Donovan began to expound about the nearness of St. Patrick's Day, about the fact that one of the women was Irish and about how important it was not to deny a request of an Irishman like himself on such a day. Tired of listening to Donovan's monologue, Castro is said to have shouted out from impatience, "Give him the women. Give him the women."[84]

After the meeting with Castro, Donovan visited the American prisoners in the Isle of Pines prison. He especially wanted to free one who had apparently suffered a breakdown in custody. Donovan also visited the nine skin divers. He interviewed them, listening carefully to their story, since he would be representing them as a virtual defense attorney.

On St. Patrick's Day, Donovan returned to Florida taking with him both O'Neal and Shamma. Several days later he hired Chris McGrath, a young lawyer, to assist him in gathering evidence on the innocence of the skin divers. He also made arrangements for Dr. Scheele to return to Havana in order to evaluate the specific problems that the Cubans were having with the food and medicine. On the twenty-first, he returned to Cuba for a five-hour conference with Castro. Meanwhile, McGrath, in Miami, worked with Betsy Brown, captain of the skin diving crew, to get depositions showing that the boat was outfitted only for fishing. He also got an affidavit from Robert Baugartner, a mechanical engineer who boarded the *Shrub* in 1962 on three occasions to investigate the fishing equipment. The vessel had had a contract with the Dominican Republic that allowed them to fish in that country's waters.

Apart from Donovan's primary negotiations, eleven missionaries who had been detained in Cuba since March 13 were deported to Miami. A twelfth, Floyd Woodworth, was still held. Donovan would later see to his release.

Dr. Scheele had had several discussions with Donovan at the end of March and the beginning of April. Scheele believed that there was substance to the Cuban complaints about some of the contents of the shipments and planned to discuss this in Cuba. For his part, Donovan met on April 1 with a number of American ship owners at the Maritime Administration office in New York City to present plans for using their ships to complete the transportation of food and drugs to Cuba.

At about this same time, Donovan decided to bring the wet suit that he had promised Castro in the fall of the previous year. After discussing the idea with Milan Miskovsky, the latter asked a CIA official, Frank DeRosa, to purchase such a suit. DeRosa agreed, but before he did so, other agency employees cautioned him to use care in maintaining custody of the suit at all times until Donovan had it in his possession. The warning was based on the knowledge that some lower echelon figures in the agency had a plan to give a poisoned wet suit to Castro, using Donovan as the unwitting intermediary. The poisoned suit was to contain a fungus that caused a chronic skin disease and a contaminated breathing apparatus with a tubercule bacillus. According to Miskovsky, DeRosa purchased a new wet suit at

Abercrombie and Fitch in Manhattan and then took evasive steps to avoid being followed until he reached Donovan's Brooklyn home where he turned the wet suit over to him.[85]

On April 2, Donovan left for Miami.[86] Five days later, he, his son, John, John Nolan, Milan Miskovsky, and Frank DeRosa traveled to Cuba.[87] Taking his son was very purposeful for Donovan:

> Bringing along my son was, I thought, the ultimate in gamesmanship. I had gotten wind that some of Castro's advisors were telling him that I was dangerous, that I intended to play the same decoy role that the Japanese ambassador played here for Pearl Harbor. Castro has a fourteen-year-old boy. I hoped that the presence of my eighteen year old would inspire confidence and make a favorable impression on Castro.[88]

On the night of their arrival, they attended a baseball game. The next day, they went to Santa Maria for swimming and another baseball game. Finally, Donovan and Castro, excusing themselves from John Donovan and John Nolan, sat down to talk. After two hours, Donovan gave Castro a list of the American prisoners that he sought to have released. He also presented his evidence on the innocence of the skin divers that McGrath had gathered. Castro indicated that the divers would be released on April 9.

The next day, John Donovan spent some time snorkeling with Castro in his new wet suit while his father fished. John asked the Cuban leader at one point if his system hadn't resulted in the loss of some freedoms for his people. Castro replied, "Freedom! Hah. What is freedom? Is a man free when he can't read or write? Is he free if he can't be admitted to a public health hospital without a note from an important political official? If his food and housing is barely enough for him to survive?"[89] It was John's impression at the time, and currently, that Castro wanted a significantly improved relationship with the United States. John described Castro's attitude as open to better relations.[90] John Nolan also remembered a number of discussions that he, James, and John Donovan had had with Castro. They traveled for hours together at this time and some of their talks focused on such things as the participation of Cuba in the upcoming World's Fair, American constitutional law, and even a new Cuban constitution with Donovan as a special adviser in developing it.[91]

As he had promised, Castro released the skin divers on April 9, and they returned to Florida with Donovan and his party. The remaining missionary, Woodworth, left with them.

Only one more trip to Cuba remained for Donovan. Just before the trip, Donovan asked Milan Miskovsky for a last gift to give the

Cuban leader. Miskovsky personally purchased a new Polaroid camera for Donovan to give Castro.[92] He had further discussions with Castro on April 21 and 22. On the latter day, the American prisoners were released. Twenty-one returned to the United States, three chose to remain in Cuba, and three elected to go to South America.[93] On the following day, the three Cubans who had been indicted in Brooklyn were moved to Miami and then returned to Cuba. They were joined by Francisco "The Hook" Molina del Rio, whose sentence Governor Nelson Rockefeller had commuted at the request of the federal government, on the condition that he be deported, never to return to the United States. Molina had been serving a twenty-year to life sentence for the accidental killing of a nine-year-old Venezuelan girl in New York City during an exchange of gun fire with anti-Castro Cubans in 1959.

For Donovan, his work was now complete. He had successfully negotiated the release of 9,703 Cubans, including the 1,113 Brigade prisoners, their relatives, and many Cuban-born, naturalized United States citizens who had been living in Cuba, together with other Cubans seeking refuge, all in addition to more than thirty American prisoners.[94] The last ship bearing goods, the S.S. *Maximus,* sailed after resolving some labor and shipping problems at the end of June.[95] It returned to Florida on July 3 with 1,204 refugees. The last plane left Miami on July 3 carrying two tons of medical supplies, together with two elderly Cubans who sought to return to their homeland.[96] The work of the pharmaceutical companies, food manufacturers, airlines, truckers, railroads and ships ended at this time, as well, when the Montreal Branch of the Royal Bank of Canada notified the American Red Cross that its Letter of Credit was now fully utilized. As a final financial detail, the Grace National Bank in New York closed its account at the request of Gen. Lucius Clay in October 1964. The National Bank of Washington still had $20,359.64 plus interest in the unexpended balance of funds of the CFC.[97] On January 12, 1965, Rasenburger sent a check in the amount of $20,409.37 to the Red Cross from the CFC pursuant to the commitment of Donovan. The amount represented the entire balance of CFC funds remaining from a total of $2,369,889.20 received during its existence.[98] Notably, the Red Cross expended $245,000 that was not reimbursed.

In its final report dated July 3, 1963, the Red Cross divided the donations of supplies and their respective values into four commodity groups: 1) raw material for pharmaceutical and veterinary specialties, $29,952,829; 2) equipment, instruments and medical, dental, and veterinary expendable material $3,702,427; 3) powdered milk for children, $2,579,411; 4) children's food, $3,183,084; and miscellaneous food, $9,899,293; for a total of $49,317,044.[99]

In all, 166 companies, the CFC, and the U.S. Department of Agriculture donated supplies to the effort. Ten airlines and a number of railroads and truck companies provided transportation of the goods to Florida. Pan American Airlines donated planes to cover thirty-five flights to and from Cuba, and nine ships had made the round trips, as well.[100]

After the negotiations, Donovan received numerous citations and commendations.[101] On May 6, 1963, he received the Bronze Medal of the City of New York from Mayor Robert F. Wagner with the citation, "Presented in appreciation to James B. Donovan, Distinguished Lawyer and Ambassador of Mercy on Behalf of our nation." The medal was similar to the one his father had received in 1904 for his efforts to aid the *Slocum* victims, and for that reason alone, Donovan cherished it. Another honor had been presented earlier, on March 21, 1963, the Gold Medal Award of Brooklyn College, given to him for vital public service as an instrument of peace in Cuba. The award was accompanied by a telegram:

> I am delighted to join with the Brooklyn College community in paying tribute to the public service of James Donovan. Mr. Donovan has performed extraordinary missions in the public interest, and we all honor particularly the role he has performed in recent months in the difficult negotiations in Cuba. His intelligence, judgment and skill have richly earned him the distinction you are conferring today.
> John F. Kennedy[102]

The Mercedarian religious order, formally known as the Order of Our Lady of Mercy for the Redemption of People in Captivity, also presented him with an award, their Grand Cross. In about 1230, St. Peter Nolasco had founded the Mercedarians, whose purpose was to ransom captives, although it had more recently been concerned with the care of the sick. Since Donovan, individually, had ransomed more people than anyone in the order had, he was made a lay affiliate.[103] There were other recognitions that Donovan received for his work in the release of Brigade 2506, such as a Certificate of Appreciation from the American Red Cross on August 22, 1963, for "his service in effecting the release of prisoners held captive in Cuba and reuniting them with their families,"[104] and the First Annual Humanitarian Award, presented to him at the Waldorf Astoria on November 23, 1963, from St. Vincent's Home for Boys. Perhaps the most unusual recognition he received, however, was from Marty Glikman, an announcer at Yonkers Raceway, who was reported to have called an oncoming horse as *John B. Donovan,* rather than *John B. Hanover* in a race on April 27, 1963.

Given the relationship of respect between Castro and Donovan and the hints of possible future talks, there has always been the retrospective thought that a rapprochement was possible between the United States and Cuba at the time. In an interview with John Bartlow Martin in 1964, Robert Kennedy was asked about such an accord with Cuba. He replied:

> We always discussed that as a possibility. It was a question of trying to work it out. There were some tentative feelers that were put out by [Castro] which were accepted by us—which were done through Bill Attwood. Bill Attwood got in touch with me, and then I had him get in touch with Mac Bundy at the White House. Ultimately, I think, the President gave the go-ahead. He was to go to Havana—I don't know, in December of last year [1963] or January of this year—and see Castro and see what could be done. We had certain things that were required: the end of the military presence of the Russians and the Communists, the cut off of ties with the Communists by Cuba, and the end of the exportation of revolution. In return for those basic points and perhaps more, there would be a normalization of the relationship.[105]

Indeed, one of Robert Kennedy's primary interests when Donovan and John Nolan were in Cuba was the attitude of Castro. At one point, Kennedy asked Nolan if he thought that the United States could do business with Castro. Nolan gave a qualified assent.[106]

Donovan, himself, had hoped for improved relations, and he offered to be a part of the process. On September 4, 1963, for example, he wrote to Lawrence R. Houston, general counsel of the CIA, and proposed himself as a "special envoy to the President to study educational needs in Latin America." This would, Donovan reasoned, give him good access to Castro and would further Latin American foreign policy. He believed that he could accomplish his goals in a five-week period. If this proposal became common knowledge, Donovan humorously related, "My family and law partners would disown me."[107]

On a more serious side, however, President Kennedy recognized Castro's initial feelers for a normalization of relations with the United States as the Cuban leader revealed them in his talks with Donovan during the first months of 1963. The president also knew that the present opportunity to begin the process toward rapprochement with Cuba was the greatest since Castro was extremely angered with the Soviets for excluding him during the diplomacy of the Cuban missile crisis and was now seeking more independence from Moscow.[108] At the same time, Kennedy did not want to make the termination of Soviet ties by Castro as a prerequisite for any talks. In a once top secret memorandum for the record, Gordon Chase, an assistant to McGeorge Bundy, President Kennedy's national security adviser, noted,

> The President does not agree that we should make the breaking of Sino/ Soviet ties a nonnegotiable point. We don't want to present Castro with a condition that he obviously cannot fulfill. We should start thinking along more flexible lines.
>
> Donovan should resist taking his week-long walk along the beach with Castro until we have had a chance to give Donovan a very good briefing. We may want to give Donovan some flies to dangle in front of Castro.
>
> The above must be kept close to the vest. The President, himself, is interested in this one.[109]

During Donovan's talks with Castro, particularly in March and April, Castro expressed, in a sincere fashion, his hope for a normalization of relations with the United States. He continued to voice this desire both in public and private thereafter. Nevertheless, it was difficult for many American politicians, particularly republicans, to accept this sincerity at face value. Even the Cuban exile community in Florida was split on the concept of rapprochement.[110]

Donovan briefed the Central Intelligence Agency, and thus the president, after each visit to Cuba. His negotiations ended in April, however, and there was no reason associated with the prisoner exchange for him to return. As it happened, an ABC news reporter, Lisa Howard, was also interested in Castro and better relations between Cuba and the United States. In fact, she had been writing to Castro for many months seeking an interview with him. Prior to Donovan's departure from Cuba in April, he provided an introduction for her to the Cuban leader. Within days, she succeeded in obtaining a taped television interview with the premier.

During his interview with Howard on April 24, which she described in an article for the journal, *War/Peace Reports*, Castro indicated his desire to discuss "all points of contention" that existed between the United States and Cuba.[111] He pointed out that he was willing to discuss the Soviet presence in Cuba, compensation for expropriated American property and the concept that Cuba was a base for communist subversion in the Americas.[112]

As Howard pointed out, Castro was extremely disappointed with the Soviet Union in leaving him entirely out of the diplomatic maneuverings during the missile crisis in October 1962. In fact, Castro removed all pictures of Khrushchev and expelled the Soviet ambassador, Sergei Kudrayavtsev, soon after that episode. It appeared to Howard that Castro needed the United States, not so much for its goods as for the opportunity to become more independent of the Soviet Union. Following her interview and return to the United States, Howard was debriefed by the CIA on the full extent of her discussions in Cuba. However, the agency was cool toward the reporter, and five months passed before any progress was made.

In September 1963 Lisa Howard spoke with William Atwood, special adviser for African Affairs to the United States Delegation to the United Nations. He, too, believed that rapprochement with Cuba was both important and achievable. Several days later, President Kennedy agreed to allow Atwood to approach the Cuban ambassador to the United Nations, Carlos Lechuga, in order to open discreet discussions. Toward that end, Howard arranged a small, private party in her New York City apartment on the evening of September 23 during which Atwood and Lechuga privately discussed a process that could lead to improved relations. Thereafter, there was a flurry of contacts among Atwood, Lechuga, and René Vallejo, Castro's personal physician and advisor, in planning for a more formal, but private, face-to-face meeting at which Castro himself wished to be present.

Meanwhile, as described by Peter Kornbluh,[113] President Kennedy sent two clear messages to Castro—one in the form of a speech to the Inter-American Press Association on November 19, 1963, in which he implied that normalization of relations was possible; and a second, through a French journalist, Jean Daniel. Kennedy had instructed Daniel in a White House meeting, to tell Castro that the trade embargo against Cuba could be lifted if Cuba ceased supporting leftist movements in the Americas.[114] However, during a meeting between Daniel and Fidel Castro, the announcement came that President Kennedy had been assassinated.

Castro was saddened and dismayed at the ramifications of the president's death. Nevertheless, he continued his pursuit of normal relations through Kennedy's successor, Lyndon Johnson. Meanwhile, in late 1963, Donovan and Milan Miskovsky presented themselves to Sol M. Linowitz, the United States permanent representative to the Organization of American States, with the suggestion that better relations with Cuba were very possible. Linowitz informed them, however, that the Johnson administration was simply not interested.[115]

Despite the nonresponsiveness of the administration, Castro persisted. In an unusually clear note to President Johnson on February

12, 1964, delivered by Lisa Howard to Adlai Stevenson, the American ambassador to the United Nations, Castro revealed his hopes for détente. He said, in part:

> Tell the President that I understand quite well how much political courage it took for President Kennedy to instruct you [Lisa Howard] and Ambassador Attwood to phone my aide in Havana for the purpose of commencing a dialogue toward a settlement of our differences. Ambassador Attwood suggested that I prepare an agenda for such talks and send the agenda to my U.N. Ambassador. That was on November 18th. The agenda was being prepared when word arrived that President Kennedy was assassinated. I hope that we can soon continue where Ambassador Attwood's phone conversation to Havana left off . . . though I'm aware that pre-electoral political considerations may delay this approach until after November.
>
> Tell the President (and I cannot stress this too strongly) that I seriously hope that Cuba and the United States can eventually sit down in an atmosphere of good will and of mutual respect and negotiate our differences. I believe that there are no areas of contention between us that cannot be discussed and settled in a climate of mutual understanding. But first, of course, it is necessary to discuss our differences. I now believe that this hostility between Cuba and the United States is both unnatural and unnecessary—and it can be eliminated.[116]

The Johnson administration did not respond to this communication, but Castro would not rest. When Lisa Howard returned to Cuba for a visit with the Cuban leader in April 1964, he stressed his intention of not precipitating any crisis before the upcoming elections in the United States so as not to jeopardize possible talks. Soon after his meeting with Howard, he tried to communicate again with Johnson's administration through an interview on July 5, 1964, with Richard Eder, a reporter for the *New York Times:* "He [Castro] suggested that the time had come when extensive discussion of issues between the two countries would be useful."[117] As the years passed, there were other indications of Fidel Castro's interest in better relations, but the United States has never followed through.

The lack of success in reaching an accord with Cuba was summed up briefly in 2000 by Richard Goodwin, the individual who had initially dealt with the CFC:

> Then [President Kennedy] died, and the embargo was frozen in place for four more decades, long after the reasons for it had evaporated. In this time, Soviet Communism weakened and tumbled. The Communist-led movements in Latin America disappeared. We welcomed trade with the Soviet Union and China.

Yet through it all the embargo on Cuba stayed in place, the historical artifact of a cold war that had ended.

This anomalous policy owed its durability to Florida politics. A large and passionate exile community in Miami turned against any party and any politician who seemed willing to dilute our hostility toward the Cuban government . . .

No president and no candidate for president was willing to take that risk [of losing Florida's electoral votes]. So for political reasons—and only for political reasons—the embargo has remained.[118]

Had Donovan lived longer, it would not have been different. But it would not have been for his lack of effort. Thus, as Richard Goodwin has written, "the embargo has remained."

10

The Board of Education

THE PROBLEMS CONFRONTING THE NEW YORK CITY PUBLIC SCHOOLS at mid-century were of long-standing. As early as 1931, Allen Raymond studied the city's educational system for a series of articles in the *New York Herald Tribune*. He found that the quality of elementary education was poor, teacher promotions were too readily provided, teacher morale was low, and the entire system was open to political patronage.[1] In addition, the public distrusted the administration of the system. Board members were appointed as a reward for political service, and no minority representation existed among those constituting the board.[2] Two decades later, little had changed. As Diane Ravitch has observed:

> During the 1950's and early 1960's, the schools were at the center of one crisis after another: juvenile delinquency, a soaring high school dropout rate, a perennial teacher shortage, union-management conflict, increasing racial segregation, the staggering cost of replacing old buildings and adding new ones. The stormy course of the integration battle, particularly in the early 1960's, contributed to the public sense that the Board of Education was incapable of providing forceful leadership and had lost touch with its public; scarcely a week went by without a demonstration against board policies, by one side or the other.[3]

Indeed, it was the result of a corruption inquiry by the New York State Investigating Commission in 1961 that led the State Board of Regents and Commissioner of Education James E. Allen to request that the governor call a special session of the legislature to address the crisis in the city's school system and the related foundering of public confidence in its administration. Governor Rockefeller complied and convened the special session in August. After a hearing, the legislators enacted Chapter 971, Laws of New York, 1961 on August 21, 1961.[4] Under this new statute the existing board of education was dissolved and its members' services, terminated. An eleven-member selection panel was created and directed to compile a list of twenty-

163

six qualified individuals for consideration in the formulation of a new board. Mayor Wagner was given the authority to make a final selection of nine from that list.

Wagner's appointments to this new, "reform" board included Max J. Rubin, a lawyer and former president of the Great Neck, New York, Board of Education; Brendan Byrne, executive director of the American Heritage Foundation; Lloyd K. Garrison, an attorney in private practice and a former dean of the University of Wisconsin Law School; John F. Hennessey, an engineer by training, but also the president of the Board of Managers of Lincoln Hall, a Catholic school for delinquent boys; Morris Iushewitz, a labor leader and secretary of New York City's Central Labor Council; Samuel R. Pierce, an attorney, former judge of the city's Court of Special Sessions and the only black member; Anna M. Rosenberg, the sole female, a public relations consultant and former assistant secretary of defense; Clarence O. Senior, a professor of sociology, consultant to the Ford Foundation, and an authority on Puerto Rican affairs; and James B. Donovan.[5] The board consisted of three Jews, three Roman Catholics, two Protestants, and one "free thinker." Seven members represented Manhattan; Brooklyn and Queens each had one; the Bronx and Staten Island had none.[6] The new legislation required that the terms of the new board be staggered, with subsequent replacement members being sworn in for full seven-year terms. Donovan's term was one of the longest of this original board, with an expiration of May 1967.

Board members, sworn in by Mayor Wagner for service beginning on September 20, selected from among themselves Max Rubin as president and James Donovan, vice-president. These were temporary selections until annual elections in the following May. All members served without pay and met monthly as a group at board headquarters, 110 Livingston Street, Brooklyn. Their responsibilities included one million students, 43,000 teachers, thousands of administrative and support staff, a plethora of contracts and over 800 buildings.

The reform board moved quickly after appointment. Meeting on Saturday, September 23, they decided upon an overhaul of some existing practices and procedures including an end to the availability of full-time chauffeurs and limousines for each member, a reduction in support staff serving the board, fewer closed executive sessions, more public meetings in the evening hours to provide an opportunity for working parents to participate, and the abolition of standing committees. Donovan proposed that the city's Corporation Counsel define the precise "lines of demarcation of authority" on matters involving the board and other departments in order to address past criticisms that the board yielded too much authority to others.[7] Five days later, at an evening public meeting, a decision was made to request that the city's Department of Labor select a collective bargaining agent for the system's forty-three thousand teachers, thus addressing the cause of their one-day walkout that occurred a year earlier in November 1960. At this same time, the superintendent of schools, Dr. John J. Theobald, was given power over the appointment and transfer of teachers, school construction, maintenance, and supplies, while the board retained control of the selection of architects and new school sites, and the awarding of contracts and the provision of payments. The board, in turn, then delegated to the local school boards the responsibility to assist in site selections and in gathering data to make recommendations regarding the board's budget.

Within the first half year of its existence the board also addressed the problems of school construction and maintenance. Private architects were employed to provide supervision for new constructions, and they were placed on an Advisory Commission on School Construction with other experts in the field. The Manual of School Planning was also revised at this time. On February 20, 1962, the board began a series of hearings to determine if it should reinstate some previously disqualified contractors and permit them to bid again on new construction proposals. Donovan and other members met with the heads of many of these firms at board headquarters. Some remained suspended from bidding, but others were allowed to resume participation as long as they understood that the potential existed for subsequent prosecution if they engaged in any illegal act.

In other actions, the board of education reduced the number of local school boards from fifty-four to twenty-five in order to increase efficiency and control. It began to look into custodial service, as well. Long a problem in the educational system, custodians were not true employees of the board of education, but were actually independent contractors who, at times, received more compensation than their services required. In fact, they were given a prearranged lump sum of money for work to be done, and they were allowed to retain for themselves any unspent funds. It was a practice that didn't encourage quality service. Eventually, this abuse would be curtailed entirely. In order to provide additional classroom space, the use of portable buildings was developed with their placement in almost any available site. A repair program for the schools was one of the first orders of business for the board. The Office of School Buildings, Bureau of Plant Operations, for example, had reported that in 1961 alone 163,736 panes of glass were broken at a replacement cost of

$818,680.[8] The board also had to contend with revitalizing their committee structure and evaluating Staten Island's call for its own seat because of its unique school problems as a more rural borough.

The new board did much to improve the infrastructure of the school system during their first year of service. However, its teachers were not satisfied with internal improvements. Seeking better pay and working conditions, these educators whose union, the United Federation of Teachers (UFT), had recently secured the collective bargaining agreement with the city, called a strike for April 11, 1962.

The teachers' action lasted only one day, but on that day 20,558 of their number did not report for work. Five thousand rallied at City Hall. Meanwhile, twenty-five schools were forced to close entirely since there was an insufficient number of teachers to provide for the safety of pupils. In other schools, students were massed into auditoriums and cafeterias and given reading assignments. Many had to be released early. The striking teachers did not engage in violence, themselves, but at some schools, the students upturned desks, broke windows, and threw eggs and rocks.

Donovan was among the majority of the board who voted on the afternoon of the work action to seek an injunction from State Supreme Court to halt the strike, and it was immediately granted. Not only did the board not anticipate the severity of the strike, but it had also relied on an exiting law in the state, the Condon-Wadlin Act, that prohibited strikes by government employees.[9] The teachers complied with the court order and returned to work on the following day. Contract talks then resumed, but the problem that both sides faced was the lack of existing funds. Teachers had demanded salary increases totaling $53 million. The board ultimately offered a package that amounted to $36.25 million, and then only if it could obtain this additional money from the city and state. Eventually, talks broke down again in June when the UFT refused to accept a no-strike pledge in their contract, despite the fact that striking was against the law in any event. Donovan concluded, then, in a statement to the press, "Until a no-strike pledge is given, the board sees no constructive purpose in carrying on further negotiations."[10] Despite the rift in negotiations, Donovan did not retract the agreement on salary increases that had already been proposed,[11] and teachers continued to work without a contract. While another strike would loom for some time to come, it was not the intractable problem that Donovan and the board would face for several years, namely, the quest for full integration of the New York City public school system by many civil rights groups, together with the intransigence of numerous white groups to the involuntary transfer of their children from their neighborhood schools. It would contribute to Donovan's later heart condition and, eventually, his resignation.

The board of education had been created in 1842 and consisted of thirty-four commissioners. Eleven years later, it absorbed the Public School Society, which had been managing the city's schools. In 1902, a centralized board was created and the position of superintendent was added and given authority to administer the schools directly. The board began with forty-six members. It was reduced to seven in 1917 and increased to nine in 1948.[12] Segregation in the New York City school system had been declared illegal in 1920, but communities of ethnically homogenous groups continued to grow over the years. The result was de facto segregation in the schools since these facilities served the neighborhoods in which they were located. Between 1945 and the early 1960s 800,000 whites had moved out of the city, while 700,000 blacks and Hispanics had moved in. By 1964 there would be 1,037,575 public school students in 860 schools. Of these pupils, 440,000 represented minorities. In Manhattan, alone, 77 percent of the students were nonwhite.[13] Two years later, in 1966, nonwhite students exceeded half of all enrollments.[14] Full integration, therefore, was becoming an impossibility, simply because there was a consistently dwindling number of white pupils who could have potentially provided racial balance in the schools. Nevertheless, during Donovan's time on the board, civil rights groups ignored the reality of these statistics. The board of education, for its part, turned a blind eye to the same evidence and frequently promised to do what it did not have the capacity to accomplish in order to avoid conflict.

The integration efforts of the board actually began some years before Donovan and his colleagues took office. The most notable action was the modification of zoning in 1959. Until that year, students attended school in the neighborhood, or zone, in which they lived. In the modified plan, actually just an experiment involving no more than 302 pupils, black students were permitted to attend underutilized white schools in the borough of Queens. Despite a brief boycott by white parents who kept 971 children home for one day, the experiment was continued.[15] It was followed by a broader, but less successful, open enrollment program that allowed black and Hispanic students to enter certain primarily white schools out of their neighborhood. The expanded program failed because, in practice, minority students for the most part did not leave their neighborhood schools. Ravitch has insightfully theorized that this could have been because "minority parents did not feel as stigmatized by participating in neighborhood institutions as their [civil rights] leaders thought they did, that black parents feared that their children might not be welcome in predominantly white schools, or that many parents might prefer to send their children to school near home."[16]

In 1962, with de facto segregation in the schools continuing, the New York City Commission on Human Rights recommended that black students be bused to white schools and that white students be bused to black schools. The board, however, did not follow the commission's advice for fear of creating greater conflict. Instead, they instituted one-way busing, that is, transporting black children, on a voluntary basis, into predominantly white schools while allowing white students to remain in their neighborhood facilities. It was a plan that would not satisfy any group for long. The *New York Times*, in an editorial in May 1963, said that busing black children would still result in their feeling as outsiders and suggested, in the alternative, that new schools be built on neighborhood borders in order to provide "a natural bridge between the races."[17] Civil rights groups, on the other hand, wanted forced transfers of both white and black students and a specific timetable for full integration, and the dynamic Brooklyn minister, Milton A. Galamison,[18] began calling for a citywide boycott of the schools by minority students toward those ends.

On August 23, the board of education, through the superintendent of schools, Calvin Gross, submitted its "Plan for Integration" to the state commissioner of education in Albany. The board's plan included permitting students in de facto segregated schools to transfer to other schools of their own choosing; adding zoning changes to increase integration; recruiting additional black and Puerto Rican teachers; providing more frequent dialogue with the community; and including texts that portrayed the societal contributions of minorities. It also suggested the possibility of pairing, that is, linking two ethnically distinct schools, which were located in close proximity to each other, and transferring certain grades between them with the result producing a better racial balance in both. However, the board refused to compel white students to transfer to primarily black schools.[19] Four days after the release of the "Plan for Integration," Superintendent Gross, board president Rubin, and members Rose Shapiro and Aaron Brown met with a number of civil rights leaders including the Reverend Milton A. Galamison, Elaine Bibauld of the Congress of Racial Equality (CORE), June Shagaloff of the National Association for the Advancement of Colored People (NAACP) and Edward Lewis of the Urban League of Greater New York. Stanley H. Lowell, chair of the City Commission on Human Rights, mediated the session. Essentially, the board agreed to provide a precise, school-by-school timetable for integration. It also agreed to establish a standing committee, to include civil rights groups, for the purpose of reviewing progress toward integration. Lowell later announced agreement by all parties. Galamison, however, would not yet agree to call off his planned boycott.[20]

Although Commissioner Allen described the integration plan as "an imaginative and constructive program of action,"[21] neither extreme whites nor blacks accepted it. Civil rights groups deemed it insufficient. Their spokesperson, Rev. Galamison, inspired by Dr. Martin Luther King Jr.'s March on Washington on August 28, called for a boycott of the schools in September. White parents, on the other hand, saw the board's plan as excessive because they feared the loss of neighborhood schools and were adamantly opposed to the forced transfers of their children into schools in ghettos. In fact, they had already boycotted schools twice, keeping 7,000 pupils out for a day in March in Brooklyn, and another 3,600 out for a day in Queens in June.[22] Local white groups organized into a citywide Parents and Taxpayers Coordinating Council (PAT) that filed suit in court to halt the zoning of schools for the purpose of racial integration.[23] A lower court found in favor of the group on September 6, 1963.

In addition to the threatened boycott by civil rights groups scheduled for the opening day of school, the United Federation of Teachers also called for a boycott beginning at the same time, September 9. They were not motivated by the integration issue, but rather by the desire to increase salaries. The board warned the UFT against striking and, as opposed to their inaction in the teachers' earlier boycotts, they indicated that the Condin-Wadlin Act, with its attendant penalties, would be invoked this time. Donovan, Garrison, and Brown were then appointed as a committee to study the implementation of legal sanctions. Ultimately, the teachers did not strike, and the civil rights boycott was called off after intervention by the City Commission on Human Rights.

The new school year opened peacefully in the city, but elsewhere around the nation a number of acts of racial hatred occurred. Earlier in the year, for example, Medgar Evers, a young civil rights leader, was murdered in his driveway in Jackson, Mississippi, by members of the Ku Klux Klan at midnight on June 11, 1963. Three months later, on September 15, the Sixteenth Street Baptist Church was dynamited in Birmingham, Alabama. Four young black girls were killed.

Two months into the new school year, board of education president Max Rubin announced his intention to retire for health reasons, as of December 10. Vice-president Donovan succeeded him in an acting capacity and was officially voted into office by his colleagues several days later. On his first day in office, Donovan issued a statement that reflected the philosophy that he would follow to the end of his service on the board. Briefly, he indicated that the school system would move "steadily and surely" toward meaningful integration, which he termed the system's number one educational problem.[24] He said, however, that he would not "yield to every pressure group and go to ends which are both impractical and self-defeating as well as educationally unsound."[25] He was also opposed to long-distance, forced busing. "To order a child to attend school far from his own home solely on the grounds of his race, creed or color is alien to our way of life." Donovan favored the neighborhood concept, but only to a degree. "Basically, in the elementary schools, I think that the concept of the neighborhood school is sound educationally," he said. "However, this follows only if you have a fine neighborhood school. Therefore, at the same time we are permitting parents to participate in the open-enrollment program and extensions of it, we are trying to raise the standards of schools in areas which desperately need improvement. We hope to make available to the least privileged child in the city the finest public education that can be provided in a free society."[26]

Several days before Donovan's statement, the board and the UFT met to discuss recruiting more black and Puerto Rican teachers and for improving their promotional opportunities. The board also started a special tutoring program for 250,000 black and Puerto Rican students as part of a voluntary after-school program to enhance the pupils' educational success. On December 11, the board appointed three consultants on integration.[27] They also approved an increase in the number of black and Puerto Rican supervisors together with educational seminars to prepare them for promotional examinations. Finally, Jacob Landers, the coordinator of the Higher Horizons Program,[28] was named to the newly created position of assistant superintendent in charge of integration. Five days later, still dissatisfied, Rev. Galamison attempted to stage a sit-in in the offices of the board of education.

Annoyed at the progress described in an interim report of the board several days earlier, 1,100 protestors marched around 110 Livingston Street in Brooklyn on December 16. Galamison, two other ministers and eleven supporters went into the building and attempted a sit-in in Gross' office on the tenth floor. Eleven other demonstrators went to Donovan's office on the floor below. While the first group was arrested peacefully and without incident, those in Donovan's office had to be carried out. All were charged with misdemeanor offenses.[29]

Despite the integration initiatives of the board of education, but perhaps in light of the new president's position supporting measured progress and neighborhood schools while opposing forced transfers, Galamison indicated that the boycott of the schools was on again and set for February 3, 1964, the opening day of the new term. According to the civil rights leader, "anyone who talks about integration and is against busing is not serious about the matter."[30] Donovan, in turn, was equally upset over the fact that Galamison was not offering what the board president believed would be sound alternatives to the board's plans. "You simply cannot get from these people," Donovan said, "a constructive, practical plan . . . You simply cannot put one million children on wheels and send them all over the city of New York."[31] The integration conflict then began to boil, and Donovan was in the center of the action.

Donovan had few vocal supporters at this time. However, he did receive a letter of encouragement in December from Theodore H. White, author of *The Making of a President*. White said, in part:

> Sometimes a man like you feels alone. I can assure you—with whatever authority twenty-five years of journalism and political reporting give me—that you are not alone. You speak the majority opinion—the liberal, reasonable, decent majority opinion. If you, in your position let yourself be pushed by the dogmas of goodwilled people who blindly style themselves "liberal," then this entire city may be pushed to chaos . . . So be firm—because you are right.[32]

To which Donovan replied, "While recognizing the explosively emotional factors in the current Negro Revolution, I continue to believe that in the long run logic and common sense will prevail. Meanwhile, extraordinary patience is required on the part of many."[33]

Not yet convinced that the school boycott would actually take place, Donovan nevertheless took steps to avoid it. On January 9, 1964, at board headquarters, he let it be known that the interim plan on integration that schools' superintendent Calvin Gross released in the previous month fell far short of illustrating the board of education's commitment in that area. He indicated that the board was preparing its own plan on integration that would "leave no doubt as to what the system intends to do to promote integration and improved education."[34] While Donovan was announcing that he was going to meet with numerous civil rights organizations during the following week, three hundred demonstrators, sponsored by PAT, paraded outside the Livingston Street headquarters chanting "Neighborhood schools for neighborhood children" in protest against changing school zones "on the basis of color."[35] That same day, Roy Wilkins, executive secretary of the NAACP, came out in support of Galamison's boycott.

On January 13 Donovan met with representatives of thirty-six civil rights and civic (white) organizations and took comments on Gross's earlier plan. He announced that a new plan, the first to be drafted by the board itself, would be ready by February 1. And in obvious recognition of one of the main objectives of the rights groups, he said that the plan would include a "specific timetable for every specific item where it is possible."[36] He also released a copy of a letter he had recently written to Roy Wilkins and other civil rights leaders to correct misunderstandings that they might have had concerning his position on integration. "I can assure you," he wrote, "that every effort is being made in good faith and with a sense of urgency to take every possible step to solve the integration problem now, with due regard to the rights of all children in the City of New York."[37]

Rev. Galamison's response to Donovan's proposed plan was not antagonistic. He said he was willing to wait and see it before commenting. However, almost immediately after saying that, he and an organization known as the Harlem Parents Committee met with twenty Harlem ministers and obtained the religious leaders' support for the upcoming boycott. In an interview on WOR–TV on January 15, Donovan denounced the boycott and attacked Galamison: "The grave danger here has been that the responsible leaders, I think, are having their leadership threatened by some irresponsible publicity seekers."[38]

Nevertheless, still trying to avoid the approaching boycott, Donovan met with thirty citywide civic organizations and twenty-five local school board representatives on the twentieth. Six days later, he joined with Rev. Galamison as a panelist at a conference of the Bedford-Stuyvesant Registration Crusade in Brooklyn. It was the first time that the two had met, and it was reported that "their encounter . . . was restrainedly cordial."[39] At that meeting, Donovan told the mostly black audience of three hundred that the forthcoming plan would encompass "the principles of racial integration announced recently by the New York City Board of Education." Rev. Galamison, in his turn, replied, "We are not boycotting principles, we are boycotting existing segregation in the schools."[40] The audience's loud applause following the civil rights leader's talk reflected strong community support for action against the schools. Three days later the board issued its "Plan for Better Education through Integration." That same night, on WABC–TV, Donovan discussed the new proposal.[41]

In substance, the "Plan for Better Education through Integration" primarily called for (1) bringing racial balance to thirty of the city's 165 schools that were more than 90 percent black and Puerto Rican; (2) extending time in school to a full day; (3) "pairing" twenty schools such that students would attend one school for grades one to three and the paired school for grades four to six (the paired schools, located in different ethnic neighborhoods, would not be more than 1.5 miles apart and students would not have to travel more than thirty minutes from their homes); (4) zoning changes for junior and senior high schools that would shift some students, both white and minority, to schools they would not normally attend, thus racially balancing nearly one-third of these schools; (5) closing Girls High School; and (6) possibly extending zoning changes to other high schools. The plan also specified the elimination of standardized intelligence testing, reduction in class size, improvement of reading and language arts curricula, enhancement of programs to reduce the dropout rate, better recruitment and advancement programs for black and Puerto Rican teachers and supervisors, more equitable distribution of experienced teachers, more guidance and clinical services, utilization of more text books that covered contributions to society by minority group members and the study of "educational parks," i.e., facilities that contained all levels of schooling through high school at one site with all related support services. The enactment of the plan would begin with the new school year in September and take three years to be fully implemented.

Immediately following the release of the "Plan for Better Education through Integration," Rev. Galamison, as chair and spokesperson for the citywide Committee for Integrated Schools, rejected the proposal. Speaking for the NAACP, CORE, the Harlem Parents Committee, and the Parents Workshop for Equality, he said, "We are in full agreement that the proposals completely fail to provide for substantial and meaningful school desegregation throughout the city."[42] In addition, the Urban League of Greater New York switched at this time from nonsupport to full support for the boycott. A hastily called meeting among the board and civil rights leaders on January 31 failed to change circumstances. The emotional pressure on Donovan was also heightened. On this same day, January 31, an extremist wrote to him, "The only time whites will understand and correct the integration problem is 'when blood runs in the streets.' You have my personal assurance that yours will be the first to be spilled."[43]

Bayard Rustin, the boycott's chief organizer, said, "There are no means by which this boycott could be stopped, and to put it quite crudely, I think if the Negro leaders did decide to call it off, the Negro people would still go into the streets."[44] On the eve of the boycott, the board urged all teachers to report for work the next day and encouraged parents to send their children to school. And in an evening television program, "Page One" on WABC–TV, Donovan debated the national director of CORE, James Farmer. Rev. Galamison had said earlier that the boycott would be followed by other protests and warned that a protracted boycott might be called if the school system did not devise an appropriate plan, meaning full racial balance in all schools. Donovan used the television forum to respond, calling the boycott a "lawless course of action" and putting Rev. Galamison on notice, saying that he would do all in his power to hold the civil rights leader " 'personally and criminally responsible' if any child, Negro or white, were injured during the boycott. [Donovan] charged that the Negro leader, by repeatedly referring to the possibility of violence, had conducted a 'campaign of intimidation' to keep pupils at home."[45]

On February 3, the boycott took place. Although Donovan called it a "fizzle,"[46] it was actually a significant success. Nearly 45 percent, 464,361 students out of a total enrollment of 1,037,757, did not attend classes. Of the number of pupils absent, about 25 percent were Puerto Rican. Many teachers too participated in the boycott. Of 43,865 on staff, 3,537 were absent.[47] In addition to pickets at 300 of the city's 860 schools, 3,500 individuals, mostly children, demonstrated at the board's headquarters on Livingston Street. The marchers and pickets were orderly and peaceful throughout the day. Demonstrators on Livingston Street demanded instant integration and the removal of Donovan, while pickets at the various schools chanted "Jim Crow must go" and "We shall overcome."[48]

Immediately following the boycott, the board dug in. It refused, for example, to meet with representatives of the civil rights groups at a meeting called by Stanley H. Lowell, the chairperson of the City Commission on Human Rights. Donovan, in Connecticut on February 4 addressing an insurance group, said that any teachers who participated in the boycott would lose a day's wage. "We don't pay people to march around buildings," he said.[49] He also added that the teachers' actions "would be taken into consideration" when the time came for promotions.[50]

Criticism of Donovan began to emerge with some vigor. The UFT immediately described his statement on the promotional considerations for teachers as akin to a form of blacklisting. Donovan eventually backed off, but said that teachers would still not be paid for failing to work on the day of the boycott. Rev. Galamison, Harlem congressman Adam Clayton Powell Jr., and Eugene T. Reed, New York State president of the NAACP, continued to call for his removal.[51] Even the board felt internal strains based on their president's extemporaneous utterances without prior consultation with fellow members. The *New York Times,* in an editorial on February 10, declared, "We cannot afford the luxury of tolerating indefinitely in the crucially important presidency of the board a man, no matter how good his intentions, who is simply not right for the job."[52] Several days later, it clarified its position saying essentially that, in its opinion Donovan could remain on the board, just not seek the presidency again in the upcoming board election in May.[53] Having drawn some community fire for its original statements, the *New York Times* also printed letters of support for Donovan in the later issue including ones from Cornelius W. Wickersham Jr., a prominent New York attorney, Chester Brisky and Stuart C. Lucey, president of the Vocational High School Principals Association.[54]

The after-effects of the boycott notwithstanding, Donovan traveled to Albany on February 12 to address a joint hearing of the State Finance Committee and the assembly's Ways and Means Committee at Chancellor's Hall. At that time he requested that a constitutional convention be called for the first time in twenty-five years, to explore better ways to assist education through financing.[55]

Meanwhile, Rev. Galamison, elated with the results of the first boycott, called for a second at some time between March 9 and April 17. It was his hope, he said, to "penalize the Board of Education economically" by having a large number of students absent during a period when state aid was calculated based on attendance.[56] His intent to financially disrupt the educational system was the primary cause of a rift among the city's civil rights groups. The thirteen local city branches of the NAACP immediately halted their participation in Galamison's organization, the Citywide Committee for Integrated Schools. In apparent reaction to the loss of support, Galamison modified his call for a second boycott by suggesting that it was only a possibility, rather than a definite plan. Instead, he said that his three remaining groups in the Citywide Committee would support and participate in a "silent prayer march" on both city hall and the board of education headquarters on Sunday, March 1. It was an event planned previously by the newly formed National Association for Puerto Rican Rights. Galamison also said that he and the Urban League were each going to develop integration plans to be submitted to the board of education. After receiving the board's response, he and his remaining groups would decide on whether or not to continue with the second boycott. The Urban League, however, while still a part of the Citywide Committee, announced in late February that it would not support a boycott that hurt state aid to education. They also did not support the removal of Donovan although they found that some of his remarks were intemperate.

As Rev. Galamison was setting the date for a new boycott, March 16, the national leadership of CORE joined with others in refusing to support it. They actually called for a new organization for integration to replace Galamison's. The Brooklyn minister was now left with only two groups, his own, the Parents Workshop for Equality, and the Harlem Parents Committee.[57] Meanwhile, on March 1, the "silent prayer march" of the National Association for Puerto Rican Civil Rights took place without incident. Eighteen hundred marchers walked silently across the Brooklyn Bridge from Manhattan to board headquarters on Livingston Street. Their goals were twofold: an increase in the number of Puerto Rican teachers and the appointment of a Hispanic on the board of education. Since it was a Sunday, there were no officials at headquarters, only police who ringed the building.[58]

In opposition to another boycott, as well as to forced transfers, a white response was also growing at this time. On February 17, Assemblyman Lucio F. Russo Jr., a Republican from Staten Island, introduced legislation in the state that would prohibit the forced transfer of pupils to promote racial balance.[59] Dr. John H Fischer, president of Columbia University's Teachers College said in a talk that boycotts undermined "the child's respect for the very school which is his surest hope of attaining equal opportunity."[60] And in his strongest statement to date, Dr. James E. Allen, the state's commissioner of education said that "a boycott of the schools is against the law and completely irresponsible."[61] The Parents and Taxpayers Coordinating Council planned a protest march around the board of education headquarters on March 12. A spokesperson for the organization and its lead counsel, Frederick M. Reuss, berated Commissioner Allen and Stanley H. Lowell for being in opposition to the neighborhood school. He also charged that Donovan was inexperienced in educational matters and presented a "disturbing" attitude on involuntary transfers.[62] A rally involving five hundred parents at a Brooklyn public school on March 8 encouraged the planned protest march, and several elected officials, a state senator, an assemblyman, and two city council members announced that they would participate in the demonstration. Donovan, meanwhile, had gone to Boys High School in the Bedford-Stuyvesant area of Brooklyn, a virtually all-black neighborhood, to seek support for the board's integration plan. While parent groups were favorably moved, Rev. Galamison's followers jeered Donovan as he spoke. "Do not play into the hands of those who have started 32 law suits to stop our program," Donovan told his audience of 150. "Our plans are only a beginning. What has slowed them has been a great many irresponsible people—your enemies as well as ours."[63]

The march by white parents around the board of education, then over the Brooklyn Bridge to City Hall, took place as planned on the twelfth. Unofficial police estimates put the number of demonstrators at about fifteen thousand of which 70 percent were women. (Two days before the march, the Appellate Division of New York State Supreme Court had upheld the concept of the neighborhood school, but it also noted that the board of education had the authority to rezone schools for the purpose of obtaining racial balance.[64]) During the march, protestors carried placards saying, "Have child—won't travel," a play on the title of a popular television program at the time, and "Princeton Plan in the garbage can," referring to the concept of pairing, which was first attempted in Princeton, New Jersey.[65] For his part, Donovan said that the demonstration would not alter the board's integration plan.[66] Four days later, Galamison's second boycott took place.

The civil rights action of March 16 was less dramatic than the first although Galamison termed it a success. Twenty-six percent (267,459) of the city's students stayed away from classes. Donovan said that he was encouraged by the fact "that the boycott method of expressing a point of view is regarded with markedly diminishing favor."[67] Indeed, most civil rights groups that supported the first boycott did not approve of the second. Nearly all of the predominantly white schools were virtually unaffected as were most primarily Puerto Rican schools.[68] Nevertheless, Rev. Galamison was sufficiently buoyed by the crowd at the board of education headquarters on the day of the boycott that he vowed, "If we have to come down here again, we are going to take this building."[69] In retrospect, however, the use and effectiveness of the boycott diminished and would eventually cease, although white groups would utilize it one more time in the fall, and Galamison would employ it at a limited number of specific schools.

With a strong belief in his board's integration plan and still anxious to share it with the community, Donovan visited a Harlem church in April and presented his "Prayer for the City of New York" as a Sunday sermon. Speaking at the Church of St. Thomas the Apostle to about three hundred congregants, he said:

> Today I come to ask you, as fellow Christians, to join with me in a prayer for the future of the great City of New York. Ours is a community which has prided itself for generations on an approach to social problems which

should merit the approbation of all decent, liberal, responsible people of good will, regardless of race, creed or color. In New York City, for generations, we have attempted to afford all children without discrimination the opportunity to obtain a free public education through elementary and secondary schools, as well as college. We are a community never self-satisfied; we are our own worst critics. We do not deny our shortcomings, but our history does show a determined effort to overcome them . . .[70]

While the primary problem of all minorities today is the lack of fair opportunity in employment and housing, it would be cowardly for our educational system to avoid its responsibilities by doing nothing until the problems in those two primary areas were first eradicated. Your Board of Education, serving you without compensation, has refused to take no action.[71]

He then presented the highlights of the board's efforts and concluded with a recitation of a prayer of St. Francis of Assisi. Outside the church, one hundred members of the Rev. Galamison's Harlem Parents Committee picketed with chants of "Jim Crow must go—Donovan must go." Inside, however, the congregants appreciated his presence and his words.[72]

On the following day, schools' superintendent Calvin Gross met for the first of several sessions with twenty civil rights leaders including James Farmer, Roy Wilkins, and Rev. Galamison. The purpose of the meeting, called by Gross without the board's awareness, was to discuss unresolved issues arising from the board's integration plan. That plan's final form was to have been released on the day of the second boycott, but it was withheld instead, in favor of sending it to Dr. Allen for comment.[73]

In their discussions with Gross, civil rights groups demanded a crash program in the education of minorities, centering on improvements in local schools, but with less emphasis on immediate integration. Based on the modified position of the rights representatives, Gross gradually started backing away from school pairings. It marked the beginning of a split with the board that ultimately led to Gross's dismissal. Meanwhile, Donovan reserved comment and waited for the receipt of the commissioner of education's report that was due soon. It was released on May 12 and was an extremely critical and contradictory document, standing in marked contrast to Dr. Allen's earlier, laudatory evaluation of the school system's integration plan.

Allen's report said bluntly, "We must conclude that nothing undertaken by the New York City Board of Education since 1954 and nothing proposed since 1963 has contributed or will contribute in any meaningful degree to desegregating the public schools of the city."[74] It criticized the board's school pairing plan, noting that of twenty-one anticipated, only four were to be put into effect in the forthcoming September session; it criticized the zoning changes that were devised; and it even suggested that the board of education could somehow alter the prediction that by 1980 minority students would constitute nearly 75 percent of the system's enrollment. Then, in contrast to its initial criticism, the report admitted that total desegregation was "simply not attainable in the foreseeable future."[75] It also supported the neighborhood school for the lower grades and opposed long-distance busing. The report concluded with several new—and expensive—recommendations concerning the structure of the educational system.

Under the proposed restructuring, the current elementary schools (kindergarten to fifth grade), junior high schools (sixth to ninth grades) and high schools (tenth to twelfth grades) were to be changed to primary units (pre-kindergarten to fourth grade), middle schools (fifth to eighth grades) and high schools (ninth to twelfth grades). The primary schools were to remain as neighborhood schools but would feed the middle schools in such a manner that these latter facilities would be better integrated. Four-year high schools were to be located outside of ghetto areas entirely and would be fed by students from around the city. The plan also recommended some educational complexes or "parks" in which primary and middle schools would be located in the same cluster of buildings.

Civil rights groups, although they disliked the prediction of never eliminating segregation entirely, favored the Allen report. In fact, Rev. Galamison called it "a giant step in the right direction," and Frederick Jones of the NAACP referred to it as "a breath of fresh air."[76] White parents, on the other hand, vowed to oppose the elimination of the neighborhood concept for their children in junior high schools. Donovan, for his part, was willing to try to implement additional changes. He said, at a board meeting on May 12, "The comprehensive recommendations of the report, including some new concepts, are in line with the board's enunciated policy on school integration—high quality education and improved ethnic distribution. The urgency of the need for school integration is such that we must adopt some further action in time for the next school year."[77] On this same day, Donovan was reelected president by a unanimous vote of the board of education. Lloyd K. Garrison was similarly re-elected vice-president. Before the meeting ended, the board also approved the acceptance of a grant to fund a study of the role of educational parks in fostering integration.[78]

In Donovan's estimation, the implementation of Commissioner Allen's plan would require several hundred million dollars. Thus he decided to seek federal and state funds. Having already spoken to Sargent Shriver, director of the Office of Economic Opportunity, Donovan announced that he intended to ask Governor Rockefeller, again, to call a special session of the legislature. "If the Governor can call a special session of the Legislature to lower the price of whiskey by $1, then he certainly should be able to call a special session to appropriate extra funds for education."[79]

Meanwhile, Bayard Rustin, the organizer of the March on Washington in 1963 and the first school boycott in New York City in February 1964, led a demonstration on May 18 in front of city hall in Manhattan. His purpose was twofold: to commemorate the tenth anniversary of the Supreme Court's decision in *Brown v. Board of Education of Topeka, Kansas*[80] and to encourage support for the Allen Plan, as it became known. Attendance was estimated at only 4,000 to 5,500, far short of the organizer's goal. Nevertheless, James Farmer of CORE, speaking to the throng, warned "that unless the Allen committee plan was implemented by September there would be 'not only a long hot summer, but a longer and hotter fall.'"[81] He also threatened many "study-ins," an action in which black students would be brought to white schools for the purpose of sitting alongside white pupils and studying with them. In fact, twenty-six black students did just that on the day of the demonstration at city hall. They were very well received by their white counterparts, and the unexpected study-in turned out to be a pleasurable event for all of the students.[82]

Donovan was not in the city on the eighteenth for Rustin's demonstration. He and Mary had sailed on a combination business and pleasure trip to Europe several days earlier and did not return until June 2. Before he left, however, he wrote, in a single article, a review of five recently published books on integration matters.[83] Within Donovan's comments, he credited Malcolm X with identifying white supremacy as what Donovan believed was the true issue in African American literature at the time. He also praised the eloquent advocacy of Dr. Martin Luther King for nonviolent direct action. He took issue, however, with one writer's position that the government should not impose integration in public schools because it actually stemmed from segregated housing. "Both such areas," Donovan wrote, "must be attacked and will be most effectively as soon as urban whites realize that they must stop running. However, is this [segregated housing] justification for taking no steps in the school system to lessen harmful tensions and to provide broader educational horizons for the children? . . . It is unfair to the most fortunate white child not to educate him to cope with the multi-racial power world of tomorrow."[84]

On the day after Donovan returned from his European cruise, the board of education met with representatives of civil rights groups together with the Parents and Taxpayers Coordinating Council. It was an extremely heated, seven-hour session. Prompting the debate was the board's new plan entitled "Blueprint for Further Action Toward Quality Integrated Education."[85] It was so heated that, at one point, Donovan lost his temper and had to give the chair to Garrison for half an hour. By this time, his wife, Mary, had asked him on numerous occasions for the past five months to resign from the board for his own health. It would be another year before he did so.

Under the "Blueprint," sixth graders in forty-four elementary schools would be transferred to ten junior high schools. Ninth graders in those junior highs would be assigned to already racially balanced high schools. Eight elementary schools would be paired and the junior high schools rezoned to achieve a better racial balance. In all, forty-thousand students would be involved.[86] PAT groups remained opposed to any forced transfers of white students. Civil rights groups, on the other hand, saw the plan as diluting the Allen committee's recommendations. Rev. Galamison called it "a colossal deception" and announced that he was proceeding with a "permanent school boycott" in the fall.[87] By the end of the day, despite community opposition, the board voted unanimously to institute the "Blueprint."

Nine days later, Donovan was rushed to St. Luke's Hospital from his home. He was diagnosed with having angina pectoris, a serious heart condition, but short of an attack. He was released from the hospital on July 13 to continue his convalescence at home.

Meanwhile, in order to reach an accord, at least with civil rights groups, school representatives met on five separate occasions between June 4 and June 15 with the New York Urban League, the NAACP, CORE, the Harlem Parents Committee, the Citywide Committee for Integrated Schools, EQUAL (a white organization that was supportive of integration), and the Conference for Integrated Quality Education (representing church, union and community groups).[88] Some of the objectionable features of the board's plan, particularly involving sixth-graders, were modified. Instead of transferring to junior high schools that were largely segregated, the sixth-grade pupils would attend integrated or white elementary schools.[89] As recommended by the Allen Plan, additional educational parks would be established and ready for the fall 1965 term. Following this series of meetings, the civil rights groups altered their stance and accepted the board's Blueprint for Further Action. The two major white organizations, PAT and the Joint Council for Better Education, did not. While some portions of it were acceptable, they continued to oppose forced transfers and busing and vowed to boycott at the start of the school year.

The summer of 1964 was not a good one, not for Donovan who was hospitalized, not for the nation and certainly not for New York City. In Philadelphia, Mississippi, three civil rights workers, Mickey Schwerner, Andy Goodman, and James Chaney were delivered by a local deputy sheriff to a country field where they were murdered by the KKK. In New York City on July 16, a police officer shot and killed a fifteen-year-old black youth. Although the officer was later exonerated, the incident touched off a riot in Harlem on the night of the eighteenth, spreading soon to the Bedford-Stuyvesant area of Brooklyn. One Harlem demonstrator, William Epton, gave a street corner speech that included the now infamous call of "Burn, Baby, Burn." The riot was short-lived, but it was bloody and tragic. One person was killed, numerous individuals were injured, buildings were burned and stores were looted.

On August 10, one month after his release from the hospital, Donovan was back doing board business. At that time, he directed that each school in Harlem and Bedford-Stuyvesant be identified as inferior, average, or superior. If it was characterized as inferior, he demanded to know what was being done to correct it. He also directed that it be found out why a 95 percent black Bedford-Stuyvesant school refused to be paired with a white school.[90]

Meanwhile, PAT and the Joint Council for Better Education were gathering momentum for a white boycott of the schools when classes resumed in the fall.[91] The two organizations claimed a combined strength of 900,000 members. Donovan denounced the parents' action saying that it would not deter the board from its plans for racial balancing. "This is not a question of how big a mob you can get out to support your point of view. It's a question of what is right, decent and in the best interests of all the children. The school boycott weapon, using children as pawns, is indefensible in a liberal community such as New York. Whether used by a minority or majority, a school boycott may induce great numbers of youngsters to take a holiday from school but it is a tragic failure in terms of achieving progress."[92]

The Joint Council asked Donovan to intervene on the night before the boycott, but he refused. "The policy of the board has been established, and any idea that we are going to take steps based on how many children, either white or Negro, are kept out of schools is ridiculous."[93] Civil rights groups never planned to participate in the forthcoming boycott calling it a problem for white parents. Frederick D. Jones, representing the New York City chapters of the NAACP said, "I have been informed that PAT does not represent the white community, but only a frightened minority within it. The boycott will show where the white community stands."[94] Opposing the boycott as well were the UFT, the 400,000-member United Parents Association and EQUAL.

On Monday, September 14, the schools opened for the new term and the integration plan of the board was in place. It included four paired schools, rezoning, and both compulsory and voluntary transfers of students.[95] In practice, it only affected 13,000 students. On this same day, 275,638 pupils, nearly all of whom were white, did not attend school, 175,000 more than the number usually absent.[96] The second day of the boycott revealed a lessening of the number of absentees, down to 233,306.[97] The boycott was only scheduled to last two days, but at the insistence of PAT, several hundred students continued it, primarily at the paired schools.[98]

In the late afternoon of the boycott's first day, Donovan issued a press release. He said, in part:

> This new weapon of child boycott is not only reprehensible, it is at a minimum a conspiracy to disrupt the public education system and, at maximum, a conspiracy to destroy it. We will not stand idly by and see children urged to disobey the law and follow a course of action which foments racial hatreds and risks violence in the city streets.
>
> I am communicating with the District Attorney of each county to inform him of the facts and to determine whether criminal violations of the law have been committed or are threatened. We cannot wait for the first tragic incident. The school boycott must be outlawed as a weapon in controversies over educational matters regardless of its use by a minority or a majority.[99]

One week later, in a meeting with the district attorneys or assistants from the five boroughs of the city, Donovan and the prosecutors reached an agreement to prosecute future organizers of school boycotts.[100] A test came quickly in October. When sixty-five parents forced their way into a Queens elementary school protesting pairing, Superintendent Gross ordered their arrests. In support of Gross's decision, Donovan said, "There are those who criticize Dr. Gross and the Board for not doing enough and those who criticize us for doing too much. There are some who will not give the plan a fair chance."[101] There were eleven similar cases of arrests of parents at this time.[102]

Donovan was not only subject to criticism by a variety of community groups during demonstrations and by the press in editorials, but also through court filings, as well. At the end of 1964, in fact, there were twenty-three lawsuits pending against him as president of the board of education, generally regarding the issue of busing. However, judges were beginning to rule, with favorable findings for the board. The case of *In the Matter of the Application of Walter Van Blerkom v. James B. Donovan*[103] was typical. In this instance, the board had decided to rezone Public School 6 in Manhattan between Fifth and Lexington Avenues from Sixty-third to Ninety-fourth Streets to achieve a fixed racial quota, thus preventing children from attending their neighborhood school. The petition was dismissed originally and on appeal. The State Court of Appeals noted in its decision, "It is within the province of the board to conclude that racial imbalance is harmful to education, and to draw school zones in order to effectuate a better racial balance in the school system."[104]

Before the year 1964 ended, the board published its "Five Year Crash Program for Quality Education: An Attack on Unemployment and Poverty Through Improved Educational Opportunity." The plan would restore at least 10 percent of teachers assigned outside of class to inside; halt supervisory appointments outside of the schools themselves; and defer filling vacant administrative and clerical positions. It would also promote quality integrated education, provide an extension of kindergarten and pre-kindergarten classes, reduce class size on all levels, provide teachers for special and remedial subjects and increase the number of textbooks.

The plan also established priorities: 1) Every child would receive a full day of schooling (48,000 did not because of a lack of facilities); 2) kindergarten classes would provide classes for all who apply (3,000 were now turned away; 2,100 had been sent outside their own neighborhoods); 3) pre-kindergarten for three and four year olds would be extended to 7,000 more (of 30,000 estimated to be eligible); 4) class size would be reduced; and 5) the number of teachers was to be increased.

Other needs that were addressed included a provision for more teachers and aides in transitional areas; an increase in repairs and maintenance; an expansion of the "More Effective Schools" program (twenty-two students per class) primarily for minority and low-income groups; and the development of a better data processing system.

Donovan sent the proposed crash program to all federal and state legislators representing New York. He also sent a copy to Sergeant Shriver, the director of the federal Office of Economic Opportunity. Included with the document was a request to President Johnson for $1.5 billion to be made available to the board of education over the next five years.[105] Shriver denied the request fairly quickly saying, "the total amount requested . . . is roughly the same amount of money authorized for all federal aid to education in 1964–1965." He did, however, agree that the needs of New York City were pressing.[106] In December 1964, Mayor Wagner also cautioned Donovan not to add new programs noting that the general fund was expected to be short because the World's Fair and the city's special income tax reduction did not generate the volume of business that had been anticipated.[107] Nevertheless, Donovan continued to seek more school aid throughout the balance of his term as president. On March 16, 1965, for example, he and other board members met in Albany at Keeler's Restaurant with leaders of the New York State Legislature including the chairs of the committees on Education, Ways and Means, Finance and New York City Affairs. The sole topic of discussion was the urgent need for increased state aid for the New York City school system.[108]

The last six months of Donovan's term as president were no less frenetic than those of the past. Rev. Milton Galamison continued with small boycotts, this time aimed at schools for difficult and disruptive students;[109] teachers threatened work actions in opposition to longer school years,[110] but more so for fear of involuntary transfers to ghetto neighborhoods; school bus drivers struck;[111] and Calvin Gross, the superintendent of schools, was asked to resign.

Donovan and the board of education, for their part, developed and published a significant plan that would alter the structure of the school system in a positive way. Entitled "A Statement of Policy on Excellence for New York City Schools," the dramatic statement essentially brought the school system into line with the recommendations of the Allen Plan by the planned abolition of all 138 junior high schools by 1973.[112] These schools, which covered grades seven, eight, and nine, would be replaced by middle schools for grades six, seven, and eight in a manner that provided better racial balance. In addition, high schools were changed to provide instruction for four grades, nine through twelve, with both college preparatory and vocational tracks. Finally, experienced teachers were to be allocated to all schools in an equitable fashion to include facilities in the city's poorer neighborhoods.[113] In a press conference on April 22, Donovan summarized the policy as "a declaration by the board that both quality instruction and integration are essential components of excellence in education. It is possible to conceive of quality instruction without integration or integration without quality instruction, but not of excellence of education without both in this multiracial city at this time."[114]

The NAACP immediately endorsed the statement, as did the Public Education Association and the United Parents Association. The Council for Better Education was opposed because it believed that the board had gone too far in promoting integration. The United Federation of Teachers (UFT) generally favored the new policy although it adamantly opposed the involuntary transfer of experienced teachers to the ghettos.[115] The UFT would strike in a later year for this reason.[116] James E. Allen, the state commissioner of education, was most admiring of the board's new efforts, and he called the statement "a sound and vigorous approach to the problems of education in New York City."[117]

On May 15, 1965, Donovan was reelected president by board of education members in a unanimous vote. He had previously told his colleagues, however, at a meeting before the election that, if he was reelected, it would be with the understanding that it was only to complete some unfinished business and that he would resign effective June 30. He added that his resignation was based on "the pressure of my private law practice and my family obligations."[118] It was clear to Donovan, also, that his potential successor, Lloyd Garrison, was a very competent individual who was well respected by his colleagues and the community and could carry on the work of the board in a professional fashion.[119]

After Donovan announced his retirement, the *New York Times* offered a somewhat backhanded compliment calling it "an act of civic responsibility."[120] The *New York Herald Tribune* was more positive saying, "Of course, Mr. Donovan managed to irk practically everybody, including his fellow board members at one time or another. But he was earnest and dedicated. And plain speech for public benefit should be appreciated. The city gets little enough blunt talk from its leaders."[121] But it was C. B. Powell, editor of New York City's *Amsterdam News*, the voice of many blacks in the city, who was the most laudatory in summing up Donovan's presidency:

> This week a tough iron-jawed Irishman who says what he means and means what he says will step down from the hot tin roof which the City of New York calls chairman of the Board of Education. We expect to hear a lot more of him in the future and we wish him well in all of his undertakings. For James Donovan was a pillar of strength for the Board of Education when sheer strength was the most important thing that was needed. Anyone who recalls the great first and second school boycotts in this city must now realize that Jim Donovan was a lion in the fight. Shackled with internal bickering and a school superintendent who at times didn't seem to know which end was up, and faced with a morally correct resourceful

adversary in the person of the Rev. Milton Galamison and hundreds of thousands of irate parents, Jim Donovan waded into the fray on the side of the children of the City of New York. We fought him at times and we certainly know that at times the odds were heavily against him. But he asked for no odds for himself and the absence of strife which we find in our schools today testifies to the tenacity and determination of Jim Donovan to provide a tranquility in which our children could be educated.

He fought the fight and he kept faith with the children of New York City. And, as he rides off to other service, he is a warrior, tall in the saddle. Good luck, Jim.[122]

11

Driving Mr. Donovan:
A Man Called Doctor Taylor

In 1943, Jamaica was still a British crown colony. The world-wide depression had destroyed the banana-based economy and widespread rioting continued on the island, in part because of the depression's lasting effects and in part because of a desire for self-government. The United States, at the same time, was fully involved in World War II, which drained the human resources away from many jobs. Jamaica, a poor country, thus became an ideal source for the inexpensive labor that was required on American farms. And so it was in 1943 that a party of white Americans traveled to Jamaica in search of agricultural laborers. The selection process was fairly simple—if one was strong enough and fit enough, he was chosen. Among those Jamaicans chosen was Aston George Taylor who, with fifty-two other men, was taken by boat to New Orleans and from there by train to Wisconsin. Taylor, as he prefers to be called, had always held the United States in high regard, and he looked forward to a new life in the States. "In school," he wrote in notes of his life, "we learn that USA is best in the world. Nothing about some of people in it. Mabe [sic] if we did hear, told about Jim Crow and discrimination and lynching we would not leave home."[1]

Indeed, Taylor's early experiences on farms in Wisconsin, Michigan, and Florida were replete with incidents of racial hatred and violence and led to his brief return to Jamaica. He reentered the United States in 1946, however, and eventually reached New York City after stays in Florida and Connecticut. Paying fees of up to $100 for temporary jobs, he finally obtained a position as a deliveryman for a Manhattan pharmacy working from 3:00 p.m. to midnight for $36 weekly. Such jobs, however, did not last long. After working for the drugstore, he loaded produce for a year, and later drove a taxi. Eventually, he took a training course in oil burner repair and thought he had finally found more permanent work. Yet, when he learned

188

that race precluded him from entering a union, he left the job and returned to driving a taxi.

When Martin Luther King was organizing his march to Washington, Taylor joined it, but returned to New York immediately after, his antipathy to whites still strong. It was so strong, in fact, that when a friend who worked at the Drug and Chemical Club in lower Manhattan asked him if he wanted a chauffeur's job driving a white lawyer, he adamantly refused twice. "I told him I don't want to go in white people home. I must admit the reason for these excuse because of the hate I develop in me for white people. The third time he asked me to take the job, trying to get rid of him, I said to him to give me the man name and his home phone number. The name was a man who I read about daily when he was President for the Board of Education of NY."[2] But after meeting James Donovan on a Monday and being offered the position to start the following day, Taylor's negative racial feelings began to abate. "My life change when I start to drive JBD," he wrote in his notes. On his first day on the job, he accompanied Donovan to a Cadillac dealership where the attorney traded in his 1965 vehicle for a new 1966 model. Donovan handed Taylor the keys and told him that the car was his to use whenever he wished, as long as he was present and on time when he was needed. During many drives between appointments, Donovan and Taylor had numerous discussions about issues of the day and a strong bond developed between them that lasted until Donovan's death.

On a number of occasions in the mid- to late-1960s, Taylor recalled driving Donovan to meetings in the company of two to three Jewish leaders. One of these men was the president of the Jewish Nazi Victims Organization of America, Moshe Yisrael Sochotchevsky. Because of his interest in the plight of concentration camp survivors, Donovan had become the unpaid general counsel to the organization. On May 9, 1965, he had chaired a memorial assembly at Hunter College to commemorate the twentieth anniversary of the liberation from the German death camps. Participants with Donovan included Mayor Wagner, U.S. ambassador to the Soviet Union Katriel Katz, and Senator Jacob Javits.[3] Eventually, Donovan and the organization were able to persuade the Israeli government to donate land for two housing projects in Tel Aviv for Holocaust survivors living in the United States and Canada who might wish to emigrate to Israel. By 1966, three hundred survivors had applied for the apartments.[4] Although Sochotchevsky wanted the complex to be named after their general counsel,[5] Donovan commented that an Irish surname would hardly fit in Tel Aviv and countered with the suggestion that it be called Reunion City.[6] By 1969, he was still engaged in the design and financing of the project, which had an anticipated completion date in 1973.[7]

In the mid-1960s, Donovan was also active in another international organization, initially known as the Hostages for Peace Foundation. The idea for "peace hostages" originated with Stephen D. James, a New York advertising copywriter, in 1962. He had hoped that such an organization would eventually contribute to the exchange of one million Americans and a similar number of Russians with the goal of reducing the possibility of nuclear war between the two countries through an increase in their mutual understanding. On September 9, 1963, James announced that Donovan and three others were to form the core of negotiators who would eventually go to Geneva in order to develop an agreement with the Russians that would lead to a pilot exchange.[8] At first, Donovan felt that the peace hostage idea was unworkable, but he liked its "emphasis on human values." He said, "If something constructive comes out it's all to the good."[9]

Nearly two years later, the first group of 140 Americans arrived in Moscow for a three-week tour sponsored by the foundation, the name of which had since been changed to the Citizens Exchange Corps, a less threatening title that avoided a reference to hostages. The group included teachers, students, doctors, lawyers, and their spouses and children. Also among the travelers were Stephen James's wife, Denise; Melvin J. Gordon, the chairman of the board of the Sweets Company, manufacturers of Tootsie Rolls; and Thomas Wellington of Donovan's law firm.[10] Donovan, now general counsel to the foundation, had the task of traveling to Moscow at the end of August 1965 in order to negotiate a return trip by Russians to the United States. He arrived in the Soviet capital on August 26.

In his negotiations, Donovan tried to persuade the Russians to form a return delegation that represented a cross-section of the population, but they, at least initially, favored small, specialized groups. The first group to be sent would be composed of machinists.[11] Donovan was not disheartened, however, saying that "From a small beginning we have good reason to hope that this search for mutual understanding will continue to grow . . . A wide variety of Russian organizations—writers, artists, trade unionists—have agreed in principle to our exchange proposal."[12] And, in fact, the idea and the organization have continued to flourish. It is currently known as "CEC International Partners" with headquarters in New York City.[13]

Not all of Donovan's activities following his departure from the board of education were international in scope.[14] Much closer to home, he had requested that the Brooklyn Chamber of Commerce sponsor a project to "substantially increase the number of Little

League Softball and Baseball Teams in the Bedford-Stuyvesant area."[15] And in concert with the talented musician Eubie Blake, he also tried to have jobs created at the dormant Brooklyn Navy Yard for residents of the same community.[16] In another area, Donovan assisted the Federal Defender Program of San Diego, Inc., an organization that provided legal services for indigent defendants in the federal court in the Southern District of California. On February 15, 1967, he was the guest speaker at a fund-raising dinner for the organization at the Hotel del Coronado in San Diego. The nonprofit agency ultimately met its income goal that enabled it to receive matching funds from the Ford Foundation.

Throughout all of his pro bono activities, Donovan also continued the practice of law as a livelihood. One of his more important and far-reaching cases in insurance law involved the Brotherhood of Railroad Trainmen (BRT), which had struck the Long Island Railroad, stopping commuter line operations from July 10 to August 3, 1960. The BRT demanded a reduction of a six-day work schedule to five days, with no reduction in pay. Such a "whipsaw" action, in which a union focuses on a single railroad, could potentially impact subsequent labor negotiations of all other railroads. Workers were entitled to receive strike benefits from a fund to which all railroads were legally required to contribute, while for its part, the railroad covered itself with a Service Interruption Policy (strike insurance). The BRT claimed that strike insurance was illegal and unconstitutional because it provided the railroad with incentive not to settle, suggesting that the railroad could conceivably receive more income from insurance than from the fares of its commuters. Donovan, as lead counsel, won the case for the Long Island Railroad and the insurers, in both the U.S. District Court for the Southern District of New York and in the Court of Appeals for the Second Circuit.[17] When the BRT appealed to the Supreme Court for a writ of certiorari, Donovan argued against it and won again.[18] Essentially, the courts ruled that the critical issue in the case was not the strike insurance policy of the railroad, which was neither illegal nor unconstitutional, but the railroads' good faith in the bargaining process that the courts found to be fair.[19]

By the mid-1960s Donovan had become the principal partner in his firm, Watters and Donovan. Thomas Watters, the senior partner, was of retirement age and was no longer active in the operation of the office. Daniel McNamara, Donovan's actuarial colleague who joined his friend on numerous court cases, had noted Donovan's ability for bringing talented young attorneys into the firm. One of these lawyers was Thomas P. Parry, who was hired as an associate in 1967. Parry described Donovan as a patrician, soft-spoken leader whose quiet suggestions were always understood to be firm directions. Donovan, Parry recalled, was never referred to by first name, but always as "Sir." If anyone ever acted with less decorum than was expected, Donovan was the last person they wanted to learn of it. On occasion, however, unusual things did occur.

Parry recalled a summer's day shortly after he was hired when Donovan was conducting a noon meeting with several guests in a conference room. At the same time, a young associate had decided to take his lunch break on the balcony of the offices. He slipped out of his window, stripped to the waist to bask in the sun, and rested for an hour. When it was time to return to work, he couldn't reopen the window from the outside. His fear had nothing to do with height as he inched from window to window, crouching low to avoid being seen. Reaching Parry's office, he tapped on the window to be let in. None too pleased with his colleague's antics, Parry permitted him to stay, but left quickly to avoid repercussions. Parry remembers that he did not go back to his office for a substantial period, well after the associate had safely dressed and made it to his own workspace.[20]

In addition to his other interests, Donovan also wrote another book at about this time, *Challenges: Reflections of a Lawyer-at-Large*.[21] The work was a compilation of several addresses Donovan had given over the years, providing observations on his experiences in the OSS, at the Nuremberg trial, and with the board of education. He also discussed the necessity for foreign intelligence, the ramifications of defending Rudolf Abel and other unpopular defendants, and his negotiations with Castro, together with an evaluation of the future of Latin American politics. While the book was not as popular as *Strangers on a Bridge*, the reviews were quite positive.[22]

In 1967, Pratt Institute in Brooklyn, a private college with a curriculum of art, design, and architecture, was without a president. A search committee, chaired by Dr. Dwayne Orton, a trustee and the editor of IBM's journal, *Think*, with representatives from the administration, faculty, students, and trustees had sought a candidate for nearly a year. In October 1967, the board of trustees, chaired by Leo J. Pantas, voted to offer the presidency to James Donovan.[23] Donovan accepted the position during a convocation at the college's eightieth Founders Day. Following chairman Pantas's opening remarks and a speech by Mayor Wagner, Donovan, dressed in academic garb, rose to address the attendees. In a brief statement, he said, "Today I pledge to the trustees, officers, faculty, student body and alumni of Pratt that my every effort in the years ahead shall be directed toward the strengthening and enhancement of this college's proud heritage. . . . I shall seek at all times the counsel and support of each and every one of these components of the Pratt community."[24] The next phase of Donovan's career would begin on the following January 1.

Pratt Institute had been founded in 1887 by Charles Pratt (1830–1891), a wealthy New York industrialist and cofounder of the Standard Oil Company. The school began with a class of twelve drawing students, and by the time of Donovan's selection, it had grown to a total student body of 4,689 including 300 foreign students and 200 blacks and Puerto Ricans.[25] Its twenty-acre campus was open and pleasant and situated in the otherwise congested residential community of Clinton Hill in Brooklyn. During the same time that a committee was searching for Pratt's next president, a private company was examining the school under a special commission it had received. The Knight and Gladieux Management Study on "The Future of Pratt Institute" was released shortly before Donovan's selection. It had found that the school was marked by programs of poor quality, an obsolete physical plant, a lack of financial resources, an absence of student government, and a dwindling enrollment. It suggested that the institute merge with a public institution such as the City University of New York or the State University of New York. It was also recommended that the institute relocate to Manhattan.[26]

In the face of the recently released study, Donovan took the first opportunity available to him to assure the campus on several points. In a talk in Memorial Hall on January 10, 1968, he informed the student-teacher assemblage that Pratt Institute would remain private, that it would be refurbished rather than relocated to another part of the city, and that Pratt's reputation both nationally and internationally would be strengthened. Donovan added that he hoped to put an exchange program in place by the end of the year. In view of the fact that a student government, known as the Student Coordinate, had been created two months earlier, after the publication of the negative Knight and Gladieux report, Donovan repeated an earlier assurance. "The Institute," he said, "will make no policy decisions directly affecting the student body without prior consultation with the duly elected student representatives."[27] Far from being fearful of students who voiced their opinions, Donovan encouraged comment. Shortly after his selection as president, for example, he told a reporter for the institute's newspaper, the *Prattler*, in November 1967 that "the only thing that can kill a campus is student apathy."[28]

The ever-present boycotts, strikes, and marches in New York City's public schools during Donovan's tenure with the board of education, had been, for the most part, nonviolent. The college environment was far different.

Students for a Democratic Society (SDS) had been formed in 1960 and was well underway by 1968 in radicalizing many as it grew and spread. As Diane Ravitch has written, "Whether it was called alienation or boredom, would-be political activists found in direct action an opportunity to live what they believed and to give meaning to their comfortable but unchallenging lives."[29] Students at colleges and universities from around the country began to make strong demands on their administrations in a number of areas including having a greater voice in the operation of educational institutions, in creating new curricula and in participating in the selection of professors. They protested the war in Viet Nam and the presence of ROTC units on campuses. Student demonstrations took the form of sit-ins and take-overs of college buildings, often destroying property and rifling confidential documents in the process. Police, when called, were frequently assaulted, not only with words, but also with rocks and other projectiles. If Pratt Institute was to be protected from these destructive elements in the national climate of student unrest, its president would have to be bold. Other college and university leaders often gave in to students' demands to end a demonstration, takeover, or other violence. However, it was later found that such administrative behavior most often fueled further demands and hostilities.[30] Donovan was instinctively aware of the truth of this, but he also believed in listening to students, not just because they were in his charge, but also because they might be correct.[31] His first test came little more than three months into his term as president.

After "four years of stress and confrontation" the architectural school students went on strike on April 4, 1968.[32] Among their concerns were a lack of adequate facilities and programs of quality, infrequent field trips, few intercollegiate cooperative events, little preparation for future employment, and the absence of a visiting critics program. They also called for the resignation of their dean. Students had met with Donovan two days before, and although he was sympathetic to most of their concerns, he refused to fire the dean.

Several other events also tested Donovan's leadership. On the morning of the first day of the architectural students' strike, a number of students attempted to block a Reserve Officer Training Corps (ROTC) inspection. One hundred students set up a picket line in front of the entrance to the ROTC meeting place, but later in the afternoon they withdrew. That same evening, the campus received the tragic word that the Reverend Martin Luther King had been assassinated in Memphis, Tennessee. Members of the Black Student Union immediately asked President Donovan to formally close the campus for a period of mourning, to which he unhesitatingly agreed.

Barely had the campus begun to cope with the death of the courageous civil rights leader when an International Student/Faculty Strike was called for April 26 to take place on campuses around the country, while Pratt's own strike by the architectural students had still to be resolved. Nationally, April 26 was a day of campus talks by teachers and students, some picketing and "guerrilla theater."[33] At Pratt, it was characterized by a paint-in on the main lawn. There were more substantive discussions among the administration, faculty, and students that lasted for three days. As a result, a "New School Committee" was designed to work on institute-wide problems. In addition to Pratt students and faculty, the committee would also consist of outside professionals and a representative from the bordering black community. The committee's formation was ratified by the Faculty Council, and students returned to classes at the end of April.[34]

The presence of military figures on campus, however, was still a sore spot for some students. The April 4 demonstration against the ROTC was actually their second expression of dissatisfaction. In the previous year, on November 22, sixty students protested the presence of recruiters on campus. Thus, in May, after classes resumed, the Student Coordinate called for a vote on the issue of recruiters. With slightly over one-third of the students participating, 560 students voted to close the campus to recruiters, but 825 cast ballots to keep it open.

With the students' return to classes and the favorable vote for recruiters, the campus settled down to complete the spring semester. On Alumni Day that year, Donovan addressed the returning graduates as well as the faculty, students, and alumni in a talk entitled "Stewards of Excellence." He used the opportunity again to support his students:

> Can we categorically condemn the young for refusing to accept a complacent dictatorship over their lives and futures? Surely, as we look about the world we inherited and developed, we should be humble about our having demonstrated any genius in organizing a decent human society on this planet. The young know this and, suspicious of all over 30, believe that they are entitled to a voice in almost every phase of decision-making which affects the future of themselves and the world in which they live. Without saying that their opinions should be determinative, without ab-

dicating the responsibility of the older to share their experience with the young, can we not agree that at least they should have a fair hearing?[35]

But Donovan's openness to the concerns of students had limits as he shared with the attendees:

At the same time, no group of undergraduates on this campus for a relatively few years should pretend to assume final responsibility for deciding policies to be binding long after their graduation upon thousands of successor students.

There shall be proper opportunity for all groups to be heard but ultimate decisions must be made by those entrusted with this task by our charter and the law. Meanwhile no form of violence, or interference with the rights of any responsible student seeking to learn, will be permitted on this campus.[36]

After the semester had ended, Donovan was still trying to find a balance between student concerns and college administrators' responsibilities, and in so doing he wrote to Dr. James E. Allen, the state commissioner of education, in July 1968. In requesting a convention of university leaders to examine the problems associated with student unrest, he stated, "The question now concerning us is how far we can go in delegating the formulation of policy decisions to committees, faculty or independent advisors without violating the responsibilities vested in our board of trustees and our officers."[37]

In that same summer of Donovan's first year, an auxiliary campus was opened at 46 Park Avenue in Manhattan known as Pratt Center. It was also a time when Pratt responded to a request from the neighboring Bedford-Stuyvesant community for assistance with a youth program. Calling it "Campaign Culture," Pratt enlisted forty-five faculty members and student teachers to work with 940 community youths in an on-campus Youth-in-Action project that lasted throughout the summer.

Meanwhile, by 1968, as Donovan's presidency was beginning, his family had grown. Jan was twenty-three and had completed her studies at Marymount and in Lausanne. She was married, and her first child was one year old. John, twenty-two, had been discharged from the Marines after service in Viet Nam where he lost a portion of his hearing as a result of his duties as a machine gunner. He planned to enter Boston University shortly. In 1968, too, Mary Ellen was completing her freshman year at Marymount Junior College in Arlington, Virginia, and Clare, James and Mary's youngest child, was already thirteen. And about this same time, James and Mary, having ceased vacationing at Lake Placid, purchased a summer home in Spring Lake, New Jersey, that would provide a quiet oceanside substitute.

As Donovan saw his work increase with the presidency of Pratt Institute, he realized that it would be beneficial to increase his law firm staff through a merger with another firm. Toward this end, he discussed the matter with his cousin, James J. Donovan, then a partner in Kelly, Donovan, Robinson, and Maloof, a firm located at 70 Pine Street close to his own. Cousin James was fifty-three years old at the time. He had graduated from Fordham College a year after Donovan and obtained his law degree three years later, also from Fordham. He agreed to the merger, and the combined firm was thereafter known for a time as Donovan, Donovan, Maloof and Walsh. Cousin James's firm moved into 161 William Street where the total staff amounted to seven partners and eleven associates.[38]

Donovan was not formally installed as president of Pratt Institute until October 18, 1968, in a special ceremony in the Sculpture Court of the Brooklyn Museum.[39] Before an audience of one thousand, including faculty, students, and two hundred visiting professors, in an address entitled "The Role of the University in Urban Affairs 1970–2000," Donovan took the opportunity to comment on student radicals:

> But we must place in a special category a tiny minority of students, noisy though they be, who come to our institutions only to indulge in so-called freedom of expression for a few years and who are not sincerely interested in the primary obligation of every student to seek learning from those who have earned the right to teach. These self-alienated youths are not so much misunderstood as they are unwilling to be understood, perhaps because they do not understand themselves. To a point they should be tolerated on a campus, but the outer limit of toleration is reached the moment they interfere with the rights of others to learn or to teach in the academic community. Such students should be told in advance the bounds of freedom but they are also entitled to explicit notice that they cannot be permitted to exceed those limits for one day, if a university is to serve the very purposes for which it exists. The overwhelming majority also have rights, which must be respected and protected.[40]

Notably, during the address, a very small group of students tried to interrupt Donovan with shouts of obscenities. They left when the attendees ignored them. Earlier, a student distributed a flyer denouncing Donovan as "a Central Intelligence Agency lawyer who was doing the bidding of the establishment."[41]

Donovan also used the address to sum up the work of his first year. Since his appointment, he told his audience at the Brooklyn Museum, "We have listened to students calling for significant shifts in curricula and administration in two of our major schools. Because the legitimacy of student concerns soon became apparent, many of the changes are now well on the way toward accomplishment."[42] Donovan described the institute's summer work with the Bedford-Stuyvesant community on which the school bordered. And he pointed out the institute's success in obtaining twenty graduate fellowships through a Ford Foundation grant as a memorial to Dr. Martin Luther King. Noting that black enrollment at Pratt was twice the national average, Donovan added that still more had to be done. "Education is essential to the responsible exercise of any black power," he said. "If the present imbalance in the student population is to be corrected, as it must be, additional sources of scholarship funds must be found."[43] Following Donovan's remarks, he was presented with a medal, created in his honor. Its design, by Paul Fjelde, a professor emeritus at Pratt, contained Donovan's likeness on one side and that of Charles Pratt, the institute's founder, on the other.

The year, however, did not end well for James, for in December he was hospitalized once again with an angina episode. Nevertheless, a month later, he had recovered and was pursuing an interest in art. He described the purchase for his home of an old painting in a letter to his son, John, then at Boston University:

> You will be pleased to know that I obtained a 17th century Russian icon of St. Nicholas, which now hangs on the wall leading upstairs to the 15th floor [the Donovans occupied a duplex apartment on the 14th and 15th floors]. This took two days of hard negotiation with your mother because she says that St. Nicholas has a very mean and disappointing expression on his face because his eyebrows are raised and his forehead is furrowed. My contention was that the man was simply asking, "What the hell is going on around here?" On that basis St. Nicholas has become part of the household.[44]

The spring 1969 semester began quietly. However, when Donovan announced two new initiatives in March 1969, including a $300-per-year tuition increase and an intent to purchase two neighboring properties for student housing, students were immediately angered. To them, he appeared to have reneged on his promise to include them in decisions. Adding a little more fuel to the fire were Donovan's mention that a popular instructor would not receive tenure and that a faculty wage package would be less than anticipated.[45] While students protested that they were not consulted on either of the main issues, they were particularly concerned with the fate of the existing tenants in the nearby buildings at 185 Hall Street and 195 Willoughby Avenue. The *Prattler* wrote a strong editorial throwing back at the president his promise of student participation in all key decisions.[46] Student and tenant picketing began almost immediately. Although Donovan explained that he could not have prematurely disclosed the intended purchase of the two buildings for fear that the sale price would increase, he also assured the students and tenants that all leases could be renewed and that no one would be forced out.

Despite Donovan's assurances, two hundred students showed up in front of the Montauk Club near Grand Army Plaza on March 25 where Donovan and the board of trustees were meeting to discuss the new housing for students and faculty.[47] The demonstrators distributed a "Student Manifesto" that essentially demanded an increased voice in policy-making, personnel issues, and financial aid.[48]

On the following day, March 26, nearly one thousand students met in Memorial Hall and voted for the first general strike in the institute's history. This was followed by more picketing accompanied by the beating on empty oil drums in front of the president's office.[49] The next day the faculty met, in part for their own needs and in part to support the students. After a discussion, they issued a paper itemizing seven specific concerns. These included a call for inclusion of faculty and students on the board of trustees; a similar inclusion of a community representative on the board;[50] meaningful representation of faculty and students on an institute finance committee; rectification of the tuition problem; the meeting of reasonable salary demands; involvement of the current tenants residing in the proposed new purchases; and a renewal of Donovan's promise made in January for increased student involvement in the institute.[51]

Meanwhile, Donovan met with representatives of the Student Coordinate and received their complaints. While he did not recognize the strike, he did suggest that student-administration communication could be improved, and he favored additional meetings. There was only one heated moment in all of the talks. It occurred when it was hinted that strikers might try to take over the president's office. Donovan was quick to respond. "Anybody who tries a stunt like that," he told the student government representatives, "will last as long as it takes a patrol car to get there."[52] After the meeting, Donovan wrote another letter to Commissioner Allen suggesting a convocation of college and university heads to explore common problems involving student unrest, but he was rebuffed.[53] On April 7, a suspicious fire gutted three floors of the East Building. No one was ever charged, nor did any person or group ever claim responsibility.[54]

During the spring break, Donovan and the board of trustees discussed the students' concerns. The board then approved the creation of an All-Institute Policy Committee to study and evaluate proposals for restructuring Pratt. Shortly thereafter, Donovan agreed to support the idea of student, faculty, and community representation on the board of trustees. As soon as he revealed his position, the student strike ended.[55] Unfortunately, it did not put an end to all discontent.

In the early morning hours of May 5, members of the Black Student Union and several white supporters padlocked the gates to the college. When other students arrived and objected to the locked gates, a confrontation developed and eleven young people, including ten students, were arrested for disorderly conduct. Police officers were on hand outside the institute and made the arrests without consulting the administration since the confrontation was off-campus. The demonstrators had sought an open enrollment policy for the Bedford-Stuyvesant community; more black and Latin American courses; additional black faculty and clerical personnel; a cessation of negotiations for the purchase of homes in the black community; and a 20 percent representation of students on the board of trustees.[56]

Although Donovan did not request or authorize the arrest of the demonstrators, he made it clear that illegal behavior would not be tolerated. "This institute has always been and is open to negotiate on all levels on all demands," he wrote in a hastily drawn policy statement. "However, destruction of property, inciting to riot, injury to persons and threats of physical harm are crimes and will be treated as such."[57] He then presented a four-point program that outlined the circumstances when arrests would be authorized:

In view of these disorders, we now state to all students: 1. Any student, student group or organization responsible for personal damage or willful damage to Institute property for any purpose will be subjected to arrest and summary expulsion from the Institute. 2. Any student, student group or organization that denies a student's rights (i.e., barring access to Institute facilities, classes or functions, etc.) or threatens, terrorizes or physically harms another person, will be subject to arrest and summary expulsion from the Institute. 3. Any student, student group or organization that exhorts, incites or conspires with any non-student to carry out either of the first two violations, will be subject to arrest and summary expulsion from the Institute. 4. Outsiders will be dealt with in accordance with the law.[58]

On the following day, Donovan met for two and a half hours with twenty members of the faculty who had demanded that he rescind his four-point program. He refused to do so, but said that once order was restored, he would review the problem with them and with representatives of the students.[59] The next day, all four hundred members of the faculty struck. Meanwhile, Francis X. Smith, the president of the New York City Council, was so pleased with Donovan's program that he sent him a congratulatory telegram and also called on the chairman of the board of higher education to adopt Donovan's four-points "for all city educational institutions."[60]

In the days immediately following the gate incident, Donovan met with members of the Black Student Union and several black faculty members. The faculty met during this same period and adopted a number of recommendations. They believed that disciplinary actions should remain with an existing committee of administrators, faculty, and students, and that punitive law enforcement measures should be abandoned. For his part, Donovan stated that his four-point program was an emergency measure, and he noted that he was willing to reevaluate it with a faculty-student senate that he hoped would be created soon. He added that he had asked police not to enter campus grounds.

By May 10, after a number of productive meetings with Donovan, the Black Student Union issued a statement indicating that an accord had been reached that would provide greater student involvement in the institute. Pratt's campus once again settled down to its academic work. However, the many conflicts were taking their toll on the president. As Margaret Latimer described it: "Donovan was more and more the target of verbal attacks. He was accused of being impossible to find, and when he did appear at a meeting, his every word was recorded, to be scrutinized later. Rumors were also circulating that he was in poor health, and that perhaps his inability to climb stairs might be preventing him from attending some of the meetings."[61]

Aston Taylor remained Donovan's chauffeur during his presidency at Pratt. At times, some of Donovan's colleagues would travel with him to various meetings. During the late spring of 1969, one associate was particularly condescending to Taylor, a circumstance that irritated the institute's president. As soon as Donovan returned to his office, he drew up a letter to the Universal Life Church for Taylor's signature. Soon after, when the associate was next in Donovan's car and spoke again in a rather haughty manner to Taylor, Donovan interjected and corrected the man. He told him that he was actually speaking to "Doctor Taylor" and then to Taylor, said, "Show him. Show him your certificate." Taylor reached down, picked up his certificate and proudly showed the obnoxious rider his doctor of divinity degree that Donovan had purchased for him earlier.[62]

It was perhaps because of his weariness with the prevalence of student unrest across the nation that Donovan developed his own radical solution, that of abandoning the system of selective service through a draft or lottery and instituting, instead, a policy of genuine universal conscription, calling it a National Youth Service. He first presented this idea before the twenty-first Annual Women's Forum on February 22, 1969, in a talk entitled "The Limits of Campus Liberty."[63] After discussing the responsibility of students to be educated and to be presented with the limits of their collegiate liberties, he suggested that it might be preferable for all youths to participate in a national service program prior to entering a university. He envisioned that such service would include all young people between the ages of seventeen and eighteen, both men and women, and he cited the State of Israel as providing such a precedent. Youths would not necessarily have to fulfill their service requirement in the armed forces, but could enter a number of alternative organizations such as the Peace Corps, Volunteers in Service to America, or public health or environmental agencies. It was Donovan's belief that young people would mature in this service and be "better prepared and better motivated to absorb the benefits of college." It would give them, as well, "an opportunity to express their idealism in meaningful action beneficial not only to themselves but also to future American generations."[64]

In his last year at Pratt, Donovan also participated in a significant conference in Manhattan in June on managing campus disorders. It was held at the John La Farge Institute, the same body to whom he had donated some of the proceeds from his book, *Strangers on a Bridge*. The conference, which included nine university and college presidents, drew up a set of twelve guidelines to help institutions in dealing with student protests. Briefly, the guidelines covered three areas of administrative concern: faculty, students, and media. The guidance suggested, for example, that administrators develop and publish clear procedures in the event of campus disorders, emphasizing that any negotiations should not be conducted under duress. They encouraged early participation of faculty in crises, more involvement of serious students in campus affairs, and a reduction in inflammatory news coverage.[65]

Pratt's campus was quiet during the fall 1969 semester. In a welcome to the incoming freshman class, Donovan was able to tell the new students that an institute senate was forthcoming and that the board of trustees had approved in principle the representation of both faculty and students on the board. He noted that a new curriculum in the School of Architecture was in place, that there were changes in library science to make it more relevant to employment in the outside world, and that there were a number of new black and Latin American studies courses added. Donovan also pointed out, "You will be interested to know that although Pratt has experienced campus disorders within the last year, unlike many other universities we have not found it necessary to expel, suspend, or even reprimand a single student. Furthermore, we have lodged no criminal complaint against a student and never have summoned police to this campus."[66]

On October 14, 1969, at a board of trustees meeting, Donovan reported that after the May arrests of students, he had asked the police during the trial if they would withdraw their charges. When they vigorously objected, even on the advice of the district attorney, Donovan asked the court to consider deferring prosecution by ordering the students to report to the Youth Control Board once a month for three months. If they didn't violate the law again, he suggested that the charges then be dismissed automatically. The assistant district attorney agreed and the court so ordered Donovan's suggestion. Donovan reported to the trustees that neither he nor anyone else was really satisfied with the results of the hearing, but asserted that it was the best that could be accomplished. At this same meeting, the board also approved Donovan's concept of a Pratt Institute Senate that would be composed of faculty, students, and administrators for the purpose of deliberating on all matters affecting, institute-wide operations and plans.[67]

The day after the board meeting, Pratt students stayed out of class in observance of a national Vietnam Moratorium in conjunction with other campuses across the country. Donovan had opposed the suspension of classes as being unfair to students who wanted to attend. The Faculty Council initially voted with the Student Coordinate, but eventually supported the president. Nevertheless, most students refrained from attending classes, but the day was otherwise uneventful at Pratt.

For Pratt students, the Christmas break came and went. In the following month, as they returned to class and embarked on the spring semester, Donovan was taken ill. He was rushed to Methodist Hospital in Brooklyn. This time it was a major heart attack. Mary and the children were with him most of the time during his brief hospital stay. At one point, as he rested in his hospital bed, he asked Aston Taylor to watch over his family in his absence.[68] Then, on the night of January 18, Mary gave James a kiss goodbye and went home to get some much-needed sleep. Shortly after, in the early morning hours of January 19, 1970, she received a call that her husband had died.

The funeral service was held at St. Patrick's Cathedral on January 21, 1970. The mass said by Terence Cardinal Cooke, archbishop of New York, and Father Robert I. Gannon, former president of Fordham University, delivered a moving eulogy before four hundred mourners.[69] Eight pallbearers bore the casket of James Donovan to a waiting hearse as a choir intoned "The Strife Is O'er." He was buried at Gate of Heaven Cemetery in Mt. Pleasant, New York.

Epilogue

IN HIS BRIEF BUT INTENSE FIFTY-THREE YEARS, JAMES DONOVAN UN-selfishly contributed far more of his intellect and time to the service of the law, human rights, education, and peace than he kept for himself. A number of precedent-setting decisions affected both the insurance industry and consumers on a national level. His income, commensurate with his talents, allowed him to care well for his family and freed him also for the public service labors that he prized. Indeed, even a portion of his later legal work was pro bono.

Though much of what he did in the Office of Scientific Research and Development and later in the Office of Strategic Services could not be made public, it was critical in furthering America's war effort during World War II. His high-level position as general counsel in both agencies required brilliance, wisdom, and integrity in advising on significant legal issues arising from the tumult of war. Negotiating for the virtually blind commitment of insurance companies to support secret government programs was nothing less than astounding.

While not a dominant prosecutorial figure at the Nuremberg Trial of 1945, his oversight and development of three graphic films shown during court sessions provided the visual evidence against Nazi leaders to expose their nefarious behavior to the tribunal and the world better than the thousands and thousands of pages of documentary evidence. Even Justice Jackson, a strong proponent of textual evidence, extolled before the tribunal the anticipated impact of Donovan's photographic compilations. "We will show you these concentration camps in motion pictures," Jackson said in his opening statement, "just as the Allied Armies found them when they arrived. Our proof will be disgusting to you and you will say that I robbed you of your sleep."

The defense of Rudolf Abel, high-ranking Soviet military officer and spy, was certainly an unpopular task in the Cold War era. The social impact of the hearings of Senator Joseph McCarthy and the Committee on Government Operations and the launching of the

205

Soviet satellite, Sputnik I, had fostered a national sense of insecurity in the face of the rise and spread of communism. Nevertheless, Donovan provided a model defense when other attorneys shrank from the prospect. Certainly, in terms of courage and talent, he can be ranked with such litigators as John Adams and Josiah Quincy, who defended British soldiers accused of murdering American patriots in the Boston Massacre; with Lloyd Paul Stryker, who defended Alger Hiss against the allegations of espionage by Whittaker Chambers; and more recently, with lawyers who have accepted the task of defending alleged terrorists charged with attacks against the United States.

A principal element of Donovan's character was his willingness to take on several major projects at once, sometimes "burning the candle at both ends," as he was once described as doing. No clearer example of this can be seen than in the year 1962 when he was negotiating the exchange of Rudolf Abel for Francis Gary Powers, making an ultimately unsuccessful run for the U.S. Senate and negotiating with Castro for the release of Cuban prisoners, all while engaged with the New York City Board of Education in his role as vice-president. Such diverse work in so concentrated a period of time provides an opportunity to evaluate his strengths and weaknesses.

In his personal discussions with Ivan Schischkin and Fidel Castro, Donovan excelled where he could apply his negotiating skills on a one-to-one basis. He was similarly successful when arguing in court. However, he was less effective when his opposite number was a large bloc, like the voters of New York State or the civil rights groups of New York City, where his quick wit and extemporaneous remarks could be perceived as caustic and, on occasion, especially in his term on the board of education, polarizing.

In his Senate bid, his opponent was far more popular and politically experienced, and Donovan's campaign was almost a distraction in view of his other major commitments at the time. He would have liked to become a senator. In fact, he, drove hard for the nomination, but with his concern to reestablish a dialogue with Fidel Castro, and the ever-present crises of the board of education always in the forefront, his six-week campaign never really developed beyond the negative and extemporaneous. The Democratic Party was viewed in the press as the underdog in the election even before Donovan entered the race. With that background, and in the face of a polished, politically experienced opponent, it was very creditable for him to have succeeded in appealing to 41 percent of the voters of New York.

He was clear and forceful during his service on the board of education, and within the demographic constraints that he faced, he fostered integration in the schools and encouraged harmony among the races. The problem was virtually intractable, yet he persevered by sheer strength of character in the face of—and often in the middle of—two significant and competing interests: the goals of African American parents and those of white parents. After stepping down as president, Donovan described the difficulty in integrating New York City's schools in his characteristically frank manner in a speech at Howard College on November 29, 1966: "unless enough white bodies are retained in the classrooms by plans for enriching the quality of education, any plan for desegregation is not only futile but a hypocritical hoax."

The New York City Board of Education continues to undergo reforms, but it has retained the structure of primary, middle, and high schools, together with other improvements, that were begun during Donovan's tenure. These improvements included the establishment of pre-kindergarten classes, massive specialized services, an increase in the number of teachers and volunteers, the addition of textbooks that revealed the role of minorities, and improved management of bus and custodial services contracts. However, his predictions that a continuing decline in white students would preclude the ability to integrate the city's schools have proved correct. As of October 2000, white students accounted for but 15.3 percent of the public schools' total enrollment. At the same time, the school population had increased to over 1.1 million students and nearly 80,000 teachers in 1,198 school buildings. Busing still exists for 168,076 pupils. In 2002, the New York state legislature eliminated the board of education and permitted the creation a new Department of Education. The primary feature of the reorganization is direct mayoral control of the nation's largest school system and the elimination of local community management. The position of schools' chancellor exists, and there is a Panel for Educational Policy that replaces former board members. Neither, however, has substantial authority. Mayor Bloomberg devised this approach so that he could personally ensure a uniform education of students at all levels. There are also plans to separate administrative tasks from educators and to reduce class size. If the new educational plan is successful, it will still depend upon the individual talents of future mayors, who may or may not want such power over a specialized field.

Donovan's ability to work successfully with Fidel Castro was inextricably tied to the personality John F. Kennedy, who believed that as president he had the strength to overcome the public's fear of Communism in seeking a more normal relationship with the Cuban government. In his own dealings with Castro, Donovan was always straightforward, using his Irish charm at appropriate times to gain the Cuban leader's trust. The coinage of the term "metadiplomat" in reference to Donovan was not misplaced. Operating as a private individual, he was able to obtain the release of all the Bay of Pigs prisoners being held, in addition to thousands of their family members, political prisoners, refugees, and a number of Americans, including three CIA agents. Someone less indefatigable would not have fared so well. While Donovan's hope for an accord between Cuba and the United States nearly died with the assassination of President Kennedy, it is significant to note that as recently as March 2001, Fidel Castro, in cosponsorship with the National Security Archive of George Washington University, hosted an extraordinary event that brought together a group of former leaders of Brigade 2506 and surviving members of President Kennedy's administration, including the CIA, with representatives of the University of Havana and the Cuban government. Fourteen months later, former President Jimmy Carter went to Cuba on the first visit by any American president since Fidel Castro had been in power. Castro, in an unprecedented decision, permitted Carter to address the nation in a live, uncensored broadcast from the University of Havana during which the former president called for reforms by Cuba and the lifting of the economic embargo by the United States. Both events suggest strongly that the Cuban leader even now desires improved relations with the United States—a process originally begun with Donovan.

Donovan's interest in international harmony and human rights did not focus solely on Cuba. As the pro bono general counsel for the Hostages for Peace Foundation, he fostered an exchange program between the United States and the Soviet Union that continues in substance to the present. Similarly, as pro bono general counsel for the Jewish Nazi Victims Organization of America, Donovan was able to elicit a donation from the West German government to help in the construction of housing in Israel for many survivors of Nazi atrocities who had taken refuge in the United States immediately after World War II but who later desired to relocate to Israel. He also persuaded the Israeli government to set aside lands for this same purpose.

In stark contrast to the more typical responses of college presidents to radical student activities in the late sixties (when four hundred police in riot gear had been summoned to remove protestors from Harvard's main administration building, or a thousand police had been needed to quell a violent confrontation at Columbia), Donovan did not believe in summoning the law to handle his students at Pratt Institute. Certainly, there were demonstrations and even a brief building takeover, but he preferred to speak to them directly. He believed in the need for student growth and the opportunity to question, but just as clearly he had set out the responsibilities not only of the school but of the students attending the school. He had formulated stringent rules, but had also created a constructive outlet for student opinion. During his tenure, no student was ever expelled or arrested; and law enforcement was never summoned to the campus to maintain order. He held fast to the belief he had expressed early in his presidency: "the only thing that can kill a campus is student apathy."

James Donovan was a brilliant attorney and a sensitive and humane individual who possessed a genuine interest in all peoples. He had an appealing sense of humor, and he valued his family and his Roman Catholic faith. He was not only bold, but brave in the face of death threats and intimidation. He rose above rebuffs aimed at his defense of a Communist spy and opposition to his prodding the community and the board of education toward integration to the extent that it was then possible. His courage was apparent in facing down demonstrators, hecklers, racists, and pickets, and in dealing with calculating Russian agents, hostile Cuban officers, and angry students.

Is it fair, then, to speak of a Donovan legacy? Do the ideas and ideals that he represented hold more than situational appeal for a single historical period? Certainly, honesty, high moral standards, the significant role of faith and family, enthusiastic public service, even the importance of humor transcend place and time. They provided the foundation on which his gift for negotiating rested. That gift is perhaps his greatest legacy. He believed in resolving impasses through dialogue, and he applied this principle in the service of others, when it was difficult, when it was unpopular. It is what made James Donovan a role model for his time, for our time, and for future generations.

Appendices

APPENDIX A
Texts of Cmdr. James B. Donovan's Presentations to the International Military Tribunal

1. Text of Cmdr. James B. Donovan's presentation to the International Military Tribunal on November 29, 1945:

COMMANDER JAMES BRITT DONOVAN, USNR. (Prosecution Counsel for the United States): May it please the Tribunal, I refer to Document Number 2430-PS, concerning the motion picture entitled "Nazi Concentration Camps" and to the affidavits of Commander James B. Donovan, Lieutenant Colonel George C. Stevens, Lieutenant E. R. Kellogg and Colonel Erik Tiebold contained therein. The affidavits of Colonel Stevens and of Lieutenant Kellogg are also contained in the motion picture, and thus will be in the record of the Tribunal. With the permission of the Tribunal, I shall now, however, read into the record those affidavits not appearing in the film.

THE PRESIDENT: In the absence of any objections by the Defense Counsel, we don't think it is necessary to read these formal affidavits.

COMMANDER DONOVAN: Yes, Sir. The United States now offers in evidence an official documentary motion picture report on Nazi concentration camps. This report has been compiled from motion pictures taken by Allied military photographers as the Allied armies in the West liberated the areas in which these camps were located. The accompanying narration is taken directly from the reports of the military photographers who filmed the camps.

While these motion pictures speak for themselves in evidencing life and death in Nazi concentration camps, proper authentication of the films is contained in the affidavits of the United States Army and Navy officers to which I have referred.

As has been stated, this motion picture has been made available to all defense counsel and they possess copies in their Information Room of the affidavits duly translated.

If the Tribunal please, we shall proceed with the projection of the film, Document 2430–PS, Exhibit USA–79.

[*Photographs were then projected on the screen showing the affidavits while at the same time the voices of the respective affiants were reproduced reading them.*]

"I, George C. Stevens, Lieutenant Colonel, Army of the United States, hereby certify:

"1. From 1 March 1945 to 8 May 1945 I was on active duty with the United States Army Signal Corps attached to the Supreme Headquarters, Allied Expeditionary Forces, and among my official duties were direction of the photographing of the Nazi concentration camps and prison camps as liberated by Allied Forces.

"2. The motion pictures which will be shown following this affidavit were taken by official Allied photographic teams in the course of their military duties, each team being composed of military personnel under the direction of a commissioned officer.

"3. To the best of my knowledge and belief, these motion pictures constitute a true representation of the individuals and scenes photographed. They have not been altered in any respect since the exposures were made. The accompanying narration is a true statement of the facts and circumstances under which these pictures were made.

"[Signed] George C. Stevens, Lieutenant Colonel, AUS.

"Sworn to before me this 2nd day of October 1945.

"[Signed] James B. Donovan, Commander, United States Naval Reserve."

"I, E. R. Kellogg, Lieutenant, United States Navy, hereby certify that:

"1. From 1929 to 1941 I was employed at the Twentieth Century Fox Studios in Hollywood, California, as a director of film effects, and am familiar with all photographic techniques. Since 6 September 1941 to the present date of 27 August 1945, I have been on active duty with the United States Navy.

"2. I have carefully examined the motion picture film to be shown following this affidavit and I certify that the images of these excerpts from the original negative have not been retouched, distorted or otherwise altered in any respect and are true copies of the originals held in the vaults of the United States Army Signal Corps. These excerpts comprise 6,000 feet of film selected from 80,000 feet, all of which I have reviewed and all of which is similar in character to these excerpts.

"[Signed] E.R. Kellogg, Lieutenant, United States Navy.

"Sworn to before me this 27th day of August 1945.

"[Signed] John Ford, Captain, United States Navy."

[*The film was then shown.*]

COLONEL STOREY: That concludes the presentation.

[*The Tribunal adjourned until 30 November 1945 at 1000 hours.*]

Office of United States Chief of Counsel for Prosecution of Axis Criminality, *Nazi Conspiracy and Aggression* (Washington, DC: United States Government Printing Office, 1946), 2:432–33.

2. Text of Cmdr. James B. Donovan's presentation to the International Military Tribunal on December 11, 1945:

Morning Session

COLONEL STOREY: If the Tribunal please, the United States next offers in evidence some captured moving pictures through Commander Donovan, who had charge of taking them.

COMMANDER JAMES BRITT DONOVAN (Assistant Trial Counsel for the United States): May it please the Tribunal, the United States now offers in evidence Document Number 3054–PS, United States Exhibit Number 167, the motion picture entitled *The Nazi Plan.* This document contains several affidavits with exhibits, copies of which have been furnished to Defense Counsel. I ask the Tribunal whether it believes it to be necessary that I formally read the affidavits at this time. Since the motion pictures themselves will be presented to the Tribunal and thereafter be in its permanent record, I respectfully submit that the reading be waived.

In the past 3 weeks the Prosecution has presented to this Tribunal a vast amount of evidence concerning the nature of the Nazi conspiracy and what we contend to be its deliberate planning, launching, and waging wars of aggression. That evidence has consisted of documentary and some oral proof, but the Nazi conspirators did more than leave behind such normal types of evidence. German proficiency in photography has been traditional. Its use as a propaganda instrument was especially well known to these defendants, and as a result the United States in 1945 captured an almost complete chronicle of the rise and fall of National Socialism as documented in films made by the Nazis themselves. It is from excerpts of this chronicle that we have compiled the motion picture now presented, entitled *The Nazi Plan,* which in broad outline sums up the case thus far presented under Counts One and Two of the Indictment.

The motion picture has been divided into four parts. This morning we first offer to the Tribunal Parts 1 and 2, respectively entitled "The Rise of the NSDAP, 1921 to 1933," and "Acquiring Total Control of Germany, 1933 to 1935." These will be concluded by 11:20, at which time we assume the Tribunal will order its customary morning adjournment. At 11:30 we shall present Part 3, entitled "Preparation for Wars of Aggression, 1935 to 1939." This will be concluded shortly before 1 o'clock. At 2 p.m. we will offer Part 4, "Wars of Aggression, 1939 to 1944," and this will be concluded by 3 p.m.

Parts 1 and 2 now to be presented, enable us to re-live those years in which the Nazis fought for and obtained the power to rule all life, in Germany. We see the early days of terrorism and propaganda bearing final fruit in Hitler's accession to the Chancellery in 1933, then the consolidation of power within Germany, climaxed by the Parteitag of 1934, in which the Nazis proclaimed to the nation their plans for totalitarian control. It is in simple and dramatic form the story of how a nation forsook its liberty.

I wish again to emphasize that all film now presented to the Tribunal, including, for example, pictures of early Nazi newspapers, is the original German film, to which we have added only the title in English. And now, if it please the Tribunal, we shall present Parts 1 and 2 of *The Nazi Plan*.

THE PRESIDENT: It may be convenient for the United States Prosecutor to know that the Tribunal propose to rise this afternoon at 4 o'clock instead of 5.

[*The film, The Nazi Plan, was then shown in the court room until 1125 hours, at which time a recess was taken.*]

COMMANDER DONOVAN: May it please the Tribunal, in the films which have just been shown to the Tribunal we have watched the Nazi rise to power. In Part 3 of our documentary motion picture now to be presented, we see the use they made of that power and how the German nation was led by militaristic regimentation to preparation for aggressive war as an instrument of national policy. Part 3, "Preparation for Wars of Aggression, 1935–1939; 1935—Von Schirach urges Hitler Youth to follow principles of Mein Kampf."

[*The showing of the film then continued and at the end a recess was taken until 1400 hours.*]

Afternoon Session

COMMANDER DONOVAN: This morning we presented photographic evidence of the history of National Socialism from 1921 to September 1939. We saw the dignity of the individual in Germany destroyed by men dedicated to perverted nationalism, men who set forth certain objectives and then preached to a regimented people the accomplishment of those objectives by any necessary means, including aggressive war.

In September 1939 the Nazis launched the first of a series of catastrophic wars, terminated only by the military collapse of Germany. It is this final chapter in the history of National Socialism that the Prosecution now presents.

May I again remind the Tribunal that all film presented and all German narration heard is in the original form as filmed by the Nazis.

[*The showing of the film, part 4, then continued.*]

COMMANDER DONOVAN: The Prosecution has concluded its presentation of the photographic summation entitled *The Nazi Plan*. We shall deliver for the permanent records of the Tribunal, as soon as possible, the original films projected today.

Office of United States Chief of Counsel for Prosecution of Axis Criminality, *Nazi Conspiracy and Aggression* (Washington, DC: United States Government Printing Office, 1946), vol. 3:400–2.

3. Text of Cmdr. James B. Donovan's presentation to the International Military Tribunal on December 13, 1945:

COMMANDER DONOVAN: May it please the Tribunal, the United States now offers in evidence Document Number 3052–PS, Exhibit Number USA-280, entitled "Original German 8–millimeter Film of Atrocities against Jews." This is a strip of motion pictures taken, we believe, by a member of the SS and captured by the United States military forces in an SS barracks near Augsburg, Germany, as described in the affidavits now before the Tribunal. We have not been able to establish beyond doubt in which area these films were made, but we believe that to be immaterial.

The film offers undeniable evidence, made by the Germans themselves, of almost incredible brutality to Jewish people in the custody of the Nazis, including German military units.

It is believed by the Prosecution that the scene is the extermination of a ghetto by Gestapo agents, assisted by military units. And, as the other evidence to be presented by the Prosecution will indicate, the scene presented to the Tribunal is probably one which occurred a thousand times all over Europe under the Nazi rule of terror.

This film was made on an 8-millimeter home camera. We have not wished even to reprint it, and so shall present the original, untouched film captured by our troops. The pictures obviously were taken by an amateur photographer. Because of this, because of the fact that part of it is burned, because of the fact that it runs for only 1½ minutes, and because of the confusion on every hand shown on this film, we do not believe that the Tribunal can properly view the evidence if it is shown only once. We therefore ask the Tribunal's permission to project the film twice as we did before Defense Counsel.

This is a silent film. The film has been made available to all Defense Counsel, and they have a copy of the supporting affidavits, duly translated. [*The film was shown.*]

COMMANDER DONOVAN: [*Continuing.*] May it please the Tribunal, while the film is being rewound I wish to say that attached to the affidavits ordered in evidence is a description of every picture shown in this film. And, with the Tribunal's permission, I wish to read a few selections from that at this time, before again projecting the film, in order to direct the Tribunal's attention to certain of the scenes:

Scene 2—A naked girl running across the courtyard.

Scene 3—An older woman being pushed past the camera, and a man in SS uniform standing at the right of the scene.

Scene 5—A man with a skullcap and a woman are manhandled.

Number 14—A half-naked woman runs through the crowd.

Number 15—Another half-naked woman runs out of the house.

Number 16—Two men drag an old man out.

Number 18—A man in German military uniform, with his back to the camera, watches.

Number 24—A general shot of the street, showing fallen bodies and naked women running.

Number 32—A shot of the street, showing five fallen bodies.

Number 37—A man with a bleeding head is hit again.

Number 39—A soldier in German military uniform, with a rifle, stands by as a crowd centers on a man coming out of the house.

Number 44—A soldier with a rifle, in German military uniform, walks past a woman clinging to a torn blouse.

Number 45—A woman is dragged by her hair across the street.

[*The film was shown again.*]

COMMANDER DONOVAN: [*Continuing.*] We submit to the Tribunal for its permanent records this strip of 8-millimeter film.

Office of United States Chief of Counsel for Prosecution of Axis Criminality, *Nazi Conspiracy and Aggression* (Washington, DC: United States Government Printing Office, 1946), vol. 3: 536–37.

APPENDIX B
LAW PRACTICE

Year	Firm	Partners	Associates
1941–42	Townley, Updike & Carter 220 E. 42nd Street New York, NY *General practice*		
1942–43	Office of Scientific Research & Development		
1943–46	United States Navy: Office of Strategic Services		
1945	United States Navy: Office of Chief Counsel for Prosecution of Major Axis War Criminals		
1946–51	National Bureau of Casualty Underwriters 116 John Street *Insurance*		

1950	Watters & Donovan 161 William Street New York, NY Watters, Cowan & Donovan 1139 Shoreham Building Washington, DC *General practice; corporation, insurance, and tax law; and departmental matters*	Thomas Watters; James B. Donovan	John P. Walsh; Hersey B. Eggington; John J. Saracino; John N. Reid; Edward T. Brown
1953			John P. Walsh; John J. Saracino; John N. Reid; Edward T. Brown; Chester E. Kleinberg
1954			John P. Walsh; John J. Saracino; John N. Reid; Edward T. Brown; Clarke S. Ryan; Geoffrey E.R. Davey; Delroy C. Thomas
1955	Watters & Donovan 161 William Street New York, NY Watters & Donovan 1139 Shoreham Building Washington, DC		John P. Walsh; Edward V. Gross; John J. Saracino; John N. Reid; Edward T. Brown; Geoffrey E.R. Davey; Delroy C. Thomas
1956		Thomas Watters Jr; James B. Donovan; John P. Walsh	Edward V. Gross; John J. Saracino; John N. Reid; Edward T. Brown; Geoffrey E. R. Davey; Thomas A. Harnett

1957	Watters & Donovan *General practice; corporation, insurance and tax law; and administrative law*		Edward V. Gross; John J. Saracino; John N. Reid; Edward T. Brown; Thomas A. Harnett; DeRoy Clinton Thomas; Vincent P. de Venoge; Patrick J. Hughes
1958		Thomas Watters Jr; James B. Donovan; John P. Walsh; Edward V. Gross	John J. Saracino; John N. Reid; Edward T. Brown; Thomas A. Harnett; DeRoy Clinton Thomas; George J. Fritz; Vincent P. de Venoge; Patrick J. Hughes
1959			John J. Saracino; John N. Reid; Edward T. Brown; Thomas A. Harnett; George J. Fritz; Vincent P. de Venoge; Patrick J. Hughes
1960		Thomas Watters Jr; James B. Donovan; John P. Walsh; Edward V. Gross; John N. Reid	John J. Saracino; Edward T. Brown; Thomas A. Harnett; George J. Fritz; Vincent P. de Venoge; Patrick J. Hughes; Richard J. Barnes
1961		Thomas Watters Jr; James B. Donovan; John P. Walsh; Edward V. Gross; John N. Reid; Edward T. Brown; Thomas A. Harnett; George J. Fritz	John J. Saracino; Vincent P. de Venoge; Patrick J. Hughes; Richard J. Barnes; Jay Goldberg

1962		Thomas Watters Jr; James B. Donovan; John P. Walsh; Edward V. Gross; John N. Reid; Edward T. Brown; Thomas A. Harnett; Patrick J. Hughes	John J. Saracino; Vincent P. de Venoge; Richard J. Barnes; Thomas D. Wellington; Gerald E. Bodell; Walter C. Reid; Emil Sebetic
1963	Watters & Donovan 161 William Street New York, NY		John J. Saracino; Vincent P. de Venoge; Richard J. Barnes; Thomas D. Wellington; Gerald E. Bodell; Walter C. Reid; James M. FitzSimons
1964			John J. Saracino; Vincent P. de Venoge; Thomas D. Wellington; Gerald E. Bodell; Walter C. Reid; James M. FitzSimons; Victor N. Farley
1965		Thomas Watters, Jr.; James B. Donovan; John P. Walsh; Edward V. Gross; John N. Reid; Edward T. Brown; Patrick J. Hughes	John J. Saracino; Vincent P. de Venoge; Thomas D. Wellington; James M. FitzSimons
1966	Watters & Donovan *General practice; corporation insurance and tax law and administrative law; estate*	Thomas Watters Jr; James B. Donovan; John P. Walsh; Edward V. Gross; John N. Reid; Edward T. Brown; Patrick J. Hughes. *Counsel:* John V. Bloys	John J. Saracino; Vincent P. de Venoge; Thomas D. Wellington; Richard J. O'Keefe

1967		Thomas Watters Jr; James B. Donovan; John P. Walsh; John N. Reid; Edward T. Brown; Patrick J. Hughes. *Counsel:* John V. Bloys	John J. Saracino; Vincent P. de Venoge; Thomas D. Wellington; Stanton D. McMahon; George M. Mulligan; Elizabeth A. Palewski; David H. Hall; Thomas R. Kennedy; Thomas P. Parry
1968	Watters & Donovan 161 William Street New York, NY *General practice; corporation, insurance, and tax law; and administrative law*	Thomas Watters, Jr.; James B. Donovan; John P. Walsh. *Counsel:* John V. Bloys	John J. Saracino; Vincent P. de Venoge; Thomas D. Wellington; Stanton D. McMahon; George M. Mulligan; Thomas R. Kennedy; Raymond J. Messina; Thomas P. Parry
1969	*General practice; corporation, insurance, and tax law; administrative law; wills and estates*	Thomas Watters Jr; James B. Donovan; John P. Walsh; Stanton D. McMahon. *Counsel:* John V. Bloys	John J. Saracino; Vincent P. de Venoge; George M. Mulligan; Thomas R. Kennedy; Raymond J. Messina; Thomas P. Parry; Warren A. Herland; Maurice Adelman Jr.
1970	Donovan, Donovan, Maloof & Walsh 161 William Street New York, NY *General practice; corporation, insurance, aviation, admiralty, and tax law; administrative, wills and estates*	James B. Donovan; James J. Donovan; David L. Maloof; John P. Walsh; Stanton D. McMahon; Henry J. Robinson; Francis V. Elias	John V. Bloys; John J. Saracino; Vincent P. de Venoge; Maurice Adelman Jr.; Joseph M. Mangino; Thomas R. Kennedy; James M. Kenny; Thomas P. Parry; Michael J. Pangia; Warren A. Herland; Mary Ellen Sweeney

Minnie E. McInturff, JBD Secretary, 1948–70
Primary Source: *Martindale-Hubbell Law Directory* (Summit, NJ: Martindale-Hubble, annually. 1941–70).

APPENDIX C
CUBAN FAMILIES COMMITTEE FOR LIBERATION OF PRISONERS OF WAR, INC.: NATIONAL SPONSORS' COMMITTEE

Amoss, Walter J., director, New Orleans Port Authority
Fonteyn de Arias, Dame Margot, prima ballerina
Baragwanath, John G., executive consulting mining engineer
Beinecke, Walter Jr., president, Osceola Foundation, Inc.
Brennan, Ledwith, retired executive
Brundage, Charles E., investment counselor
Byrne Joseph Jr., business executive
Clay, Gen. Lucius D., chairman, Continental Can Co.
Clore, Charles, British financier
Connelly, Geo. A., president, Eastland Oil Co.
Craig, Hon. George N., former governor, State of Indiana
Cushing, Richard, cardinal
de Berardinis, H.W., executive *Shreveport (La.) Times*
de Jesus Toro, Roberto, president, Bank of Ponce, Puerto Rico
de Saint Phalle, Claude, Financier
Donnelly, George A., executive
Donovan, James B., attorney
Eager, A. Gifford Jr., broadcasting executive
Ely, Roland T., professor, Latin American Economic History, Rutgers University
Farley, Hon. James A., chairman, Coca-Cola Export Corporation
Ferre, Luis A., industrialist, Ponce, Puerto Rico
Finklestein, Rabbi Louis, chancellor, Jewish Theological Seminary of America
Franklin III, Mrs. Benjamin, philanthropist
Golden, Daniel L., attorney
Gordon, Dean Ernest, clergyman and author
Hackley, Sherlock D., executive
Hanna, Rev. Philip M., auxiliary bishop, Washington, D.C.
Harr, Karl G Jr., attorney
Hayden, Mrs. Charles M. (Phyllis McGinley), poet
Hickey, Thomas J. Jr., broker
Hiller, Eldredge, executive
Horan, Miss Ellaway, educator and author
Hortzer, J. Z. retired executive
Jaffe, Herman, printer-publisher
Johnson, John, educator

Kean, Robert W. Jr., business executive
Kelley, Nicholas, attorney
Kemper, James S. Jr., vice chairman, Lumbermens Mutual Casualty Company
Kirchner, Edward J., president, Kossuth Foundation
Leavitt, Nathan R., banker
Lehman, Hon. Herbert H., former U.S. Senator and governor of New York
Lehman, Orin, chairman, Just One Break, Inc.
Lowe, Donald V., industrialist
Lyons, Leonard, columnist
Magner, Richard T., insurance executive
McClintic, H. H. Jr., contractor
McDonald, David J., president, United Steel Workers of America
Meyer, Mrs. Tom Montague (Fleur Cowles), editor and author
Monroe, Vernon Jr. attorney
Oates, James F. Jr., president, Equitable Life Assurance Society
O'Connor, Richard A., chairman, Magnavox Company
Osborn, Mrs. A. Perry, philanthropist
Parker, Dr. Ben H., chairman, board of trustees, Colorado School of Mines
Patterson, Hon. Henry S., mayor, Princeton, New Jersey
Pawley, William D., former United States Ambassador to Peru and Brazil
Perrilliat, Claiborne, president, Perrilliat & Rickey Construction Company
Perry, Mrs. John H., publisher
Pierce, Roger V., international consulting mining engineer
Pike, Rev. James A., bishop, Episcopalian Diocese of California
Pinkham, Richard A. R., senior vice president, Ted Bates & Company, Inc.
Pipes, Fort, publisher
Quesada, Gen. Elwood R., former Chief of Air Staff, U.S. Air Corps
Radziwill, Princess Lee
Riesel, Victor, columnist
Rockwell, Willard F., chairman, Rockwell Manufacturing Company
Smith, Gen. C.R., President, American Airlines, Inc.
Smith, Mrs. Joseph Kingsbury, wife of Pulitzer Prize-winning journalist
Sobol, Louis, columnist
Spivey, Gen. Delmar T., superintendent, Culver Military Academy
Sullivan, Ed, broadcaster and columnist
Swanstrom, Bishop Edward E., director, Catholic Relief Services
Taylor, Dr. Gardner C., pastor, Concord Baptist Church, Brooklyn, NY
Vanderwilt, John W., president, Colorado School of Mines
Wade, Gen. Leigh, retired Air Force officer
Whitehead, Vice-Admiral Richard, U.S. Navy (ret.)
Whitsett, W. Gavin, vice president, Louisville and Nashville railroad

Compiled from sponsor lists in *HIA*, Box 44.

Appendix D
The Poisoned Wet Suit

When Donovan was conducting his negotiations with Castro, someone in the Central Intelligence Agency conceived the idea to buy a skin diving suit, lace it with harmful materials, and have Donovan give it to Castro as a gift. Donovan was not to be told of the plan, but as is known now, he did learn of it. The scheme first came to light within the CIA in 1967 (but not publicly) when an inspector general of the agency investigated a number of such plans to kill Castro. With respect to the wet suit plot, the inspector general's report, now declassified, states:

Skin Diving Suits

At about the time of the Donovan-Castro negotiations for the release of the Bay of Pigs prisoners a plan was devised to have Donovan present a contaminated skin diving suit to Castro as a gift. Castro was known to be a skin diving enthusiast. We cannot put a precise date on this scheme. Desmond Fitzgerald told us of it as if it had originated after he took over the Cuban task force in January 1963. Samuel Halpern said that it began under William Harvey and that he, Halpern, briefed Fitzgerald on it. Harvey states positively that he never heard of it.

According to Sidney Gottlieb, this scheme progressed to the point of actually buying a diving suit and readying it for delivery. The technique involved dusting the inside of the suit with a fungus that would produce a disabling and chronic skin disease (Madura foot) and contaminating the breathing apparatus with tubercle bacilli. Gottlieb does not remember what came of the scheme or what happened to the scuba suit. Sam Halpern, who was in on the scheme, at first said the plan was dropped because it was obviously impractical. He later recalled that the plan was abandoned because it was overtaken by events: Donovan had already given Castro a skin diving suit on his own initiative. The scheme may have been mentioned to Mike Miskovsky, who worked with Donovan, but Fitzgerald has no recollection that it was.

Halpern says that he mentioned the plan to George McManus, then a special assistant to the DD/P (Helms). McManus later told Halpern that he had mentioned the scheme to Mr. Helms. Those who were in on the plot or who were identified to us by the participants as being witting are the following:

Richard Helms
William Harvey (denies any knowledge)
Desmond Fitzgerald
Samuel Halpern
George McManus
Sidney Gottlieb
XXXXXXX Name still classified

J. S. Earman, Inspector General, Central Intelligence Agency. Memorandum for the Record: *Report on Plots to Assassinate Fidel Castro.*, May 23, 1967, pp. 76–77; Reprinted in toto in *CIA Targets Fidel: Secret 1967 CIA Inspector General's Report on Plots to Assassinate Fidel Castro* (Melbourne, Australia: Ocean Press, 1996).

In 1975, Senator Frank Church began a series of public hearings into the areas that the CIA inspector general had explored eight years earlier. With respect to Donovan, the Senate Select Committee's report states:

A second plan involved having James Donovan (who was negotiating with Castro for the release of prisoners taken during the Bay of Pigs operation) present Castro with a contaminated diving suit. [A footnote here in the original states that "Donovan was not aware of the plan."—author].

The Inspector General's Report dates this operation in January 1963, when Fitzgerald replaced Harvey as Chief of Task Force W, although it is unclear whether Harvey or Fitzgerald conceived the plan. It is likely that the activity took place earlier, since Donovan had completed negotiations by the middle of January 1963. Helms characterized the plan as "cockeyed."

The Technical Services Division bought a diving suit, dusted the inside with a fungus that would produce a chronic skin disease (Madura foot), and contaminated the breathing apparatus with a tubercule bacillus. The Inspector General's report states that the plan was abandoned because Donovan gave Castro a different diving suit on his own initiative. Helms testified that the diving suit never left the laboratory.

Church Committee, *Alleged Assassination Plots Involving Foreign Leaders: An Interim Report of the Select Committee to Study Governmental Operations with Respect to Intelligence Activities* (New York: W.W. Norton, 1976), 85–86.

After the public revelations of the Church Committee, there was still speculation about whether or not Donovan knew of the CIA scheme. For example, Daniel Schorr wrote in 1977 that Donovan may have suspected the CIA scheme: "The idea (of the assassination planners of CIA's Task Force W) was that an unwitting Donovan, who was going to Cuba for President Kennedy to negotiate the release of Bay of Pigs prisoners, would present the diving suit to Castro as a gift. Donovan was so unwitting that, on his own initiative, he presented Castro with a different diving suit." *Clearing the Air* (Boston: Houghton Mifflin Co., 1977), 164. Most simply say that he was an unsuspecting, potential participant. See, for example, Dick Russell, *The Man Who Knew Too Much* (New York: Carroll & Graf Publishers, 1992), 291; Ernest Volkman and Blaine Baggett, *Secret Intelligence* (New York: Doubleday, 1989), 134; John Ranelagh, *The Agency: The Rise and Decline of the CIA* (New York: Simon & Schuster, 1987), 389; Thomas Powers, *The Man Who Kept the Secrets: Richard Helms and the CIA* (New York: Alfred A. Knopf, 1979), 150; Evan Thomas, *The Very Best Men:*

Four Who Dared—The Early Years of the CIA (New York: Simon and Schuster, 1995), 295; Brock Brower, "Why People Like You Joined the CIA," *Washington Monthly* 8, 9 (November 1976): 59; and Warren Hinckle and William W. Turner, *The Fish Is Red: The Story of the Secret War Against Castro* (New York: Harper & Row Publishers, 1981), 190–91. One author actually changed the circumstances, even in the face of the Select Committee report. See John Prados, in *Presidents' Secret Wars: CIA and Pentagon Covert Operations from World War II Through the Persian Gulf,* (Chicago: I.R. Dee, 1996), 215.

APPENDIX E
KATZENBACH LETTER TO PHARMACEUTICAL MANUFACTURER'S ASSOCIATION

NdeBK:meg

December 8, 1962

Pharmaceutical Manufacturers Association
1411 K Street, N.W.
Washington, D.C.

    Attention: Mr. Eugene N. Beesley
             Chairman of the Board

Gentleman:

We have your letter of December 8, 1962, which you have submitted on behalf of the Pharmaceutical Manufacturers Association and each of its constituent members. Your letter outlines a proposed plan for the contribution of drugs by the members of your Association to the Cuban Families' Committee for the Liberation of Prisoners of War, Inc., or to the American Red Cross. These contributions, together with contributions of food, such as dried milk and baby foods, and medical supplies, will be used in connection with the Committee's efforts to obtain the release of certain prisoners presently held by the Cuban government.

Pursuant to the plan, the Committee or the Red Cross will submit to the Association and its members, a list of the types and quantities of pharmaceutical products which are desired. The responsibility for contributing the various items on the list will then be allocated among the manufacturers of the necessary products. For various reasons, the mechanics of the allocation may require the Association to obtain from the participants information relating to costs, prices, levels of taxable income, and other items, and may involve the exchange of this information and pledge agreements among the participants themselves.

The contributing manufacturers will receive no consideration for their products. Execution of the plan—including completion of the allocation among manufacturers and all necessary exchanges of information—will be accomplished within a determinable and relatively short span of time. Manufacturers in the industry who are not members of the Association will be invited to participate in the plan.

The Department has carefully considered the plan described in your letter. I am authorized to advise you that the Department does not intend to institute any criminal or civil proceedings under any of the antitrust laws against the Association, any of its members, any officers or employees of the Association or its members, any non-members who accept invitations to participate or their officers or employees, on account of their actions in formulating or executing the contributions plan.

If the formulation or execution of the plan does not occur in the manner described in your letter, you should advise the Department so that prompt reconsideration may be made of the plan in terms of such variations. You should also advise the Department when the action contemplated by the plan has been completed or terminated for any reason.

Sincerely yours,

Nicholas deB. Katzenbach
Deputy Attorney General

cc: James B. Donovan, Esq.
161 William Street
New York, N.Y.

From *HIA,* Box 44.

APPENDIX F
IRREVOCABLE LETTER OF CREDIT ISSUED BY THE ROYAL BANK OF CANADA

The Royal Bank of Canada
Post Office Bag Service 6007
Montreal, P.Q.

LML/as-L/C

Banco Nacional de Cuba,   December 20, 1962
Apdo. 736,
Havana, Cuba.

Our irrevocable Letter of Credit 8310

For account of The American National Red Cross we open our irrevocable Letter of Credit in your favour for an amount not exceeding Fifty-Six Million, Nine Hundred and Eighty-Nine Thousand, Two Hundred and Forty-Seven Canadian dollars (Can$56,989,247) available by your draft drawn on us at sight, subject to the following:

(1) Our engagement will become effective upon delivery to the Canadian Consul at Havana for transmission to us of your written statement countersigned by James B. Donovan, Esq., in the presence of the said Consul that you have received advice from The American National Red Cross that foodstuffs and medical supplies valued at not less than Ten Million Six Hundred Thousand U.S. Dollars (US$10,600,000) are in the process of actual shipment to Cuba and the Brigade taken prisoner in connection with the attempted invasion at the Bay of Pigs and any other persons named in such statement have been released from imprisonment and have left Cuba;

(2) The amount of this Letter of Credit shall be reduced from time to time by the amount of invoices including invoices relating to the foodstuffs and medical supplies referred to in paragraph (1) above, of The American National Red Cross describing shipment to you C.I.F. a Cuban port, free of payment, of foodstuffs and medical supplies with an aggregate stated value not exceeding Fifty-Six Million, Nine Hundred and Eighty-Nine Thousand, Two Hundred and Forty-Seven Canadian Dollars (Can$56,989, 247) based upon an exchange rate of U.S.$0.93 per Canadian Dollar, which invoices The American National Red Cross shall certify to us up to the close of business in Montreal on July 15, 1963, as having been despatched to you on or before July 15, 1963.

(3) Any draft drawn by you under this Letter of Credit shall be presented for payment not later than July 31, 1963 and shall not be drawn on or presented prior to July 16, 1963 provided, however, that if The American National Red Cross shall certify to us in writing prior to July 9, 1963 that it has been prevented by circumstances beyond its control other than an act or omission of the Government of the United States of America from making any contemplated shipment, and is therefore unable to despatch to you the invoices stipulated in (2) above on or before July 15, 1963, we shall so advise you and thereupon the first date upon which you may draw on or present this Letter of Credit shall be postponed by us for such period as may be required to permit such shipment and despatch to you of the relevant invoices, but under no circumstances shall this postponement be for longer than 6 months from July 16, 1963 and the abovementioned expiry date shall be postponed for a like period not exceeding 6 months.

Yours truly,

Original signed by E. Darby
Authorized Signature

Original signed by L. W. Lee
Authorized Signature

From *HIA*, Box 44.

APPENDIX G
EXPORTS TO CUBA — SHIP AND PLANE SUMMARY

No.	Date	Via	From	Short Tons	Value
1	12/22–24	S.S. *AFRICAN PILOT* Pan American (13)	Ft. Lauderdale Miami	1,844.5 142.6	$ 8,544,771 4,468,809
2	1/9	Pan American	Miami	7.8	290,492
3	1/13	Pan American	Miami	6.4	616,230
4	1/14 1/17	S.S. *SHIRLEY LYKES*	Baltimore Ft. Lauderdale	7,249.6 963.3	8,085,213 454,223
5	1/18	Pan American	Miami	6.5	2,349
6	1/25	Pan American	Miami	9.0	204,851
7	2/1	Pan American	Miami	3.6	106,087
8	2/7	S.S. *SANTO CERRO*	Baltimore	2,156.0	2,151,389
9	2/8	Pan American	Miami	5.3	165,945
10	2/15	Pan American	Miami	5.9	9,262
11	2/22	Pan American	Miami	6.9	11,940
12	2/23	M.V. *PRIAMOS*	New Orleans	2,812.5	1,471,128
13	3/5	Pan American	Miami	7.3	12,960
14	3/7	Pan American	Miami	7.3	269,851
15	3/14	Special Plane	Miami	0	2,619
16	3/15	Pan American	Miami	4.9	59,390
17	3/22	Pan American	Miami	5.9	7,520
18	3/27	Pan American	Miami	4.8	86,576
19	3/29	Pan American	Miami	7.0	2,425
20	4/3	M.V. *COPAN*	Philadelphia	2,710.1	4,208,703
21	4/4	Special Plane	Miami	.3	34,918
22	4/10	Pan American	Miami	.2	45,000
23	4/17	S.S. *AMERICAN SURVEYOR*	New York	8,499.0	3,160,726
24	4/20	Pan American	Miami	7.4	2,596
25	4/22	Pan American	Miami	5.1	1,789
26	4/27	Special Plane	Miami	.5	413
27	5/2	Pan American	Miami	.9	552
28	5/8	S.S. *AMERICAN SURVEYOR*	Philadelphia	7,351.5	7,465,548
29	5/14	S.S. *MORNING LIGHT*	New Orleans	6,176.7	3,618,739
30	5/16	Pan American	Miami	.2	8,401
31	6/23	S.S. *MAXIMUS*	Philadelphia	5,701.9	3,676,106
32	7/1	Pan American	Miami	1.3	31,920
33	7/3	Pan American	Miami	2.2	37,603
		TOTAL		45,714.4	**$49,317,044**

From *HIA*, Box 44.

Appendix H
Memorandum of Agreement, December 21, 1962

Between representatives of the Government of Cuba and the Cuban Families Committee for the Liberation of Prisoners of War Inc. made in Havana this 21st. day of December, 1962.

1. The basic understanding of the parties, on matters previously agreed upon, is ratified and confirmed.
2. This memorandum is designed for the further assurance of the Government that the Committee in good faith and to the best of its ability will perform its pledges to the Government.
3. The Committee agrees that it will exert every effort to supply the Government with medical and pharmaceutical supplies, including foodstuffs nutritious for the children before July 1st. 1963 and in conformity with the list prepared by the Government.
4. The values shall be determined as provided in the Letter of Credit issued to the Government today by the Royal Bank of Canada, Montreal.
4A. 15% shall be the agreed percentage to cover all cost of transportation (land, sea and air), all insurances, all overseas packing and any and all other charges beyond the FOB prices.
5. To the extent that the Committee certifies that it is absolutely unable to supply any items in whole or in the quantities specified in the Government list, the Government shall specify other alternatives and the Committee shall make every effort to obtain such substitute materials. However, in the event the Committee finally certifies that it has exhausted all such alternatives, the Government shall have the right to have the equivalent value supplied in the basic foodstuffs nutritious for children, such as the materials referred to in the first list supplied to the Committee by the Government.
6. This is an agreement in which the utmost good faith is required on the part of both parties, who agree that time is of the essence and every effort humanly possible will be made to effect the exchange of the prisoners upon delivery of the first shipment covered by the Letter of Credit. To that end the Government shall send today to Miami, Florida, U. S. A. several representatives of the Cuban Red Cross who shall, together with the representatives of the American Red Cross and the Committee inspect the shipments.
7. Dr. Donovan will remain in Havana to complete the attestation in the Canadian Embassy to make effective the Letter of Credit in accordance with its items.
8. A copy of this memorandum shall be deposited with the Royal Bank of Canada, to clarify the intent of the parties under the Letter of Credit.

9. The Government states its intention that the materials supplied under the agreement satisfy the indemnity fixed by the Revolutionary Tribunals which passed judgement, upon the happenings of the Bay of Pigs.

For the Government

/s/ Regino Boti

/s/ René Vallejo

For the Committee

/s/Alvaro Sanchez, Jr.
Chairman

/s/ James B. Donovan
General Counsel

HIA Box 39, *Cuban Chronology*, 298–99.

APPENDIX I
VENDOR DONATIONS ACCEPTED BY THE AMERICAN NATIONAL RED CROSS AND WHOLESALE VALUE OF GOODS INVOICED UNDER CUBAN PRISONERS PROJECT

ARC No.	Name of Vendor	Category	Value of Goods Sent to Cuba (in U.S. dollars)
100	Beech-Nut Life Savers, Inc.	Food	193,926
100A	Beech-Nut Life Savers, Inc.	Milk	148,296
100A	Beech-Nut Life Savers, Inc.	Food	299,311
101	Gerber Products Co.	Food	1,022,188
102	American Cyanamid Co. (Lederle Labs)	Drugs	2,402,166
102A	American Cyanamid Co. (Lederle Labs)	Drugs	783,630
103	Eli Lilly & Co.	Drugs	1,857,798
104	Armour Pharmaceutical Co.	Drugs	52,302
105	S. B. Penick & Co.	Drugs	18,749
106	Merck and Co.	Drugs	2,502,212
107	Clay-Adams, Inc.	Equipment	5,477
108	Carter Products, Inc.	Drugs	441,000
109	Cutter Laboratories	Drugs	47,880
110	Richardson Merrell, Inc.	Drugs	1,272,292
111	Pitman-Moore Company	Drugs	220,433
112	Eaton Laboratories	Drugs	65,153

113	Davis & Geck	Equipment	100,175
114	Savage Laboratories	Drugs	9,459
115	Empire State Thermometer Co., Inc.	Equipment	17,895
116	The Upjohn Company	Drugs	1,491,127
117	Warner Lambert Pharmaceutical Co.	Drugs	1,457,221
118	The Stuart Co.	Drugs	149,281
119	Burroughs Wellcome & Co., Inc.	Drugs	329,058
120	Ethicon, Inc.	Equipment	1,011,285
121	Hynson, Westcott & Dunning, Inc.	Drugs	24,396
122	Sandoz Pharmaceuticals	Drugs	137,259
123	Sterling Drugs	Drugs	605,041
124	Smith, Kline & French Laboratories	Drugs	1,112,590
125	C.R. Bard, Inc.	Equipment	20,543
126	Bristol-Myers Co.	Drugs	336,596
127	Abbott Laboratories	Drugs	1,000,495
128	G.D. Searle & Co.	Drugs	902,646
129	Rohm & Haas Co.	Drugs	493,243
130	Ritter & Co.	Equipment	31,357
131	The Borden Company	Food	1,486,868
132	Chas. Pfizer & Co., Inc.	Drugs	1,022,097
133	Seamless Rubber Co.	Equipment	4,298
134	Ayerst Laboratories	Drugs	383,993
134A	Ayerst Laboratories	Drugs	182,400
134B	Ayerst Laboratories	Drugs	12,800
135	Ciba Pharmaceutical Co.	Drugs	577,859
136	Hoffman-LaRoche, Inc.	Drugs	1,098,226
137	Irwin, Neisler & Co.	Drugs	6,600
145	WTS Pharmaceuticals	Drugs	199,984
146	American Home Products (Whitehall Labs)	Drugs	323,487
147	Pillsbury Company	Food	226,804
148	The Kendall Co., Inc.	Drugs	14,275
148	The Kendall Co., Inc.	Equipment	145,212
148A	The Kendall Co., Inc.	Equipment	170,711
149	Baxter Laboratories, Inc.	Drugs	185,839
149	Baxter Laboratories, Inc.	Equipment	5900
150	Wyeth Laboratory	Drugs	1,463,122

151	Taylor Instrument	Equipment	4,650
152	The Mentholatum Co., Inc.	Drugs	49,939
153	Glenbrook Laboratories	Drugs	12,745
154	S.S.S. Co.	Drugs	37,554
155	Dome Chemical Co., Inc.	Drugs	105,211
156	Ames Co., Inc.	Drugs	302,162
157	Pet Milk Company	Milk	65,007
157	Pet Milk Company	Food	126,000
158	Becton, Dickinson & Co.	Equipment	9,910
158A	Becton, Dickinson & Co.	Drugs	24,035
159	The Mennen Co.	Drugs	201,585
160	Miles Laboratories, Inc.	Drugs	464,958
161	American Hospital Supply Co.	Drugs	41,724
161	American Hospital Supply Co.	Equipment	8,586
162	General Foods Corp.	Food	726,367
163	General Mills, Inc.	Food	448,275
164	Austenal Co.	Equipment	48,876
165	McKeeson & Robbins, Inc.	Drugs	1,190,767
166	G.C. Hanford, Mfg. Co.	Drugs	10,773
167	Lehn & Fink Products Corp.	Drugs	81,584
170	W.F. Young Inc.	Drugs	52,500
172	Parke, Davis & Co.	Drugs	621,481
172A	Parke, Davis & Co.	Drugs	648,680
173	H. J. Heinz Company	Food	1,556,835
174	National Biscuit Co.	Food	203,624
175	American Optical Co.	Equipment	175,091
176	Plough, Inc.	Drugs	154,685
177	Sterilon	Equipment	15,869
178	Winn-Dixie Stores, Inc.	Food	15,648
179	Pharmacraft Laboratories	Drugs	78,234
182	Chesebrough-Pond's, Inc.	Drugs	38,155
183	Corning Glass Works	Equipment	181,711
184	Green Giant Co.	Food	135,500
186	Owens Illinois Glass Co.	Equipment	238,595
187	Campbell Soup Co.	Food	735,000
189	Union Carbide Corp.	Drugs	1,525,105

190	Bausch & Lomb, Inc.	Equipment	153,887
191	Standard Brands, Inc.	Food	300,230
192	General Aniline & Film Co.	Equipment	45,183
194	Orthopedic Equipment Co.	Equipment	13,108
194A	Orthopedic Equipment Co.	Equipment	4,851
195	White Dental Co.	Equipment	2,325
196	Difco Laboratories	Drugs	64,586
197	E. R. Squibb & Sons	Drugs	408,393
198	Truett Labs (Div. Southwestern Drug Corp.)	Drugs	13,627
199	Anderson Clayton Co.	Food	10,021
200	The Wheatena Corp.	Food	574
201	Eastman Kodak Co.	Equipment	360,884
203	Westinghouse Electric Corp.	Equipment	73,603
204	E. Leitz Inc.	Equipment	2,970
205	Tecumseh Refrigeration Co.	Equipment	79
206	Acme Cotton Products Co.	Equipment	2,694
207	Dade Reagents, Inc.	Drugs	8,456
208	Machlett Laboratories, Inc.	Equipment	1,800
209	Richards Mfg. Co.	Equipment	13,756
210	Proctor & Gamble	Food	208,006
211	Church & Dwight	Food	4,375
212	George P. Pilling & Son Co.	Equipment	184
213	J.H. Emerson Co.	Equipment	450
214	Warren E. Collins, Inc.	Equipment	2,967
215	Ohio Chemical and Surgical Equipment Co.	Equipment	34,714
216	General Electric Co.	Equipment	60,533
217	American Sterilizer Co.	Equipment	38,955
218	Corn Products	Food	971,273*
219	Bird Corp.	Equipment	10,000
220	Acme Markets, Inc.	Food	4,633
222	Chemtron Corp.	Equipment	878
223	International Chemical Corp.	Drugs	691
224	The Birtcher Corp.	Equipment	970
225	Bon Vivants Soups, Inc.	Food	590

*Includes $8,889 of supplies presumed loaded on S.S. *Morning Light.*

226	Zenith Laboratories, Inc.	Drugs	6,776
228	Monsanto Chemical Co.	Drugs	18,357
229	Hellige, Inc.	Equipment	476
230	Dentist's Supply Co. of N.Y.	Equipment	330,574
233	Murine Co.	Drugs	5,039
247	Purdue Frederick Co.	Drugs	118,517
249	Airshields, Inc.	Equipment	7,850
252	A.E. Staley Mfg. Co.	Drugs	29,700
253	McNeil Laboratories	Drugs	800
254	Organon	Drugs	11,950
255	(See No. 102A)		
256	U.S. Dept. of Agriculture	Milk	2,354,950*
256	U.S. Dept. of Agriculture	Food	3,150,267
258	United Fruit Co.	Food	276,951
259	Mortemoth Chemical Laboratories	Drugs	19,592
259	Mortemoth Chemical Laboratories	Equipment	2,205
260	Schering Corp.	Drugs	103,434
261	Geigy Chemical Corp.	Drugs	199,076
262	Bio Rama Drug	Drugs	7,550
263	Allied Supermarkets	Food	1,859
264	Hunt Foods & Industries, Inc.	Food	196,073
265	Food Fair Stores	Food	9,262
266	California Packing Corporation	Food	344,343
267	Universal Foods Corp.	Food	49,903
268	Jewel Tea Co., Inc.	Food	11,534
269	Hershey Chocolate Corp.	Food	318,165
270	Vaponefrin Company	Equipment	36,012
271	Alcon Laboratories, Inc.	Drugs	51,408
272	North Star Dairy	Milk	1,161
273	T.J. Lipton Co.	Food	47,981
274	American White Cross Laboratories	Equipment	627
275	Lawton Company	Equipment	2,475
276	Aero Plast Corp.	Equipment	7,184

*Donation of $2 million from Union Carbide established as credit with Department of Agriculture; difference includes 3,800 lbs. milk ($635) and 950 lbs. shortening ($150) in dispute on shipments nos. 28 and 31 and not billed.

277	Cameron Miller Surgical Instrument Co.	Equipment	257
278	McKesson Appliance Co.	Equipment	1893
280	Torit Manufacturing Co.	Equipment	557
281	The Forregger Co., Inc.	Equipment	17,804
282	Crown Surgical Manufacturing Corp.	Equipment	144
283	Blue M Electric Co.	Equipment	426
285	Pfeiffer Glass, Inc.	Equipment	28,545
286	American Wheel Chair (Div. Institutional Industries, Inc.)	Equipment	6,072
287	Chase Chemical Co.	Drugs	5,040
288	Minnesota Mining & Mfg. Co.	Equipment	5,635
289	Baker Laboratory, Inc.	Milk	9,997
290	E.I. Dupont de Nemours & Co.	Equipment	20,938
291	Welch-Allyn, Inc.	Equipment	4,532
292	Cuban Families Committee	Drugs	78,750
292	Cuban Families Committee	[not identified]	617
292A	Cuban Families Committee	Equipment	1,168
292B	Cuban Families Committee	Drugs	473
292C	Cuban Families Committee	Drugs	63
292D	Cuban Families Committee	Equipment	1,875
3	Zimmer Manufacturing Co.	Equipment	3,550
295	Johnson & Johnson	Equipment	42,059
296	Fuller Pharmaceutical Co.	Equipment	620
297	Coleman Instruments, Inc.	Equipment	82,297
298	Mizzy, Inc.	Equipment	2,500
301	Homer Higgs Sales Corp.	Equipment	3,444
301	Halperin Company	Equipment	6,824
303	W.D. Hudson Manufacturing Co.	Equipment	12,042
304	The Lufkin Rule Co.	Equipment	21,258
305	Association of American Medical Book Publishers	Equipment	5,000
	GRAND TOTAL		**$49,317,044**

From *HIA,* Box 44.

APPENDIX J
VERBAL MESSAGE OF FIDEL CASTRO TO PRESIDENT JOHNSON THROUGH LISA HOWARD*

To: President Lyndon B. Johnson

From: Prime Minister Fidel Castro

Verbal Message given to Miss Lisa Howard of
ABC News on February 12, 1964 in Havana, Cuba.

1. Please tell President Johnson that I earnestly desire his election to the Presidency in November . . . though that appears assured. But if there is anything I can do to add to his majority (aside from retiring from politics), I shall be happy to cooperate. Seriously, I observe how the Republicans use Cuba as a weapon against the Democrats. So tell President Johnson to let me know what I can do, if anything. Naturally, I know that my offer of assistance would be of immense value to the Republicans—so this would remain our secret. But if the President wishes to pass word to me he can do so through you [Lisa Howard]. He must know that he can trust you; and I know that I can trust you to relay a message accurately.

2. If the President feels it necessary during the campaign to make bellicose statements about Cuba or even to take some hostile action—if he will inform me, unofficially, that a specific action is required because of domestic political considerations, I shall understand and not take any serious retaliatory action.

3. Tell the President that I understand quite well how much political courage it took for President Kennedy to instruct you [Lisa Howard] and Ambassador Attwood to phone my aide in Havana for the purpose of commencing a dialogue toward a settlement of our differences. Ambassador Attwood suggested that I prepare an agenda for such talks and send the agenda to my U.N. Ambassador. That was on November 18th. The agenda was being prepared when word arrived that President Kennedy was assassinated. I hope that we can soon continue where Ambassador Attwood's phone conversation to Havana left off . . . though I'm aware that pre-electoral political considerations may delay this approach until after November.

4. Tell the President (and I cannot stress this too strongly) that I seriously hope that Cuba and the United States can eventually sit down in an atmosphere of good will and of mutual respect and negotiate our differences. I

---

*This document, in PDF format, can be found at http://www.gwu.edu/~nsarchive/NSAEBB/
NSAEBB103/640212.pdf.

believe that there are *no* areas of contention between us that cannot be discussed and settled in a climate of mutual understanding. But first, of course, it is necessary to *discuss* our differences. I now believe that this hostility between Cuba and the United States is both unnatural and unnecessary—and it can be eliminated.

5. Tell the President he should not interpret my conciliatory attitude, my desire for discussions, as a sign of weakness. Such an interpretation would be a serious miscalculation. We are not weak . . . the Revolution is strong . . . very strong. Nothing, absolutely nothing that the United States can do will destroy the Revolution. Yes, we are strong. And it is from this position of strength that we wish to resolve our differences with the United States and to live in peace with all nations of the world.

6. Tell the President I realize fully the need for absolute secrecy, if he should decide to continue the Kennedy approach. I revealed nothing at that time . . . I have revealed nothing since . . . I would reveal nothing now.

Appendix K
New York City Board of Education: Report of Progress and Growth for the Period September 1961 to May 1965

1. Statement of Policy on Excellence for New York City schools.
   a. Quality education for all children
   b. Better ethnic distribution of pupils to prepare for multi-racial world
   c. Creation of an Assistant Superintendent for Integration
   d. A proposal to add 3 additional school days in 1966–1967 school year to bring up to the formerly customary 190 days.
2. Pre-Kindergarten for 3 and 4 year olds
3. After-school study centers
4. Expanded summer instruction
5. "More Effective Schools" program started in September 1964 in disadvantaged neighborhoods with massive specialized services.
6. Group intelligence tests abolished in February 1964.
7. September 1965: Board of Education educational TV program.
8. New type of high school. Experiment will begin with progress at students' own rate.
9. An increase in the number of day school teachers since 1961 to 46,502.
10. Reading clinics increased
11. An increase in the number of special teachers for improved reading by almost 500 to 928.
12. 650 lay volunteers to assist teachers.
13. More guidance counselors.

14. Playgrounds open everyday for entire year.
15. Manpower Development Training Program for young people who have already dropped out, together with a job-counseling program. Drop out rate lowered from 30.23% to 23.68%.
16. Textbooks which show role of minorities in the United States and New York.
17. Puerto Rican Discovery Day started on November 19, 1964. Puerto Rican children in schools total 190,465 or 18.2% of the student population.
18. Ethnic balance: Open enrollment and Free Choice Transfer Programs; transfer of students, with parents consent, from over-crowded to under-utilized schools; site selections in fringe areas and rezoning of existing schools; school pairings; transfer of 9th grade pupils from 10 junior high schools which were classified as *de facto* segregated to 9th grade in better integrated schools; changes in junior high school feeder patterns; alternate assignment program in connection with transfer of pupils in 30 elementary schools to 6th grade in junior high schools.
19. Move toward four-year comprehensive high schools; Girls High School closed in the fall of 1964, a step away from segregated schools.
20. Courses in human relations mandatory for all teachers.
21. The city was divided into 15 zones so that small bus carriers could bid for contracts; action broke the monopoly held by large companies.
22. Custodians income better controlled.
23. 400 portable classrooms placed in use in September 1964, in addition to another 150 which were converted from non-instructional space.
24. Fiscal flexibility: Board broke the financial straight jacket by a Memorandum of Agreement on July 18, 1963, among the Mayor, the President of the Board of Education and the Comptroller. Essentially, the Board gained the right to expend all monies appropriated to it as it sees fit without further Board of Estimate approval. The only exception was repairs in excess of $25,000.

HIA, Box 70.

Appendix L
Eulogy by Father Robert I. Gannon
St. Patrick's Cathedral, January 21, 1970

It seems like yesterday—actually it was more than 33 years ago—that a quiet, shrewd young member of the senior class came into my office at Fordham to size me up. He was the editor of the college weekly and wanted to let the student body know what they could expect from the new administration.

When he finished and left I said to myself "Well, I hope that Donovan is typical of his generation. I can live with boys like him." The impression deepened as the year wore on. He knew the door was open and came regularly to talk about every new development on campus: the visit of the future Pope Pius XII; the incredible record of the football team with its Seven Blocks of Granite; the completion and dedication of the graduate school and all the other headline events of 1936.

The draft was not even anticipated as yet, still less World War II, but I came to know Jim Donovan as the kind of student we had in mind when we started the place in 1841; the kind we wanted to graduate in 1937: intelligent, fearless and good—a man of principle. While he was at the Harvard Law School I stopped by one day to have lunch with his little group of friends. He was evidently their leader and deserved to be.

After Pearl Harbor we followed his record in the service and later at the trials in Nuremberg where he was in charge of all the visual evidence. Even that early in his career a pattern began to develop that soon became consistent. He was always unpopular with extremists of the Right and Left and always seemed quite indifferent to such unpopularity. He once gave a lecture at Cornell entitled: "The Privilege of Advocating Unpopular Causes." Reactionaries called him a "Commie-lover" because he once saw to it that even a Communist spy received a fair hearing. Others labeled him a racist because he defended the rights of all American children, white as well as black. But Fidel Castro and J. Edgar Hoover, who agreed on nothing else, both trusted Jim Donovan because they recognized a man of principle.

After the war he was quietly building a law practice, when the Brooklyn Bar Association asked him to undertake the defense of the top Soviet spy in the U.S., Rudolf Ivanovich Abel. He accepted the invitation as a public duty and became headline news overnight. His success in this venture led Cardinal Cushing, Bishop Pike and New York's own Dr. Finklestein, together with parents and brothers and wives of prisoners in Havana, to seek his help in freeing the thousands of unfortunate Americans and Cubans who were victims of the disastrous Bay of Pigs. His handling of the situation was nothing short of brilliant and brought him a nomination to the United States Senate. He would have liked to be a senator but did not regard that as being quite as important as the safety of the 10,000 human beings he was working to release so he neglected his campaign and lost the election.

Now that he had been conditioned to modern warfare by Nuremberg, Moscow and Havana, it was appropriate that he become head of the largest educational complex in the world. Anyone who willingly becomes president of the New York City Public School System is looking for martyrdom and Jim very nearly achieved that goal. He went through picketing, rioting and demands for his resignation as a racist because he would not yield to political pressure and bus little children to schools that were far from home. In the end, the Board of Education re-elected him.

As the violent 1960s wore on, the unrest reached the college campuses. Racism and Viet Nam, acting on certain types of students, certain types of professors and certain types of administrators, brought educational chaos and disgrace to many universities and colleges. It was said that only five per cent of the students were actually throwing things but the other ninety-five per cent seemed strangely unable to defend themselves. So, logically enough at this point, Jim Donovan accepted the Presidency of Pratt Institute. This distinguished institution with an international reputation was soon caught in a national crisis. When the riots and strikes developed, its President attracted attention by taking the stand of a red-blooded American, interested in higher education. It was to be his last "unpopular cause."

Once more he was denounced as a racist and even worse than that, as a conservative. The fact was that although he could always see the good in men who were not like himself, men like Rudolf Ivanovich Abel, Fidel Castro and Malcolm X, he was still a conservative in the best sense of the Latin word "conservare," which means to treasure what is best from the past and the present so that the future may know what is meant by wisdom.

Of course, a man of principle is never one thing in public and another in private, so Jim was a family man in the best sense of the word. He had married Mary for love and there was always love in the home. As a husband and a father, he measured up to his reputation in the public service and as a Catholic he developed just as his Alma Mater hoped he would. He became a Knight of Malta and of the Holy Sepulcher who observed all the ideals of these historic orders.

To his friends, of course, it seems that he was taken from them twenty years too soon, but who knows? Life for so many of us can become such an anti-climax. It is wonderful to go when everyone is saying, "stay." In such a death as his, there is no sorrow. The tears that are shed are tears of sentiment, not of regret. As we read in the Preface of the Requiem Mass, "For those who are faithful, life is not ended but merely changed." For such, death is just a kindly usher who opens the door to eternity and beckons to us to cross the threshold. Every priest reads in the office for many martyrs this beautiful passage from the Book of Wisdom: "*Justorum animae in manu Dei sunt.*" "The souls of the just are in the hands of God and the torment of death will not touch them. In the sight of the unwise they seem to die . . . but they are in peace."

Rev. Robert I. Gannon, S.J. *A Eulogy for James B. Donovan.* Fordham University, 1970. Pamphlet. The eulogy is also reprinted in its entirety in the *Pratt Alumnus* 72, 2 (Spring 1970): 19–30.

APPENDIX M
MEMBERSHIPS AND HONORS

Memberships

American Bar Association, Chair, 1961–62, Insurance Negligence and
    Compensation Law Section
American College of Trial Lawyers, fellow

American Judicature Society, member
American Law Institute, member
American Legion Auxiliary Poppy Club, 1964
American Legion, Post Commander, Clavin Post, Brooklyn, 1960–61
American Organization of Jewish Survivors of Nazi Concentration Camps, honorary general counsel
American Society of International Law, fellow
Art Commission, City of New York, Member 1951–61; president, 1966–68
Association of the Bar of the City of New York, chair, Committee on Insurance Law
Association of the Bar of the City of New York, member
Association of Insurance Attorneys, 1965
Authors' Guild, member
Bath and Tennis Club of Lake Placid, member
Bathing and Tennis Club of Spring Lake, member
Brooklyn Club, member
Brooklyn Institute of Arts and Sciences, trustee
Brooklyn Museum, member, Governing Committee
Campaign Culture for the Reconstruction of Bedford-Stuyvesant, organizer
Cardinal's Committee of the Laity, member
College of Insurance, trustee and chair, Library Committee
Drug and Chemical Club of New York, member
Fordham College Alumni Association, vice-president
Forest Press, director, 1960 (publisher of Dewey Decimal System)
Friendly Sons of St. Patrick, New York and Brooklyn, member
Golf and Country Club of Spring Lake, New Jersey, member
Grolier Club of New York, member
Harvard Club of New York, member
Harvard Law School Association of New York, trustee
Insurance Society of New York, chair, Library Committee, 1957–61
International Academy of Trial Lawyers, fellow
International Association of Insurance Counsel, member
Irish-American Historical Society, member
Junior League of Brooklyn, Advisory Committee, 1961
Knight of the Holy Sepulcher, member
Knights of Malta, member
Lake Placid Club Education Foundation, president (1960)
Lake Placid Club, member
Maritime Law Association of the United States, member
Marymount College (VA), Board of Advisors, 1961
Mearin Foundation, trustee
Methodist Hospital, trustee
Metropolitan Club of New York, member
Montauk Club, member
Municipal Art Commission of the City of New York, secretary, 1951–61

National Lawyers Club of Washington, DC, member
New York State Bar Association, chair, Committee on Administrative Law, 1959–61
New York State Bar Association, chair, Committee on Insurance Section, 1951
Northwood School for Boys, trustee, Lake Placid, New York
Phi Delta Phi, member
Rembrandt Club of Brooklyn, member
Richmond County (Staten Island) Country Club, member
St. Francis College, trustee; chair, Council of Regents, 1960–61
St. John's University Law School, Phi Delta Phi, honorary member
Veterans of Foreign Wars, member

Awards

Legion of Merit—World War II Service
Tyne Award, Federation of Insurance Counsel, 1953
Gold Medal Award, General Insurance Brokers' Association of New York, 1958
Public Service Award, Brooklyn Bar Association, December 4, 1958
Alumni Achievement Award in Law, Fordham University, 1960
Civil Liberties Award, New York State Bar Association, New York County Lawyers Association, and the Association of the Bar of the City of New York, 1961
CIA Distinguished Intelligence Medal, 1962
Law Day Award, Decalogue Society of Illinois, 1962
Americanism Award, Kings County American Legion, 1962
Encaenia Award, Fordham College, 1962
Honorary Colonel on the Governor's Staff, State of Oklahoma, 1962
Award of Honor, Emerald Lawyers Society of New York, 1963
Award of Merit, Lotus Club, 1963
Award of Honor, Dutch Treat Club, 1963
Catholic Layman of the Year, 1st recipient, Associated First Friday Clubs
Fifth Annual Award of the Hispanic Society of the New York City Police Department, 1963
Gold Medal, Interfaith Movement, 1963
American Red Cross Decoration, 1963
Gold Medal Award by Brooklyn College, 1963
Grand Cross of the Order of Mercedarians (award subsequently blessed by Pope Paul VI in special audience)
Distinguished Service Medallion of the City of New York, 1963
Andrew Carney Centennial Award, Carney Hospital, Boston, MA, 1963
First Annual Humanitarian Award, St. Vincent's Home for Boys, 1963
Strangers on a Bridge selected by Literary Guild, Catholic Book Club, and Readers Digest Condensed Book Club, 1964
Bishop Griffin General Assembly Patriotic Award, 1964

Laurel Wreath for Achievement, Doctorate Association of New York Educators, 1964
John F. Kennedy Memorial Award, Holyoke College, 1964
St. Francis Xavier Medal, Xavier University, 1965
Scribes Organization of the ABA selects *Strangers on a Bridge* as best portrayal of legal profession to general public, 1965
Humanities Award, College of Insurance, 1966

Honorary Degrees

LLD, Fordham University, 1962, Bronx, New York
LittD, St. Francis College. 1963, Brooklyn, New York
LHD, Villanova University, June 3, 1963, Villanova, Pennsylvania
LHD, Bryant College, 1963, Smithfield, Rhode Island
LLD, Albany Law School, 1965, Albany, New York
LLD, Gannon College, 1965, Erie, Pennsylvania
JD, Harvard Law School, 1969, Cambridge, Massachusettes

Notes

CHAPTER 1. THE EARLY YEARS

1. "The Survivor," *Life*, June 1998, 106. Catherine died in 2002 at the age of 109. *New York Times*, October 19, 2002, sec. A, national edition. The last survivor, Adella Wotherspoon, died on January 26, 2004, at the age of 100. *New York Times*, February 4, 2004, sec. C, national edition. Citations from the *New York Times* are based on the metropolitan New York edition unless otherwise noted.

2. Clarence Axman, "James B. Donovan," *Eastern Underwriter* (April 25, 1958).

3. Claude Rust, *The Burning of the General Slocum* (New York: Elsevier/Nelson Books, 1981); see also John S. Ogilvie, *History of the General Slocum Disaster* (New York: Ogilvie, 1904); I. N. Phelps-Stokes, *The Iconography of Manhattan Island* (New York: R.H. Dodd, 1915–28); John Steele Gordon, "The Wreck of the *General Slocum*," *Seaport: New York's History Magazine* 23, 1 (Summer 1989): 28–35; and New York City Board of Health, *Annual Report* of 1904 (New York: Martin Brown Press, 1905). The captain of the *General Slocum*, William Van Schaick, was eventually sentenced to ten years imprisonment. The ship, itself, which had burned down to the waterline, was reconditioned as a barge. It sank in a storm off Atlantic City, New Jersey, in 1911.

4. *New York Times*, December 13, 1950. John Donovan's obituary, and his family's tradition, are the only sources of information on his receipt of a gold medal. The New York City Department of Records and Information Services does not have listings of award recipients for that time (letter to the author, June 21, 2000), nor does the *General Slocum* Memorial Committee (letter to the author, August 4, 2000). A search of the records relating to the *Slocum* at the New York Historical Society and South Street Seaport Museum Library proved similarly fruitless with respect to John Donovan.

5. National Genealogical Society, Arlington, Virginia. Index card record of John Donovan, MD, transferred with other deceased physicians' records from the America Medical Association.

6. 1880 *U.S. Census*, Vol. 66, ED 662, Sheet 12, Line 4. John Donovan's father, James, a painter, was born in Ireland in July 1850. His future wife, Catherine, was also born in Ireland, in November of the same year. According to family tradition, John's father was born in Klonikilty, County Cork. He is believed to be related to a Father Donovan of Cork who was a chaplain of the Irish Brigade in Napoleon's army. See letter of James B. Donovan, November 6, 1958, to Rev. Francis P. Donovan, St. Teresa Church, Campbell, MD. James B. Donovan Papers, Hoover Institution Archives, Hoover Institution on War, Revolution and Peace, Stanford University (hereafter *HIA*), Box 3.

243

7. The area east of the Bronx River was annexed to New York County in 1895. Both areas were originally part of Westchester County. The Bronx did not become a county in its own right until 1914.

8. Xavier Alumni Sodality *Register Book*, 203. Cited in a letter of Rev. Daniel J. Gatti, S.J., to the author, March 24, 2001. John was a member from 1904 to 1911.

9. *New York Times*, September 29, 1935, Sec. 2.

10. James Joseph Donovan (New York City Birth Certificate, # 3089) was also known as James Aloysius. He became James B. Donovan at a later date. See note 12.

11. Fordham University, *Bulletin of Information* 12, 3 (April 1919). Originally founded as St. John's College, Fordham, on June 24, 1841, it became Fordham University on March 7, 1907.

12. James's sponsors were T. Louis A. Britt and Sarah Bolger. Britt, a cousin of Harriet Donovan, was an attorney and a president of the Catholic Club. He also managed Dr. Donovan's real estate holdings. Later in life, James would cease using his given middle name and adopt that of "Britt" in memory of this friend and relative.

13. The art editor of the avant-garde art and literary quarterly, *The Yellow Book* (published from April 1894 to April 1897), was English artist and illustrator, Aubrey Beardsley.

14. James B. Donovan, "Memories of One Book Collector" (speech, annual dinner, Antiquarian Booksellers Association, New York City, October 14, 1969).

15. Incunabula (pl. of Lat. *incunabulum*, meaning cradle) are early books printed before 1500. The multifaceted Woollcott (1887–1943), journalist; actor, starring in *The Man Who Came to Dinner* in 1940; and radio host of "The Town Crier," was a member of the literary circle, the Algonquin Round Table. Carolyn Wells (1862–1942) wrote 170 books including mysteries and children's stories.

16. The school has no surviving copies of its newspaper for the time that Donovan attended (1929–33), or the yearbook for 1933. According to Paul Krebs of the Development Office, the yearbook may not have been printed during the Depression years. Conversation with the author, November 2001.

17. Henry Lee, "James B. Donovan: Metadiplomat," *Catholic Digest* 28, 5 (March 1964): 56.

18. Conversations with James's wife, Mary, between 1999 and 2001.

19. Letter of Edward J. Calhoun, MD, October 18, 1962, *HIA*, Box 3.

20. The scripts for many of the one-act plays are no longer extant. According to an article in the *Ram*, the play *Deadline* was a newspaper story concerned with the attempts of a corrupt candidate for the office of mayor to hide a sensational revelation about his record. Near midnight, the star reporter comes into the editorial offices with the proof of the politician's intrigue. The assistant editor puts the copy on the presses knowing the probable consequences. Mills, the politician, appears and, when his bribe is refused, approaches the editor-in-chief. The latter, despite threats by the candidate, holds to the journalist's code of "Print the News." *Ram*, May 3, 1934. James, himself, played one of the reporters in the performance.

21. *Ram*, October 19, 1934. The late Vince Lombardi was one of Fordham football's line known as the "Seven Blocks of Granite." He later went on to coach the Green Bay Packers from 1959 to 1967. Wellington Mara was president of the New York Giants football team.

22. *New York Times*, September 29, 1935, sec. 2. The newspaper listed some of the guests: Judge and Mrs. William E. Slevin, Mr. and Mrs. James J. Donovan, Mr. and Mrs. T. Louis A. Britt, Mr. and Mrs. Harry Ulmer, Dr. and Mrs. Edwin R. Crowe, Dr. and Mrs. Thomas Haynes Curtin, Mr. and Mrs. George A. Weigel, Dr. and Mrs. Edward L. Corbett, Mr. and Mrs. James J. Donovan Jr., Dr. and Mrs. William P.

Doran, Mrs. Daniel J. Hennessey, Dr. and Mrs. John J. McMahon, Mrs. William T. Wallace, Miss Anna G. Byrne, Miss Helen Curtin, John J. Donovan Jr., James A. Donovan, William T. Wallace Jr. and Dr. Louis M. Mooney.

23. *Ram,* November 22, 1935; December 20, 1935; March 20, 1936; March 6, 1936; December 11, 1936; February 19, 1937.

24. Ibid., December 11, 1936.

25. Central to most student demonstrations that occurred was the recitation of the *Oxford Oath* ("I refuse to support the Government of the United States in any war it may conduct"). The *New York Times,* on the day following the rallies, cited an editorial written by Donovan in the *Ram* in which James called for an immediate investigation of the "radical activities of student organizations involved in the peace strike." April 23, 1937.

26. *Ram,* April 23, 1937.

27. "Anti-War Strike Is Anti-Peace Movement: College Students Led By Communist Strategists," *America,* 57, 6 (May 15, 1937): 126–28.

28. *Ram,* October 16, 1936.

29. Ibid., March 19, 1937.

30. *America* 54, 10 (December 14, 1935): 220.

31. *Ram,* February 28, 1936.

32. Ibid., October 23, 1936.

33. Ibid., March 13, 1936.

34. *Vogue,* "College Man's Vote," December 15, 1935, 84.

35. *Ram,* January 17, 1936.

36. Ibid., January 15, 1937 and February 19, 1937. The play was written in 1936 before it became well known that the Nazis and fascists were providing significant men and materiel to General Franco and the rebels.

37. *Ram,* May 21, 1937. Prohibition ended in December 1933.

38. "Informal Confession of a Pipe-lover," *Fordham Literary Monthly* 52, 1 (November 1934): 8–9.

39. Letter to James B. Donovan, May 11, 1939, *HIA,* Box 6.

40. "Communication and Study Relating to the Defense of Fair Comment in Actions for Libel or Slander: Report of the Law Revision Commission of New York State." Undergraduate thesis, Harvard University Law School, April 1940.

41. Thomas Parry (Donovan, Parry, McDermott and Radzik), in discussion with the author, June 30, 2000. Parry was present when Judge Edelstein related the story.

42. *Shay v. Metropolitan Life Insurance Co.,* 172 Misc. 202, 14 N.Y.S. 2d 347, aff'd. 260 App. Div. 958, 24 N.Y.S. 2d 870 (1940).

43. *New York Times,* December 18, 1940.

44. Charles Moritz, ed., *Current Biography Yearbook, 1961* (New York: H. W. Wilson, 1961), 138.

45. This case was not recorded and was most probably withdrawn or dismissed upon publications of the apologies.

46. *New York Daily News,* September 26, 1940; see also Ray Robinson, *Iron Horse: Lou Gehrig and His Time* (New York: W.W. Norton, 1990), 269–70.

47. *Edmund Kilroy and May Kilroy v. The News Syndicate Co., Inc.* 263 A.D. 961; 32 N.Y.S. 2d 210 (1942).

48. Other cases in which Donovan was a part included *Patricia Wilder v. The Daily News and Danton Walker* (NY, 1941); *Jerzy L. Potocki v. The News Syndicate Co., Inc.* (NY, 1941); and *Edward L. Walsh v. The News Syndicate Co., Inc.* (NY,1941). As in the case of Lou Gehrig, these cases were not reported and were perhaps settled out of court.

49. Mary Donovan Busch, conversation with author, Spring Lake, NJ, June 2, 2000.

CHAPTER 2. THE LAWYER IN WORLD WAR II

1. This was a stellar group of scientists. Vannevar Bush (1890–1974), an electrical engineer, developed the differential analyzer. Robert A. Millikin (1868–1954), a research physicist at the University of Chicago, later directed the Norman Bridge Laboratories at the California Institute of Technology and received the Nobel Prize in 1923. Ernest O. Lawrence (1901–1958), physicist, invented the cyclotron in 1930 and received the Nobel Prize in 1939. James B. Conant (1893–1978), a research chemist at Harvard, was elected president of the university in 1933, later U.S. High Commissioner for West Germany, then ambassador, and devoted his final years to education. Karl T. Compton (1887–1954), physicist, graduate, then researcher in atomic physics at Princeton University, after World War II chaired the National Military Establishment (later Department of Defense). Harold C. Urey (1893–1981), chemist, discovered deuterium.

2. James B. Donovan, "Byways of Law: An autobiographical retrospection delivered as the annual Arant Lecture at the Ohio State University College of Law, Columbus, Ohio, on January 21, 1966," in *Challenges: Reflections of a Lawyer-at-Large* (New York: Atheneum House, 1967), 4–5.

3. *Eastern Underwriter*, December 28, 1956.

4. *From William Street to a Bridge in Berlin: Profile of Lawyer Jim Donovan* (n.d., ca. 1962). New York Democratic State Committee campaign flyer, *HIA*, Box 2.

5. *Eastern Underwriter*, December 28, 1956.

6. *HIA*, Box 37.

7. At the time of his selection to OSS, James Donovan felt that some individuals in Congress suggested nepotism in his appointment. James B. Donovan, "Major General William J. Donovan: A Pioneer in U.S. Intelligence," *Columbia Library Columns* 14, 3 (May 1965): 4. William Joseph "Wild Bill" Donovan (1883–1959) was a Columbia University Law School classmate of Franklin D. Roosevelt, a WW I recipient of the Congressional Medal of Honor. From 1924–25 he served President Coolidge as assistant attorney general and later headed the Office of Strategic Services 1942–45. He was ambassador to Thailand 1953–54.

8. "COI Came First," in *The Office of Strategic Services: America's First Intelligence Agency*, Article 2 (Washington, DC: Central Intelligence Agency, 2000), http://www.cia.gov/cia/publications/oss/art02.htm.

9. "What Was OSS," in *The Office of Strategic Services: America's First Intelligence Agency*, Article 3 (Washington, DC: Central Intelligence Agency, 2000), http://www.cia.gov/cia/publications/oss/art03.htm.

10. Arthur M. Schlesinger Jr. (1917–) graduated Harvard University 1938. After WWII, he taught at Harvard until 1961. He was a campaign adviser to Adlai Stevenson and John F. Kennedy and later Kennedy's special assistant for Latin American affairs. His historical works have earned two Pulitzer Prizes. Richard M. Helms (1913–) came to prominence when he was successful in interviewing Adolf Hitler for United Press International. He joined the navy in 1942, and served in the OSS in Europe throughout the war. He remained in Germany working for the Central Intelligence Group and its successor, the Central Intelligence Agency (CIA), which he directed from 1961–73. Arthur J. Goldberg (1908–1990) was in private law practice until joining the OSS. In 1962 he was nominated to the Supreme Court, and remained on the bench for three years, resigning to become ambassador to the United Nations from 1965 to 1968, then Ambassador-at-Large from 1977–78. Allen W. Dulles (1893–1969) brother and law partner of John Foster Dulles, served with the OSS in Europe, was director of the CIA 1953–61, and was a noted author on foreign affairs and intelligence.

11. James B. Donovan, *Challenges,* 5–6. General Donovan himself had posed the question of tampering with an enemy's water supply. *HIA,* Box 37.

12. James B. Donovan, *Challenges,* 8–10.

13. Ibid., 10–11.

14. Ibid., 12–14.

15. John English, interviewed by Richard Dunlop in Dunlop's *Donovan, America's Master Spy* (Chicago: Rand McNally, 1982), 362.

16. Mary Donovan, telephone conversation with author, May 2001.

17.The name of the commission was eventually changed to the United Nations War Crimes Commission, which, by 1945, was chaired by Lord Wright of Australia.

18. Joseph E. Persico, *Nuremberg: Tyranny on Trial* (New York: Viking, 1994), 15.

19. George C. Stevens (1904–1975) had been a director/producer since the silent era, including *Dr. Jekyll and Mr. Hyde* (1920). Later movies included *Gunga Din* (1939) and *Woman of The Year* (1942). After the war, his credits included *I Remember Mama* (1948), *Shane* (1953), *Giant* (1956), *The Diary of Anne Frank* (1959), and *The Greatest Story Ever Told* (1965). Jay Robert Nash and Stanley Ralph Ross, *The Motion Picture Guide* (Chicago: Cinebooks, 1987), I–1532.

20. Dan Ford, *Pappy: The Life of John Ford* (Englewood Cliffs, NJ: Prentice-Hall, 1979), 202; Ford's citation for the Legion of Merit is in Andrew Sinclair, *John Ford* (New York: Dial Press/James Wade, 1979), 125.

21. Telford Taylor, *The Anatomy of the Nuremberg Trials: A Personal Memoir* (New York: Alfred A. Knopf, 1992), 47 (citing NA Box 1, File 000.51, Donovan to McCloy, October 5, 1944, transmitting OSS R&A No. 2577, September 28, 1944, "Problems Concerning The Treatment of War Criminals" OSS Micro.24).

22. Drexel A. Sprecher, *Inside The Nuremberg Trial: A Prosecutor's Comprehensive Account* (Lanham, MD: University Press of America, 1999), I:52.

23. *Executive Order 9547.* Russell Houghwout Jackson returned to the Supreme Court after Nuremberg in 1946 and continued to serve as associate justice until his death on October 9, 1954.

24. Justice Robert H. Jackson, interviewed by Harlan Phillips, February 1955, cited in Persico, *Nuremberg,* 28.

25. *HIA* Box 34, Folder 29.

26. Taylor, *Anatomy,* 47. From 1939–40 Taylor was a special assistant to Jackson as U.S. attorney general.

27. Western Union WY138 DL PD-New York NY 17 220 P 1945 May 17 PM 2 41 Lt. James B. Donovan, Office of Strategic Services.

28. "Program Report," 10, *HIA,* Box 35.

29. Taylor, *Anatomy,* 49. Taylor later was appointed chief prosecutor at the subsequent Nuremberg trials, replacing Justice Jackson. Lemkin, who died in 1959, was only recently honored by the United Nations for his work in developing an international convention opposing genocide. *New York Times,* June 13, 2001, national edition.

30. That Donovan won the New York Democratic senatorial nomination over Taylor in 1962 could have contributed to this feeling in Taylor's later writings.

31. Robert G. Storey, *The Final Judgement? From Pearl Harbor to Nuremberg* (San Antonio, TX: Naylor, 1968), 81. Storey refers to the home in "McClain."

CHAPTER 3. THE AFTERMATH OF WAR

1. R. R. Palmer and Joel Colton. *A History of the Modern World* (New York: Alfred A. Knopf, 1965), 895.

2. Ibid., 841.

3. Donovan's widow, Mary Donovan Busch, provided the author with access to forty-one personal letters from her husband written in the mid-1940s spanning the time he spent in the OSRD through his assignment in Nuremberg. The original letters remain with Mrs. Busch and are hereafter cited as JBD, Personal Letters. Photocopies of these letters may also be found in *HIA*, Box 34. For the most part, Donovan never provided a specific date when he wrote, often just noting the day of the week. However, there was sufficient information in his letters to determine the approximate, if not exact, date. Bracketed dates are those estimated by the author. Other bracketed data is included for clarification only; parenthetical remarks are those of Donovan.

4. Taylor, *Anatomy*, 86.

5. Of these individuals, Alderman, Bernays and Donovan constituted the Executive Committee of Jackson's staff.

6. JBD, Personal Letters, Friday [June 22, 1945].

7. Cable from Justice Jackson to Forrestal, labeled Priority, Secret in *HIA*, Box 7.

8. Storey and Thomas J. Dodd were co-executive trial counsels at the first Nuremberg trial. Storey had the task of finding additional attorneys for the prosecution. While in Paris, he recruited Ralph G. Albrecht, an attorney from New York with international experience, as a future trial counsel with Sidney Alderman, Telford Taylor and Col. John Harlan Amen. Amen, who was also establishing his office in the same building as Storey, was responsible for the interrogation of potential prosecution witnesses. Dodd (1907–1971) was executive trial counsel in subsequent trials in Nuremberg, later represented Connecticut as a congressman (1953–1957) and as a U.S. senator (1959–1971). *Biographical Directory of the United States Congress, 1774–1989* (Washington, DC: U.S. Government Printing Office, 1989), 917. Hereafter, *BDUSC*.

9. Storey, *The Final Judgement?*, 82–85.

10. JBD, Personal Letters, Monday [July 9, 1945].

11. Nuremberg is the English spelling; in German it had been Nürnberg.

12. Taylor, *Anatomy*, 56.

13. JBD, Personal Letters, Tuesday [July 17, 1945].

14. Taylor, *Anatomy*, 78–79.

15. Ibid., 79.

16. Office of United States Chief of Counsel for Prosecution of Axis Criminality, *Nazi Conspiracy and Aggression* (Washington, DC: U.S. Government Printing Office, 1946), 1:1–3. Hereafter, *Nazi Conspiracy and Aggression*. The record of negotiations that led to the agreement can be found in *Report of Robert H. Jackson, United States Representative To The International Conference on Military Trials* (Washington, DC: U.S. Government Printing Office, 1949), Department of State Publication No. 3080, International Organization and Conference Series II, European and British Commonwealth 1. Donovan's picture at the signing appeared in the *London Times*, August 9, 1945.

17. Ibid., 4–12.

18. *Nazi Conspiracy and Aggression*, 1:5.

19. Bernays later became a partner in the firm of Gale, Bernays, Falk, Eisner and Nathan, 40 Wall Street.

20. *Nazi Conspiracy and Aggression*, 1:13–82.

21. Shawcross, England's attorney general, was required to be in London for most of the trial. As a result, Sir David Maxwell-Fyfe performed most of the prosecutorial work in his place. Lord Ellwyn-Jones, *In My Time: An Autobiography* (London: Weidenfeld & Nicolson, 1983), 102. Lord Shawcross died at the age of 101 on July 10, 2003. *New York Times*, July 11, 2003, national edition.

22. JBD, Personal Letters [September 12, 1945]

23. A record of Donovan's military travel is located in *HIA*, Box 7. According to E. H. Cookridge in *Gehlen: Spy of the Century* (New York: Random House, 1971), 135, it was at about this same time that Reinhard Gehlen, a lieutenant general in Nazi Germany, surrendered to allied forces. He was immediately seen as an invaluable resource for information, especially about the USSR. His own plan was to assist the allies, but it also included establishing himself as the head of the German intelligence service after the war. At the time that Gehlen submitted his "plan," Cookridge relates that he first asked James Donovan to review it from a legal point of view. There is no evidence, however, in Donovan's personal papers that he ever spoke to or corresponded with Gehlen either at the time or later. It would have been unlike him not to note it, had this incident occurred, for he would certainly have seen it as a coup in his own career. As to Gehlen, the United States did accept his plan and later, in 1956, he became the leader of one of Germany's intelligence services until his retirement in 1968. See also R. Harris Smith, *OSS: The Secret History of America's First Central Intelligence Agency* (Berkeley and Los Angeles: University of California Press, 1972), 239.

24. *Nazi Conspiracy and Aggression*, 1:xvii.

25. JBD, Personal Letters, Nurnberg, September 24 [1945].

26. Storey, *The Final Judgement?*, 96.

27. Ibid.

28. JBD, Personal Letters, Paris, October 2 1945.

29. English later led a team of OSS members who captured the Wehrmacht film library in St. Johannes, near Bayreuth. Dunlop, *Donovan*, 536.

30. JBD, Personal Letters, Berlin, October 15, [1945].

31. Ibid., Berlin, October 16, [1945].

32. Memorandum issued on October 22, 1945. Taylor, *Anatomy*, 138.

33. Amen was a prosecutor from Brooklyn, New York who, since 1942, had been in the Army's Inspector General's branch.

34. JBD, Personal Letters, Thursday [November 1, 1945].

35. Soon after, the remaining trial counsel were chosen: Col. Leonard Wheeler Jr.; Lt. Col. William H. Baldwin; Lt. Col. Smith W. Brockhart Jr.; Cmdr. James B. Donovan; Maj. William F. Walsh; Maj. Warren F. Farr; Capt. Samuel Harris; Capt. Drexel A. Sprecher; Lt. Cmdr. Whitney R. Harris; Lt. Thomas F. Lambert Jr.; Lt. Henry K. Atherton; Lt. Brady O. Bryson; Lt. Bernard D. Meltzer; Dr. Robert M. Kempner and Walter W. Brudno. Only 23 attorneys actually spoke before the Tribunal during the course of the trial.

36. JBD, Personal Letters, Tuesday [November 6, 1945].

37. Dunlop, *Donovan*, 482.

38. JBD, Personal Letters, Thursday [November 8, 1945].

39. Joseph E. Persico, *Nuremberg: Tyranny on Trial* (New York: Viking, 1994), 119–20; see also Storey, *The Final Judgement?*, 97–98; Robert E. Conot, *Justice at Nuremberg*, (New York: Harper & Row, 1983), 151–52; Dunlop, *Donovan*, 482–83; Robert H. Jackson, *The Nürnberg Case* (New York: Alfred A. Knopf, 1947), viii.

40. JBD, Personal Letters, [November 7, 1945].

41. *New York Daily News*, November 17, 1945 (Pink Edition).

42. Those not being tried included Gustav Krupp van Bohlen, head of the Krupps Munitions Works, who had become senile; Robert Ley, chief of the Labor Front, since he had committed suicide before the trial; and Alfred Krupp who was to be tried later.

43. *Nazi Conspiracy and Aggression*, 1:115–16.

44. JBD, Personal Letters, Friday [November 23, 1945].

45. Persico, *Nuremberg*, 143–44. For a similar chilling reaction to the film, see Telford Taylor, *Anatomy*, 186–87.

46. December 2, 1945, Sec. 4.

47. Justice Jackson's son had arranged for simultaneous translations of all courtroom speakers with a technology newly developed by IBM.

48. JBD, Personal Letters, Wednesday [December 5, 1945].

49. *Nazi Conspiracy and Aggression*, 3:400–403. John Ford (Sean O'Fearna) (1895–1973), produced several major films before his military service including *Drums Along the Mohawk* (1939) and *The Grapes of Wrath* (1940).

50. *New Yorker*, December 1, 1945, 106–11. The *New Yorker* correspondents in Nuremberg also included journalists Rebecca West, Janet Flanner and Andy Logan.

51. December 12, 1945.

52. Sprecher, *Inside the Nuremberg Trial*, 293.

53. December 12, 1945.

54. *Nazi Conspiracy and Aggression*, 3:536–37.

55. As a naval commander, Donovan might have been directed to stay longer. However, Justice Jackson agreed to his departure, with the understanding that if Jackson believed Donovan was needed again, he would return. Letter of Donovan to Sidney Alderman, March 22, 1946, *HIA*, Box 34.

56. Letter of Maj. Gen. William J. Donovan to Cmdr. James B. Donovan, October 1, 1945, *HIA*, Box 1.

57. Persico, *Nuremberg*, 227.

58. Office of United States Chief of Counsel for Prosecution of Axis Criminality, *Nazi Conspiracy and Aggression: Opinion and Judgment*, (Washington, DC: U.S. Government Printing Office, 1947),189–90.

CHAPTER 4. PRIVATE PRACTICE

1. Donovan was also later accorded a Commendation Ribbon with clusters, the Victory Ribbon of World War II, the American Area Campaign Ribbon and the European-African Campaign Ribbon.

2. Letter to David K. Niles, January 10, 1946, *HIA*, Box 34.

3. Letter of Ray Kellogg to Donovan, March 14, 1947, *HIA* Box 34. Kellogg continued his work in special effects as well as writing and producing, after the war. Among his credits were *The Desert Fox* (1951), *You're in the Navy Now* (1951), *The Robe* (1953), *Titanic* (1953), *Demetrius and the Gladiators* (1954), and *The Seven Year Itch* (1955). The last of the fifty-seven movies with which he was associated was *The Green Berets* (1968). Nash and Ross, *The Motion Picture Guide*, I-2741.

4. The NBCU was an unincorporated nonprofit group, with a membership of 118 insurance companies and 87 subscriber companies. The bureau was not itself an insurer or re-insurer, but represented its members on issues affecting the industry such as underwriting rules, risk classifications, coverages, policy provisions, and rates. It also defended them in court cases. In 1968 it became known as the Insurance Rating Board.

5. *Eastern Underwriter*, April 25, 1958.

6. Speech of July 3, 1946, *HIA*, Box 35.

7. Address of October 24, 1946, *HIA*, Box 35.

8. With public interest still high years later, *Playhouse 90* presented "Judgement at Nuremberg" on April 16, 1959 on WCBS-TV; Turner Network Television presented

"Infamy on Trial" on July 16–17, 2000; and the History Channel broadcast "The Last Days of World War II" on August 5, 2001. None of the programs, however, mentioned James Donovan.

9. 322 U.S. 533, 64 S. Ct. 1162 (1944).

10. James B. Donovan, "Insurance Becomes Commerce (Part I)," *Insurance Counsel Journal* 17, 2 (April 1950): 142.

11. Robert Kramer in the foreword to *Law and Contemporary Problems*, 15, 4 (Autumn 1950): 471.

12. *Public Law* 15, 15 *U.S. Code* §1011–1015, 59 *Stat.* 33, 34.

13. James B. Donovan, "Insurance Becomes Commerce," 144.

14. *New York Times*, November 14, 1946.

15. September 25, 1947, " 'Other Insurance' Clauses in Casualty Policies," cited in *Eastern Underwriter*, September 26, 1947.

16. Kramer, foreword to *Law and Contemporary Problems*, 472.

17. James B. Donovan, "Regulation of Insurance Under the McCarran Act," *Law and Contemporary Problems* 15, 4 (Autumn 1950): 484. This article was the most substantial written by Donovan on the topic. However, he also wrote several other related essays including "State Regulation of Insurance," *Insurance Law Journal* 368 (September 1953): 627–30; "State Regulation of Insurance," *Insurance Law Journal* 396 (January 1956): 11–15; "Public Regulation of Title Insurance," *Title News* 32 (December 1953): 74–77; "Insurance Becomes Commerce," *Insurance Counsel Journal* 17, 2 (April 1950): 141–45 (Part 1) and 17, 3 (July 1950): 249–53 (Part 2); and "Insurance-The Case in Favor of Existing Exemptions from the Antitrust Laws," *The Federal Bar Journal* 20 (Winter 1960): 56–65. He also lectured on the subject. See, for example, his talk on September 6, 1949, before the American Bar Association concerning "National Standard Provisions for Casualty Policies," St. John's University Library, Manhattan (formerly the College of Insurance), (hereafter *SJU*) File CA410 and "Rate Regulation Revisited," a presentation during the Symposium on Insurance and Government, School of Commerce, University of Wisconsin, September 20, 1960, *SJU*, File 710R19 (1960).

18. Proceedings, National Association of Insurance Commissioners 45 (76th Sess. 1945) in Donovan, "Rate Regulation Revisited," 6.

19. For example, see *Prudential Insurance Co. v. Benjamin*, 328 U.S. 408 (1946), *Robertson v. California*, 328 U.S. 440 (1946) and *Panhandle Eastern Pipeline Co. v. Public Service Commission of Indiana*, 332 U.S. 507 (1947).

20. Seven *Fire and Casualty Cases* 144, 181 F. 2d 174 (8th Cir. 1950), *aff'g* 85 F. Supp. 961 (E.D. Ark. 1949), cert. denied, 340 U.S. 823 (1950).

21. *In the Matter of the Appeal of Daniel Kornblum . . . and The Nation*, The University of the State of New York, the State Department of Education, Before the Commissioner, Francis T. Spaulding, No. 5321 (May 29, 1949).

22. *In the Matter of the Appeal of Daniel Kornblum . . . and The Nation*, ibid.

23. *New York Daily News*, July 25, 1945.

24. *New York Times*, September 12, 1950.

25. *New York Times*, September 12, 1950; November 8, 1950.

26. Jennie Sue Daniel, *Eastern Underwriter*, December 14, 1951.

27. *Eastern Underwriter*, July 24, 1953; *Brooklyn Eagle*, September 21, 1953.

28. *New York Times*, March 13, 1955.

29. *New York Times*, January 16, 1952; January 28, 1953; January 29, 1953; January 26, 1955; and January 28, 1955.

30. *New York Times*, March 14, 1955; March 16, 1955.

31. James B. Donovan, "Recent New York Developments in Liability Insurance,"

New York State Bar Bulletin, (December 1951): 437–41; "Our Association's Program To Aid Victims of Financially Irresponsible Motorists," *New York State Bar Bulletin,* (October 1953): 302–14; "Hardy Perennials of Insurance Contract Litigation," *Insurance Law Journal,* 374 (March 1954): 163–70; "Wife Cannot Recover for Loss of Husband's Consortium," *Insurance Counsel Journal* 21, 2 (April 1954): 143–45; "The Lawyer and the Uninsured Motorist," *Insurance Counsel Journal* 21, 3 (July 1954): 319–24; "When Does an Accident Become Two Accidents?," *Insurance Counsel Journal* 23, 2 (April 1956): 194–95; "An Accident Is an Accident Is an Accident," *The Journal of Insurance Law,* 409 (February 1957): 71–78; and "Insurance Problems Created by the Peacetime Use of Atomic Energy," *Insurance Law Journal,* 417 (October 1957): 623–68.

32. For example, see review of Roger Hilsman, *Strategic Intelligence And National Decisions* (Glencoe, IL: The Free Press, 1956) in *University of Pennsylvania Law Review,* 105 (November 1956): 133–34.

33. *Truck Insurance Exchange v. Roy Rohde, a minor; Omega Mae Shaw; Priscilla Kathleen Knudeson; Leslie Davis Anderson; Lloyd Grant Knudeson, deceased, by Blaine Hopp, Jr.; Robert Dean Shaw, deceased, by Blaine Hopp, Jr.,* 49 Wash. 2d 465; 303 P.2d 659 (November 8, 1956).

34. 303 P.2d 663. Other examples of amicus curiae briefs included *Cardinal v. United States Casualty Company,* 277 A.D. 1140, 101 N.Y.S. 2d, 421 (December 18, 1950) in which Donovan represented the NBCU and the National Automobile Underwriters' Association; and in two cases of *State Compensation Insurance Fund, et al. v. F. Britton McConnell, as Insurance Commissioner of the State of California,* 285 P.2d 29 (June 20, 1955) and 294 P.2d 440 (March 28, 1956) where he represented the insurance commissioner.

35. McNamara was later vice-president of the Chubb Insurance Group and president of both the Casualty Actuarial Society and the American Academy of Actuaries; he was also a member of the American Bar Association and the New York State Bar Association. Interview with author, August 25, 2000; hereafter, *McNamara interview.* See also, Donald E. Wolff, ed. *Who's Who in Insurance, 1987* (Englewood, NJ: The Underwriting Printing & Publishing Co., 1987), 392.

36. *New York Times,* January 19, 1957.

CHAPTER 5. ARREST AND TRIAL

1. Bard Lindeman, "He Defended a Soviet Spy," *Coronet,* October 1960, 46.

2. The true infant Goldfus had died two months after birth.

3. *New York Times,* August 24, 1957.

4. His identity, that is, as "Rudolf Abel." Here only the name Rudolf Abel is used and refers to the captured spy, though vastly different accounts of his life abound. His true name could have been William August Fisher. One source relates that Abel had been born in Newcastle Upon Tyne, England on July 11, 1903, under the name of Vilyam ("Willie") Genrikhovich Fisher. See Christopher Andrew and Valili Mitrokhin, *The Sword and the Shield: The Mitrokhin Archive and the Secret History of the KGB* (New York: Basic Books, 1999). According to retired FBI Agent Wallace Erichsen, Mitrokhin was in charge of the KGB archives from 1972 until he defected to the British in 1991. He was exfiltrated to Britain in 1992 with a large archive of handwritten notes that he had compiled and hidden in his dacha during the thirty years that he was the KGB archivist. Note to author, November 26, 2000. By contrast,

Norman Polmar and Thomas B. Allen, *The Encyclopedia of Espionage* (New York: Gramercy Books, 1997), 3, relate that Abel was born in a town on the Volga River. As a youth he helped his father, a metal worker, distribute Bolshevik literature, later joining the Young Communist League (*Komsomol*) in 1922. He studied engineering and was learned in chemistry and nuclear physics. He was also fluent in English, German, Polish, Yiddish, and Russian. Abel reportedly served in a Red Army communications unit and later taught languages until 1927 when he joined the OGPU. Drafted into the Red Army as a radio specialist during World War II, he served as an intelligence officer on the Russian front until he reportedly was successful in penetrating the German *Abwehr*, working as a chauffeur under the name of Johan Weiss. After the German invasion of Russia, Polmar and Allen report that he was promoted to lance corporal and given a decoration. In the Russian NKVD, he held the rank of major at the conclusion of the war. In 1947 Abel illegally entered Canada from France under the name of Andrew Kayotis. A year later, he entered the United States under the same assumed name.

5. *New York Times*, August 9, 1957; James B. Donovan, *Strangers on a Bridge: The Case of Colonel Abel* (New York: Atheneum House, 1964), 19.

6. *New York Times*, August 9, 1957.

7. Minutes of Initial Appearance, August 9, 1957, *U.S. v. Rudolf I. Abel*. Case File 45094, 1144. Records of the U.S. District Court for the Eastern District of New York, RG 21. National Archives Branch Depository, New York, NY.

8. 18 *U. S. Code* §2385.

9. *New York Times*, August 11, 1957, sec. 4.

10. Donovan, *Strangers*, 17.

11. *New York Times*, August 13, 1957.

12. Minutes of Hearing, August 13, 1957, *U.S. v. Rudolf I. Abel*. Case File 45094, 1152. Records of the U.S. District Court for the Eastern District of New York, RG 21. National Archives Branch Depository, New York, NY. See also *New York Times*, August 14, 1957. Normally, the court would appoint counsel immediately, without obtaining any recommendations. Not only did Abel's request reveal someone who had anticipated the possibility of arrest, but also it could have been taken as a slight to the court and its capacity to appoint counsel on its own.

13. *New York Times*, August 15, 1957.

14. Minutes of Hearing, August 16, 1957, *U.S. v. Rudolf I. Abel*. Case File 45094, 1158–59. Records of the U.S. District Court for the Eastern District of New York, RG 21. National Archives Branch Depository, New York, NY. See also *New York Times*, August 17, 1957.

15. Donovan, *Strangers*, 11. A personal diary entry for August 19, in Donovan's hand, notes a telephone call this date from Goodnough and Cross asking, "would I accept since they believed they would recommend me," *HIA*, Box 28.

16. Letter of Judge Harold R. Soden to Donovan, March 12, 1964, *HIA*, Box 15.

17. Donovan, *Strangers*, 14. The case was probably that of *Danish v. Guardian*, U.S. District Court for the Southern District of New York, in which the insurance company refused to pay over policy proceeds to the Polish state on behalf of a beneficiary on the grounds that it was unlikely that the proceeds would be released by the state.

18. *New York Times*, August 21, 1957.

19. Ibid.

20. Donovan, *Strangers*, 36.

21. *New York Times*, August 30, 1957. Although the newspaper related that it took the Bar Association nine days to deliberate among the candidates, Fraiman was actually appointed one day after his selection.

22. Thomas McElrath Debevoise II (1930–1995) later served one term as Vermont's attorney general. He was also dean of Vermont Law School (1974–1982). *New York Times*, February 9, 1995.

23. Donovan, *Strangers*, 20. Donovan was very conservative when it came to publicity for a case, viewing it as akin to advertising and, hence, unbecoming in the practice of law.

24. Popularly, the Espionage and Sabotage Act of 1954, Public Law 777, 68 *Stat* 1219 (1954). The revised statute provided for a maximum penalty of death in the disclosure of information relating to the national defense in peacetime. Previously, the death penalty was only available for wartime offenses of this nature.

25. Donovan, *Strangers*, 21.

26. Ibid., 17.

27. Memorandum in Support of Petitioner's Application, In the Matter of the Application of Rudolf Ivanovich Abel, Civil No. 124–200, U.S. District Court for the Southern District of New York located in *U.S. v. Rudolf I. Abel*. Case File 45094, Records of the U.S. District Court for the Eastern District of New York, RG 21. National Archives Branch Depository, New York, NY.

28. *U.S. v. Rudolf I. Abel*, 155 F. Supp. 11 (E.D.N.Y. 1957).

29. Donovan, *Strangers*, 50.

30. Ibid., 51.

31. Trial Minutes, vol. 1, 23–25 (October 14, 1957), *U.S. v. Rudolf I. Abel*. Case File 45094, U.S. District Court for the Eastern District of New York, RG 21, National Archives Branch Depository, New York, NY.

32. Donovan asserted that the dark hair was actually dyed for Hayhanen's own security. He was reportedly naturally blond. *New York Times*, October 15, 1957.

33. *Komitet Gosudarstvenoi Bizopasnosti* (Committee for State Security).

34. *U.S. v. Jencks:* "We hold that the criminal action must be dismissed when the Government, on the ground of privilege, elects not to comply with an order to produce, for the accused's inspection and for admission in evidence, relevant statements or reports in its possession or Government witnesses touching the subject matter of their testimony at trial." 353 U.S. 657 (1957).

35. Hayhanen died in a mysterious automobile accident on the Pennsylvania Turnpike in 1961.

36. *New York Times*, September 22, 1957. This hollow nickel never led to any arrest and could not be deciphered until Hayhanen defected and revealed the key. It did, however, alert the FBI to possible espionage activity in the New York area. Given Hayhanen's character, it was most likely he who inadvertently passed it.

37. Trial Minutes, vol. 1, 713–14 (October 21, 1957), *USA v. Rudolf I. Abel*. Case File 45094, U.S. District Court for the Eastern District of New York, RG 21, National Archives Branch Depository, New York, NY. Rhodes was tried before a military court martial from February 11–February 21, 1958. Found guilty, he was dishonorably discharged, ordered to forfeit all benefits, and committed to five years hard labor. A Robert W. Hicks, associate member of the District of Columbia bar, was given a press pass to Rhodes's trial based upon his fraudulent representation that he was a member of the Rudolf Abel defense team. In actuality, he had written to Donovan to offer his services, but they were declined. Letter of Lt. Col. Allen B. Clark to Donovan, February 25, 1958, *HIA*, Box 29.

38. Trial Minutes, vol. 2, 946 (October 24, 1957), *USA v. Rudolf I. Abel*. Case File 45094, U.S. District Court for the Eastern District of New York, RG 21, National Archives Branch Depository, New York, NY.

39. Ibid., 953–54.

40. Ibid., 956–57.

41. Ibid., 971.

42. Donovan, *Strangers*, 247. Donovan was referring to the words of Emmanuel Block, Julius Rosenberg's attorney in the famous trial of 1951. After the execution of Julius and his wife, Ethel, Block went too far in the other direction, calling Attorney General Herbert Brownell and FBI Director J. Edgar Hoover, murderers. It prompted Louis Nizer to comment, "Suddenly, he was dislodged from his role of doughty fighter for unpopular clients, a role highly honored by Americans and praised by the Supreme Court." Louis Nizer, *The Implosion Conspiracy* (Garden City, N.Y. : Doubleday & Co., 1973), 488. Nizer, writing in 1973, may well have had Donovan in mind as that fighter.

43. *New York Times*,. October 26, 1957.

44. *New York Times*, November 15, 1957.

45. John Kaplan, "Evidence in Capital Cases," *Florida. State University Law Review* 11, 3–4 (1983): 376–77.

46. Sentencing Minutes, 1048–49 (November 15, 1957), *U.S. v. Rudolf I. Abel.* Case File 45094, U.S. District Court for the Eastern District of New York, RG 21, National Archives Branch Depository, New York, NY.

47. Donovan, *Strangers*, 257.

48. *New York Times*, December 24, 1957.

49. *United States v. Rudolf Ivanovich Abel*, 258 F. 2d 485 (2d Cir. 1958).

50. *Rudolf Ivanovich Abel v. U.S.*, 79 S. Ct. 59 (1958).

51. Donovan was admitted to practice before the United States Supreme Court while he was serving with the OSS in 1944. Shortly before Donovan was to appear before the Supreme Court, General William J. Donovan passed away on February 8, 1959. *New York Times*, February 9, 1959. The general's death had greatly saddened him, and in later years, Donovan wrote a tribute to his former mentor. See James B. Donovan, "Major General William J. Donovan: a Pioneer in U.S. Intelligence," *Columbia Library Columns* 14, 3, (May 1965): 3–10. The article was written in conjunction with the donation by the general's widow to Columbia University of her late husband's collection of espionage material from the American Revolution.

52. Donovan, *Strangers*, 301.

53. Records of the Supreme Court of the United States, *Rudolf Ivanovich Abel v. U.S.*, case no. 263, argued February 24, 1959, RG 267, audiotape no. 267.188, National Archives II, College Park, MD.

54. Ibid., 306. At his request, Donovan also received a picture of all the justices, signed by each.

55. The payments and dates were: July 27, 1959: $3,471.19; October 19, 1959: $6,529.81. Regarding the source of the money, see Craig R. Whitney, *Spy Trader: Germany's Devil's Advocate and the Darkest Secrets of the Cold War* (New York: Times Books-Random House, 1993), 31. Whitney's work contains a very well balanced account of the events leading to the Abel-Powers exchange. It is based in part on his lengthy personal interviews with Vogel and numerous individuals involved in government and espionage.

56. Donovan had received permission from the District Court, with no objection from the government, to receive these funds. Order (September 22, 1957), *U.S. v. Rudolf I. Abel.* Case File 45094, U.S. District Court for the Eastern District of New York, RG 21, National Archives Branch Depository, New York, NY.

57. Letter to Kings County (NY) Supreme Court Judge Miles F. McDonald, April 21, 1959, *HIA*, Box 30.

58. *New York Times*, March 29, 1960.

59. *Rudolf Ivanovich Abel v. U.S.*, 80 S. Ct. 683 (1960).

60. *New York Times*, May 17, 1960.

61. *US v Abel*, 362 U.S. 217 (1960).

62. By this time, state superintendents of insurance were not only empowered to oversee the insurance companies, but as political appointees, were sensitive to public opinion that, during this period, ran against insurance companies *(McNamara interview)*. In one instance, the New York State Supreme Court agreed with Donovan that the superintendent improperly disapproved rate increases by the NBCU *(In the matter of the Application of National Bureau of Casualty Underwriters v. the Superintendent of Insurance of New York*, 174 N.Y.S. 2d 836 [June 17, 1958]). In another, the Wisconsin Supreme Court found that the superintendent was justified in his order to temporarily halt a rate increase sought by the Fire Insurance Rating Bureau, but allowed the rate bureau time to resubmit its rate calculations. *(Fire Insurance Rating Bureau v. Paul J. Rogan, Commissioner of Insurance of the State of Wisconsin*, 91 N.W. 2d 372 [June 26, 1958]).

63. *New York Times*, September 17, 1958.

CHAPTER 6. THE ABLE-POWERS EXCHANGE

1. Formally, the *Staatsicherheit* or state security. The Stasi was created in 1950 by the (East) German Democratic Republic and remained in existence for forty years.

2. *Los Angeles Times*, February 10, 1956.

3. Whitney, *Spy Trader*, 29–30.

4. May 26, 1960.

5. *New York Times*, June 17, 1960.

6. Straud Talbott, ed. and trans., *Khrushchev Remembers: The Last Testament* (Boston: Little, Brown, 1974), 458.

7. Interview with Milan C. Miskovsky by author, March 10, 2003, hereafter, Miskovsky interview. Admitted to the District of Columbia Bar in 1957, Miskovsky joined the CIA as assistant general counsel in 1958 and served in that capacity until 1964. For his service, he received the Distinguished Intelligence Medal.

8. David Wise and Thomas B. Ross, *The U-2 Affair* (New York: Bantam Books, 1962), 130.

9. *New York Times*, August 17, 1960.

10. *New York Times*, August 20, 1960.

11. Rev. L. C. McHugh, "The Powers Espionage Trial (An interview with) James B. Donovan, *America*, October 29, 1960, 144. A comparison of the two cases may also be found in *The New York Times*, sec. 3 August 20, 1960.

12. Miskovsky interview.

13. Donovan, *Strangers*, 324.

14. This letter from the pardon attorney was drafted by Miskovsky and was quickly approved by the State and Justice Departments. Miskovsky interview.

15. In a dramatically written article for *True* magazine, Jimmy Breslin asserted several times that Donovan carried a .32 caliber pistol that he had brought from home. "The Lawyer Who Horse-Traded The Russians," *True*, September 1962. While it made for interesting reading, it does not seem plausible that Donovan would risk the entire exchange by carrying a weapon. The Berlin Wall had been erected in August 1960. East German security was heightened, and a number of people had been killed attempting to flee over the wall. Twelve years earlier, the Soviets had virtually laid siege to the entire city of Berlin, and it took the Berlin airlift to break

the stranglehold. There was simply no point in increasing the danger that Donovan would face by his carrying of a tape recorder or weapon.

16. Donovan, *Strangers*, 374.

17. Peter Wyden, *Wall: The Inside Story of Divided Berlin* (New York: Simon and Schuster, 1989), 310n.

18. David Snell, "Inside Story of a Lawyer's Adventure," *Life*, February 23, 1962, 26.

19. *HIA*, Box 27. Although Donovan gives the distinct impression in *Strangers* that his family did not know the true nature of his European trip, his wife, Mary, remarked, rather matter-of-factly that, of course she knew where he was. Mary Donovan Busch, conversation with author, Spring Lake, NJ, June 2, 2000.

20. Whitney, *Spy Trader*, 40.

21. Ibid., 41.

22. Secretary of State Dean Rusk wrote a strong rejoinder and the matter was never broached again. Clay's letter and that of the secretary of state have since been lost. Miskovsky interview. Lucius Clay (1897–1978), a son of U.S. senator Alexander S. Clay, graduated from West Point in 1918. During World War II he earned the Bronze Star, the Legion of Merit, and the Distinguished Service Medal with Oak Leaf Cluster. Clay was military governor of Germany and directed the Berlin Airlift between 1948 and 1949. He retired from service in the latter year. Frances Carol Locher, ed., *Contemporary Authors* (Detroit, MI: Gale Research, 1979), 77–80: 92; 81–84: 93; Roger J. Spiller, ed., *Dictionary of American Military* (Westwood, CT: Greenwood Press, 1984), 1, 185–88.

23. So designated for being the third of three military points of entry or exit from East Berlin. In the military alphabet, the first check point was Alpha (Helmstedt); the second was Bravo (Dreilinden); and the third was Charlie (Friedrichstrasse).

24. *HIA*, Box 27.

25. Whitney, *Spy Trader*, 40.

26. Miskovsky interview.

27. *New York Times*, February 10, 1962.

28. Donovan, *Strangers*, 421. Powers never really showed any appreciation of Donovan's efforts, not even in his own book, *Operation Overflight: The U-2 Spy Pilot Tells His Story for the First Time*, that he wrote with Curt Gentry (New York: Holt, Rinehart & Winston, 1970), 286. However, after divorcing Barbara and remarrying, his second wife may have urged him to send the twelve-pound Virginia ham that Donovan received at his office on December 20, 1963. Donovan, however, never represented Powers before the military.

29. Interview with Jane Ann Amorosi, February 2001.

30. Miskovsky interview. Donovan, *Strangers*, 423; *New York Times*, February 12, 1962.

31. *New York Times*, February 13, 1962.

32. *New York Times*, April 15, 1963. Donated to Georgetown University after Donovan's death, the volumes can still be viewed at the university's Lauinger Library.

33. *HIA*, Box 29. Finally, after an additional ten months, Marvin W. Makinen was released on October 11, 1963, by the Soviets, together with an American priest, Walter Martin Ciszek, who had been held for twenty-three years on espionage charges. In return, the United States deported two Soviet spies, Ivan D. Egorov and his wife, Aleksandra. The couple were facing trial on November 4 in the same court where Abel was prosecuted. *New York Times*, October 12, 1963.

34. *New York Times*, June 28, 1964. Mrs. Minnie McInturff was Donovan's longtime secretary.

35. Mary Ellen was enthralled with the trip. She had never traveled far before this, and it was her sixteenth birthday. She recalls staying at the fashionable Claridge

Hotel in London and being introduced by her father to Woody Allen, Gregory Peck, and Sophia Loren at a cocktail party. Leaving London, the two went on to Oslo and spent time with Donovan's son, John, who was there at the time as well. After a stay in Stockholm, Donovan and Mary Ellen proceeded to Moscow. Conversation with Mary Ellen, January 25, 2002. John had spent the summer of 1963 in Oslo. During that time, he recalls, he took a side trip to East Berlin. While behind the Berlin Wall, a young boy approached him and asked that he mail a letter from the western side. John related that he agreed to do so, but was then almost immediately approached by local police. Thinking quickly, John asked the officers to bring him to Ivan Schischkin who was well known to his father. When John asked that General Clay be notified as well, the police took John straight to the border and saw him across. Conversation with John Donovan, July 1, 2002.

36. Whitney, *Spy Trader*, xv.

37. *New York Times*, May 5, 1965.

38. *HIA*, Box 25.

39. *New York Times*, March 18, 1962.

40. Donovan, after the exchange, referred to himself as a metadiplomat. The term was popularized at the ceremony. It has been defined as "1. Diplomacy that is carried out in channels above and beyond the ordinary; 2. A contact with a foreign government patterned after James B. Donovan's negotiations with the Communist bloc over the Powers-Abel spy exchange." *San Francisco Monitor*, August 17, 1962. See also Henry Lee, "James B. Donovan: Metadiplomat," *Catholic Digest* 28, 5 (March 1964): 56*ff.*

41. Fordham University Press Release, June 13, 1962, 2; Gertrude Samuels, "How Metadiplomacy Works: James Donovan and Castro." *Nation* 196, 15 (April 13, 1963): 301.

42. Snell, "Inside Story," 26–27.

43. *HIA*, Box 25. Some water damage to the file, occurring before it was transferred to the Hoover Institution, made a few words of the letter illegible. Those sections are so noted.

44. *New York Times*, February 19, 1962.

45. *New York Times*, February 20, 1962. Actually, the newspaper did not print a retraction. They simply published Donovan's denial.

46. David Wise and Thomas B. Ross, *The U-2 Affair* (New York: Random House, 1962); and Sanche de Gramont (Ted Morgan, pseud.), *The Secret War: The Story of International Espionage Since World War II* (New York: G.P. Putnam's Sons, 1962).

47. *New York Times*, November 3, 1994. Vogel was arrested in 1993 on several charges including blackmailing his clients into leaving their property behind in East Germany, perjury, and working for the Ministry of State Security from 1953 to 1989. A conviction was overturned on appeal. *New York Times*, 1996; January 10; November 30.

48. See, for example, "Privilege of Advocating Unpopular Causes," *Albany Law Review*, 30 (January 1966): 52 (Text of address at Albany Law School Commencement, June 1, 1965); *Louisiana State Bar Journal* 12, 2 (August 1964): 83–87; *Challenges: Reflections of a Lawyer-at-Large* (New York: Atheneum House, 1967): 72–82; and *Brooklyn Barrister* 16, 9 (November 1964).

49. Letter of Thomas Debevoise, February 18, 1964, *HIA*, Box 3.

50. Donovan letter of January 9, 1961; letter of Simon Michael Bessie, Atheneum Publishing Company, to Donovan, May 23, 1963, *HIA*, Box 15.

51. James B. Donovan, letter to Allen Dulles, January 7, 1964, *HIA*, Box 64.

52. James B. Donovan, letter, April 10, 1964, *HIA*, Box 3.

53. See, for example, Allen Dulles, "A Spy for a Spy," *New York Times*, sec. 7, April 12, 1964; William Kunstler, *Chicago Tribune*, sec. 9, March 22, 1964; "An American Example," *Newsweek*, March 30, 1964, 75–76; and Paul Mandel. "It's Just as Cold for a Real Spy," *Life Magazine*, April 17, 1964, 11–14.

54. For example, David Brinkley, NBC *David Brinkley's Journal*, February 21, 1962; again on April 16, 1964 (Brinkley, on August 17, 1961,had broadcast a reconstruction of Abel's capture based on Hayhanen's information); NBC *Today Show* with Hugh Downs, March 30, 1964; and the Martha Deane program on WOR radio, March 24, 1964. Other appearances included the Ed Joyce show, CBS radio; the Casper Citron show, WRFM; Mike Wallace, "Personal Closeup," WCBS-TV; the Victor Riesel show, WEVD radio; and the Lee Graham show, WNYC radio.

55. Perhaps prompted by the lack of production of a movie, Donovan's son, John, began to develop a teleplay, "Defense of a Spy," based on the trial. A rough draft covering the period from October 13 to October 19, 1957, is in *HIA*, Box 15 and is entitled "The Defense of Colonel Abel."

56. Letter of Donovan to Thomas E. Ambrose, S.J., April 12, 1967. The royalties for *Strangers* were 15 percent of the $6.95 cover price ($1.0425 per copy sold).

57. *New York Post*, October 6, 1967. A copy of the picture that Donovan viewed can be found in the *London Sunday Telegraph*, October 8, 1967, *HIA*, Box 14.

CHAPTER 7. CUBAN NEGOTIATIONS — I

1. John E. Nolan Jr. who accompanied Donovan to Cuba in April 1963 recorded some of Castro's own reflections on the revolution and after. The "Memorandum On Castro's Statements and Notes on Cuban Trip, April 5–9, 1963" written to the attorney general were donated to the National Security Archive of the George Washington University, Gelman Library.

2. Santana actually died in a training accident before the invasion. Haynes Johnson, *The Bay of Pigs* (New York: W.W. Norton, 1964), 56. Johnson provides a detailed history of the Brigade and invasion of Cuba from first-person recollections. He also includes a chapter on Donovan's role in the negotiations with Castro through December 1962 (303–41).

3. Fabian Escalante Font (head of Cuban State Security), *The Secret War: CIA Covert Operations against Cuba, 1959–1962*, trans. Maxine Shaw (Melbourne, Australia: Ocean Press, 1995), 170. In 1999, the United States government released previously confidential information indicating that four Americans, members of the Alabama Air National Guard were also killed in a support action during the invasion. Two of four guardsmen's B-26s were shot down by Castro's forces on the third day of the attack. Warren Trest and Donald Dodd, *Wings of Denial: The Alabama Air National Guard's Covert Role at the Bay of Pigs* (Montgomery, AL: New South Books, 2001), 13–15.

4. Johnson, *The Bay of Pigs*, 231–35.

5. The CFC ultimately had offices at 527 Madison Avenue in New York City and 1714 Biscayne Boulevard in Miami, Florida. Officers included Alvaro Sánchez Jr., president; Virginia B. de Rodriguez, Julio Lobo, Enrique Godoy, and Manuel Arca Campos, vice-presidents; José I. De la Cámara, treasurer; Eudaldo A. Suárez, vice-treasurer; Ernesto Freyre, secretary; Marcelo Hernández, vice-secretary; and Enríque Llaca, Carlos Lalla, and Caridad R. de Alzugaray, directors.

6. Goodwin originally attained notoriety for his part in exposing the quiz show scandals in the 1950s. He continued as a special counsel to President Johnson. He has spoken and written extensively on American history.

7. While 1,180 men were captured, two of the ten sent as a commission by Castro defected and never returned to Cuba.

8. Hurwitch (1921–97) served in World War II, earning the Bronze Star. Joining the Foreign Service in 1950, he was vice-consul in Peru and labor attaché in Columbia before his appointment as a special assistant. He was later ambassador to the Dominican Republic from 1973 to 1978.

9. Family and friends paid the fines for five prisoners and obtained their release. With the sixty wounded prisoners released as well, 1,113 remained imprisoned. *New York Times*, August 30, 1962.

10. Johnson, *The Bay of Pigs*, 303.

11. 1 *Stat.* 613 (1799). The statute provided a penalty of from six months to three years for any citizen who carried on any correspondence or intercourse with any foreign government.

12. See Appendix D for a complete list of Sponsors as of August 16, 1962.

13. Johnson, *The Bay of Pigs*, 307. The official resolution to appoint Donovan as general counsel to the CFC was passed on August 21, 1962 (*HIA*, Box 44).

14. Morse (1928–73) was in private practice when Donovan involved him in the prisoner release project. He was also associated with Donovan when he served the board of education as a special counsel investigating various criminal activities. *New York Times*, December 5, 1973.

15. The entire speech may be found at the University of Texas web site database: http://lanic.utexas.edu/la/cb/cuba/castro/1961/19610520. It had also been in this talk that Castro announced his suggestion of exchanging tractors for the prisoners.

16. *HIA*, Box 39, Cuban Chronology. The Hoover Institution archives contains, in several boxes of Donovan's papers, a chronological record of his involvement with the prisoner release project. This was probably Donovan's method of keeping a daily diary. It is a paginated work which extends over more than eight hundred pages, but it is untitled and unsigned. However, an entry at the bottom of a page typed on December 5, 1962, bore the initials, "JBD:jls." It is termed the Cuban Chronology here and hereafter for simplicity. Donovan's style in this document is similar to that in *Strangers on a Bridge*, and suggests that he may also have had publication in mind at some future date. In addition to the Cuban Chronology, Box 46 contains part of another document entitled "Factors Affecting the Outcome of the Bay of Pigs Prisoner Talks" without a date or author and appears to have been part of some larger work that was not contained among his papers.

17. *HIA*, Box 39, Cuban Chronology.

18. *New York Times*, August 25, 1962.

19. *HIA*, Box 41, Cuban Chronology.

20. *HIA*, Box 39, Cuban Chronology.

21. Johnson, *The Bay of Pigs*, 312.

22. *HIA*, Box 39, Cuban Chronology.

23. Ibid.

24. *HIA*, Box 39, Cuban Chronology.

25. Ibid.

26. McGeorge Bundy (1919–96) was a Yale graduate. He served as an intelligence officer in World War II, and after the war was dean of the School of Arts and Sciences at Harvard University. He was special assistant for National Security Affairs from 1961

to 1966; later president of the Ford Foundation (1966–79) and professor of history at New York University (1979–89).

27. Miskovsky Interview. Miskovsky related this same incident to John D. Amorosi (a grandson of Donovan) on April 23, 1990, and is contained in Amorosi's "The Donovan-Castro Talks: A Potential Opportunity or an Historical Anomaly," a paper completed for Foreign Policy, Deerfield Academy, Deerfield, MA, May 14, 1990. See also C. David Heymann, *RFK: A Candid Biography of Robert F. Kennedy* (New York: Dutton, 1998), 270.

28. *HIA*, Box 38.

29. Bard Lindeman, "Cuban Prisoner Exchange," *Saturday Evening Post* 236 (February 2, 1963), 20.

30. *HIA*, Box 39, Cuban Chronology. In these same notes for that day, Donovan added, "Needless to say, I had no cousin Tom and hadn't been to Abercrombie & Fitch in fifteen years! A government man would do this for me." The episode of the skin diving suit has received a degree of notoriety since several officials at the CIA, months later, would conceive a plan to assassinate Castro with such equipment, using Donovan as the unwitting giver. See Chapter 9.

31. *HIA*, Box 39, Cuban Chronology.

32. The name of Jim McIntosh appears several times. However, it is believed that it is not his true name.

33. *HIA*, Box 39, Cuban Chronology.

34. Ibid.

CHAPTER 8. SENATE RACE

1. *HIA*, Box 9.

2. Sec. B, February 15, 1962, One-Star Final Edition.

3. Paul Screvane (1914–2001), commissioner of sanitation for the City of New York, 1957, later briefly acting mayor, 1962. James A. Farley (1888–1976) earlier chair of the Democratic National Committee from 1932 to 1940 and the U.S. postmaster general from 1933 to 1940.

4. *New York Journal American*, May 20, 1962.

5. The popularity of both Javits and Rockefeller was very strong. One newspaper even suggested that the Democratic Party "assume that the election is lost but to campaign as if it isn't," so as to be more prepared in the next election. *Long Island* (NY) *Newsday*, July 30, 1962.

6. *HIA*, Box 9.

7. The newspaper is not identified on the clip that is in *HIA, Box 9*.

8. Ibid.

9. *HIA*, Box 9; see also *New York Herald Tribune*, August 7, 1962, and *New York Times*, August 7, 1962.

10. *New York Times*, August 7, 1962.

11. See *New York World Telegram and Sun*, August 31, 1962. Wagner (1910–91) in past years had taken on many Democratic bosses and won. Son of a U.S. senator of the same name, he entered the political arena in 1937 as an assemblyman, was elected Manhattan borough president in 1949 and mayor in 1953, later chair of the New York State delegation to the Democratic National Convention in 1960. Jackson, *The Encyclopedia of New York City*, 1231; *Syracuse* (NY) *Post-Standard*, September 16, 1962.

12. His certificate as delegate is in a file of campaign papers that were never transferred to the Hoover Institution archives. They remain in the possession of Donovan's wife and are hereafter referred to as the Donovan Campaign Papers.

13. September 16, 1962.

14. *New York Times,* September 12, 1962.

15. The state Democratic Party Platform can be found in its entirety in *Proceedings of the Democratic State Convention,* War Memorial Auditorium, Onondaga County, Syracuse, New York, September 17 and 18, 1962 (New York: Sills Reporting Services, n.d., ca.1962), 45–85.

16. *New York Herald Tribune,* September 18, 1962.

17. Despite some opposition at the convention, Morganthau was a popular figure among the electorate in the state. A Democrat from Bronx County, he worked for John F. Kennedy's campaign in 1960, was later United States attorney for the Southern District of New York (1961–70); and has been district attorney for New York County (Manhattan) since 1975. *Syracuse* (NY) *Post-Standard,* September 16, 1962; Jackson, *The Encyclopedia of New York City,* 770; http://www.manhattanda.org/history/index.htm.

18. Campaign Press Release, September 27, 1962, in Donovan Campaign Papers.

19. Corning (1909–83) had been mayor since 1941. He served in that capacity for eleven consecutive terms and died in office in 1983.

20. *Proceedings of the Democratic State Convention,* 271.

21. Four delegates had voted for James Farley, but he had not been nominated, neither had Telford Taylor nor William L. Cary.

22. *HIA,* Box 39. The last person from Brooklyn was William Musgrave Calder, 1869–1945, a Republican who served in the United States Senate from 1917 to 1923.

23. "Acceptance Speech of James B. Donovan, Democratic Candidate for United States Senator," in *Proceedings of the Democratic State Convention,* 289–91.

24. Mary Donovan Busch, conversation with author, Spring Lake, NJ, June 2, 2000.

25. *New York Post,* September 19, 1962.

26. *New York Times,* September 23, 1962.

27. Campaign Press Release, September 27, 1962. Donovan's *Political Committee Statement,* dated November 26, 1962 and filed with the New York State Secretary of State reflects campaign income of $38,215 including $5,000 of his own money. Expenses totaled $47,451 including a $10,000 loan to be repaid. A copy of the filing is located in the Donovan Campaign Papers.

28. *New York Times,* October 14, 1962. Actually, CIA director John McCone had briefed Javits on October 4 about the Cuban negotiations so that he would not be in the dark.

29. *Long Island* (NY) *Newsday,* November 1, 1962.

30. Ibid.

31. *New York Times,* October 14, 1962.

32. *Newsmakers,* transcript, 5, *HIA,* Box 48.

33. *HIA* Box 39, Cuban Chronology, 189. He was referring to the New York State Election Laws of 1922 and 1949 that did not permit the removal of a candidate's name from the ballot, except under very limited circumstances, after a candidate filed a Certificate of Acceptance of designation. Currently, Articles 6–146 and 6–158(2) of the Election Law. Information provided to the author by Brian Quail, Election Law Counsel to the New York State Assembly Election Committee, January 18, 2002. Actually, Kennedy told Donovan that he did not think Donovan could defeat such a formidable opponent, suggesting that a campaign would not be worth the effort. However, Kennedy never told Donovan not to run. Miskovsky Interview. In

contrast, Arthur M. Schlesinger Jr. wrote that Donovan was asked earlier by Robert Kennedy to withdraw but declined to do so. *Robert Kennedy and His Times* (Boston: Houghton Mifflin, 1978), 471.

34. *HIA*, Box 39, Cuban Chronology, 192; *New York Times*, October 17, 1962.

35. *New York Post*, 1962: October 29; October 30; October 31; November 1; November 2; and November 4.

36. *New York Times*, October 22, 1962.

37. *New York Times*, October 23, 1962. For Donovan's part, he did have the research unit of the Democratic Senatorial Campaign Committee in Washington compare defense contracts in the eastern and western parts of the United States, and to compare, as well, the efforts of Senators Warren G. Magnuson and Jacob Javits in obtaining federal funds in their respective states. Letter from the Democratic Senatorial Campaign Committee to the New York State Democratic Committee, October 12, 1962, in Donovan Campaign Papers.

38. Debate transcript, *HIA*, Box 39. Donovan's foreign policy was essentially one of toughness. In a letter written on October 30, Donovan said, "So far as I am concerned, our principal difficulty in foreign policy for the past fifteen years has been that we have been leading from weakness when we should have been leading from strength. You will find that I have repeatedly agreed with General Lucius D. Clay that, both in the Havana uprising and when they commenced to build the Berlin Wall, we should have taken as firm a stand as President Kennedy has now taken with respect to Cuba. In my opinion, if we had done so we today would have a free Hungary and no wall in Berlin, and the Russians would not have fired a shot." Letter to Victor K. Scavillo, *HIA*, Box 3.

39. *New York Times*, October 27, 1962.

40. *New York Times*, October 30, 1962.

41. Taylor Branch, *Parting the Waters: America in the King Years, 1954–1964* (New York: Simon and Schuster, 1988), 633–72.

42. Ibid., 412–91. Preceding the Freedom Rides, the year-long Montgomery, Alabama bus boycott had been launched on December 1, 1955, triggered by Rosa Parks when she refused to give up her forward seat on a bus to a white person. It led to court-ordered desegregation on buses in November 1956. On February 1, 1960, four black college students had staged a sit-in at a "white only" lunch counter in North Carolina. The sit-in, eminently successful, was continued by the Student Nonviolent Coordinating Committee (SNCC) that came into being in that same year. Robert J. Norrell, "Civil Rights Movement in the United States," Microsoft Encarta99, CD-ROM, 9–10.

43. "I am surprised by your statement on television Monday night that additional civil rights legislation is not necessary at this time. Your position is at odds with the Democratic and Liberal Party platforms, and as I am sure you know, is also at odds with the position of the NAACP, which believes legislation is vitally needed in many areas. Also, the Civil Rights Commission has recommended the urgent enactment of 27 civil rights laws. I call upon you to correct your position immediately, for you are doing the cause of civil rights much harm by such statements." Basil Paterson, Chairman, Political Action Committee, NY City Branch, NAACP. The telegram, dated October 30, 1962, is in the Donovan Campaign Papers.

44. *New York Times*, October 31, 1962.

45. Ibid.

46. *New York Times*, October 15 and 16, 1962.

47. *New York Times*, November 7 and 11, 1962. On November 6 Donovan sent a telegram to Javits from his Hotel Commodore headquarters: "The people of our state have given you their mandate. I know that you will fulfill that mandate in the

best interests of all the people of our state. In this endeavor I pledge my whole-hearted support." *New York World Telegram and Sun,* November 7, 1962. For his part, Javits never gloated over his success. In his autobiography, he only mentioned the size of the vote. Jacob K. Javits, with Rafael Steinberg, *Javits: The Autobiography of a Public Man* (Boston: Houghton Mifflin, 1981), 366.

48. James B. Donovan, letter to Raymond Reisler, Esq., November 21, 1962, Donovan Campaign Papers.

CHAPTER 9. CUBAN NEGOTIATIONS — II

1. *Palace Meeting Notes, HIA,* Box 39. John Nolan, who accompanied Donovan on later trips to Havana, remembered Donovan's telling Castro about the prisoners, "They're your problem; they're your cross. What are you going to do with them? You can't shoot them. If you do you'll go down as one of the greatest butchers in world history. Maybe you could have done that at one time, but you can't do it now. And it's difficult for you to keep them here, to keep them in jail for a prolonged period of time. If you want to get rid of them, if you're going to sell them, you've got to sell them to me. There's no world market for prisoners." John Nolan, recorded interview by Frank DeRosa, April 25, 1967, 6, John F. Kennedy Library Oral History Program. Hereafter, John Nolan interview, April 25, 1967.

2. *Chronology of Cuban Prisoner Release Negotiations, HIA,* Box 40. This is a twelve-page synopsis of Donovan's activities, of unknown authorship, but probably composed by Donovan's secretary. It is a document different from the Cuban Chronology.

3. The diplomatic maneuvering in the Cuban missile crisis has been described in Roger Hilsman, *To Move a Nation: The Politics of Foreign Policy in the Administration of John F. Kennedy* (New York: Doubleday & Company, 1967), 157–229. See also Robert F. Kennedy, *Thirteen Days: A Memoir of the Cuban Missile Crisis* (New York: W.W. Norton, 1969).

4. Johnson, *The Bay of Pigs,* 318–19. Prior to publishing his book, Johnson sent relevant parts of his manuscript to Donovan on March 3, 1964, for review and comment. *HIA,* Box 2.

5. For the Logan Act, see Chapter 7. With respect to antitrust violations, the pharmaceutical companies had been the subjects of investigation between 1959 and 1962 by Senator Estes Kefauver (1903–63) and the Antitrust and Monopoly Subcommittee. Since they would be sharing information among themselves about the setting of prices of their commodities, they did not want to be open to prosecution in return for helping in this matter. Joseph Bruce Gorman, *Kefauver: A Political Biography* (New York: Oxford University Press, 1971), 351–55; see also Charles L. Fontenay, *Estes Kefauver: A Biography* (Knoxville: University of Tennessee Press, 1980), 379–93.

6. Louis F. Oberdorfer (1919–   ) graduated from Yale Law School in 1946. He served in World War II from 1941 to1946 and was in private practice for fourteen years before joining the Justice Department. In 1965, he returned to private practice, but in 1977 he was appointed a United States District Court Judge for the District of Columbia.

7. Miskovsky Interview.

8. *HIA,* Box 39, Cuban Chronology.

9. Nicholas Katzenbach (1922–   ) served in World War II and was captured by

the Germans who held him as a prisoner of war for two years. He graduated from Yale Law School in 1947 and in the same year became a Rhodes Scholar studying in England. He was a professor of law at Yale University (1952–55) and at the University of Chicago (1956–60). Katzenbach entered government service in 1961 as an assistant attorney general. He was appointed attorney general in 1965 and undersecretary of state in 1966. Leaving government service in 1969, he worked for IBM for sixteen years before returning to private practice.

10. Louis F. Oberdorfer, recorded interview by Francis J. Hunt DeRosa, May 14, 1964, 2, John F. Kennedy Library Oral History Program.

11. Lawrence R. Houston (1913–95) was the first general counsel of the CIA and served in that capacity from 1947 until he retired in 1973.

12. C. Douglas Dillon (1909–   ) graduated from Harvard University in 1931, was appointed ambassador to France, 1953–59, and later secretary of the treasury 1960–65. Mortimer Caplin (1916–   ) graduated from the University of Virginia Law School in 1940 returning as a law professor in 1950, later teaching both Robert F. and Edward M. Kennedy; he was commissioner of the IRS 1961–64; Stanley Surrey was assistant secretary of the treasury for tax policy, 1961–69.

13. As Oberdorfer recollected, "As far as 'price' was concerned, I left with the impression . . . that there was a substantial markup and that costs were to be the market value of $53,000,000. It was reasonable to assume abstractly on the basis of early experience in attempting to raise this material that it would actually cost about $17,000,000." Louis F. Oberdorfer, recorded interview by Francis J. Hunt DeRosa, June 2, 1964, 6, John F. Kennedy Library Oral History Program. Hereafter, Oberdorfer Interview, June 2, 1964.

14. Ibid.

15. *HIA*, Box 39, Cuban Chronology.

16. Oberdorfer Interview, June 2, 1964, 6.

17. Ibid., 4.

18. John C. Wilson, recorded interview by Francis J. Hunt DeRosa, July 1, 1964, 2, John F. Kennedy Library Oral History Program. Hereafter, Wilson Interview, July 1, 1964.

19. Ibid., 3.

20. Ibid., 4.

21. Several historians have covered the government's role in securing the release of the prisoners, especially Haynes Johnson, *The Bay of Pigs*, 323–29 and David Wise and Thomas B. Ross, *The Invisible Government*, 281–89.

22. Miskovsky interview.

23. Joseph Dolan, recorded interview by Francis A. Hunt DeRosa, July 8, 1964, 3, John F. Kennedy Library Oral History Program, hereafter, Dolan interview, July 8, 1964. John E. Nolan Jr. has been with Steptoe and Johnson, LLP since 1956. A law clerk for Supreme Court Justice Tom C. Clark (1955–56), he was subsequently administrative assistant to Attorney General Robert Kennedy (1963–64); E. Barrett Prettyman Jr. has been in private practice in Washington, DC, since 1955. John W. Douglas, son of Senator Paul H. Douglas, later headed the civil division of the attorney general's office. Raymond Rasenburger was an adviser to Senator Edmund Muskie during the senator's 1972 presidential campaign.

24. Nolan interview, April 25, 1967; and author's interview with John Nolan, January 11, 2002, hereafter, Nolan interview, January 11, 2002. Nolan also knew Robert Kennedy from the time that he assisted with his brother's earlier presidential campaign.

25. Nolan interview, January 11, 2002.

26. Dolan interview, July 8, 1964, 14.

27. *New York Times,* December 26, 1962.

28. Michelle Rogovin, recorded interview by Francis J. Hunt DeRosa, June 2, 1964, 12, John F. Kennedy Oral History program,. Hereafter, Rogovin interview, June 2, 1964.

29. Foley had already discussed the prisoner exchange on November 13 with CIA Director John McCone after Donovan had talked to Foley about it. *The Avalon Project at the Yale Law School: The Cuban Missile Crisis.* Document No. 178, November 14, 1962. Memorandum of Conversation Between Attorney General Kennedy and CIA Director McCone at: http://www.yale.edu/lawweb/avalon/diplomacy/forrel/cuba/cuba178.htm.

30. Oberdorfer interview, May 14, 1964, 25–26.

31. Ibid. 26–27.

32. See Appendix F for a copy of the letter.

33. *HIA,* Box 39, Cuban Chronology, 262.

34. Ibid., 258. Rogovin interview, June 2, 1964, 7.

35. Miskovsky interview.

36. Ibid., 258. Rogovin interview, June 2, 1964, 7.

37. John B. Jones, recorded interview by Francis J. Hunt DeRosa, June 2, 1964, 7, John F. Kennedy Library Oral History Program. Hereafter, Jones interview, June 2, 1964.

38. Rogovin Interview, June 2, 1964, 8.

39. Johnson, *The Bay of Pigs,* 328.

40. *HIA,* Box 39, Cuban Chronology. Manufacturers also wanted to be sure that their products would be used within Cuba and not transshipped to other countries, an occurrence that would impact on their own foreign markets. Dolan Interview, July 8, 1964, 9.

41. The members of the PMA also made clear at this meeting that they would only provide "first class products," no samples and no expired drugs. Rogovin interview, June 2, 1964, 10.

42. Mary Ellen Donovan Fuller, interview with author, January 25, 2002.

43. Oberdorfer interview, May 14, 1964, 32.

44. Ibid., 31. John Nolan voiced the same opinion. John Nolan interview, April 25, 1967, 15.

45. Don Coppock of the Border Patrol, stepping outside of his usual duties, assisted the Red Cross by tracking pledge amounts and their status of movement toward the port of embarkation in an office down the hall from Oberdorfer. Dolan Interview, July 8, 1964, 7. Dolan felt that Coppock, Oberdorfer, and himself had gained experience in working with crises through their involvement in the civil rights incidents in Oxford, Mississippi, and Montgomery and Birmingham, Alabama, in the recent past. Dolan Interview, July 8, 1964, 12.

46. Robert F. Shea, recorded interview by Francis J. Hunt DeRosa, July 1, 1964, 6–9. Hereafter, Shea interview July 1, 1964.

47. Ibid., 9–10.

48. Ibid., 10.

49. John Wilson Interview, July 1, 1964, 14.

50. Jones interview, June 2, 1964, 17.

51. Title 7 *U.S. Code* §1431.

52. Jones interview, June 2, 1964, 19–20.

53. *Time,* January 4, 1963, 14.

54. Oberdorfer interview, May 14, 1964, 9–10.

55. Wilson interview, July 1, 1964, 4–5. See Appendix G for a copy of the Letter of Credit.

56. "The Cuban Prisoners' Release," a speech by James Donovan before the Health Insurance Association of American, Roosevelt Hotel, New Orleans, May 15, 1963, 2–3, *HIA,* Box 39.

57. For a complete list of ships and planes over the course of the entire effort see Appendix H.

58. Nolan interview, January 10, 2002.

59. See Appendix I for the full text of the Memorandum of Agreement.

60. *HIA,* Box 39, Cuban Chronology.

61. John Nolan had described the fury of soliciting drug companies and the fact that "we took everything we could get. We had seventy-five thousand dollars' worth of Ex-Lax, five hundred thousand dollars' worth of Listerine. We had something called Gil's Green Mountain Asthmatic Cigarettes and thirty-seven different kinds of menstrual remedies. It was a great shelf-clearing operation for the drug companies, and we took all of this stuff and loaded it either on an airplane or on a ship." Haymann, *RFK: A Candid Biography,* 276.

62. Nolan interview, January 10, 2002.

63. Johnson, *The Bay of Pigs,* 333, and Nolan interview, January 10, 2002.

64. *HIA,* Box 39, Cuban Chronology.

65. Nolan interview, January 10, 2002.

66. According to Robert Shea of the Red Cross, ships returning with refugees required that the Coast Guard be called upon to escort these ships from the territorial limits of Cuban waters to Port Everglades because the freighters were carrying far in excess of their rated passenger loads. Shea Interview, July 1, 1964, 22.

67. John Nolan recalls that about this time, a pilot brought a handwritten note from Gen. Lucius Clay to either Castro or Donovan but to be opened first by Nolan who was to decide what to do with the note. It said, in effect, "Oh, about that 2.9 million, we are going to do the best we can to get it. We're going to use our best efforts to get it, and we feel reasonably sure that we should be able to raise it within thirty days. We don't want you to be disturbed about it, and we want you to go ahead on this assurance and just act as if you already had it." Nolan continued, "Well, as soon as I saw the letter, I knew that it wouldn't wash as far as either Donovan or Castro was concerned." Ultimately, Nolan gave the note to Donovan who read it, put it away, and never mentioned it again. Nolan interview, April 25, 1967, 20, and repeated in Nolan interview, January 10, 2002.

68. Nolan interview, January 10, 2002.

69. Nolan interview, April 25, 1967, 23, and January 10, 2002; and Miskovsky interview.

70. Nolan interview, April 25, 1967, 24.

71. Ibid., 25, and *HIA,* Box 39, Cuban Chronology.

72. Cardinal Cushing later recalled that the attorney general "wanted to know if I could get them $1,000,000 before the day was over. It was then only a couple of days before Christmas, and they wanted these prisoners in the United States prior to that day. I replied, 'I'll call you back in a few hours.' I did so, and I promised to have the money delivered to him at the White House about 6 p.m. Where did I get the money? I borrowed it from Latin American friends and those in the United States and promised to pay it back within three months." Heymann, *RFK: A Candid Biography,* 277.

73. "He [Clay] then solicited contributions from American business firms to cover that amount. Texaco, Standard Oil of New Jersey and the Ford Motor Company Fund [for example] each contributed $100,000." Johnson, *The Bay of Pigs*, 285.

74. *HIA*, Box 39, Cuban Chronology.

75. December 24, 1981.

76. One such problem, that is illustrative, arose when the Red Cross accepted $500,000 worth of Salk vaccine. John Wilson explained that the vaccine, which had to be refrigerated continuously, was shipped to Cuba. However, the Cubans had already been immunized against polio with a vaccine from the Soviet Union, and the shipment had to be returned. The donating company did not want the vaccine back, and thus the Red Cross had to look for another recipient. Ultimately, it was shipped to several South American Red Cross Societies. John Wilson Interview, July 1, 1964, 17.

77. In addition to simply providing ships, the shipping companies took on substantially more. For example, United Fruit Company's *Santo Cerro* had to feed all of its refugee passengers during the fourteen-hour return trip with previously stocked food. It also had to be rigged as a "mercy ship" with latrines, sleeping and eating accommodations, etc. In addition, the company had arranged with Pan American Airlines to fly down blankets and cots for the return trip. Other ships provided similar necessities.

78. Johnson, *The Bay of Pigs*, 344.

79. Leonard A. Scheele, letter to Donovan, April 10, 1963, *HIA*, Box 34.

80. Donovan was also asked to obtain the release of Robert Geddes, a British subject married to a United States citizen. However, there is no mention of such a discussion with Castro in Donovan's papers.

81. The three Cubans referred to were Roberto Santiestebán Casanova, an attaché to the Cuban mission to the UN; Marino Antonio Esteban del Carmen Sueiro y Cabrera; and José García Orellano. The three had been indicted by a federal grand jury in Brooklyn on November 16, 1962, as members of a sabotage ring that had planned to blow up defense installations and public buildings in the metropolitan New York area.

82. The United States had issued a NOTAM, that is, a Notice to Airmen, warning against flying to or over Cuba. This effectively halted all flights to the island and particularly effected Pan American Airlines.

83. *HIA*, Box 40, Cuban Chronology.

84. Donovan, "The Cuban Prisoners Release," speech, 6, *HIA*, Box 39.

85. Miskovsky Interview. Donovan, then, was most certainly aware of the plot, but was also assured that he had a safe suit to present to Castro. The public disclosure of the wet suit incident was not made until the Church Committee hearings in 1975, but at that time, it was still not clear that Donovan knew what was planned for him. A fuller discussion can be found in Appendix D.

86. On March 28 Donovan received a letter from Helen Strauss of the William Morris Agency, Inc. inquiring as to his interest in a motion picture about him and Cuba. In a response the following day, he declined. *HIA*, Box 46.

87. John Nolan donated "Notes re. Cuban Trip, April 5–9, 1963" to the National Security Archive, the George Washington University. It is essentially a three-page topical outline of the discussions with Castro.

88. *HIA*, Box 40, Cuban Chronology.

89. Ibid. John Donovan's account of his visit with Castro is contained in an unpublished article, "I Spent Five Days in Communist Cuba," *HIA*, Box 40, Chronology of events March 8–April 13, 1963.

90. John Donovan, conversation with author, January 19, 2001.

91. Nolan interview, April 25, 1967, 16.

92. An Associated Press photograph captured Castro on a visit to Moscow in late April 1962 taking a picture with the camera—the one purchased by a CIA attorney. *New York Times*, May 1, 1962. Miskovsky interview.

93. The returning Americans included Gilberto Rodriguez Fernandez, Hector E. Varona, John Robert Gentile, Eustace Van Brunt, Daniel Lester Carswell, James D. Beane, Donald Joe Green, Thomas L. Baker, Leonard L. Schmidt, Edmund K. Taransky, Alfred Eugene Gibson, George R. Beck, Lamar E. DeZaldo, Guillermo Vidal Morales, Dario Prohias Bello, Joaquin Ossorio, Fernando G. Sanchez, Austin F. Young, Juan Pedro Koop, Richard Allen Pecoraro and Leslie N. Brandley. Three of the Americans, it was later revealed, were actually members of the CIA (Carswell, Van Brunt and Taransky).

94. The list of persons released from Cuba was coordinated through the Swiss Embassy in Washington, DC. See letter of April 25, 1963, from Abba P. Schwartz to Victor Martin of the embassy in *HIA*, Box 38.

95. A jurisdictional dispute among labor unions had arisen and had to be resolved first. In addition, there was a question about whether or not some goods were suitable for shipment to Cuba. Those goods, retractable steel rulers, fell into a questionable area of suitability. "When this question came up at a meeting in the Attorney General's Office," related Robert Shea, "he [Kennedy] asked, 'Are they bombs?' His question resolved the problem. The rulers were included in the final shipment." Robert Shea Interview, July 1, 1964, 24–25.

96. *New York Times*, July 4, 1963.

97. Lucius Clay, letter to Donovan dated October 27, 1964, *HIA*, Box 44.

98. *HIA*, Box 44.

99. A copy of the Red Cross Final Report is in *HIA*, Box 44. Later in the month, Castro claimed that the Cubans were shorted by $10 million. The Red Cross responded that their Cuban counterparts had checked each ship on delivery. *New York Times*, July 27, 1963. Donovan asserted that this was either propaganda or a simple misunderstanding. *New York Times*, July 28, 1963. Castro, however, always spoke highly of Donovan and never implied that he tried to dupe his people. "Playboy Interview: Fidel Castro," in *The Playboy Interview: The Best of Three Decades, 1962–1992* (Chicago: Playboy Enterprises, 1992), 68. Before leaving Havana for Moscow at the end of April 1963, Castro had told a crowd at the university, "Donovan is intelligent and, at least with us, handled himself in very serious form. . . . He is skillful and a great worker." *New York Times*, April 27, 1963.

100. See Appendix H for a list of the carriers. See Appendix J for a list of all companies making donations.

101. While awards were an acceptable form of recognition for Donovan, he was still opposed to undue publicity. When his son, John, for example, was asked to be on the television program, *To Tell the Truth*, his father did not approve. John Donovan, conversation with the author, January 19, 2001.

102. *HIA*, Box 40.

103. Neil McKenty, "A Modern Mercedarian," *America*, August 1, 1964, 101; "Man in Havana," *New Yorker*, July 6, 1963, 23. Later, while in England, Donovan purchased a vellum manuscript of the history of the Mercedarian Order that was written in 1445 in Spain, before printing, in its original leather binding. He was able to export it to his home, but only after agreeing to let the British Museum microfilm it first. *HIA*, Box 2.

For years after Donovan's work in the release of Cuban prisoners, numerous families and individuals from around the world wrote requesting his assistance in obtaining the release of relatives. It extended to at least April 1968. When Major Richard H. Pearce, for example, defected to Cuba on May 21, 1967, Mrs. John C. Mitchell, wife of the then attorney general, contacted Donovan. Two years earlier, Pearce's wife had obtained a divorce in Beaumont, Texas, and was awarded custody of their son, Richard. Major Pearce, believed to be distraught at the loss of his four-year-old son, took him to Cuba. In another instance, an individual wrote in behalf of Edwardo Arango Cortina who was captured in Cuba in 1959. His father, Enrique Arango, was a lawyer and member of the Lake Placid Club, as was his grandfather, José M. Cortina, a lawyer, too, and a lifetime member of the Club. *HIA*, Box 38. In each instance, characteristic of numerous requests, Donovan was asked to secure the release of the loved one. While he could pass on the information to the U.S. State Department, Donovan was simply not in a position to provide assistance as an intermediary.

104. Press release, August 22, 1963, *HIA*, Box 38.

105. Edwin O. Guthman and Jeffrey Shulman, eds., *Robert Kennedy: In His Own Words. The Unpublished Recollections of the Kennedy Years* (New York: Bantam Books, 1988), 376. Attwood had been a former editor of *Look* magazine and was a Kennedy campaign aide in 1960. He was ambassador to Guinea between 1961 and 1963 during which time he kept chronological notes of discussions related to a normalization of relations with Cuba. These may be found in Mark J. White, ed., *The Kennedys and Cuba: The Declassified Documentary History* (Chicago: Ivan R. Dee, 1999), 337–40 and 343–44.

106. John Nolan, interview with Richard D. Mahoney cited in Mahoney's *Sons and Brothers: The Days of Jack and Bobby Kennedy* (New York: Arcade Publishing, 1999), 219.

107. *HIA*, Box 51.

108. W. W. Atwood, *The Reds and the Blacks: A Personal Adventure* (New York: Harper & Row, 1967), 142–44.

109. March 4, 1963. The full memorandum is at http://www2.gwu.edu/~nsarchiv/NSAEBB/NSAEBB103/630304.pdf

110. Robert Dalleck, *An Unfinished Life: John F. Kennedy, 1917–1963* (Boston: Little, Brown, 2003), 661.

111. Lisa Howard, "Castro's Overture." *War/Peace Reports* 3, 9 (September 1963): 3.

112. Ibid.

113. Peter Kornbluh, a senior analyst at the private National Security Archive at George Washington University, wrote a detailed history of the search for rapprochement from Donovan's initial discussions with Castro in 1963 through December 1964. Peter Kornbluh, "JFK & Castro: The Secret Quest for Accommodation," *Cigar Aficionado*, October 1999 at http://www.cigaraficionado.com/Cigar/CA—Archives/CA—Show—Article/0,2322,320,00.html.

114. Kornbluh, "JFK & Castro," 11; Schlesinger, *Robert Kennedy*, 552–56.

115. Miskovsky Interview; Atwood, *The Reds and the Blacks*, 146.

116. The document is provided in full in Appendix J. It can also be found at: http://www.gwu.edu/~nsarchive/NSAEBB/NSAEBB103/640212.pdf.

117. *New York Times*, July 6, 1964. Lisa Howard had no further meetings with Castro after July 1964. Suffering from personal crises in the following year, she committed suicide on July 4, 1965, at the age of thirty-five. *New York Times*, July 5, 1965.

118. *New York Times*, July 5, 2000.

CHAPTER 10. BOARD OF EDUCATION

1. Allen Raymond, *A Study of New York's Public School System* (New York: New York *Herald Tribune,* n.d.). The booklet contains reprints of Raymond's articles published between February 23, 1931, and March 6, 1931.

2. Ibid., 41.

3. Diane Ravitch, *The Great School Wars: A History of the New York City Public Schools* (New York: Basic Books, 1988), 265.

4. The actual powers of the board of education can be found in the New York State Education Law, Article 52, §2554*ff.*

5. *New York Times,* September 19, 1961.

6. *New York Times,* September 20, 1961.

7. *New York Times,* September 24, 1961.

8. *HIA,* Box 80.

9. N.Y. Civil Service Law, §210 (McKinney 1999).

10. *New York Times,* June 16, 1962.

11. Ibid.

12. Kenneth T. Jackson, ed., *The Encyclopedia of New York City* (New Haven: Yale University Press, 1995), 121–22.

13. *Congressional Record,* February 4, 1964, 1773.

14. Diane Ravitch, *The Great School Wars,* 272.

15. Ibid., 259. See also *New York Times,* February 4, 1964.

16. Ravitch, *The Great School Wars,* 262–63.

17. May 22, 1963.

18. Milton Arthur Galamison (1923–1988), pastor of the Siloam Church in Brooklyn from 1948 until his death, he used his position to foster the civil rights movement. See Clarence Taylor, *Knocking at Our Own Door: Milton A. Galamison and the Struggle to Integrate New York City Schools* (New York: Columbia University Press, 1997). See *New York Times,* March 11, 1988 for his obituary.

19. *New York Times,* August 26, 1963.

20. *New York Times,* August 28, 1963.

21. *New York Times,* September 3, 1963.

22. *New York Times,* February 4, 1964.

23. *New York Times,* September 7, 1963; Ravitch, *The Great School Wars,* 271.

24. *New York Times,* December 11, 1963.

25. Ibid.

26. Ibid. Donovan had stressed the need to create educational opportunities earlier in the year. On March 21, 1963, upon receipt of the Brooklyn College Medal for his Cuban efforts, he spoke of his goal for New York City school children: "It is terribly important to all of us . . . to safeguard the concept that every child in the City of New York [who] wishes . . . is afforded the opportunity to gain an education, not only through elementary, secondary and college, but through the Doctorate degree as well." *Ken* (Brooklyn College), March 25, 1963.

27. Edward S. Lewis, executive director of the Urban League of Greater New York; Dan W. Dodson, director of New York University's Center for Human Relations and Community Studies; and Antonia Pantoja, executive director of ASPIRA, an organization designed to assist Puerto Ricans in obtaining an education.

28. Higher Horizons began in 1956 and offered enhanced services and remedial services, first to an experimental group, and later to many students. Ravitch, *The Great School Wars,* 260.

29. *New York Times,* December 17, 1963.

30. Ibid.

31. Ravitch, *The Great School Wars,* 273.

32. Theodore H. White, letter to James B. Donovan, December 27, 1963, *HIA,* Box 75.

33. James B. Donovan, letter to Theodore H. White, January 7, 1964. *HIA,* Box 75.

34. *New York Times,* January 10, 1964.

35. Ibid.

36. *New York Times,* January 14, 1964.

37. The letter was sent to Roy Wilkins; James Farmer, president of the Congress of Racial Equality (CORE); C. B. Powell, editor of the *Amsterdam* (New York City) *News;* A. Philip Randolph, president of the Brotherhood of Sleeping Car Porters; and Whitney Young, executive director of the National Urban League, January 10, 1964. *HIA,* Box 75. The letter was essentially a reproduction of a statement, "Responsibility of the Schools in Integration," which he helped to develop in August 1963. It is quoted, in part, in the *New York Times,* January 14, 1964. The document is similar in tone to one of Donovan's statements issued late in the prior year: "We feel integration is an urgent problem now and not a generation from now." However, he believed that overemphasizing integration would drive whites from the city. "The last thing we should do is take action so precipitously as to turn New York City into a Negro ghetto." *New York World Telegram & Sun,* November 29, 1963.

38. *New York Times,* January 16, 1964.

39. Ibid., January 27, 1964.

40. Ibid.

41. The full text of the board's seventeen-page plan can be found in *New York Times,* January 30, 1964.

42. Ibid.

43. Quoted in the *New York Journal American,* February 9, 1964.

44. *New York Times,* January 31, 1964.

45. *New York Times,* February 3, 1964. In fact, civil rights leaders had already met with police officials on February 1 and assured them of the nonviolent nature of the boycott. *New York Times,* February 2, 1964. However, Donovan may also have been concerned because of the number of threatening letters he had been receiving from integration extremists such as that quoted in this chapter. Since the end of January he was continually accompanied by a police guard. After the debate ended, Donovan said, "I like James Farmer. I think we speak the same language, but I also think the radicals have got the good men like him running scared on this boycott thing [of Galamison's]. . . . You know though, this isn't our first bout with prejudice. We're Irish. My father, who worked his way through med school, collected ads from newspapers only years ago which advertised jobs with the last line reading 'Irish need not apply.'" *New York Herald Tribune,* February 3, 1964. To Mylas Martin of the *Herald Tribune* staff he also said, "There comes a time when you have to forsake the so-called language of diplomacy. You have to use simple, blunt, Anglo-Saxon that the least educated can understand." Ibid.

46. *New York Times,* February 4, 1964.

47. Ibid.

48. Ibid.

49. *New York Times,* February 5, 1964.

50. Ibid.

51. Dr. Reed created an eight-point program for Integration, the first of which called for Donovan's removal. His other points included desegregating all predomi-

nantly black and Puerto Rican high and junior high schools by September 1964; adoption of a citywide plan to racially balance all New York City public schools; a temporary halt to new construction (to avoid building more schools in entirely segregated neighborhoods); adoption of a program to raise educational standards; appointment of a Puerto Rican to the board of education; improvement of the employment and assignment of minority teachers; and a revision of textbooks to include the contributions of minorities. *New York Times*, February 18, 1964.

52. *New York Times*, February 10, 1964.

53. *New York Times*, February 15, 1964.

54. Ibid. Senator Javits, Donovan's former opponent in 1963, also supported the embattled president of the board saying, "The New York City Board of Education has prepared a positive plan to create better balance in even the 19 percent of the schools to which I have referred. Principally, the plan involves pairing adjoining elementary schools in the case of approximately 20 pairs of schools and distributing the feeder patterns from elementary schools to junior high schools, at the same time keeping travel time for the elementary school students to a maximum of 30 minutes and for the junior high schools to a maximum of 45 minutes. This is only a beginning, of course. Much more must be done, and will be done." *Congressional Record*, February 4, 1964, 1773.

55. Months earlier, on June 4, 1963, Donovan had asked that a convention be called to review the state constitution in order to "re-examine the basic rights of all people in the state, including the basic right of every child to a satisfactory education." *New York Times*, June 5, 1963.

56. *New York Times*, February 11, 1964.

57. *New York Times*, February 28, 1964.

58. On February 27, in anticipation of the march, Donovan had invited a Puerto Rican committee to assist the board, and he also expressed the hope that the demonstration would impact on the legislature for additional funds for education.

59. *New York Times*, February 18, 1964.

60. *New York Times*, February 19, 1964.

61. *New York Times*, February 28, 1964.

62. *New York Times*, March 2, 1964.

63. *New York Times*, March 9, 1964. Donovan had met, too, with an organization, Negro Women on the March, two days earlier and listened to their recommendations for more experienced and licensed teachers in disadvantaged areas, together with the purchase of new textbooks that illustrated black accomplishments. Donovan responded that these two initiatives were already underway.

64. It was, in fact, a decision that made everyone happy. White groups saw it as preserving the neighborhood school and black groups perceived it as increasing the opportunity for integration. *New York Times*, March 11, 1964.

65. *New York Times*, March 13, 1964.

66. Soon after the demonstration, however, the number of schools to be paired was substantially reduced. David Rogers, *110 Livingston Street: Politics and Bureaucracy in the New York City School System* (New York: Vintage Books, 1969), 93.

67. *New York Times*, March 17, 1964.

68. The National Association for Puerto Rican Civil Rights did not support the boycott. Ibid.

69. Ibid.

70. *Prayer for the City of New York*, pamphlet, 1–2. Reprinted in its entirety in Donovan, *Challenges*, 125–36.

71. Donovan, *Prayer*, 3.

72. *New York Times*, April 6, 1964.

73. At the request of Donovan, Allen had set up a committee to review the New York City school system. It included Drs. John H. Fischer, president of Columbia University's Teachers College; Kenneth B. Clark, professor of sociology at City College; and Judah Kahn, a rabbi of the Metropolitan Synagogue. Rogers, *110 Livingston Street*, 26; *New York Times*, April 8, 1964.

74. "Desegregating the Public Schools of New York City," a Report Prepared for the Board of Education of the City of New York by the State Education Commissioner's Advisory Committee on Human Relations and Community Tensions, May 12, 1964, 8, *HIA*, Box 77. A synopsis of the report can also be found in *New York Times*, May 13, 1964.

75. "Desegregating the Public Schools of New York City," 8.

76. *New York Times*, May 14, 1964.

77. *New York Times*, May 13, 1964.

78. Ibid.

79. *New York Times*, May 14, 1964.

80. 347 U.S. 483 (1954).

81. *New York Times*, May 19, 1964.

82. Ibid.

83. They included *Why We Can't Wait* by Martin Luther King Jr.; *Assimilation in American Life* by Milton M. Gordon; *Equality in America* by Alan P. Grimes; *Integration vs. Segregation* by Hubert H. Humphrey; and *Baseball Has Done It* by Jackie Robinson.

84. *New York Herald Tribune*, June 7, 1964, Book Section.

85. A copy is in *HIA*, Box 78.

86. *New York Times*, June 4, 1964.

87. Ibid.

88. *New York Times*, June 16, 1964.

89. Ibid.

90. *HIA*, Box 73.

91. Notably, the two candidates in the U.S. Senate race in New York State, Robert F. Kennedy and the incumbent, Kenneth B. Keating, each stated that they were opposed to long distance busing of pupils. In fact, it was a nonissue since such long bus rides did not exist. Civil rights groups criticized both individuals, and Donovan said that they had to have been talking about some other city. Donovan also criticized them for trying to make an educational matter a subject in a partisan political campaign. *New York Times*, September 9, 1964.

92. *New York Times*, September 9, 1964.

93. *New York Times*, September 13, 1964.

94. Ibid.

95. Detailed, school-by-school changes can be found in *New York Times*, September 14, 1964.

96. *New York Times*, September 15, 1964.

97. *New York Times*, September 16, 1964.

98. *New York Times*, September 17, 1964.

99. News Bureau, Office of Education Information Services and Public Relations, Board of Education, September 14, 1964, N15-64/65; quoted, in part, in *New York Times*, September 15, 1964.

100. Summary minutes of the meeting are located in *HIA*, Box 64; quotes from those minutes are in *New York Times*, September 22, 1964.

101. *New York Times*, October 15, 1964.

102. Ibid.

103. 22 AD2d 72 (November 12, 1964) affirming 44 Misc 2d 356 (September 2, 1964).

104. Similar cases included *Remo J. Addabbo. v. James B. Donovan,* 16 N.Y. 2d 619, 209 N.E. 2d 112 (1965); *cert. denied,* 382 U.S. 905, 86 S. Ct. 241 (1965), which concerned pairing; and *In the Matter of Isidore Balaban v. Rubin,* 20 AD 2d 450 (March 10, 1964). In the Balaban case Judge Beldock summarized, "The choice of schools must be left to the sound discretion of the Board; otherwise, there would be chaos in the administration of the school system."

105. Letter to Sergeant Shriver, October 22, 1964, *HIA,* Box 74.

106. Letter to James B. Donovan, October 30, 1964, *HIA,* Box 74.

107. Letter of Robert of Wagner to James B. Donovan, *HIA,* Box 61.

108. *New York Times,* March 17 and April 14, 1965.

109. *New York Times,* January 20, 1965.

110. See, for example, a letter from Albert Shanker, president of the UFT, to James B. Donovan, February 10, 1965, *HIA,* Box 88.

111. *New York Times,* 1965; April 10; April 12; April 26; and April 27. In a request for bids on school bus routes, the board had divided the city into fifteen districts in order to enhance the competitive process. (Request Serial No. RT950, *HIA,* Box 87.) A bus company could bid on one, some or all of the contracts for the fifteen areas. The Children's Bus Service, which held the major contract for years planned to go out of business at the end of the school year. While Donovan informed that company's drivers that they would be hired by the new companies who won the bids, the workers were still fearful of losing their current income and benefits and had struck in a wildcat action. After the drivers received written assurances, the strike ended.

112. *HIA,* Box 86.

113. *New York Times,* April 23, 1965.

114. Ibid.

115. *New York Times,* April 23 and 24, 1965.

116. Understanding that teachers did not agree with the concept of involuntary transfers, Donovan said that a mutually agreeable method would be worked out with the union. Unfortunately, he then added, "It still remains that if we find the right carrot, it's better than the stick with most donkeys." *New York Times,* May 9, 1965. It brought immediate denunciations from teachers. Several days earlier, Donovan also irked blacks with another off-the-cuff remark during a public hearing on a different issue when he referred to their organizations as "so-called civil rights groups." *New York Times,* April 16, 1965.

117. *New York Times,* May 1, 1965.

118. *New York Times,* May 11, 1965.

119. Had Donovan not discussed his resignation before the election, the vote may have been different as some board members were very concerned about a number of his extemporaneous public remarks. The unfinished business that Donovan referred to was the oversight over the removal of Calvin Gross. Earlier in March, Donovan had written to Robert A. Morse, the attorney who had worked with him on the Cuban prisoner release project: "By direction of the Board of Education you are hereby assigned as Special Counsel to compile the evidence of the causes for the suspension and ultimate dismissal of the Superintendent of Schools" (*HIA,* Box 64). Briefly, the board did not see Gross as being a strong figure in the position of chief executive officer of the school system. They felt that he failed to develop an integration plan with due diligence, did not move quickly to draw up a decentralization scheme that the board had wanted and had failed to fill important vacancies on his administrative

staff. "Educational Politics." *Reporter* 32 (March 25, 1965): 12. Gross had been put on three months' suspension as of March 1, 1965. *New York Times*, 1965, March 3; March 4; March 5; and March 7, sec. 4. He was ultimately terminated and succeeded by Bernard E. Donovan (no relation to James Donovan), the acting superintendent. During May, following his announced departure, Donovan prepared a "Report of Progress and Growth for the period September 1961 to May 1965 to the people of the City of New York." It was a summary of what he saw as the board's accomplishments during his tenure. In outline form, it may be found in Appendix K.

120. *New York Times*, May 12, 1965.

121. *New York Herald Tribune*, May 12, 1965.

122. *Amsterdam News*, July 3, 1965.

CHAPTER 11. DRIVING MR. DONOVAN

1. From a handwritten notebook of Aston Taylor, who provided a copy to the author.

2. Ibid.

3. *New York Day-Jewish Journal*, April 30, 1965, 3. Page translation provided by Global Translation Systems, Chapel Hill, NC.

4. *New York Times*, May 28, 1966.

5. Ibid.

6. Aston Taylor and Mary Busch in conversation with author, May 2, 2000.

7. Letter of James Donovan to Dr. Ernst Coenen, Fritz Thyssen Stiftung, Hapsburgerring, Germany, October 23, 1969, *HIA*, Box 7. The Fritz Thyssen Stiftung is a German charitable foundation that was founded in 1959. Donovan also participated in other events regarding the plight of European Jews. For example, on April 25, 1968, he gave an address at a Times Square rally held by the Warsaw Ghetto Uprising Anniversary Committee.

8. The other negotiators included the Rev. Pierson, a son-in-law of Governor Nelson Rockefeller, and professors J. D. Singer and Anatole Rapoport of the University of Michigan. *New York Times*, September 10, 1963.

9 Ibid.

10. *New York Times*, August 22, 1965.

11. *New York Times*, August 28, 1965.

12. Ibid.

13. It remained the Citizen Exchange Corps until 1985, although it was dormant in the early 1980s during the Russian conflict with Afghanistan. In 1985 it was renamed the Citizen Exchange Council. When it ultimately became CEC International Partners, it focused on artists and museums. Stephen James died on January 30, 1998. *New York Times*, February 23, 1998.

14. However, he never shied from an opportunity to engage in international negotiations. On August 11, 1966, for example, at a Jockey Club roundtable discussion in Albany, he stated that he would be willing to try to negotiate with North Viet Nam, although he hadn't been asked yet. When questioned if an exchange were possible, Donovan stated, "Anything is possible. If a person has enough confidence, enough patience and enough 'tradable' items, an exchange would certainly seem possible." *New York Knickerbocker News*, August 16, 1966.

15. Brooklyn Chamber of Commerce memo to its Board of Directors, June 23, 1965. *HIA*, Box 64.

16. Aston Taylor and Mary Busch in conversation with author, May 2, 2000. Mary still retains a Eubie Blake record album that the artist autographed for her husband.

17. *W.P. Kennedy v. The Long Island Railroad.*, 211 F. Supp. 478; 319 F. 2d 366 (1962).

18. 375 U.S. 830, 84 S. Ct. 75 (1963).

19. For a very brief analysis of the decision's impact, see *Insurance* 64, no. 45 (November 16, 1963): 1:1.

20. Thomas Parry, in conversation with author, August 1, 2001.

21. James Donovan, *Challenges: Reflections of a Lawyer-at-Large* (New York: Athenaeum, 1967).

22. One reviewer hoped for an autobiography: "The book indicates that when the author has an opportunity for a lengthy biography, the experience will be well worth it. His speeches can give the reader only a taste of what has been and continues to be, a fascinating career." *Harvard Law Record* 45, no. 5 (October 26, 1967): 13. In a symposium on *Challenges* at St. Francis College, Brooklyn on January 10, 1968 it was favorably critiqued by a panel that included Francis X. Altimari, then a district judge of Nassau County and later a federal judge; Jerome Prince, dean of Brooklyn Law School; Frank Pino, justice of the New York State Supreme Court; and John Murphy, dean of St. John's University Law School. *Prattler* (St. Francis College), January 16, 1968.

23. *Newsletter* (Pratt Institute), October 30, 1967, 3.

24. *Prattler,* October 24, 1967, 1.

25. *New York Times,* May 6, 1969.

26. Margaret Latimer, "Field of Influence: A Centennial History of Pratt Institute" (Brooklyn: Pratt Institute, February 15, 1988, unpublished manuscript), 128.

27. *Prattler,* January 16, 1968.

28. Ibid., November 7, 1967.

29. Diane Ravitch, *The Troubled Crusade: American Education, 1945–1980* (New York: Basic Books, Inc. 1983), 189.

30. Ibid., 224, citing Alexander W. Astin, et al., *The Power of Protest* (San Francisco: Jossey-Bass, 1975), 45, 180.

31. Even as a student, himself, Donovan was always opposed to giving radical minorities too much recognition since it would appear to exaggerate their importance in the collegiate community. "Anti-War Strike is Anti-Peace Movement," 126.

32. Latimer, "Field of Influence," 130.

33. Conceived about 1965, guerrilla theaters attempted to address current social issues through radical concepts and biting satire, with plays usually performed in public places such as parks.

34. Latimer, "Field of Influence," 132.

35. *Wall Street Journal,* September 19, 1968; *Prattler,* May 21, 1968.

36. *Wall Street Journal,* September 19, 1968. Before and after the address, the returning alumni also had the chance to view some of Donovan's rare books in an exhibit he had set up. The selections included the *Nuremberg Chronicle of 1493,* the world's first illustrated book, a page of the Guttenberg Bible, a print of Durer's *Ship of Fools;* and a work by Chaucer with a woodblock from Kelmscott Press.

37. *New York Times,* July 16, 1968.

38. About two years before the two Donovans merged, former Vice President Richard Nixon asked James B. Donovan to consider a merger with his own firm, Nixon, Mudge, Rose, Alexander and Mitchell. Nixon's firm was a large one with twenty-three attorneys and was located at 20 Broad Street in Manhattan with offices

in Washington, DC, and Paris, France. Donovan declined the offer since his politics differed substantially from those of Nixon.

39. Pratt historian, Margaret Latimer, characterized the event not so much as an installation as a "coronation." Latimer, "Field of Influence," 133. Whether the remark was intended to be humorous or sarcastic could not be determined.

40. James B. Donovan, "Adventure in Education," *Pratt Alumnus* (Winter 1969): 6. The article is a reprint of his talk at the Brooklyn Museum.

41. *New York Times*, October 19, 1968.

42. Donovan, "Adventure in Education," 7.

43. Ibid., 8.

44. Letter to John at Boston University, January 17, 1969, *HIA*, Box 4.

45. *Prattler*, March 18, 1969, 1.

46. *Prattler*, March 25, 1969.

47. *New York Times*, March 26, 1969.

48. The Manifesto can be found in its entirety in *Prattler*, April 8, 1969. Grand Army Plaza was practically on the doorstep of the Donovan family residence. James's daughter Mary Ellen recalled that the pickets were also in front of their home. In fact, she remembers "thirteen years of pickets" from the time of the Abel case, through her father's presence on the board of education up to his presidency of Pratt. Mary Ellen Donovan Fuller, in conversation with author, January 25, 2002.

49. Latimer, "Field of Influence," 135.

50. Late in the previous year Donovan had said, "I intend to give greater accent to my pledge, that on every major issue of policy the voices of the students and faculty will be heard." He followed the statement by making arrangements to permit the president of the Student Coordinate and the chair of the Faculty Council to meet with him before each trustees meeting, review the entire agenda, offer comments, add items and either attend the meetings or submit a report. *Prattler*, October 8, 1968. They were not members of the board, however. The request for community participation on the board was new.

51. Latimer, "Field of Influence," 136.

52. *Prattler*, April 8, 1969.

53. Donovan's letter and Allen's response is in *Prattler*, April 8, 1969.

54. *Prattler*, April 18, 1969.

55. Ibid.

56. *New York Times*, May 8, 1969; *Prattler*, May 13, 1969.

57. *New York Times*, May 6, 1969.

58. Ibid.

59. *New York Times*, May 7, 1969.

60. Ibid.

61. Latimer, "Field of Influence," 139.

62. Aston George Taylor, letter to the Universal Life Church, June 11, 1969, *HIA*, Box 4, and conversation of Aston Taylor with author, May 2, 2000.

63. Congressman Hugh L. Carey later entered the talk in its entirety in *The Congressional Record— Extension of Remarks*, May 14, 1969, E3966. It was also featured as an article, "Conscription, . . . With a Choice," *America* (June 28, 1969), 726—27.

64. *New York Times*, February 23, 1969.

65. The twelve guidelines are reported in full at *New York Times*, July 1, 1969.

66. *Prattler*, September 25, 1969. Just before Donovan took office, in October 1967, students, themselves, had sought police protection after the rape of a graduate student in Emerson Hall and an assault and robbery of another student near the school at Myrtle and Waverly Avenues. *Prattler*, November 7, 1967.

67. "Report from the President," a memorandum to alumni and friends of Pratt Institute, October 24, 1969.

68. Now retired (2004) and living in Florida, Aston George Taylor continues to drive north to visit with Mary and her family in fulfillment of his friend's request.

69. See Appendix L for the full eulogy.

Bibliography

PRIMARY SOURCES

Donovan, James B. "Adventure in Education." *Pratt Alumnus* 71, 2 (January 1969), 6–12.

———. "An Accident Is an Accident Is an Accident." *Insurance Law Journal*, no. 409 (February 1957): 71–78.

———. "Anti-War Strike Is Anti-Peace Movement: College Students Led By Communist Strategists." *America* (May 15, 1937), 126–28.

———. *Challenges: Reflections of a Lawyer-at-Large.* New York: Atheneum House, 1967.

———. "Communication and Study Relating to the Defense of Fair Comment in Actions for Libel or Slander: Report of the Law Revision Commission of New York State." LLB thesis, Harvard University Law School, April 1940.

———. "Conscription . . . With Choice," *America* (June 28 1969), 726–27.

———. "The Dropout." *Mediatrix* (Angel Guardian Home. Brooklyn, NY) May–June 1964).

———. "Hardy Perennials of Insurance Contract Litigation." *Insurance Law Journal*, no. 374 (March 1954): 163–70.

———. "Informal Confession of a Pipe-lover," *The Fordham Monthly* 52, 1 (November 1934): 8–9.

———. "Insurance—The Case in Favor of Existing Exemptions from the Antitrust Laws." *Federal Bar Journal* 20 (Winter 1960): 56–65.

———. "Insurance Becomes Commerce." (Part I), *Insurance Counsel Journal* 17, 2 (April 1950): 141–45.

———. "Insurance Becomes Commerce." (Part II), *Insurance Counsel Journal* 17, 3 (July 1950): 249–53.

———. "Insurance Problems Created by the Peacetime Use of Atomic Energy." *Insurance Law Journal*, no. 417 (October 1957): 623–28.

———. Introduction to *Trials: An Encyclopedic Guide to Modern Practices, Techniques, and Tactics Used in Preparing and Trying Cases, with Model Programs for the Handling of all Types of Litigation.* 82 vols., through 2002. San Francisco: Bancroft-Witney, 1964.

———. "The Lawyer and the Uninsured Motorist." *Insurance Counsel Journal* 21, 3 (July 1954): 319–24.

———. "Major General William J. Donovan: a Pioneer in U.S. Intelligence." *Columbia Library Columns* 14, 3 (May 1965): 3–10.

———. *Memories of One Book Collector.* Speech, annual dinner, Antiquarian Booksellers Association, New York City, October 14, 1969.

———. "National Standard Provisions for Casualty Policies." Speech, American Bar Association, St. Louis, MO, September 6, 1949. Typescript. St. John's University Library, Manhattan (formerly The College of Insurance), file no. CA410.

———. "New York: A National Problem." *New York County Lawyers Association Bar Bulletin* 18 (September-October 1960): 53–55.

———. "Opening Statements by Counsel for the National Automobile Underwriters Association at a Hearing Held in November 1951 Before the New York State Insurance Department." St. John's University Library, Manhattan (formerly The College of Insurance), File AU574 N.Y.

———. "Our Association's Program to Aid Victims of Financially Irresponsible Motorists." *New York State Bar Bulletin* 25 (October 1953): 295–345.

———. "Privilege of Advocating Unpopular Causes." *Albany Law Review* 30 (January 1966): 52 (text of address at Albany Law School Commencement, June 1, 1965); also in the *Louisiana State Bar Journal* 12, 2 (August 1964): 83–87; *Challenges: Reflections of a Lawyer-at-Large,* 72–82; and in the *Brooklyn Barrister* 16, 9 (November 1964). Presented as a lecture on numerous occasions such as the Stevens Lecture, April 14, 1962, Cornell University Law School, Ithaca, New York.

———. "Public Regulation of Title Insurance." *Title News* 32 (December 1953): 74–77.

———. "Rate Regulation Revisited," Symposium on Insurance and Government, School of Commerce, University of Wisconsin, September 20, 1960. Copy in St. John's University Library, Manhattan (formerly The College of Insurance), File 710 R19 (1960).

———. "Recent New York Developments in Liability Insurance." *New York State Bar Bulletin* 23 (December 1951): 437–41.

———. "Regulation of Insurance Under the McCarran Act." *Law and Contemporary Problems* 15, 4 (Autumn 1950): 473–92.

———. Review of *Assimilation in American Life,* by Milton M. Gordon, *New York Herald Tribune,* June 7, 1964.

———. Review of *Baseball Has Done It,* by Jackie Robinson, *New York Herald Tribune,* June 7, 1964.

———. Review of *Equality in America,* by Alan P. Grimes, *New York Herald Tribune,* June 7, 1964.

———. Review of *Integration vs. Segregation,* ed. Hubert H. Humphrey, *New York Herald Tribune,* June 7, 1964.

———. Review of *Strategic Intelligence and National Decisions,* by Roger Hilsman, *University of Pennsylvania Law Review* 105, November 1956, 133–34.

———. Review of *Why We Can't Wait,* by Martin Luther King, Jr., *New York Herald Tribune,* June 7, 1964.

———. Review of *With God in Russia,* by Walter J. Ciszek, *America,* December 19, 1964, 807.

———. "State Regulation of Insurance." *Insurance Law Journal,* no. 368 (September 1953): 627–30.

———. "State Regulation of Insurance." *Insurance Law Journal,* no. 396 (January 1956): 11–15.

———. *Strangers On a Bridge: The Case of Colonel Abel.* New York: Atheneum House, 1964.

———. "Strangers on a Bridge." *Saturday Evening Post,* March 28, 1964. (Excerpts.)

———. "Strategic Intelligence and Espionage." Address, the Lake Placid Club (Lake Placid Education Foundation reprint), September 4, 1960.

———. "The Standard Policy Program." Reprinted from *Casualty and Surety Journal,* November 1948, in St. John's University Library, Manhattan (formerly The College of Insurance), File CA410.

———. "When Does an Accident Become Two Accidents?" *Insurance Counsel Journal* 23, 2 (April 1956): 194–98.

———. "Why We Must Spy." *America,* May 28, 1960, 307–9.

———. "Wife Cannot Recover for Loss of Husband's Consortium." *Insurance Counsel Journal* 21, 2 (April 1954): 143–45.

Donovan Campaign Papers. In the possession of Mary Donovan Busch.

Hoover Institution on War, Revolution and Peace, Stanford University, Papers of James B. Donovan, 1919–76, 97 boxes.

Taylor, Aston George. Personal Notebook.

INTERVIEWS

Mary Donovan Busch, 1999–2003

Jane Ann Donovan Amorosi, February 2001

John Donovan, 1999–2003

Mary Ellen Donovan Fuller, January 2002

Daniel McNamara, August 2000

Milan Miskovsky, March 2003

John Nolan, January 2002

Thomas Parry, August 2001

Aston George Taylor, May 2000

GOVERNMENT DOCUMENTS

Church Committee. *Alleged Assassination Plots Involving Foreign Leaders: An Interim Report of the Select Committee to Study Governmental Operation with Respect to Intelligence Activities.* New York: W.W. Norton, 1976.

Congressional Record, 1964, 1969.

Earman, J. S., Inspector General, Central Intelligence Agency. Memorandum for the Record: *Report on Plots to Assassinate Fidel Castro.* May 23 1967. Reprinted in toto in *CIA Targets Fidel: Secret 1967 CIA Inspector General's Report on Plots to Assassinate Fidel Castro.* Melbourne, Australia: Ocean Press, 1996.

1880 *U.S. Census.*

John F. Kennedy Library Oral History Program:

Joseph Dolan, recorded interview by Francis J. Hunt DeRosa, July 8, 1964.

John Nolan, recorded interview by Frank DeRosa, April 25, 1967.

Louis F. Oberdorfer, recorded interview by Francis J. Hunt DeRosa, May 14, 1964.

Cuban Prisoner Exchange Panel [Louis F. Oberdorfer, John Jones, Mitchell Rogovin], recorded interview by Francis J. Hunt DeRosa, June 2, 1964.

Robert F. Shea and John Wilson, recorded interview by Francis J. Hunt DeRosa, July 1, 1964.

McKinney's Consolidated Laws of New York Annotated.

New York City Board of Health. *Annual Report* of 1904. New York: Martin Brown Press, 1905.

Office of United States Chief of Counsel For Prosecution of Axis Criminality. *Nazi Conspiracy and Aggression.* Washington DC: United States Government Printing Office, 1946. 9 volumes.

————. *Nazi Conspiracy and Aggression: Opinion and Judgment,* Washington, DC: U.S. Government Printing Office, 1947.

Proceedings of the Democratic State Convention, War Memorial Auditorium, Onondaga County, Syracuse, New York, September 17 and 18, 1962. New York, NY: Sills Reporting Services, 1962.

Report of Robert H. Jackson, United States Representative to the International Conference on Military Trials. Washington, DC: U.S. Government Printing Office, 1949. Department of State Publication No. 3080, International Organization and Conference Series II, European and British Commonwealth 1.

Trial of the Major War Criminals Before the International Military Tribunal, Nuremberg, 14 November 1945 – 1 October 1946. 42 volumes (reprint). Buffalo, NY: William S. Hein & Co., 1995.

United States Senate. *Hearing before the Committee on Armed Services, United States Senate, 87th Congress, 2nd Session on Francis Gary Powers, March 6, 1962.* Washington, DC: U.S. Government Printing Office, 1962.

ENCYCLOPEDIC REFERENCES

The American Catholic Who's Who, 1968–69; 1970–71. Grosse Point, MI: Walter Romig, Publisher, n.d.

American National Biography, 1999. John A. Garraty and Mark C. Carnes, eds. New York: Oxford University Press, 1999.

Biographical Directory of the United States Congress, 1774–1989. Kathryn Allamong Jacob and Bruce A. Ragsdale, eds. Washington, DC: U.S. Government Printing Office, 1989.

Contemporary Authors, vols. 9–10, 1964. James M. Etheridge, ed. Detroit: Gale Research Co., 1964. *Contemporary Authors.* vols. 89–92, 1980. Frances C. Locher, ed. Detroit: Gale Research Co., 1980.

Current Biography Yearbook, 1961. Charles Moritz, ed. New York: H.W. Wilson Co., 1961.

Dictionary of American Biography, 1988. John A. Garraty and Mark C. Carnes, eds. New York: Charles Scribner's Sons, 1988.

Dictionary of American Military, 1984, Roger J. Spiller, ed. Westport, CT: Greenwood Press, 1984.

Facts On File Yearbook, vols. 5 and 6. R. L. Lapica, ed. New York: Person's Index, Facts On File, Inc. 1945, 1946.

The National Cyclopedia of American Biography, vol. 55. Clifton, NJ: James T. White & Co., 1974.

Who's Who in America. 1961 and 1970. Chicago, IL: Marquis Who's Who.

Who's Who in Insurance, 1970, 1984, 1987, 1988. Donald E. Wolff, ed. New York: The Underwriter Printer and Publishing Co.

Who's Who in the East, 1970. Chicago: Marquis Who's Who, 1970.

Who Was Who in America, 1969–1973. Chicago: Marquis Who's Who, 1973.

NEWSPAPERS, NEWSLETTERS AND MAGAZINES

Amsterdam (New York City) *News*

Bulletin of Information, Fordham University

Catholic Digest

Chicago Tribune

Cigar Aficionado

Day Jewish Journal (New York)

Eastern Underwriter

Harvard Law Record

Jewish Daily Forward (New York)

Ken (Brooklyn College)

Knickerbocker News (Albany, NY)

Life

Long Island (NY) *Newsday*

Los Angeles Times

Maroon, Fordham University

New York Daily News

New York Herald Tribune

New York Journal American

New York Mirror

New York Law Journal

New York Post

New York Times (12/8/62–4/1/63: Western Edition used due to Printers and Engravers Strike)

Newsletter (Pratt Institute)

Newsweek

Post Standard (Syracuse, NY)

Prattler (Pratt Institute)

Ram (Fordham University)

Saturday Evening Post

Sunday Telegraph (London)

Time

Times of London

Wall Street Journal

Washington Post

World Telegram and Sun (New York)

SECONDARY SOURCES

"Abel for Powers." *Time*, February 16, 1962, 15–16.

Acheson, Patricia. *The Supreme Court: America's Judicial Heritage*. New York: Dodd, Mead, 1961.

Alderman, Sidney S. "Background and Highlights of the Nuernberg Trial," *I.C.C. Practitioners' Journal* (November 1946): 99–113.

Amorosi, John D. "The Donovan-Castro Talks: A Potential Opportunity or an Historical Anomaly." A paper completed for Foreign Policy, Deerfield Academy, Deerfield, MA, May 14, 1990.

Amory, Cleveland. *International Celebrity Register: An Irreverent Compendium of American Quotable Notables*. New York: Harper & Row, 1963.

"An American Example." Review of *Strangers On a Bridge* by James B. Donovan. *Newsweek*, March 30, 1964, 75–76.

Andrew, Christopher and Valili Mitrokhin. *The Sword and The Shield: The Mitrokhin Archive and the Secret History of the KGB*. New York: Basic Books, 1999.

Appleman, John Alan. *Military Tribunals and International Crimes*. Indianapolis: Bobbs-Merrill, Co., 1954.

Atwood, W. W. *The Reds and the Blacks: A Personal Adventure*. New York: Harper & Row, 1967.

Axman, Clarence. "James B. Donovan." *Eastern Underwriter*, April 25, 1958, 36–38.

Bernikow, Louise. *Abel*. New York: Pocket Books, 1971.

Beschloss, Michael R. *Mayday, Eisenhower, Khrushchev and the U-2 Affair*. Boston: Faber & Faber, n.d., orig. 1986.

"Biggest Fish." *Newsweek*, May 6, 1963, 24–25.

Branch, Taylor. *Parting the Waters: America in the King Years, 1954–1964*. New York: Simon and Schuster, 1988.

Breslin, Jimmy. "The Lawyer Who Horse-Traded The Russians." *True*, September 1962.

"Bridge Where Secret Meeting Took Place," *Life*, February 16, 1962, 32–34.

"Brigades Brave Men." *Newsweek*, January 7, 1963, 12–15.

Buchwald, Art. "It's Galling But We'll Pay the Ransom," in *I Chose Capitol Punishment*. 193–94. Cleveland: World Publishing, 1962.

Colitt, Leslie R. *Spy Master: The Real-Life Karla, His Moles and the East German Secret Police*. Reading, MA: Addison-Wesley, 1995.

"College Man's Vote." *Vogue*, December 15, 1935.

Conot, Robert E. *Justice at Nuremberg*. New York: Harper & Row, 1983.

"Constitutional Law—*Abel v. United States*—Issues Before the Supreme Court." *University of Pennsylvania Law Review* 107 (1958–1959): 1192–1206.

Cookridge, E. H. *Gehlen: Spy of the Century*. New York: Random House, 1971.

———. *Spy Trade*. London: Hodder and Stroughton, 1971.

Cremin, Lawrence A. *Popular Education and Its Discontents.* New York: Harper & Row Publishers, 1989.

Dallek, Robert. *An Unfinished Life: John F. Kennedy, 1917–1963.* Boston: Little, Brown, 2003.

———. "JFK's Second Term: How He Made Up with Castro and withdrew from Viet Nam." *Atlantic Monthly,* June 2003, 58–66.

de Gramont, Sanche (Ted Morgan, pseud.), *The Secret War: The Story of International Espionage Since World War II.* New York: G. P. Putnam's Sons, 1962.

Derrick, Peter. "New York's Rapid Transit System and the Development of The Bronx." *Bronx County Historical Society Journal* 36, no. 2 (Fall 1999): 51–66.

Donovan, John. "I Spent Five Days in Communist Cuba," *Northwood School Quarterly, HIA,* Box 38.

"Donovan: The Public's Man." *Brooklyn Tablet,* November 13, 1975.

Dowling, Claudia Glenn. "The Survivor," *Life,* June 1998, 106–12.

Dulles, Allen. "A Spy For a Spy." Review of *Strangers On a Bridge* by James B. Donovan. *New York Times,* April 12, 1964.

Dunlop, Richard. *Donovan, America's Master Spy.* Chicago: Rand McNally, 1982.

"Educational Politics." *Reporter* 32 (March 25, 1965).

Eisenhower, Milton S. *The Wine Is Bitter: The United States and Latin America.* New York: Doubleday, 1963.

Elwyn-Jones, Lord. *In My Time: An Autobiography.* London: Weidenfeld & Nicolson, 1983.

Escalante Font, Fabian. *The Secret War: CIA Covert Operations against Cuba, 1959–1962.* Translated by Maxine Shaw. Melbourne, Australia: Ocean Press, 1995.

Fontenay, Charles L. *Estes Kefauver: A Biography.* Knoxville: University of Tennessee Press, 1980.

Ford, Corey. *Donovan of OSS.* Boston: Little, Brown, 1970.

Ford, Dan. *Pappy: The Life of John Ford.* Englewood Cliffs, NJ: Prentice Hall, 1979.

Fordham University. *Bulletin of Information,* April 1919.

From William Street to A Bridge in Berlin: Profile of Lawyer Jim Donovan (1962). New York Democratic State Committee campaign pamphlet.

Gannon, S.J., Rev. Robert I. *A Eulogy for James B. Donovan,* Fordham University, January 21, 1970 (booklet).

Gerhardt, Eugene C. *America's Advocate: Robert H. Jackson.* Indianapolis: Bobbs Merrill, 1958.

Gibney, Frank. "Intimate Portrait of a Russian Master Spy." *Life.* November 11, 1957.

Gordon, John Steele. "The Wreck of the *General Slocum.*" *Seaport: New York's History Magazine* 23, 1, (Summer 1989): 28–35.

Gorman, Joseph Bruce. *Kefauver: A Political Biography.* New York: Oxford University Press, 1971.

Guthman, Edwin O. and Jeffrey Shulman, eds. *Robert Kennedy: In His Own Words. The Unpublished Recollections of the Kennedy Years.* New York: Bantam Books, 1988.

Harris, Whitney R. *Tyranny on Trial.* Dallas: Southern Methodist University Press, 1999.

Hermalyn, Gary. "The Bronx at the Turn of the Century." *Bronx County Historical Society Journal* 26, 2 (Fall 1989): pp. 92–112.

Heymann, C. David. *RFK: A Candid Biography of Robert F. Kennedy.* New York: Dutton, 1998.

Hilsman, Roger. *To Move a Nation: The Politics of Foreign Policy in the Administration of John F. Kennedy.* New York: Doubleday, 1967.

Hinckle, Warren, and William W. Turner. *The Fish Is Red: The Story of the Secret War Against Castro.* New York: Harper & Row, 1981.

Howard, Lisa, "Castro's Overture." *War/Peace Reports* 3, 9 (September 1963): 3–5.

Hunt, E. Howard. *Give Us This Day.* New Rochelle, NY: Arlington House, 1973.

Jackson, Kenneth T., ed. *The Encyclopedia of New York City.* New Haven,: Yale University Press, 1995.

Jackson, Robert H. *The Nürnberg Case.* New York: Alfred A. Knopf, Inc., 1947.

———. *That Man: An Insider's Portrait of Franklin D. Roosevelt.* New York: Oxford University Press, 2003 (particularly the biography of Jackson in the Introduction by John Q. Barrett, xiii–xxviii).

Javits, Jacob K. with Rafael Steinberg. *Javits: The Autobiography of a Public Man.* Boston: Houghton Mifflin, 1981.

"Jim Donovan: Newsmaker," *Journal of Insurance Information* 23, 4 (July-August 1962): 24–30.

Johnson, Haynes Bonner. *The Bay of Pigs; the Leaders' Story of Brigade 2506.* New York: W.W. Norton, 1964.

Kaplan, John. "Evidence in Capital Cases," *Florida. State University Law Review* 11, 3–4 (1983), 376–77.

Kaufman, Irving R. "The Defense of Unpopular Clients. *New York Law Journal,* June 2, 1958.

Kennedy, Robert F. *Thirteen Days: A Memoire of the Cuban Missile Crisis.* New York: W.W. Norton, 1968. Reprint, 1998.

"Kennedy's Man in Havana." *Time,* October 19, 1962, 15.

King, Robert D. "Treason and Traitors: Ethical Implications of Espionage," *Society* 35, 2 (January 11, 1998), 329–38.

Kornbluh, Peter. "JFK & Castro: The Secret Quest for Accommodation," *Cigar Aficionado,* October 1999 at http://www.cigaraficionado.com/Cigar/CA—Archives/CA—Show—Article/0,2322,320,00.html.

Kramer, Robert. Foreword to *Law and Contemporary Problems* 15, 4 (Autumn 1950).

Kunstler, William. Review of *Strangers on a Bridge,* by James B. Donovan. *Chicago Tribune,* March 22, 1964.

Latimer, Margaret. "Field of Influence: A Centennial History of Pratt Institute." Unpublished manuscript. Brooklyn, NY: Pratt Institute, February 15, 1988.

Lazo, Mario. *Dagger in the Heart: American Policy Failure in Cuba.* New York: Funk & Wagnalls, 1968.

Lee, Henry. "James B. Donovan: Metadiplomat", *Catholic Digest,* March 1964.

Lichtenstein, Nelson. *Political Profiles: The Kennedy Years.* Vol. 1. New York: Facts on File, 1976.

Lindeman, Bard. "Cuban Prisoner Exchange." *The Saturday Evening Post,* 236, February 2, 1963, 15–22.

———. "He Defended a Soviet Spy" in *Coronet,* 48, October 1960, 46–51.

Mahoney, Richard D. *Sons and Brothers: The Days of Jack and Bobby Kennedy.* New York: Arcade, 1999.

"Man in Havana." *New Yorker,* July 6, 1963, 22–23.

"Man in the News." *Insurance* 64, 45 (November 16, 1963): 3, 69.

Mandel, Paul. "It's Just as Cold for a Real Spy." Review of *Strangers on a Bridge* by James B. Donovan. *Life,* April 17, 1964, 11–14.

McHugh, Rev. L. C. "The Powers Espionage Trial." *America,* October 29, 1960, 142–44.

McKenty, Neil. "A Modern Mercedarian." *America,* August 1, 1964, 101.

McKinney's Consolidated Laws of New York Annotated. Minnesota: West Group, 1999.

McLaughlin, Gerald T. "How The Marketplace Can Help In International Crisis." *Chicago Daily Law Bulletin* 139, 10, January 15, 1993.

"Millions for Tribute?" *Time,* October 19, 1962, 15–16.

Nash, Jay Robert, and Stanley Ralph Ross, *The Motion Picture Guide.* Chicago: Cinebooks, 1987.

National Genealogical Society, Arlington, Virginia. Index card record of John Donovan, MD, deeded from the America Medical Association's deceased physicians' files.

Nizer, Louis. *The Implosion Conspiracy.* Garden City, NY: Doubleday, 1973.

Norrell, Robert J. "Civil Rights Movement in the United States," CD-ROM, Microsoft Encarta99.

Oates, Stephen B. *Let The Trumpet Sound: A Life of Martin Luther King, Jr.* New York: HarperCollins, 1994.

Ogilvie, John S. *History of the* General Slocum *Disaster.* New York: Ogilvie Co., 1904.

Palmer, R. R., and Joel Colton. *A History of the Modern World.* New York: Alfred A. Knopf, 1965.

Paterson, Thomas G., ed. *Kennedy's Quest For Victory: American Foreign Policy, 1961–1963.* New York: Oxford University, 1989.

Persico, Joseph E. *Nuremberg: Tyranny on Trial.* New York: Viking, 1994.

Phelps-Stokes, I. N. *The Iconography of Manhattan Island.* New York: R.H. Dodd, 1915–28.

"Playboy Interview: Fidel Castro." *The Playboy Interview: The Best of Three Decades, 1962–1992.* Chicago: Playboy Enterprises, Inc., 1992.

Polmar, Norman, and Thomas B. Allen. *The Encyclopedia of Espionage.* New York: Gramercy Books, 1997.

Powers, Francis Gary, with Curt Gentry. *Operation Overflight.* New York: Holt, Rinehart and Winston, 1970.

Powers, Thomas. *The Man Who Kept the Secrets: Richard Helms and the CIA.* New York: Alfred A. Knopf, 1979.

Prados, John. *Presidents' Secret Wars: CIA and Pentagon Covert Operations From World War II Through The Persian Gulf.* Chicago: I. R. Dee, 1996.

Presidents and Deans of American Colleges and Universities. Nashville: Who's Who in American Education. 1970.

Quirk, Robert E. *Fidel Castro.* New York: W.W. Norton, 1993.

Ranelagh, John. *The Agency: The Rise and Decline of the CIA.* New York: Simon and Schuster, 1987.

Ravitch, Diane. *The Great School Wars: A History of the New York City Public Schools.* New York: Basic Books, 1988.

———. *The Troubled Crusade: American Education, 1945–1980.* New York: Basic Books, 1983.

Raymond, Allen. *A Study of New York's Public School System.* New York: New York Herald Tribune, n.d.

"Return of Brigade 2506." *Time,* January 4, 1963, 14–15.

Robinson, Ray. *Iron Horse: Lou Gehrig and His Time.* New York: W.W. Norton, 1990.

Rogers, David. *110 Livingston Street; Politics and Bureaucracy in the New York City School System.* New York: Vintage Books, 1969.

Rust, Claude. *The Burning of the General Slocum.* New York: Elsevier/Nelson Books, 1981.

Samuels, Gertrude. "How Metadiplomacy Works: James Donovan and Castro." *Nation* 196, 15 (April 13, 1963): 299–302.

Sayre, Joel. "Letter From Nuremberg," *New Yorker,* December 1, 1945, 106–11.

Schorr, Daniel. *Clearing the Air.* Boston: Houghton Mifflin Company, 1977.

Sinclair, Andrew. *John Ford.* New York: Dial Press/James Wade, 1979.

Smith, Bradley F. *The Shadow Warriors: O.S.S. and the Origins of the C.I.A.* New York: Basic Books, 1983.

Smith, R. Harris. *OSS: The Secret History of America's First Central Intelligence Agency.* Berkeley and Los Angeles: University of California Press, 1972, 1981.

Snell, David. "Inside Story of a Lawyer's Adventure." *Life,* February 23, 1962, 26–27.

Sprecher, Drexel A. *Inside the Nuremberg Trial: A Prosecutor's Comprehensive Account.* 2 vols. Lanham, MD: University Press of America, 1999.

Storey, Robert G. *The Final Judgement? From Pearl Harbor to Nuremberg.* San Antonio: Naylor, 1968.

Sullivan, Edward J. "The Trouble With Donovan," *Sign,* April 1964.

Talbott, Straud, ed. and trans. *Khrushchev Remembers: The Last Testament.* Boston: Little, Brown, 1974.

Taylor, Clarence. *Knocking at Our Own Door: Milton A. Galamison and the Struggle to Integrate New York City Schools.* New York: Columbia University Press, 1997.

Taylor, Telford. *The Anatomy of the Nuremberg Trials: A Personal Memoir.* New York: Alfred A. Knopf, 1992.

Thomas, Evan. "Bobby Kennedy's War on Castro." *Washington Monthly* 27, 12 (December 1, 1995).

———. *Robert Kennedy: His Life.* New York: Simon and Schuster, 2000.

———. *The Very Best Men: Four Who Dared—The Early Years of the CIA.* New York: Simon and Schuster, 1995.

Tishkov, A.V. "Rudolph Abel Tried Before American Court." *Sovetskoye Gosudarstvo i Pravo* 4, (1969): 131–37, in Joint Publications Research Service, *Translations on USSR Political and Sociological Affairs,* 10, JPRS 48044, May 14, 1969, 1–13. English translations are also in *HIA,* Boxes 10 and 30.

Tobier, Emanuel. "The Bronx in the Twentieth Century: Dynamics of Population and Economic Change." *Bronx County Historical Society Journal* 35, 2 (Fall 1998), 69–102.

Trest, Warren, and Donald Dodd. *Wings of Denial: The Alabama Air National Guard's Covert Role at the Bay of Pigs.* Montgomery, AL: New South Books, 2001

Tuohy, William. "Wolfgang Vogel Works in Secret on a New Exchange." *Los Angeles Times,* February 10, 1986.

"Unconventional Trader." *Senior Scholastic* 81 (January 9, 1963): 14.

Volkman, Ernest, and Blaine Baggett. *Secret Intelligence.* New York: Doubleday, 1989.

Weisbrot, Robert. *Freedom Bound: A History of America's Civil Rights Movement.* New York: W.W. Norton, 1990.

White, Mark, ed. *The Kennedys and Cuba: The Declassified Documentary History.* Chicago: Ivan R. Dee, 1999.

White, William L. *The Little Toy Dog: The Story of the Two RB-47 Fliers.* New York: E.P. Dutton, 1962.

Whitney, Craig R. *Spy Trader: Germany's Devil's Advocate and the Darkest Secrets of the Cold War.* New York: Times Books–Random House, 1993.

Wighton, Charles. *The World's Greatest Spies: True-Life Dramas of Outstanding Secret Agents.* New York: Taplinger Publishing Co., 1965.

Wise, David, and Thomas B. Ross. *The Invisible Government.* New York: Random House, 1964.

———. *The U-2 Affair.* New York: Bantam Books, 1962.

Wyden, Peter. *Wall: The Inside Story of Divided Berlin.* New York: Simon and Schuster, 1989.

Young, Warren. "Door to Freedom: A Quiet Lawyer's Eloquent Patience." *Life,* January 4, 1963, 25–26.

Index

Page numbers in italics refer to illustrations.

Abbott Laboratories, 230
Abel, "Frau," 90, 92, 93, 94
Abel, Mrs. Rudolf, 82
Abel, Rudolf Ivanovich: arrest of, 70, 71; identity of, 72, 252 n. 4; espionage activity of, 72; initial detention of, 72; indictment and initial appearance of, 73; and first meeting with JBD; and illegal search argument, 77; trial of, 78–84, *131;* sentence of, 84–85; appeals by, 85–88; imprisonment of, 89; and exchange for Powers, 89–90, 92–97; intercession asked of for Makinen release, 98; and gift to Donovan, 97; and Soviet Union admission he was spy, 98; death of, 103
Abercrombie and Fitch, 113, 155
Abrahantes, Capt. José, 112, 113, 115, 116
Abruzzo, Judge Matthew T., 73, 74, 76
Abt, John J., 74
Acme Cotton Products Co., 232
Acme Markets, Inc., 232
Adelman, Maurice, Jr., 219
Ad Hoc Committee to Lift the Ban on the *Nation,* 65
Advisory Commission on School Construction, 165
Aero Plast Corp., 233
Aetna Casualty and Surety Co., 64
African Pilot, SS, 145, 147, 148, 227
Agency for International Development, 143
Agriculture, U.S. Department of, 142, 144, 157, 233 and n.
Air Force, U.S., 151

Airshields, Inc., 233
Air Transport Association, 142, 157
Alabama Air National Guard, 259 n. 3
Albrecht, Ralph G., 50, 248 n. 8
Alcazar (JBD), 27
Alcon Laboratories, Inc., 233
Alderman, Sidney S.: and British list of war criminals, 41; naming of to International Military Tribunal prosecution team, 37; as participant at International Military Tribunal, 50, 248 n. 8; and travel to London Conference, 40
Allen, James E., 163, 169, 176, 186, 196, 199, 274 n. 73
Allen, Oliver S., 98, 101
Allen, Woody, 258 n. 35
Allen Plan, 178–79, 180, 181, 185
All Hallows Elementary School, 23
All Hallows High School, 24
Allied Supermarkets, 233
Allis Chalmers, 106
All-Industry Conferences: and McCarran-Ferguson Act, 63, 64
All-Institute Policy Committee (Pratt Institute), 200
Altimari, Hon. Francis X., 277 n. 22
Amen, Col. John Harlan, 248 n. 8, 249 n. 33
America, 25, 26, 92, 103
America Fore Insurance Group, 145
American Bar Association, 62, 63, 66, 119
American Cyanamid Co. (Lederle Labs), 229, 233
American Heritage Foundation, 164
American Home Products (Whitehall Labs), 230

291

viet Union, 49–50; participates in experiment with Rudolf Hess, 50, 51; and relationship with Justice Jackson, 46, 51; describes opening of trial, 53–54, 55; and military point system, 45, 46, 47; is discharged from active duty, 58–59, 60; receives letter of commendation from General Donovan, 58; and military honors, 60; gives post-Nuremberg lectures 61–62; and heart condition, 61, 181, 182, 198, 201, 204; is hired as general counsel to NBCU, 61; and state regulation of insurance, 62–65, 88; is selected as defense attorney for Rudolf Abel, 75; selects Abel defense team, 76; and defense fee, 76, 87, 101; gives opening trial statement, 78; provides closing trial argument, 82; and picketing of his home, 278 n. 48; offers the social utility argument against death penalty, 84; and appeals for Abel, 85–88; and Abel-Powers-Pryor exchange, 89–90, 92–99; and Makinen negotiations, 94–99; is approached by CFC to assist in release of Brigade 2506 prisoners, 107; prepares for first visit to Castro, 109; has first meetings with Castro, 110–11, 112–115, 116; reaches first tentative agreement on exchange, 115, 116; continues efforts through missile crisis, 134–35; and friction with Attorney General, 141–42, 150; obtains insurance backing for the ANRC, 145; has subsequent meetings with Castro, 146, 148, 150, 152, 153, 155; prepares Memorandum of Agreement, 147, 228–29; arranges gifts for Castro, 113–15, 154, 155, 156; negotiates for American prisoners in Cuba, 114, 146, 152, 153–54, 155, 156; negotiates for captured American skin divers, 152, 153, 154, 155; obtains release of two American women, 153, 154; obtains release of missionaries, 154, 155; takes son to Cuba, 155; and summary of negotiations with Castro, 156–57; seeks Cuban-American détente, 148, 158; and media follow-up to exchange, 259 n. 54; senate ambition, of, 118;

and pre-convention planning, 118; announces candidacy for U.S. Senate, 120; addresses NY convention, 122; establishes campaign headquarters, 123; struggles with lack of political experience, 125–27; and the final tally of votes, 128; is appointed to Board of Education and elected vice-president, 164; is elected president, 169, 179, 186; and philosophy of education, 170; debates Galamison, 172; opposes boycotts, 172, 182, 183; and opinion on busing, 170; and threats to his life, 173; debates Rev. Galamison, 172; debates James Farmer, 174; seeks funds from New York State for education, 175, 180, 185; writes book reviews, 180; speaks to Bedford-Stuyvesant community, 176–77; and law suits against, 184; and integration of schools, 272 n. 37; and summary of accomplishments of board under JBD, 236–37; hires Aston George Taylor, 189; is general counsel to Jewish Nazi Victims Organization of America, 189; and "peace hostages," 190; negotiates with Soviet Union for exchange program, 190; and later law cases, 191; as president of Pratt Institute, 192, 197; supports students, 193, 195–96; and Black Student Union, 195, 200, and merger of law firm, 197; and black enrollment, 198; addresses student protests, 199, 200, 201; responds to arrests of students, 200, 203; arranges doctorate for Aston George Taylor, 201–2; calls for a National Youth Service, 202; death of, 204; and eulogy of Father Gannon; and summary of awards and honorary degrees, 241–42; and summary of organization memberships, 239

Donovan, James J., cousin of JBD 197, 219

Donovan, Jane Ann (Jan). See Amorosi, Jan Donovan

Donovan, John, brother of JBD, 23, 24, 25, 66, 67–68

Donovan, John, son of JBD: birth of, 35; education of, 90, 124, 198; and Marine Corps discharge, 196; and

Koop, Juan Pedro, 269 n. 93
Kornbluh, Peter, 160
Korotkov, Alekssandr Mikhailovich, 73
Korznikov, Nikolai A., 97
Kramer, Donald, 121
Krupp, Alfred, 249 n. 42
Krupp van Bohlen, Gustav, 249 n. 42
Kudrayavtsev, Sergei, 160
Ku Klux Klan, 169, 182

Labor, New York City Department of, 165
Labor, U.S. Department of, 142
Lafarge Institute, John, 103, 202
Lake Placid Club, 24, 28, 29, 62, 75, 86, 197, 270 n. 103
Lalla, Carlos, 259 n. 5
Lambert, Lt. Thomas F., Jr., 249 n. 35
Landers, Jacob, 170
Landis, James McCauley, 28
Langer, William L., 37
Latham Hotel, 71
Latimer, Margaret ("Field of Influence"), 201
Latin American politics, 192
Lawrence, Ernest O., 31, 246 n. 1
Lawrence, Sir Geoffrey, 48
Lawton Company, 233
Leavitt, Nathan R., 221
Lechuga, Carlos, 160
Lee, L. W. (Royal Bank of Canada), 226
Lefkowitz, Louis J., 128
"Legal Aspects of the Nuremberg Trial" (Robert Storey), 61
Lehman, Hon. Herbert H., 221
Lehman, Orin, 221
Lehn & Fink Products Corp., 231
Leitz, Inc., E., 232
Lemkin, Rafael, 37, 47, 247 n. 29
Lenin Peace Prize, 108
Leonard, Elizabeth, 40
Leslie, William, 61
Letters of Credit: in negotiations with Castro, 112, 114, 115, 116, 117, 138, 139, 142, 143, 144, 145, 146, 147, 156, 225
Levin, A. Leo, 69
Levitt, Arthur, 121, 128
Lewis, Edward S., 168, 271 n. 27
Ley, Robert, 249 n. 42
Life Magazine, 99, 100

"Limits of Campus Liberty" (JBD), 202
Lincoln Warehouse, 71, 72
Lindeman, Bard, 102
Linowitz, Sol M., 160
Lipton Co., T.J., 233
Literary Guild, 102
Literaturnaya Gazeta, 84
Llaca, Enrique, 106, 259 n. 5
Lobo, Julio, 259 n. 5
Loeb, Louis M., 69, 74
Logan, Andy, 250 n. 50
Logan Act, 107, 108, 135, 141
Lombardi, Vince, 25, 244 n. 21
London Conference (preparatory to International Military Tribunal), 41, 42, 43, 44
Long, Tania, 56
Long Island Railroad, 191
Loren, Sophia, 258 n. 35
Lovejoy, Ben, 147
Lowe, Donald V., 221
Lowell, Stanley H., 168, 169, 174, 176
Lucey, Stuart C., 175
Lufkin Rule Co., 234
Luftwaffe, 42
Lydia (daughter of "Frau Abel"), 94
Lyons, Leonard, 221

Machlett Laboratories, Inc., 232
MacLeish, Archibald, 65
Magner, Richard T., 221
Magruder, Brig. Gen. John, 60
Mahoney, Sen. Francis J., 68
Maki, Eugene Nikolai (alias of Reino Hayhanen), 79
Makinen, Marvin W.: is captured by Russians, 93; and negotiations for release of, 94, 95, 97, 98, 99, 100, 101; release of, 257 n. 33
Malcolm X, 180
Maloof, David L., 219
Manes, Mathew, 68
Manes, Sturim, Donovan & Laufer, 66
Mangino, Joseph M., 219
Manhattan College, 26
Manual of School Planning, 165
Mara, Wellington, 25, 244 n. 21
Maritime Administration, U.S., 140, 142, 154
Mark (alias of Rudolf Abel), 79
Maroon (Fordham University), 27
Martin, John Barlow, 158